The Best American Political Writing 2003

The Best American Political Writing 2003

Edited by Royce Flippin

Thunder's Mouth Press
New York

THE BEST AMERICAN POLITICAL WRITING 2003

© 2003 by Royce N. Flippin, III & Avalon Publishing Group

Published by
Thunder's Mouth Press
An Imprint of Avalon Publishing Group Incorporated
245 West 17th Street, 11th Floor
New York, NY 10011

Library of Congress Cataloging-in-Publication Data is available.

ISBN: 1-56025-517-X

9 8 7 6 5 4 3 2 1

Designed by Sue Canavan
Printed in the United States of America
Distributed by Publishers Group West

CONTENTS

Part One: Politics in the Bush Era (continued)

National Conversation: Debt and Taxes

Part Two: The State of the Union

National Conversation: Affirmative Action

National Conversation: The Iraq Conflict

Part Four: America and the World

National Conversation: Winning the Peace

Part Five: The Democratic Contenders for 2004

This book is dedicated with love to my wife, Alexis,
who makes every day a good day

Acknowledgments

I'd like to thank all of the writers who agreed to contribute their work to this anthology, as well as their publishers and agents. I'm also grateful to the many friends and family members who forwarded ideas and suggestions over the course of the past year. In particular, I want to thank Dan O'Connor and Michael O'Connor of Avalon Publishing Group for their excellent and essential input throughout the process of putting this book together. Thanks, too, to publisher Neil Ortenberg for his continuing support of this series, to Shawneric Hachey for his always-skillful efforts at securing all reprint rights, to Karen Auerbach for her work promoting the anthology, and to the Avalon production team. I'd also like to say a special thank-you to my wife, Alexis Lipsitz Flippin, for her love and support, and to Rob Esposito, for lending his valuable political expertise to this project.

Preface

Royce Flippin

Welcome to *The Best American Political Writing 2003*—the annual compendium of articles and essays from the nation's leading political writers, representing the year's most insightful, provocative, and best-written examples of political prose from across the ideological spectrum. When choosing the selections for this anthology, we sought topical pieces that provide a fresh perspective on important political subjects, presented in a clear and entertaining style. In other words, "good reads." At the same time, we worked hard to achieve a balance in the pieces we selected. By balance, I don't just mean conservative versus liberal, or domestic policy as opposed to foreign affairs; we also wanted to reflect the diversity of America's many venues for political expression. The selections cover the period beginning in early 2002 through late spring of 2003—a time frame that includes the 2002 elections, the passage by Congress of the recent 2003 tax cut legislation (which ranks as the third-largest tax reduction in history), the invasion of Iraq, and the first weeks of the post-war "rebuilding" effort.

The book's five main sections are made up mainly of longer articles, grouped into broad categories. "Part One: Politics in the Bush Era (continued)" focuses on the Bush administration—its policy decisions and its political maneuvering. "Part Two: The State of the Union" is concerned with how politics are affecting the lives of average Americans, including our ability to function as informed and empowered citizens in a democracy. "Part Three: Marching to War" contains various takes on the administration's steady buildup to the invasion of Iraq. "Part Four: America and the World" contains articles and essays about the United States and its role in international politics. Finally, "Part Five: The Democratic Contenders for 2004" features profiles of the leading candidates for the Democratic presidential nomination.

Set between these main sections are four segments called "The National Conversation," comprised mainly of column-length pieces. Each segment focuses on a fairly specific subject—our goal being to give readers a sampling of the back-and-forth dialogue taking place in the nation's newspapers and magazines around that particular issue. This year the four topics are the most recent Bush tax cut; the issue of affirmative action; the debate over whether or not to invade Iraq; and the challenges facing the U.S. in the post-war landscape.

What leaps out most clearly from the vast body of political writing published over the past year is the degree to which the Iraq war dominated the political discussion. The public-relations buildup to the invasion started in the first months of 2002, and steadily gained momentum through the summer and fall—at which point the U.N. weapons inspections and the actual war preparations took center stage. Throughout this period, the approaching conflict sucked all other political considerations into its wake. As Democratic Senator Kent Conrad notes in Eleanor Clift's article on the administration's budget priorities ("What Is He Thinking?" p. 72), President Bush hasn't had to defend his domestic policies because "the war overwhelms everything." On the international front, too, the administration's aggressive stance on Iraq overshadowed other considerations, straining America's relations with the international community—most especially with our long-time NATO allies, France and Germany—and pushing aside other hot-button issues, such as the uncertain political situation in Afghanistan and the continuing activity of the Al Qaeda terrorist network (see "The Return of Bin Laden," p. 312).

The Best American Political Writing 2003 looks at the Iraq issue from a number of different perspectives, including an interview with one of the leading "hawks" on Iraq, Deputy Defense Secretary Paul Wolfowitz ("The Unilateralist," p. 278), a description by author Bob Woodward of Colin Powell's efforts to forge an international consensus for invasion ("Bush at War," p. 193), Kenneth Pollack's influential essay on why an invasion is necessary ("Next Stop, Baghdad?" p. 182), and the text of President Bush's historic address to the United Nations General Assembly on September 12, 2002—in which he challenged the U.N. to act on Iraq, or forfeit its own relevancy ("A Decade of Deception and Defiance," p. 205).

Senator Robert Byrd's stirring speech in the Senate ("We Stand Passively Mute," p. 232), Lewis Lapham's thoughtfully contrary essay ("Cause for Dissent," p. 212) and Anna Quindlen's cautionary column ("Sounds of Silence," p. 238) all raise questions about the administration's determined march to war, and its impact on Americans' ability to speak their minds freely. On the other hand, William Kristol argues that the people protesting the Iraq war simply don't grasp the threat we're faced with ("The End of the Beginning," p. 250), while Christopher Hitchens asks why the pacifist wing is so intent on preserving an obviously evil status quo ("War and Consequences," p. 236), commentator John Leo lampoons the moral hypocrisy of certain members of the anti-war camp ("Befuddled in Baghdad," p. 241), and Thomas Friedman warns that that we'll all be losers if conservatives and liberals don't shelve their animosity over the Iraq issue and join together in the post-war rebuilding effort ("Our New Baby," p. 298).

Another thread that weaves through *The Best American Political Writing 2003* has to do with the sheer talent and skill of the White House political operation—led by President Bush's immensely gifted (and, some say, immensely powerful) political advisor, Karl Rove. The Bush-Rove team's accomplishments in the past year included engineering the Republican's historic midterm election takeover of the Senate ("W. and the 'Boy Genius,'" p. 2), and leveraging Senator Trent Lott's ill-conceived birthday toast to Strom Thurmond into a swift transfer of the Senate leadership post to White House favorite Bill Frist ("With Signals and Maneuvers, Bush Orchestrates an Ouster," p. 66). Probably the best depiction of Rove's influence, though, comes from *Esquire* writer Ron Suskind, who made headlines when he got ex-White House staffer John DiIulio on the record, complaining about how "the Mayberry Machiavellis" are riding roughshod over the administration's domestic policy apparatus ("Why are These Men Laughing?" p. 10).

Also apparent was the staunch determination of the administration and its GOP allies to pursue a tax-cutting agenda at home and a hard-line (and often unilateral) foreign policy overseas. In both cases, their stance has contributed to what can only be described as the remaking of the United States. On the home front, economist Paul Krugman paints a striking portrait of America's growing gap between rich and poor ("For Richer," p. 107), while former presidential contender Ralph Nader describes the power that the national media conglomerates have to influence the substance of a presidential campaign ("The Media: An Ongoing Non-Debate," p. 131). Looking abroad, historian Michael Ignatieff offers a thoughtful assessment of America's growing predominance in world affairs and its implications for our own political system ("The Burden," p. 254).

Finally, the theme of disarray among the Democrats drifts through this anthology like background music. The party's search for a new message is most apparent in the book's final section on the Democratic presidential hopefuls. For a particularly telling illustration of the Dems' struggles, read Jeffrey Toobin's description from *The New Yorker* of how Senator Joe Lieberman's legislation to establish the Homeland Security Department was hijacked by the Senate Republicans, then used as a club against the Democrats in last November's elections ("Candide," p. 318).

Inevitably, tomorrow's political issues are already looming on the horizon. As I write this, U.S. troops are being wounded and killed on a near-daily basis in Iraq, while a debate continues to rage over whether the Bush administration manipulated intelligence to overstate the threat posed by Saddam Hussein (see Nicholas Kristof's "Missing in Action: Truth," p. 302). Meanwhile, the nuclear programs of the other two members of the "axis of evil" are beginning to take over the headlines. There is talk from the White House of blockading all shipments coming out of North Korea, and the administration is also demanding that Iran submit to more stringent inspections by the International Atomic Energy Agency (sound familiar?). Inside our borders, there's a continuing discussion over whether the government is doing enough to protect homeland security. At the same time, the Justice Department just released the results of an internal investigation criticizing the FBI's treatment of suspected terrorists in the months following 9/11. And of course the 2004 presidential campaign is well underway, and picking up steam every day.

Where is this all headed? Check back with us next year, and we'll let you know.

The Best American Political Writing 2003

Part One: Politics in the Bush Era (continued)

W. and the "Boy Genius"

James Carney and John Dickerson

with reporting by Matthew Cooper, Karen Tumulty, Douglas Waller,
  and Michael Weisskopf
Time magazine | November 18, 2002

From its tax-cutting agenda to its hawkish foreign policy, the Bush administration has been relentlessly aggressive and unfailingly sophisticated in promoting its agenda. Nowhere was this unique mix of political hardball and state-of-the-art marketing acumen more on display than in the 2002 elections. The Republicans went into the contest with minority status in the Senate (thanks to Vermont Senator Jim Jeffords' defection from the GOP in 2000), a scant six-seat majority in the House of Representatives, and the tide of history running against them: For the past 60 years, every sitting president's party has lost seats in the off-year elections of his first term.

This year, however, White House political guru Karl Rove was determined to overturn tradition. Rove's master plan included hand-picking the GOP nominees for national office, using the president's prestige on the stump to swing close races their way, and mustering an intensive, last-minute effort to get out the vote. When the dust finally cleared, the Republicans had gained six seats in the house, giving them 229 (vs. 205 for the Dems, plus one independent), and picked up two Senate seats for a 51-seat total, leaving them in control of both houses of Congress for the first time since early in Bush's presidency. Here is an account of how Rove and Co. challenged history—and won. . . .

There is, as a rule, no smoking in the White House, but this Election Day was one for breaking the rules. The moment of sweet vindication came at midnight, up in the private quarters, where President Bush and close aides were watching the returns on the Fox News Channel. Unlike the fateful election night of 2000, when they waited for results that never came, this one was going well, and the President, who hovered close enough to the television to get static cling, was enjoying it. His strategist Karl Rove was perched on the edge of an armchair, double-thumbing e-mail messages into his Black-Berry when the call came in from Lloyd Smith, the salty 51-year-old manager of Jim Talent's campaign against Senator Jean Carnahan in Missouri.

His boys had been torturing the computer models, Smith said, and it looked as if Talent was performing well enough in the Democratic strongholds of St. Louis and Kansas City to guarantee victory. "You're the man!" Rove bellowed back into his cell phone. Then he gave the President the news: Talent's win meant they didn't have just the state; they had the Senate. They had it all.

And with that, the President lighted a cigar. It's especially heady to win the game when even playing it is a gamble. Presidents aren't supposed to bet their prestige in midterm elections, which their party traditionally loses. Rove especially, as Bush's long political shadow, could imagine the stories that would have been written if he had sent the President into every tight race and the Republicans still lost: no coattails, no mandate, no respect for the adviser who had peddled perhaps the riskiest midterm-election strategy ever to emerge from a White House. Instead he woke up Wednesday morning in a new political world, one step closer to the grand, gauzy vision Rove has been touting for the past three years: that together he and Bush are forging a new Republican majority that will rule the land for a generation. "This is part of it," Rove told *Time* last week. "It's not going to be a dramatic realignment of American politics in which one day it's deadlocked and the next day it's a blowout. The changes are gradual, but they're persistent."

The victory reflected more than a year of careful plotting: harvesting candidates, husbanding resources, refining messages. But in the crucial last weeks, it also reflected the extraordinary relationship between the President and his political adviser of nearly 15 years. What does it take to persuade a President, who has a country to run and a reputation to protect and who prefers to go to sleep in his own bed, usually before 10 P.M., to plunge from state to state as though his own survival depended on it, when in fact the opposite is true? The sheer nerve of the White House strategy left even enemies in awe. "What they did was risky as hell," marvels Tony Coelho, a veteran operative who served as chairman of Al Gore's 2000 campaign. "They rolled the dice, they won, and now Bush has a huge mandate. It's not about 9/11 anymore. He is the legitimate President."

Most campaigns begin the moment the previous one ends, and so this wild race, with its surprise ending, actually started quietly and methodically nearly two years earlier, in the weeks after Bush's presidential victory was confirmed. The Rove war room knows no armistice, and so in December 2000, when he hired Ken Mehlman, the key deputy who shares his devotion to the game, they started blocking out the map for the next election. Where had Bush done well in 2000? Where were vulnerable seats that could be picked off? And, most of all, who would carry the G.O.P. flag into the battles that mattered most?

Though Rove is often cast as Bush's conservative enforcer, his search for candidates was highly pragmatic. He wanted to know who could win; true believers did him no good if they were left smoldering at 35% on Election Day. That meant he didn't much care whose turn it was to run, who was owed a favor or whom the state-party elders had anointed. Complaints about his meddling soon spread across the country. But when it came to winning back the Senate, Rove had a strong ally in Senator Bill Frist, the Tennessee surgeon who was running the Senate campaign committee and who was determined to put enough races in play to give the Republicans a shot at getting their majority back.

The blueprint was born in the spring of 2001 in the private upstairs dining room of La Brasserie on Capitol Hill. Frist and his political director, Mitch Bainwol, ran through a PowerPoint presentation for Rove and majority leader Trent Lott that was based on some quiet polling in 10 key states. They had tested the names of potential Republican candidates—some of whom hadn't even decided to run. In Minnesota, former Democrat and St. Paul Mayor Norm Coleman, who was planning a bid for Governor, actually looked as though he could knock off Paul Wellstone if he could be persuaded to run for Senate instead. In Missouri, G.O.P. Representative Jo Ann Emerson, who had replaced her husband after his death, lagged behind Senator Jean Carnahan in a potential "battle of the widows." But former Representative Jim Talent broke even with Carnahan. South Dakota looked promising if Representative John Thune could be persuaded to give up his run for Governor and challenge Democratic Senator Tim Johnson.

Frist concluded the rundown with a prediction of Republican victory if he had the financial support of the Republican National Committee. By the end of the campaign, the R.N.C. would give $15 million to Frist, seven times as much as its 1998 payout. That dinner launched a coordinated recruitment effort unprecedented in recent memory. Bush himself made the call to Thune; in Minnesota, Vice President Dick Cheney called Tim Pawlenty, the Republican majority leader in the Statehouse, just 90 minutes before he was set to announce his bid for the Senate and asked him to stand down so that Coleman could move in. The President's father, George H. W. Bush, tried unsuccessfully to persuade ex-New Jersey Governor Tom Kean to enter the race against then Senator Bob Torricelli.

To help candidates in need of a little extra muscle, Rove dispatched surrogates in all directions—experienced political hands such as Vin Webber, Charles Black, and Don Fierce, who could keep him informed about where the money needed to flow right up to the final hours. "I was amazed at who was working these races," says a G.O.P. veteran. "Usually they have some 25-year-old kid." Shortly after Rove learned that the polls were tightening in the Senate race in North Carolina, the Republican Senatorial Committee sent an additional $1.5 million to help Elizabeth Dole. "They had the resources ready, and they didn't hesitate to pull the trigger," says consultant Ed Gillespie, one of Rove's expert surrogates who handled that race.

Through it all, Rove wore his war room on his belt—the postcard-size BlackBerry communicator that holds his unmatchable Rolodex as well as his e-mail system, through which he squirted orders and suggestions to campaign workers and lobbyists using only a few words. "It's like haiku," says a political operative who has been on the receiving end. During meetings—even ones with the President—Rove would constantly spin the BlackBerry's dial and punch out text on its tiny keyboard. "Sometimes we're in a meeting talking to each other and BlackBerrying each other at the same time," says a colleague. At times Rove's voltage got too hot even for all his outlets. He became known for breaking into song in midsentence. During games of gin rummy on Air Force One during Bush's campaign swings, Rove was always the loudest one yelling, "Feed the monkey!" when it was his turn to pick up a card. (Bush played once, Rove says, and "whipped me.")

Once they had recruited the right people, they needed the right message, and here it was the Democrats who thought they had the upper hand. On July 19, Frist's committee hosted a retreat for donors at the West Virginia resort Greenbrier. That day alone, the stock market slid 390 points; the White House was bracing for the mid-August restatement of corporate income, which was expected to increase pressure on Bush to crack down on the kind of people who had assembled at the resort. "It felt like a funeral," recalls Bainwol. Democrats were calling for the scalp of Securities and Exchange Commission chairman Harvey Pitt and citing poll numbers that pointed to big gains for their party in both houses. "They were filled with the euphoria of our misery," Bainwol says of his rivals.

Rove stepped in to stop the bleeding. Sources tell *Time* he leaned on executives to support the corporate accounting reforms written by Democratic Senator Paul Sarbanes. Three weeks later, he orchestrated the President's economic summit in Waco, Texas, which amounted to little more than a photo op for CEOs but gave the impression that Bush was focused on the economy. The Justice Department, urged on by G.O.P. political consultants, made several high-profile arrests of corporate chiefs, complete with handcuffs. In August Rove kept his boss traveling during his vacation and talking about the economy.

But come the final weeks of battle, it was Rove's ability to deliver the President, and Bush's to deliver the voters, that, when the results were finally in, left political experts in both parties speechless. The idea of sending Bush himself out into the midterm storms wasn't a last-minute decision made because Rove and the pollsters saw something that made them think the races were suddenly winnable. It stretched all the way back to a series of meetings last January of Rove's Strategic Initiatives office (nicknamed "strategery" after the *Saturday Night Live* parody of Bush's malapropisms). Bush's top aides debated whether to keep the President above the fray during the midterms—"to protect him," as Rove says—or to put his wartime popularity to political use. They decided on the latter and took their recommendation to Bush. "As far as Bush was concerned, the real risk would have been to sit on his hands when he had the opportunity to make the difference in some very close races. He and Karl were completely in synch."

So the two were prepared when Congressman Saxby Chambliss agreed to Rove's call to challenge Georgia incumbent Max Cleland, a war veteran and conservative Democrat who had voted with the President on his $1.3 trillion tax cut. Chambliss had demands beyond the buckets of money Rove promised: "I also need the President to come to Georgia twice," Chambliss said. Rove looked at him, perplexed. "Can he only come to the state two times?" "No, Karl, I mean twice a month," Chambliss said. It was an outsize request, but Bush almost lived up to it. He visited Georgia six times—including two stops just before Election Day, which local politicians believe sealed the upset.

In the final days of the campaign, Rove was not only penciling in new stops on the Bush itinerary but was also tearing up the Vice President's schedule, sometimes hours before an event, to reroute him to a more politically potent place. When Chambliss started getting traction with the homeland-security issue, Cheney was there to hit that theme hard. When John Sununu needed help in Nashua, N.H., and wanted Bush to touch down there, Rove Black-Berried the campaign strategist: "Can't do, will get back to you." Two days later, he had the First Lady there instead. The narrowcasting was so refined that Energy Secretary Spence Abraham, a former Michigan Senator, visited a Florida senior home in which half the residents hailed from his home state.

On Election Day the Republican machine was prepared to be nimble. The R.N.C. put in place a 72-hour plan that tried to match the labor unions' success in getting voters to the polls. "We decided to change the culture of Republicans running just on money," says future House majority leader Tom DeLay. "We decided to run a ground war."

Though he endorsed the idea of blitzing the country in the last week of the campaign, Bush retained his well-known distaste for spending nights away from his White House pillow. "Bush gets pretty grumpy out there, and Karl absorbs the brunt of it," says an aide to the President. Five days before the election, as Air Force One flew from South Dakota to Indiana, Rove was tugging at the President to make an extra stop in Iowa to help candidates there. Bush was having none of it. "You better have a parachute, Karl," Bush quipped, "because when we get over Iowa, we're throwing you off the plane."

There are many reasons that Bush trusted Rove's advice to wager so much on the midterms. Rove sits in Hillary Clinton's old West Wing office, and that's as good an image as any: he and the President have a long political marriage. Unlike most politicians, who change advisers the way Hollywood stars cycle through spouses, Bush has stuck with Rove even through his most disastrous misjudgments: underestimating John McCain's appeal back in the New Hampshire primaries and failing to take disgruntled Senator Jim Jeffords seriously right up to the day he switched parties and gave the Democrats the Senate back. The easy caricature of the partnership—the one to which Democrats cling at their peril—casts Rove as "Bush's Brain," the snickering puppeteer who never takes his eye off politics, so Bush can talk highmindedly about principles. But that cartoon misunderstands what a departure the Bush-Rove relationship is from recent Presidents and their operatives. Bush's father famously loved policy but scorned politics, saw campaigning as a necessary evil but banished the political hacks from the West Wing. Even Bill Clinton, as political an animal as they come, ran through advisers like Kleenex. James Carville and Dick Morris and the rest were not making White House policy.

But George W. Bush sees politics and government as seamless; his whole vision of the presidency intertwines the two, and so it makes sense that he keeps his political adviser right next to him. Rather than distance himself from Rove after the 2000 election by sending him to run the R.N.C. or set up shop as an outside consultant, Bush brought him into the West Wing. There are few decisions, from tax cuts to judicial nominations to human cloning, in which Rove is not directly involved. "It's not a real meeting if Karl isn't there," says a senior member of the domestic-policy staff. While Rove does not attend sessions of the President's war council, he regularly weighs in on foreign-policy matters during morning senior staff meetings with the President, offering opinions on everything from Middle East peace to international trade to the Cuban economic embargo. "Karl has the absolute, utter trust of the President of the United States," says Bill Paxon, a prominent G.O.P. operative and former Congressman with close ties to the White House. "That's really what makes him so good."

Bush often brags that he does not look at polls, but that is in part because he has Rove to do it for him. The two men delight in the game—a fact both the President and his staff go to great lengths to obscure. "They both love this stuff, and so they talk about it in shorthand. It's like talking about baseball," says a senior White House official. And it showed throughout the campaign: "The President knew what was in nearly every ad. He was getting that from Karl." He had a junkie's appetite for the polling data: "Bush wanted to know the polling numbers," says Brooks Kochvar, campaign manager for new Indiana Congressman Chris Chocola. "It wasn't just the top line either. He wanted to know where the undecideds stood and what was going on in depth in the polls."

The question now, after such a triumph, is whether it will go to Rove's head so that he loses his grip, like many a political genius before him. His successes have guaranteed that there are plenty of people who would love to see him fail. And more than one pundit has rubbed his hands in anticipation of Rove's overreading the message of Bush's success. But here again, it may be the nature of his relationship with Bush that saves him from the agonies of arrogance.

Bush has always known how to keep Rove in his place. To this day, Rove tells the story of seeing George W. for the first time in 1973, when he was sent by Bush's dad to deliver the car keys. Rove sounds as though he had just encountered the reincarnation of James Dean, leather jacket and all.

"He was cool," says Rove, who can still come across as the nerd in high school with the pocket protector and briefcase. Where Bush was the carefree product of a loving family, with a Yale degree and money to burn, Rove was the opposite. His father, an oil company geologist, moved the family constantly. Rove's parents divorced, and his mother eventually killed herself. Rove attended three different universities before quitting without a degree to go into politics full time.

For all the differences between Rove and Bush, their similarities bound them from the start. They bonded over their shared disdain for the snobbery of East Coast élites and the culture of permissiveness of the 1960s. They both share a faith in their own instincts: Bush boasts about trusting his gut and the clear simple wisdom of the West Texas oil patch. Rove, the college dropout turned academic, cultivates an intellectual version of the same, considering himself a Natural—a self-taught big brain who devours histories and political tomes and applies what he learns to the art of winning races.

But the President's role in their symbiotic relationship is as often about taking his adviser down a notch as it is taking direction from him—which in light of Tuesday's victory may be what saves Rove from himself. There are the now famous nicknames Bush has for Rove (Boy Genius on good days, Turd Blossom on others), and there is the evident pleasure the President seems to take in putting Rove in his place. "Thank you for that brilliant idea," Bush will say mockingly when Rove is rambling on. And Bush seems to know when not to listen to his political adviser. It was Rove who argued in the summer of 2000 against picking Dick Cheney as Bush's running mate, citing Cheney's multiple heart attacks and lack of electoral appeal. Bush disagreed, of course, and his decision has paid off so handsomely that just last week the President announced that Cheney would be his running mate again in the 2004 campaign. Which shows that Karl Rove isn't the only one planning for the next election.

Why Are These Men Laughing?

Ron Suskind

Esquire | January 2003

The following article created more controversy than any other selection in this book. In it, Ron Suskind paints a scathing portrait of a White House operation dominated by Karl Rove, where political considerations take precedence over all else; but what really got people talking were the comments of John DiIulio, erstwhile director of the White House Office of Faith-Based and Community Initiatives. In a phone conversation and a follow-up letter to Suskind, DiIulio (who resigned his position in February, 2002 to resume teaching at the University of Pennsylvania) characterized the Bush administration as "the reign of the Mayberry Machiavellis," adding that "the lack of even basic policy knowledge . . . was somewhat breathtaking."

What was truly breathtaking was how quickly the White House swung into action after The New York Times *published a preview of Suskind's article in early December. That morning, DiIulio offered a tepid response, questioning several of Suskind's quotes. At his noon briefing the same day, White House press secretary Ari Fleischer told reporters, "any suggestion that the White House makes decisions that are not based on sound policy reasons is baseless and groundless." By midafternoon DiIulio was in full retreat, issuing another statement that read, "John DiIulio agrees that his criticisms were groundless and baseless due to poorly chosen words and examples. He sincerely apologizes and is deeply remorseful."*

This left everyone to wonder what sort of pressure the White House had brought to bear on DiIulio. Meanwhile, Suskind—whose veracity had already been attacked by the Bushies over an earlier Esquire *piece on the departure of communications director Karen Hughes ("Mrs. Hughes Takes Her Leave"), in which he quoted White House chief of staff Andy Card as lamenting that "the whole balance of the place . . . is gone, simply gone"—stood by his story, as did* Esquire. *The magazine even went so far as to post DiIulio's letter on its website—where, as of this writing, it could be viewed in its entirety. . . .*

On a cool Saturday a few days before Christmas last year, Karl Rove showed up in a festive mood at David Dreyer's house in suburban Washington, D. C., to trim the tree and have a cup of eggnog. Dreyer is a liberal Democrat, formerly the deputy communications director in the Clinton White

House and also a senior adviser to Treasury secretary Robert Rubin. He now runs a small public-relations firm. His daughter and Karl's son were in the same seventh-grade class. After a few brief, friendly encounters at school functions, Dreyer invited Karl and his boy over for a tree-trimming party with the class, about fifteen kids and eight or nine parents in all. It was one of those enchanting days that you remember for a long time. Rove was the ringmaster of fun, brimming with good cheer, Mr. Silly, without a care in the world. All in attendance were warmed by his presence, and you never would have known that his job carried such awesome responsibility. Rove was far too busy decorating cookies and stringing popcorn to betray anything close to that. "Karl completely took charge, absolutely in the most endearing way possible. He had a vision of what each kid could contribute. What they could make or hang, based on how tall they were, or what they could do . . . what ornament, what Christmas ball. Need more lights? Hey, kids, let's get in the car and go get some more lights!" Dreyer, a sober man, is trying not to go overboard about how all this affected him. "You expect a partisan who's onstage all the time, and it doesn't function that way in real life. You get a father and husband." He pauses. "I think it's sad." What's sad? I ask. "That we so often have such an extraordinarily one-dimensional view of people, of our fellow human beings." Not that Dreyer, having glimpsed Karl in repose, far from his natural habitat, sees him as anything less than extraordinary. "He was magnetic," Dreyer says dreamily. "He picked up my four-year-old son, Sam, so he could place the star atop the tree. It was lovely. Just lovely."

When I heard this story, it made me like Karl Rove. It made him sound like a hero to children, and in my view, there's no better person. But I've never heard another story like this one, because people in Washington, especially Rove's friends, are utterly petrified to talk about him.

They heard that I was writing about Karl Rove, seeking to contextualize his role as a senior adviser in the Bush White House, and they began calling, some anonymously, some not, saying that they wanted to help and leaving phone numbers. The calls from members of the White House staff were solemn, serious. Their concern was not only about politics, they said, not simply about Karl pulling the president further to the right. It went deeper; it was about this administration's ability to focus on the substance of governing—issues like the economy and social security and education and health care—as opposed to its clear political acumen, its ability to win and enhance power.

And so it seemed that each time I made an inquiry about Karl Rove, I received in return a top-to-bottom critique of the White House's basic functions, so profound is Rove's influence.

I made these inquiries in part because last spring, when I spoke to White House chief of staff Andrew Card, he sounded an alarm about the unfettered rise of Rove in the wake of senior adviser Karen Hughes's resignation: "I'll need designees, people trusted by the president that I can elevate for various needs to balance against Karl. . . . They are going to have to really step up, but it won't be easy. Karl is a formidable adversary."

One senior White House official told me that he'd be summarily fired if it were known we were talking. "But many of us feel it's our duty—our obligation as Americans—to get the word out that, certainly in domestic policy, there has been almost no meaningful consideration of any real issues. It's just kids on Big Wheels who talk politics and know nothing. It's depressing. Domestic Policy Council meetings are a farce. This leaves shoot-from-the-hip political calculations—mostly from Karl's shop—to triumph by default. No one balances Karl. Forget it. That was Andy's cry for help."

But now the stunning midterm ascendancy of the Republicans boosts Rove into a new category; a major political realignment may hereby be ascribed to his mastery, his grand plan.

At the moment when one-party rule returns to Washington—a state that existed, in fact, in the first five months of the Bush presidency, before Senator Jeffords switched parties—we are offered a rare view of the way this White House works. The issue of how the administration decides what to do with its mandate—and where political calculation figures in that mix—has never been so important to consider. This White House will now be able to do precisely what it wants. To understand the implications of this, you must understand Karl Rove.

"It's an amazing moment," said one senior White House official early on the morning after. "Karl just went from prime minister to king. Amazing . . . and a little scary. Now no one will speak candidly about him or take him on or contradict him. Pure power, no real accountability. It's just 'listen to Karl and everything will work out.' . . . That may go for the president, too."

Over time, I came to know these sources to be serious people with credible information. And, of course, their fear of discovery is warranted, for this White House has defined itself as a disciplined command center that enforces a unanimity of purpose and has a well-known prohibition of leaks, a well-known distaste for openness. But still, the fact that they must veil themselves leaves them open to the charge of being disgruntled employees. I can only attest to the fact that they certainly do not seem to be that. There is, however, one man who, at some personal and professional risk, has now decided to speak openly about the inner workings of the White House.

President George W. Bush called John DiIulio "one of the most influential social entrepreneurs in America" when he appointed the University of Pennsylvania professor, author, historian, and domestic-affairs expert to head the White House Office of Faith-Based and Community Initiatives. He was the Bush administration's big brain, controversial but deeply respected by Republicans and Democrats, academicians and policy players. The appointment was rightfully hailed: DiIulio provided gravity to national policy debates and launched the most innovative of President Bush's campaign ideas—the faith-based initiative, which he managed until this past February, the last four months from Philadelphia.

"There is no precedent in any modern White House for what is going on in this one: a complete lack of a policy apparatus," says DiIulio. "What you've got is everything—and I mean everything—being run by the political arm. It's the reign of the Mayberry Machiavellis."

In a seven-page letter sent a few weeks after our first conversation, DiIulio, who still considers himself a passionate supporter of the president, offers a detailed account and critique of the time he spent in the Bush White House.

"I heard many, many staff discussions but not three meaningful, substantive policy discussions," he writes. "There were no actual policy white papers on domestic issues. There were, truth be told, only a couple of people in the West Wing who worried at all about policy substance and analysis, and they were even more overworked than the stereotypical nonstop, twenty-hour-a-day White House staff. Every modern presidency moves on the fly, but on social policy and related issues, the lack of even basic policy knowledge, and the only casual interest in knowing more, was somewhat breathtaking: discussions by fairly senior people who meant Medicaid but were talking Medicare; near-instant shifts from discussing any actual policy pros and cons to discussing political communications, media strategy, et cetera. Even quite junior staff would sometimes hear quite senior staff pooh-pooh any need to dig deeper for pertinent information on a given issue."

Like David Stockman, the whip-smart budget director to Ronald Reagan who twenty years ago revealed that Reagan's budget numbers didn't add up,

DiIulio is this administration's first credible, independent witness—a sovereign who supports his president but must, nonetheless, speak his mind.

Sources in the West Wing, echoing DiIulio's comments, say that even cursory discussion of domestic policy became much less frequent after September 11, 2001, with the exception of Homeland Security. Meanwhile, the department of "Strategery," or the "Strategery Group," depending on the source, has steadily grown. The term, coined in 2000 by *Saturday Night Live's* Will Ferrell, started as a joke at the White House, too, but has actually become a term of art meaning the oversight of any activity—from substantive policy to ideological stance to public event—by the president's political thinkers.

"It's a revealing shorthand," says one White House staff member. "Yes, the president sometimes trips, rhetorically, but it doesn't matter as long as we keep our eye on the ball politically."

This approach to policy-making is a fairly radical departure from the customary relationship between White House political directors and policy professionals. Each has always influenced the other, of course, but the political office has rarely been so central to guiding policy in virtually every area, deciding what is promoted and what is tabled.

"Besides the tax cut, which was cut-and-dried during the campaign," DiIulio writes, "and the education bill, which was really a Ted Kennedy bill, the administration has not done much, either in absolute terms or in comparison with previous administrations at this stage, on domestic policy. There is a virtual absence as yet of any policy accomplishments that might, to a fair-minded nonpartisan, count as the flesh on the bones of so-called compassionate conservatism. There is still two years, maybe six, for them to do more and better on domestic policy and, specifically, on the compassion agenda. And, needless to say, 9/11, and now the global war on terror and the new homeland- and national-security plans, must be weighed in the balance. But, as I think Andy Card himself told you in so many words, even allowing for those huge contextual realities, they could stand to find ways of inserting more serious policy fiber into the West Wing diet and engage much less in on-the-fly policy-making by speechmaking."

DiIulio calls the president "a highly admirable person of enormous personal decency . . . [who is] much, much smarter than some people—including some of his own supporters and advisers—seem to suppose." So what, then, is John DiIulio's motivation for now offering his pointed critique? There is, as he says, "two years, maybe six." He has a vision for who George W. Bush might yet become.

If you buy Isaiah Berlin's famous dictum about history being a struggle between foxes and hedgehogs, Karl Rove has, like the hedgehog, stayed focused on a single ideal and pushed it forward relentlessly. A bookish kid born in Denver on Christmas Day 1950, Rove has known George W. Bush for thirty years. He started bobbing up on senior staffs of Texas campaigns in his late twenties, with the unshakable goal of making the Republicans the permanent majority party. He's up early and works late, with an assured disdain for Marquis of Queensberry rules of political engagement. In conversation with scores of people who know him, the assessment ultimately is the same: For Karl Rove, it's all and only about winning. The rest—vision, ideology, good government, ideas to bind a nation, reasonable dissent, collegiality, mutual respect—is for later.

And Rove is disciplined in maintaining his mystery. In visiting the White House frequently from February to April of this past year, I interviewed much of the senior staff, as well as the First Lady. No one would utter so much as a word about Rove. They'd talk about one another, assessing the strengths, weaknesses, and specific roles of Hughes, Card, deputy chief of staff Josh Bolten, media adviser Mark McKinnon, communications chief Dan Bartlett, Cheney aide Mary Matalin, national-security adviser Condoleezza Rice, the vice-president, and, of course, the president himself. When I'd mention Rove, the reaction was always the same: "I can't really talk about Karl." It was odd; it was extraordinary.

Eventually, I met with Rove. I arrived at his office a few minutes early, just in time to witness the Rove Treatment, which, like LBJ's famous browbeating style, is becoming legend but is seldom reported. Rove's assistant, Susan Ralston, said he'd be just a minute. She's very nice, witty, and polite. Over her shoulder was a small back room where a few young men were toiling away. I squeezed into a chair near the open door to Rove's modest chamber, my back against his doorframe.

Inside, Rove was talking to an aide about some political stratagem in some state that had gone awry and a political operative who had displeased him. I paid it no mind and reviewed a jotted list of questions I hoped to ask. But after a moment, it was like ignoring a tornado flinging parked cars. "We will fuck him. Do you hear me? We will fuck him. We will ruin him. Like no one has ever fucked him!" As a reporter, you get around—curse words, anger, passionate intensity are not notable events—but the ferocity, the bellicosity, the violent imputations were, well, shocking. This went on without a break for a minute or two. Then the aide slipped out looking a bit ashen, and Rove, his face ruddy from the exertions of the past few moments, looked at me and smiled a gentle, Clarence-the-Angel smile. "Come on in." And I did. And we had the most amiable chat for a half hour. I asked a variety of questions about his relationship with Karen Hughes. Were there ever tensions between him and Karen? Nope. "Oh, we're both strong-willed people, but we work well together." I mentioned a few disputes others had told me of. He dismissed them all. Didn't they sort of bury the hatchet after September 11? Nope— no hatchet to bury. As the president's two most powerful aides, did they ever disagree? "Not often." Any examples? Nope. He couldn't be nicer, mind you. Finally, I asked if one of his role models was Mark Hanna, the visionary political guru to President William McKinley who helped reshape Republicans into the party of inclusion and ushered in decades of electoral victory at the turn of the twentieth century. Rove's a student of McKinley and Hanna. He has talked extensively in the past about lessons he's learned from this duo's response to challenges of their era. "No, this era is nothing like McKinley's. I'm not at all like Hanna. Never wanted to be."

Since then, I've talked to old colleagues, dating back twenty-five years, one of whom said, "Some kids want to grow up to be president. Karl wanted to grow up to be Mark Hanna. We'd talk about it all the time. We'd say, 'Jesus, Karl, what kind of kid wants to grow up to be Mark Hanna?'" In any event, it's clear, when I think of my encounter with Rove, why this particular old friend of his, and scores of others—many of whom spoke of the essential good nature of this man who was a teammate on some campaign or other—don't want their names mentioned, ever. Just like Rove's mates on the current team—the one running the free world—who go numb at the thought of talking frankly, for attribution, about him. These are powerful people, confident and consequential, who suffer gaze aversion when I mention his name. No doubt they've had extended exposure to the two Karls I saw that day last spring.

William Kristol, among the most respected of the conservative commentators—a man embraced by the Right but still on dinner-party guest lists for the center and Left—is untouchable. He is willing to speak.

"Karl and I aren't really friends. I have sort of a vague and indirect relationship with him. But we talk pretty regularly. He has always been fair and straight and honest with me, despite the stories that others have about him." He pauses, as though encountering one of those beware falling rocks signs. "I believe Karl is Bush. They're not separate, each of them freestanding, with distinct agendas, as some people say. Karl thinks X. Bush thinks X. Clearly, it's a very complicated relationship." He goes on to say that he thinks Bush is a "canny manager" who creates competing teams and plays them against one another. As for those who sometimes disagree with that point, he says, "There is criticism of Karl from the friends of the former President Bush who don't approve of the way the current President Bush is doing his job in every case." Kristol notes that "the kid is what he is, and he's different from the father, some differences that I feel good about," but that gray men around "41" who don't approve of "43" have trouble criticizing the son to the father "and ascribe everything to Karl's malign influence." In that, Rove is at the center of the most portentous father-son conversation of modern times. Sources close to the former president say Rove was fired from the 1992 Bush presidential campaign after he planted a negative story with columnist Robert Novak about dissatisfaction with campaign fundraising chief and Bush loyalist Robert Mosbacher Jr. It was smoked out, and he was summarily ousted.

Mark McKinnon, who would not speak of Rove in my earlier interviews with him for another story on the Bush White House, is now effusive. "Karl's sheer bandwidth is greater than anyone I've ever met. . . . Lots of people have planetary systems, covering history or policy or politics, but Karl covers the whole universe." He goes on: "James [Carville] and Dick [Morris]"—both advisers to Clinton whom McKinnon knows from his days, up until the mid-1990s, as a Democratic consultant—"can drive the car and drive it very well. Karl can take out the engine and put it back together. He's the best ever. And his love for policy is as great or greater than his love of politics." This is the Rove defense. He's really a policy guy, a seeker of best remedies, a nonpolitical.

Senator John McCain knows something of Karl Rove, though he'd rather not think about all that tonight, as a crowd gathers to celebrate the release of the senator's new book. In fact, lots of folks here know Rove well. "Sure, I know Karl," says one man who has worked on several campaigns with him. "At the end of long days, we'd always meet at one bar or another, everybody but Karl. Where's Karl? we'd wonder. The line was always 'Oh, he's out ruining careers.'"

These are virtually all Republicans, gathered in an elegant room off the wide atrium of Union Station. It's a good night for McCain. He and the intellectually lithe Mark Salter, his longtime aide, have produced their second book in just three years. The first, *Faith of My Fathers*, documented McCain's early life as the rebel son and grandson of legendary admirals who was shot down in Vietnam and held prisoner for five and a half years. This second book, which picks up after Vietnam, is more reflective, angry, and lyrical, as McCain bares his breast and beats it a little. At sixty-six and in middling health, he's settling, it seems, on the idea that he won't get a chance to be president. It's the kind of thing that has liberated his already libertine spirit, though it stands as tragic injustice to everyone else in the room. And people in various corners of the wide room are retelling the story again—they'll tell it forever—the moment when McCain surged in the New Hampshire primary, when he caught, and won the state in a walk. The Bush juggernaut had stalled. McCain, embraced by the media, to whom he gave extraordinary access—"just hang with me, boys, all day, everything on the record"—was seizing the high middle ground, where you win presidential elections. And someone points to a guy in the room—yeah, him over there near the curtains, tall, friendly-looking guy named John Weaver. He was the other genius wunderkind in Texas in the 1980s, along with Rove. They won campaigns left and right, those two. Rove was mostly a direct-mail fundraiser back then, Weaver more a strategist-manager type. Something happened that neither will talk about, and they stopped working together in 1988. Many of the people in this room followed Weaver, who was McCain's political director in his bid for the 2000 Republican presidential nomination, to this side of the Republican party. Since their estrangement, Weaver's relationship with Rove has gotten somewhat odd.

On the night of the vote in New Hampshire, the senator's senior staff was all gathered at the Crowne Plaza in Nashua. A call came in to the penthouse suite moments after McCain's big victory was declared by the networks. It was Rove. A junior staffer cupped his hand over the receiver and told Weaver: "Rove says he's calling to concede."

Weaver was stunned. "Karl's conceding?" He shook off disbelief, gathered himself, and said, "Tell Karl that he can't concede. He's not the candidate. The governor has to bring himself to actually call the senator." Weaver gave Karl a cell-phone number where McCain could be reached, and a few minutes later, the candidates had a brief chat. Then it was off to the showdown in South Carolina, which changed everything. . . .

I suddenly hear McCain laugh through the din. He laughs like a pirate. There's a cluster, bent in tight, as he whispers something hysterical. Heads go back. Man can tell a story. Tonight he is ebullient. On Sunday, *The Washington Post* gushed over his book, leading with what it called the strange occurrence that the president is the third-most-popular politician in America, behind Al Gore, who got more votes, and, of course, John McCain.

He loved that, God knows, and tonight he's among his lovers, his troops, cutting between them, slapping and clasping, a man of modest height and fiercely angled, always leaning a few degrees forward, a bit pinched, in his blue suit. He breaks from the cluster; I meet him in the clearing. We huddle for a moment, make small talk about this and that. I ask if historians will consider South Carolina a crossroads moment for the Republican party. "Well, it was unprecedented, South Carolina," he says softly. "But you have to put it past you and move on." He points over to the corner where his top aide, Salter, is now standing next to Weaver and a few others. "Those guys can tell you all about what happened. As for history," he says, offering a pained smile, "I think it will little note nor long remember and all that." I go over. Weaver gets asked about Rove quite often; people know about their history. He always demurs. "Not worth getting into," he says. People around him, though, will talk. "John will never work in the Republican party again, thanks to Karl," says Salter. Weaver now works for the Democratic Congressional Campaign Committee. It's commonly held that Rove ran him out of the party. The word went out: Any Republican who hired Weaver would be held in disfavor by the president. "What can I say?" Weaver says quietly. "Like me, all the moderate Republicans have been run out of the party by the Right. I'm doing what I've always done politically; these guys just call themselves Democrats now."

As for the Waterloo of South Carolina, most of the facts are well-known, and among this group of Republicans, what happened has taken on the air of an unsolved crime, a cold case, with Karl Rove being the prime suspect. Bush loyalists, maybe working for the campaign, maybe just representing its interests, claimed in parking-lot handouts and telephone "push polls" and whisper campaigns that McCain's wife, Cindy, was a drug addict, that McCain might be mentally unstable from his captivity in Vietnam, and that the senator had fathered a black child with a prostitute. Callers push-polled members of a South Carolina right-to-life organization and other groups, asking if the black baby might influence their vote. Now here's the twist, the part that drives McCain admirers insane to this very day: That last rumor took seed because the McCains had done an especially admirable thing. Years back they'd adopted a baby from a Mother Teresa orphanage in Bangladesh. Bridget, now eleven years old, waved along with the rest of the McCain brood from stages across the state, a dark-skinned child inadvertently providing a photo op for slander. The attacks were of a level and vitriol that even McCain, who was regularly beaten in captivity, could not ignore. He began to answer the slights, strayed off message about how he would lead the nation if he got the chance, and lost the war for South Carolina. Bush emerged from the showdown upright and victorious . . . and onward he marched.

Eight months after the South Carolina primary, McCain and Weaver were on a plane campaigning with the nominee. This was the kind of barnstorming finale—closing in on the last week of the campaign—that Rove normally wouldn't miss. But Weaver was with McCain on the plane, and if Weaver is present, Rove will not show. The governor was, nonetheless, ecstatic. With McCain at his side for the better part of two weeks, he'd been on fire. After a stop in Fresno, California, for a joint speech, Weaver slipped out of the hall and Bush slipped out after him. McCain, who was still inside working the crowd, was due to leave now, his promised time with Bush completed. McCain had told Representative Tom Davis, a Virginia congressman heading up the Republican congressional effort, that he'd spend the last week whistle-stopping House and Senate races.

Governor Bush approached Weaver, who was huddling with the McCain staff. They'd known each other for fifteen years. "Johnny, I want you and John to be with me until the end."

"Can't do it, George," Weaver said. "I just talked to Tom Davis, and he's really counting on us. We've made a commitment."

Bush grew agitated. "You don't seem to understand. I want you with us!" It was already clear that the race was very close. Bush was looking for every advantage. He said, "Look, I'm better when John's with me."

Bush said, "Hold on a minute," stepped away, placed a call on his cell phone, and walked back, looking relieved. "Look, I just talked to Karl, and he says don't worry about the congressional races. It's okay for you to come with me."

Weaver said, "Thanks anyway, but Karl's not in charge of us." McCain walked up. "Weav says you can't stay with me for the last week. Is that right, John?" Bush was simmering. McCain was uncertain what to do. After an awkward moment, Weaver said, "I'm sorry, we've really got to go," and hustled McCain into a waiting limo. The senator slumped into the seat, exhaled, and then, with a smile of relief, turned to Weaver and said, "Thank you."

I've come to meet John DiIulio.

It has been three weeks since our first interview, when he spoke with surprising frankness about the style and substance of the White House. Other White House officials had discussed and corroborated the range of Rove's influence, how all major decisions were passing first through his political-strategic directorate. But I was still regarding this White House in terms of the long-standing model, in which the art of political strategy is carefully balanced against serious policy discussion, in which church-state separations of these two distinct functions are respected, even championed.

It seemed that in the person of Karl Rove such distinctions had been blurred. And I hoped that DiIulio, a true believer in problem solving through sober policy analysis, could clarify how this had happened. He, after all, was present when the architecture of this White House—and the key relationships in it—was established.

But even more striking, he is the most credible independent witness to exit the administration so far.

I race into the Sofitel Hotel in downtown Washington a little late for a cocktail party held by the Nelson A. Rockefeller Institute of Government, a nonpartisan think tank based in Albany, New York, that has brought luminaries together to kick off its three-day conference on religion and social-welfare policy. The French-owned hotel has little bustle in its portico—all cool marble and polished mahogany and whispery potted hydrangeas—and I wander, searching for life, until I see an enormous man near the elevator banks. He's stuffing his hand into a shoulder-slung briefcase, looking for his glasses. He doesn't seem to fit here, or in his blue suit, pulled taut as a windbreaker across a frame a few inches shy of six feet that has to be supporting three hundred pounds. He looks up and squints at me, his glasses now slightly askew on a gentle, soft-edged mug, like Big Pussy in The Sopranos.

His story is as unlikely as it is inspiring: a working-class kid from a tough Italian-Catholic neighborhood, the son of a sheriff's deputy and a department-store clerk, who stumbled forward from a local parish school to Philadelphia's exclusive Haverford School—there through a program for lower-income kids—then to the University of Pennsylvania and Harvard for graduate school, picking up speed with each stride. By the time he got his Ph.D. in political science from Harvard—one of the best students his mentor James Q. Wilson had ever seen—his mass times velocity was bending laws of physics. At Princeton, he was made a full professor after just five years. He was thirty-two.

We talk briefly about our conversation of a few weeks ago; DiIulio knows he has collapsed a wall by offering his frank assessment. "I'm on the record," he says. And then, lightly, "It's not a problem, really not."

His appearance in Washington qualifies as a special event, a top ticket for the guests tinkling glasses inside, where John stops at the reception table.

"Hey, big man!" He turns. It's the Reverend Eugene Rivers, the former gang member who tamed urban violence in Boston, and a DiIulio buddy. They hug as the hive notices DiIulio and surrounds him. They are fans, admirers, but also part of an ideal, that there's nothing odd about Democrats and Republicans dining together and agreeing on a few things, even in regard to faultline issues like religion and social policy and the bracing possibility of connecting the two.

And disagreeing constructively. Rabbi David Saperstein, director of the Religious Action Center of Reform Judaism and a liberal opponent of federal funding for faith-based institutions, makes small talk with Rivers—a conservative black supporter of such funding—while nearby is Harris Wofford, the former Democratic senator from Pennsylvania, right beside Michelle Engler, wife of Michigan's Republican governor, John Engler. This kind of ecumenical promise, political as well as religious, is what helped get George W. Bush elected—the ideal, at its heart, of "compassionate conservatism" and the pledge of returning a more civil tone to Washington.

"There he is, the face of compassionate conservatism," says Richard Roper, who was DiIulio's colleague at Princeton. "Whatever that means." DiIulio has often found himself an enemy of the Left. During the Clinton impeachment drama, he beat the drum for Clinton's removal from office and decried the failure to do so as a signal of the "paganization" of American political culture. And before that, research he conducted in the early 1990s identified the growth of what he called "superpredators" in urban America: youths who seemed to carry a virulent strain of unchecked violence. The research, born of DiIulio's focus on urban America and prison cultures, formed an intellectual framework for mandatory-sentencing statutes that swept the country. DiIulio coauthored *Body Count* with conservative thinker William Bennett and built a thinking-writing-speaking franchise as the conservatives' favorite intellectual. Then he did something that almost no academician, especially one atop his own mountain, seems ever to do: He said, Hold on a minute. Data he'd started collecting in the mid-1990s seemed to contradict the "superpredator" theory. What this latest evolution of his research showed was that prevention, especially targeted at "at risk" urban environments, really does work.

And that brought him to church. Churches—along with mosques and, in some cases, synagogues—have long stood as a bulwark against chaos in many blighted urban cores, as true sanctuary and often an engine of homegrown social services. Urban analysts know this in a general way; DiIulio wanted to know, as a serious researcher, the whys and hows, variables, structures, etiology, and outcomes. This turned out to be a very bright idea; he swiftly captured an enormous swath of unmapped territory. The early trend line of DiIulio's research evolved into his work for the president.

DiIulio and Bush bonded. At a Philadelphia stop early in the campaign, the two spoke for nearly two hours about the possibilities of federal support for faith-based programs, a nuanced discussion that left DiIulio duly impressed. "The president is up to the task. We had an extraordinary exchange. He had significant knowledge and real sensitivity to the challenges that such an effort would face. It's not as though he's not capable."

Bush started talking about his friend "Big John," and a year later DiIulio was an anchor tenant in the new administration. He would attend the 7:30 A.M. senior-staff meeting every day and offer insights on a broad array of domestic policies while launching programs that, in some fashion, used federal financial support to enhance the efforts of faith-based institutions.

Meanwhile, the White House's political arm was asserting itself in the new Office of Strategic Initiatives, which Rove created. In this period before September 11, 2001, domestic affairs accounted for most of what the White House did every day. So John DiIulio and Karl Rove started to regularly encounter each other, forming one of the most interesting couples in the executive branch.

Each, after all, is among the most accomplished in his field. Rove, the consummate political strategist, having trained at the knee of the master, Lee Atwater, who guided Republicans, including George H. W. Bush, to electoral victory; and DiIulio, the public intellectual and academic heavyweight, the only one to join this administration. In almost every realm of public policy, there are always a few people who lead the intellectual parade, advancing the research and ideas that form the agenda for discussion in that field. It's a ferocious meritocracy, played out in symposia and academic journals, on peer-review committees and editorial pages. Generally, administrations tap several of these leaders to join them. Republicans and Democrats both have their share. In economics, for instance, think Milton Friedman or Herbert Stein; they can sometimes be young up-and-comers, like Pat Moynihan in the Nixon administration. In the Clinton White House, they were numerous, including Robert Reich at Labor and Lawrence Summers, Clinton's Treasury secretary and now the president of Harvard.

It's clear, standing in this room with DiIulio, why such men can be so valuable to a president: In the White House, where political calculation is like respiration, they can make confident, fact-based assessments of which important ideas are worth executing. Ideas, ultimately, that a presidency will be remembered for.

The cocktail party is moving toward dinner. Doors are opened to a baronial chamber that cossets a stunning forty-foot-long table. Almost time for DiIulio's speech. He doesn't seem to notice. His wide back is to the door and he's digging deep, trying as he will to make sense of his strange journey.

He says he loves Bush. He loves him as a man, as a friend. He loves his decency, his compassion, which, he says, is "not a 'feel your pain' thing like Clinton. With Bush it's more grounded, more real."

But mention of Clinton turns him inward, tapping repressed memory. He says he visited the White House five times during the Clinton presidency—Al Gore called upon DiIulio in the mid-1990s to assist with his reinventing-government initiative.

Clinton, DiIulio says, was a wonk-in-chief. "For all his flaws, he had that monster to feed. Bush is just too 'normal,'" DiIulio says, curling his thick fingers into quotation marks around the word normal, this huge man with profound hungers. "Great guy. But he doesn't have a beast to feed, that got-to-know-the-answer beast. It's a problem being president at this time, without that, without that hunger."

Then he pauses, and we're both thinking the same thing. Karl. DiIulio smiles his cockeyed smile. "Yeah, he's got a beast. One problem: He's not the president."

Two days later, I get a very long letter from John DiIulio.

It is a manifesto, really, the work of a scholar, reasoned and sober. It is designed to be constructive criticism of the White House that, in large measure, Karl Rove has created, and to give context to his remarks of a few weeks before. Early on, in its opening section, DiIulio, thinking like a historian, offers a stream of qualifiers. "I'm no 'representative sample,' as it were, but I do have some things that are maybe worth saying now on the record."

In the letter, DiIulio is charitable toward his former colleague. "Some are inclined to blame the high political-to-policy ratios of this administration on Karl Rove," DiIulio writes. "Some in the press view Karl as some sort of prince of darkness; actually, he is basically a nice and good-humored man. And some staff members, senior and junior, are awed and cowed by Karl's real or perceived powers. They self-censor lots for fear of upsetting him, and in turn, few of the president's top people routinely tell the president what they really think if they think that Karl will be brought up short in the bargain. Karl is enormously powerful, maybe the single most powerful person in the modern, post-Hoover era ever to occupy a political-adviser post near the Oval Office. The Republican base constituencies, including Beltway libertarian policy elites and religious-Right leaders, trust him to keep Bush 43 from behaving like Bush 41 and moving too far to the center or inching at all center-left. Their shared fiction, supported by zero empirical electoral studies, is that 41 lost in '92 because he lost these right-wing fans. There are not ten House districts in America where either the libertarian litany or the right-wing-religious policy creed would draw majority popular approval, and most studies suggest Bush 43 could have done better versus Gore had he stayed more centrist, but, anyway, the fiction is enshrined as fact. Little happens on any issue without Karl's okay, and often he supplies such policy substance as the administration puts out. Fortunately, he is not just a largely self-taught, hyperpolitical guy but also a very well informed guy when it comes to certain domestic issues."

According to various sources close to Rove, he and DiIulio had a wary but respectful relationship. DiIulio, like any heavyweight with his own constituency, didn't seem to fear Rove. Rove, who never graduated from college but has a deep love of academic inquiry, seemed to enjoy having DiIulio to fence with. Periodically, he would ask John to advance the administration's political agenda, and John would do what almost no one does currently at the White House now that Karen Hughes has left: tell Karl to take a hike.

For instance, there was Karl's desire to have John cozy up to the conservative evangelicals, with whom DiIulio was having problems. DiIulio recalls Karl telling him to bury the hatchet "and start fighting the guys who are against us." DiIulio says he responded: "I'm not taking any shit off of Jerry Falwell. The souls of my dead Italian grandparents are crying out to me, 'That guy's not on the side of the angels.'" Rove backed off, DiIulio recalls, and said, "Look, those guys don't really matter to this president."

"Sure, Karl," DiIulio responded. "They don't matter, but they're in here all the time."

On his primary mission—push forward ideas and policies to partner government with faith-based institutions—DiIulio says that he saw the beginning of what was to become a pattern: The White House "winked at the most far-right House Republicans, who, in turn, drafted a so-called faith bill that (or so they thought) satisfied certain fundamentalist leaders and Beltway libertarians but bore few marks of compassionate conservatism and was, as anybody could tell, an absolute political nonstarter. It could pass the House only on a virtual party-line vote, and it could never pass the Senate, even before Jeffords switched.

"Not only that, but it reflected neither the president's own previous rhetoric on the idea nor any of the actual empirical evidence. . . . I said so, wrote memos, and so on. . . . As one senior staff member chided me at a meeting at which many junior staff were present and all ears, 'John, get a faith bill, any faith bill.' Like college students who fall for the colorful, opinionated, but intellectually third-rate professor, you could see these twenty- and thirty-something junior White House staff falling for the Mayberry Machiavellis."

DiIulio defines the Mayberry Machiavellis as political staff, Karl Rove and his people, "who consistently talked and acted as if the height of political sophistication consisted in reducing every issue to its simplest black-and-white terms for public consumption, then steering legislative initiatives or policy proposals as far right as possible. These folks have their predecessors in previous administrations (left and right, Democrat and Republican), but in the Bush administration, they were particularly unfettered.

"Remember 'No child left behind'? That was a Bush campaign slogan. I believe it was his heart, too. But translating good impulses into good policy proposals requires more than whatever somebody thinks up in the eleventh hour before a speech is to be delivered."

Weekly meetings of the Domestic Policy Council "were breathtaking," DiIulio told me. As for the head of the DPC, Margaret La Montagne, a long-time friend of Karl Rove who guided education policy in Texas, DiIulio is blunt: "What she knows about domestic policy could fit in a thimble."

When DiIulio would raise objections to killing programs—like the Earned Income Tax Credit, a tax credit for the poorest Americans, hailed by policy analysts on both sides of the aisle, that contributed to the success of welfare reform—he found he was often arguing with libertarians who didn't know the basic functions of major federal programs. As a senior White House adviser and admirer of DiIulio's recently said to me, "You have to understand, this administration is further to the right than much of the public understands. The view of many people [in the White House] is that the best government can do is simply do no harm, that it never is an agent for positive change. If that's your position, why bother to understand what programs actually do?"

It was encounters with the president—displays of his personal qualities—that time and again restored DiIulio's commitment. From the way he "let detainees come home from China and did not jump all over them for media purposes" to a time, DiIulio writes, when he and Bush were in Philadelphia at a "three-hour block party on July 4, 2001, following hours among the children, youth, and families of prisoners . . . running late for the next event. He stopped, however, to take a picture with a couple of men who were cooking ribs all day. 'C'mon,' he said, 'those guys have been doing hard work all day there.' It's my favorite and, in some ways, my most telling picture of who he is as a man and a leader who pays attention to the little things that convey respect and decency toward others."

Five days later, on July 9, at the administration's six-month senior-staff retreat, DiIulio writes that "an explicit discussion ensued concerning how to emulate more strongly the Clinton White House's press, communications, and rapid-response media relations—how better to wage, if you will, the permanent campaign that so defines the modern presidency regardless of who or which party occupies the Oval Office. I listened and was amazed. It wasn't more press, communications, media, legislative strategizing, and such that they needed. Maybe the Clinton people did that better, though surely they were less disciplined about it and leaked more to the media and so on. No, what they needed, I thought then and still do now, was more policy-relevant information, discussion, and deliberation."

Part of the problem, DiIulio now understood, was that the paucity of serious policy discussion combined with a leakproof command-and-control operation was altering traditional laws of White House physics. That is: Know what's political, know what's policy. They are different. That distinction drives the structure of most administrations. The policy experts, on both domestic and foreign policy, order up "white papers" and hash out the most prudent use of executive power. Political advisers, who often deepen their knowledge by listening carefully as these deliberations unfold, are then called in to decide how, when, and with whom in support policies should be presented, enacted, and executed.

The dilemma presented by Karl Rove, DiIulio realized, was that in such a policy vacuum, his jack-of-all-trades appreciation of an enormous array of policy debates was being mistaken for genuine expertise. It takes a true policy wonk to recognize the difference, and, beyond the realm of foreign affairs, DiIulio was almost alone in the White House.

"When policy analysis is just backfill to support a political maneuver, you'll get a lot of oops," he says.

DiIulio points to the "remarkably slapdash character of the Office of Homeland Security, with the nine months of arguing that no department was needed, with the sudden, politically timed reversal in June, and with the fact that not even that issue, the most significant reorganization of the federal government since the creation of the Department of Defense, has received more than talking-points-caliber deliberation. This was, in a sense, the administration's problem in miniature: Ridge was the decent fellow at the top, but nobody spent the time to understand that an EOP [Executive Office of the President] entity without budgetary or statutory authority can't coordinate over a hundred separate federal units, no matter how personally close to the president its leader is, no matter how morally right it feels the mission is, and no matter how inconvenient the politics of telling certain House Republican leaders we need a big new federal bureaucracy might be."

One has to consider the possibility that John DiIulio just wasn't cut out for working at the White House. Government, after all, is not a graduate seminar. I need to get a reality-based assessment on what the professor himself is proffering. DiIulio's last day running the faith-based initiative was February 1, 2002. He never intended to stay for long, he says, and the commute from Philadelphia was becoming onerous. And though he remains in regular touch with former colleagues, he is not there now—not in the building. I talk to several sources in the West Wing, and one of them agrees to meet me at a neutral site: a restaurant off Pennsylvania Avenue with a dark back room. It's midafternoon. We order coffee. He is nervous about a face-to-face. "You know, this is risky, just being here."

I tell him we'll try to make this quick, and I describe DiIulio's rendering of the White House, its conduct and character, and Rove's enveloping role. Does this resemble reality, or is DiIulio mistaken or misguided?

He nods. "All of that is realistic, basically correct. It's really been even worse since after 9/11. There has been no domestic policy, really. Not even a pretense of it."

He pauses. "You know, if John had stayed, we might have actually had a domestic policy. He's just that smart, that credible. The reason is that he's rigorous, that he demands the data. He asks, What does the evidence indicate? What is the best path? He truly doesn't care about politics, which is all anyone here seems to care about. He just digs in to actually see what policy would most benefit the most people."

We talk for more than an hour. He's an honored member of the political Right with a flawless conservative pedigree and pure faith in ideas emerging from that flank of the Republican party. But he is as pointed in his critique of the processes of this White House as the more moderate DiIulio. It's clear from every word that this is not about politics or ideology. It's not about who's right or wrong. It's about a kind of regret.

"Don't you understand?" he says, his voice rising. "We got into the White House and forfeited the game. You're supposed to stand for something . . . to generate sound ideas, support them with real evidence, and present them to Congress and the people. We didn't do any of that. We just danced this way and that on minute political calculations and whatever was needed for a few paragraphs of a speech."

He says that in mid-August, Jay Lefkowitz—a longtime policy manager who was hired in early 2002 to work as Margaret La Montagne's deputy at the Domestic Policy Council—became part of an effort to create some forward motion. He and a small group of senior staffers started to meet each week or so to discuss domestic issues and long-term goals. "They're attempting to at least generate some ideas. It's a small sign of hope . . . but everything will have to go through Karl."

We sit for a while and sip coffee, now cold. He says he's not going to leave—he waited too long to get to the White House—but that increasingly he finds himself thinking in the past tense, of missed opportunities.

"Here's what would have worked," he says a bit later. "Swap DiIulio in for [deputy chief of staff for policy] Josh Bolten. Bolten's a good guy, a smart guy, but DiIulio knows more about everything, every area of policy, than anyone. He would have helped us have the balance—the considerate, thoughtful approach to everything—that administrations are supposed to have."

Shortly after this conversation came the midterm elections. Early the morning after, my White House sources were on the phone, offering the insider view.

"It's unbelievable," one of them says, awe coming across the phone line. "Could Karl be that smart? Could anyone?"

There's just silence for a bit as he maps the frontiers of possibility.

"Maybe the last two years wasn't just a case of benign neglect," says this source, with whom I spoke extensively throughout October. "Maybe it was brilliant neglect."

He went on to explain: From early on, Rove may have been focused on energizing the core, the far Right, for the midterms. An attempt to push centrist policies through a divided Congress would have done anything but that, and it would have violated the prime strategic directive: don't alienate the right wing like the first President Bush. Karl's remedy: co-opt the policy-creation process; put it in a lockbox until after genuine Republican control is established.

"Now the troops are ready to march," the source says. "The question is, What will we do? Will we finally put together a thoughtful policy team to create a coherent plan for America's future, or just push through one political favor after another dressed up like policy? I guess it's really for Karl, Karl and the president, to decide."

John DiIulio knows that because of what he's done here, he will lose friends. The White House will personally attack him. Some longtime Republican colleagues will suddenly be too busy to return his calls. Others may spread rumors. Karl Rove, who would not comment for this story, might say that DiIulio's manifesto is "duly noted." Rove likes to say that after doling out a condemnation—that someone's actions have been duly noted. It's a very adult version, with teeth, of "This will be put on your permanent record."

But DiIulio and an increasing number of people in the White House seem to have their eye on a somewhat different permanent record.

The Mind of George W. Bush
Richard Brookhiser

The Atlantic Monthly | April 2003

Whether or not you agree with the policies of George W. Bush, there is no denying that our 43rd president has evolved into a far stronger and more decisive chief executive than most people would have anticipated . In this lengthy essay, historian Richard Brookhiser—the author of numerous books, including one on that first family of father-and-son presidents, the Adamses—turns his scholarly spotlight on the inner workings of our nation's current leader. Not suprisingly, Brookhiser (who is also a senior editor at the conservative publication National Review*) finds a lot to admire in George W., including a management style that stresses accountability and follow-through. He highlights some potential limitations as well, however. One example is what he*

*calls Bush's "phantom framework"—a disinclination to articulate the philosophical
context for his various policies, which can often leave colleagues (not to mention
the rest of us) uncertain about the underlying principles guiding his decisions. . . .*

The powers of the presidency have changed almost beyond recognition since
the infancy of the office, when foreign relations were handled by a dozen clerks
and diplomats, the armed forces consisted of several thousand soldiers and
sailors, and the President himself took months-long summer vacations from
the yellow-fever-ravaged capital of Philadelphia or Washington, D.C.

One pattern of presidential decision-making was established early on, however. The process is determined not by the office but by who holds it. The
first President, George Washington, a veteran officer and a lifelong performer,
led from the front; his decisions, clear and direct, were announced—if not
made—in public. Thomas Jefferson, the third President, had a different style;
a century and a half before the political scientist Fred I. Greenstein coined
the phrase "hidden-hand presidency" to describe Dwight D. Eisenhower's time
in office, Jefferson operated behind a screen of reticence, dinner-table charm,
and the feints of congressional front men. The first Presidents also pioneered
different ways of taking advice before making decisions. Washington weighed
the counsel of often quarrelsome advisers, chiefly Jefferson, his Secretary of
State, and Alexander Hamilton, his Treasury Secretary; John Adams, the
second President, dealt with a Cabinet that was positively mutinous by firing
half its members in his last year in office. In this area, too, Jefferson introduced a new model: the men around him all sang from the same page. His
most important advisers—James Madison, at the State Department, and
Albert Gallatin, at the Treasury—had worked with him and each other for
years, and harmonized in ideology and temperament.

Presidents do not choose from a number of complete decision-making
models but gravitate toward one pole or the other on a variety of axes. The
axis of presenting decisions gives us extroverts (Truman—"the buck stops
here") or hidden hands (Van Buren, who "rowed to his object with muffled
oars"). The axis of advice-taking gives us ringmasters presiding over an endless circus (FDR) or unifiers who deplore or even hate conflict (Nixon). There
are Presidents who take in information and assign tasks through an orderly,
hierarchical structure (Eisenhower named the first chief of staff), and those
who position themselves at the center of converging spokes of counsel
(Clinton). There is an axis of learning, which runs from Presidents who seek

frankly for guidance to Presidents who know everything to begin with. (Jefferson was considered a polymath—though some weren't so sure. John Quincy Adams, then a senator, heard Jefferson tell White House dinner guests that he had learned Spanish in only nineteen days, using a grammar and a copy of *Don Quixote*. "But," Adams wrote in his diary, "Mr. Jefferson tells large stories.") No extreme on any axis guarantees success; there are heroes and dogs at either end of each one. The axis of mental health, along which are ranged the serene (Ford) and the tormented (Nixon again), might seem to be an exception—until we remember the deep depressions of Abraham Lincoln. The possible permutations have yielded almost as many kinds of decision-makers as we have had Presidents.

George W. Bush, No. 43, is not an easy man to write about. He is not contradictory, not flamboyant, and not well-spoken. He thus deprives reporters, as he will deprive historians, of three of the handles—conflict, gestures, words—they automatically reach for to describe their subjects. It is possible, though, to figure out how Bush makes decisions. Nothing reveals a man's mind, especially the mind of a man who is not articulate, better than the decisions he makes. Here his very consistency helps. To write this article I talked to insiders and outsiders, higher-ups and lower-downs, who have known him in a variety of circumstances: in Texas and in Washington, in business and in government. Their collective portrait was not of a Jekyll and Hyde sort; by and large everything they said fit together. Even when, in my view, almost all of them were mistaken in their reading of the man, they were mistaken in the same way. The picture of Bush deciding is as close as we can easily come to Bush's mind.

President George W. Bush came to office with a particular package of traits and experiences. His two most obvious personal traits are humor and seriousness.

Bush's humor was most in evidence during his campaign and in his early days in the White House. It was not universally admired: Bush has no ability to bathe a crowd in a delighted glow, as Ronald Reagan could. Yet almost all who deal with him, from loyal associates to unsympathetic reporters, testify that one-on-one he is a funny man. Evidently you have to be there. When Bush, speaking to the journalist Tucker Carlson, jeered at the condemned murderer Karla Faye Tucker's plea for clemency (Carlson's description: "'Please,' Bush whimpers, his lips pursed in mock desperation, 'don't kill me'"), you didn't want to be there.

Journeys With George, the home movie that the journalist Alexandra Pelosi shot with a camcorder on Bush's plane during the 2000 campaign, may have been the first treatment that conveyed his humor to outsiders. Bush got into the spirit of Pelosi's project and mugged without pretension—or shame. The movie shows how Bush makes his humor work for him: he charmed Pelosi and put her at her ease; he also subtly put Pelosi's colleagues, who were giving her a bit of a hard time during the campaign, in their place (*they* didn't get the next President in a home movie).

Bush uses his humor when he makes decisions. Any officeholder transforms those who come into contact with him, and this is especially true of a President. He is not just a person; he is power. But Bush, one journalist says, "gets you to relax so much you say what you know, not what you think he wants to hear." Another way of putting this is that Bush uses his humor to lower the bar for himself, and thus makes others lower their guard. The White House political adviser Karl Rove, when I asked him to compare his boss to other Presidents, mentioned Eisenhower on the grounds that both men had a "wiliness about being underestimated." Like Ike, Bush knows that low expectations work to his advantage. Eisenhower used geniality and opaque rhetoric to make people think less of him. Bush clowns.

Finally, Bush's humor helps him maintain control over his aides. "He keeps people in their place in a friendly way," says Mitchell Daniels, the director of the Office of Management and Budget. "There are no self-seekers in this group; the general ethos is one that would discourage that." Condoleezza Rice, Bush's National Security Advisor, says, "He will kid people, tease people." One of the ways he teases the earnest Rice is to call her a mother hen.

Bush's seriousness became evident after 9/11, but the signs were there earlier for those who looked. By any normal standard Bush has led a charmed life: he was born to wealth and prominence, and has carved out an even larger share. He did have a problem, however. Though Bush does not use the A-word, he drank as a young man. Then, at age forty, he stopped. Bill Clinton also had a life touched by addiction—his stepfather's drinking, his half brother's drugs. During the 1992 campaign Clinton presented these encounters to Joe Klein and other journalists as Baby Boomer, Al-Anon growth experiences. Bush may think of his own escape somewhat differently.

During the 2000 election each candidate was asked to name a favorite book. Gore said *The Red and the Black*, by Stendhal. Bush often said *The Raven*, by Marquis James—a 1930 Pulitzer Prize-winning biography of Sam Houston that was last reissued in the 1980s. It is a lushly written biography of the old school, a colorful look at a colorful subject. Houston, of course, is the founding father of Texas—the man who beat Santa Anna at San Jacinto. Houston is still a presence in Austin: he occupied the present governor's mansion when he held the office, at the end of his career. (He is also a presence in Midland, Texas, where Bush grew up: the young George attended Sam Houston Elementary School and San Jacinto Junior High School.) One of Bush's favorite stories about Houston concerns the crisis of the last years of his life, when the governor, a staunch Unionist, refused to take a loyalty oath to the Confederacy. Houston's office was declared vacant, and after he left the state capitol, a crowd showered him with abuse. The lesson Bush draws from that story is the fickleness of instant verdicts and the importance of doing the right thing. It is a tale of heroic principle and of virtue rewarded in the long run: the political nadir of Houston's life became a high point in the judgment of history.

But what may have been equally meaningful to Bush was Houston's personal nadir. In 1829 Houston, then thirty-five, a protégé of Andrew Jackson, and the governor of Tennessee, married a young belle who left him after three months. Houston's reaction was dramatic: he resigned from office, moved to Indian territory (what is now Arkansas), joined the Cherokee nation, and married a part-Cherokee woman. Always a heavy drinker, he began to drink spectacularly. Alexis de Tocqueville ran into Houston during this period; the deracinated wastrel struck him as one of the "unpleasant consequences of popular sovereignty." Yet after three lost years Houston moved to Texas, where he found himself. The victory over alcohol and despair was transformative, and it set the stage for political greatness. Believing that victory over yourself can make you great doesn't mean that you will be; but it sets a goal.

Bush also came to the White House with two kinds of experience—in business and in politics. He attended Harvard Business School from 1973 to 1975, making him the only modern President to have had such training. (Jimmy Carter and George H. W. Bush ran businesses, but neither went to business school.)

An important effect of going to business school is that it may keep one from going to law school—an especially important effect these days, when so many people in government have legal training. Many law schools and business schools, including Harvard's, use the case method, requiring students to work through historic trials or the problems of actual companies. But they use the method differently. Law school accustoms future lawyers to discerning theoretical constructs, either in past decisions or in legal principles, and applying them to the case at hand. Business school immerses future businessmen in the histories of specific companies, in order to develop problem-solving abilities. Law school worships understanding, business school worships skill. Law-school students scrutinize *what* has been done. If business-school students don't quite learn by doing, they learn *how* things have been done. Typical of the Harvard Business School's ethos is a line from the textbook *Business Policy*, by C. Roland Christensen, et al., about company presidents: in "the incomparably detailed confusion of a national company" the role and function of a president "cannot possibly be made clear [by] generalization." In a famous lecture at Harvard, Oliver Wendell Holmes Jr. declared that "the life of the law" was not logic but experience. These days the business school is actually truer to Holmes's dictum than the law school is.

The aspect of business that most interested Bush was organization. One of his favorite courses, according to Bill Minutaglio, the author of *First Son: George W. Bush and the Bush Family Dynasty*, was Human Organization and Behavior. A classmate remembered him as being "pretty concerned about how organizations worked and how people worked in those organizations." When the country was smaller, Presidents did much of the job themselves—writing their own speeches, dispensing patronage, even leading troops (Washington in the Whiskey Rebellion, Madison in the War of 1812). Now that the job requires layers of underlings, and the White House is like a company, a course like the one Bush took is no bad preparation.

After Harvard, Bush went into the oil-exploration business, founding Arbusto Energy, a small company. He was so-so at finding oil, better at selling his business to progressively larger firms. He acquired additional managerial responsibility when he and a group of partners bought the Texas Rangers, in 1989.

Critics have portrayed Bush's stint with the Rangers as the result of a favor to a politically connected young man by the real movers and shakers (the partners put up $46 million, of which Bush contributed only $600,000, largely raised from his oil-business stock). Not surprisingly, the movers and shakers don't see it that way.

Bush's role was to act as Mr. Outside, handling the team's political and public-relations problems. There was a lot for him to do. In order to move from the converted minor-league park in which they were playing, the Rangers had to persuade the town of Arlington, Texas, located midway between Dallas and Fort Worth, to build them a modern stadium, using the revenue from a half-cent increase in the sales tax. The Rangers also had to balance the interests of those twin cities, which hate each other. Bush had "fabulous instincts," Richard Gilder, one of the co-owners, recalls. "He wants to be liked, so he studies people." The reason offered is inadequate; lots of people, from movie stars to unhappy teenagers, want to be liked yet do not study people. Bush, however, paid attention to those he dealt with. He had to overcome a natural impatience. "If he wasn't running the meetings," Gilder says, "which he wasn't, he couldn't really sit still. But he became a good listener. He's not a ball hog."

Bush had already tested his business-school education in his first important political job—helping his father during the campaign for President in 1988. After the elder Bush won, his son continued to act as an adviser. Bush is "the only President with functional experience of being a White House staffer," as David Frum, a former speechwriter, told me. "Vice Presidents may know how the very top of the staff system works," Frum says, but Bush operated at a lower level, albeit with a peerless pipeline to the top. (Access is power, as the Republican strategist Lee Atwater told him.) John Quincy Adams, the only other President to have training as a presidential son, also advised his father, but he could not observe John Adams's management techniques firsthand: the son spent his father's presidency in Europe, as a diplomat, and the two communicated only by letter.

George W. Bush got to observe a White House that was notoriously badly run. The chief of staff for much of the elder Bush's term was John Sununu, the former governor of New Hampshire, who had been given the job in gratitude for his crucial support at the time of the 1988 primaries. Sununu was intelligent but abrasive and willful, picking fights with legislators and journalists: he called one Republican senator, who opposed a budget deal, "insignificant," and publicly accused a *Washington Post* reporter at a ceremonial bill signing of being a liar. Sununu also tried to shape policy—the great temptation for chiefs of staff, who are supposed to be honest brokers between competing policy advisers but to remain neutral themselves. He did not want to be liked, and he did not study people. When the elder Bush, floundering in the face of a poor economy, decided that Sununu had to go, George W. Bush went to deliver the terminal hint. He told Sununu at the end of November 1991 that he had lost his political support. In the first Bush White House even firings went amiss: Sununu did not take the hint, and had to be asked by the President himself to step aside. (Eleven years later, when the prospective Senate majority leader Trent Lott was going down in flames for praising Senator Strom Thurmond's Dixiecrat past, the fatal hint bearer was the President's brother Jeb. Lott responded, either because he had better hearing than Sununu or because the President himself had already given an unmistakable hint when he said that Lott had apologized "and rightly so.")

George W. Bush's first direct experience of political management came when he was elected governor of Texas, in 1994. The main lesson of his tenure in Austin was the importance of focusing on a handful of issues. During the 1995 legislative session these were education reform, welfare, tort law, and the juvenile-justice system. During his second term, in 1999, he pushed for parental notification in cases of abortions requested by minors, and for a tax cut. These issues, when packaged together and presented by Karl Rove, would nicely facilitate a run for the White House. Ralph Reed, the boyish former head of the Christian Coalition, who first met Bush during his Rangers days, was struck by how "focused" and "disciplined" he was as governor.

The governorship of Texas, however, scarcely allows those who hold it to get much done otherwise. It is a figurehead office, a bully pulpit that confers little power. The legislature, which meets only every other year, takes its cues from the independently elected lieutenant governor. The man who held that job during most of Bush's tenure was Bob Bullock, a conservative Democrat. Bush met with Bullock during the 1994 campaign, and they hit it off. David Guenthner, who edits *The Lone Star Report*, a conservative newsletter that criticized Governor Bush for his tax policies, says that Bullock had a large role in setting Bush's priorities. "Bullock told him, Here's what you can get done, here's what you can't get done, here's what you don't even try," Guenthner says. "Real cynics say that Bush embraced the agenda Bullock gave him. I would not go so far." Bush wanted to establish what he could realistically hope to accomplish when he took office. He also saw that Bullock was at loggerheads with the incumbent governor, Ann Richards, a liberal Democrat. Clearly, for reasons of both policy and politics, Bullock was a man worth studying. Governor Bush was not a dynamic leader, but he was effective because he saw the lay of the land and judged how to traverse it.

Bush became President after one of the most bollixed-up presidential elections in American history (interestingly, two other notorious elections, in 1800 and 1824, involved the other father-son presidential pair). How has what he learned from business school, from his father's White House, from his corporate experiences, and from the Texas statehouse been serving him now that he is the nation's chief executive?

Following are the markers of Bush's decision-making in the White House so far—the traits he has shown and the factors he pays attention to.

Thriftiness with time. Bush begins meetings promptly and runs them briskly, starts and ends his days early, and sets aside time to spend at his ranch in Crawford, Texas. His promptness is partly for public consumption. According to one aide, he often says, "It is important that the President be on time. When I come on time, that shows people I respect them, and that shows discipline."

The discipline is even more important to him. "He feels the fleeting of the presidency, which is made up of a certain number of minutes," Frum says. "That doesn't mean cramming them all with business. You have to sleep, exercise, and keep your relationships functioning well enough to keep you sane. But then there are only so many minutes left over. Every time you let someone ramble [in a meeting], you destroy a minute." All Presidents have limited time in office—John Quincy Adams wrote of the job's "perpetual motion"—and they all recognize this fact intermittently. "The key to discipline," Frum adds, "is recognizing it all the time."

The team. Newt Gingrich, formerly speaker of the House and now a consultant, has an avid interest in both history and management; when he gave a reading list to the Republican freshmen of the 104th Congress, half the books were on American history (the *Federalist Papers*, Tocqueville) and half were on management techniques. "Bush," he says, "has a very disciplined sense of himself as a team leader." Rove agrees. "I had read [the management guru] Peter Drucker, but I'd never *seen* Drucker until I saw Bush in action." What do these buzzwords—"team leader," "Drucker"—mean in practice?

Bush was determined not to reproduce the fireworks of his father's staff. "The people who control the channels of communication [in the new Bush White House]," Frum says, "have their egos carefully under control. They have fewer psychodramas than any staff since the invention of staffs." The average newspaper-reading non-political junkie may not even know the name of Bush's chief of staff (Andrew Card). That is just fine by Bush.

Bush's advisers do not rat each other out in public. Rove says, "People told me before I went to Washington that the White House would be a snake pit. Leaking and backbiting just come with the territory." But, he claims, Bush's advisers "can go to the Oval Office and advocate a perspective diametrically opposed to the point of view of the person on the sofa across from [them]." If the decision goes against you, Rove says, "you can link arms and go on, and be certain that your [losing] view won't appear in the paper." He adds, in a nod to the human condition: "Or at least be reasonably certain."

The men and women Bush has put in positions of substance are either Texans, like Rove, or veterans of the first Bush Administration or the Ford Administration. In picking Richard Cheney to be his Vice President, Bush made another correction of his father, who chose Senator Dan Quayle as a running mate. Quayle was picked for his youth. He turned out to be a man of ideas, but his penchant for flubs made him seem more callow than energetic. Cheney was picked for his experience, which was thought to outweigh even the risks of his heart condition.

The reach back to the Ford Administration, in the persons of Cheney and Secretary of Defense Donald Rumsfeld, is interesting, because Gerald Ford learned the value of a good team only on the job. He took office, after Nixon's resignation, promising to be his own chief of staff. But the storm that followed his pardon of Nixon, which was caused in part by the abrupt manner in which the pardon was announced, showed him the error of his ways. The first chief of staff Ford chose after acknowledging his mistake was Rumsfeld; when Rumsfeld became Secretary of Defense for the first time, Ford replaced him with Cheney. Significantly, Bush largely passed over the Reagan Administration in his talent search (Colin Powell began his ascent under Reagan but came into his own under the elder Bush). Reagan's inner circle was divided between true believers and convictionless operators. Bush wanted solid junior managers.

Q&L. Bush manages his team by questioning and listening. After he has put people at ease with his humor and his low-key manner, Bush wants information. Robert D. Kaplan, an *Atlantic* correspondent, whom Bush has questioned about the Balkans and the Near East, says that Bush "never asked a question that got the conversation off track." Talking with Bush, Kaplan says, is the opposite of punditry. "Guests on talk shows are asked things they can't possibly know. Some retired officer will be asked 'Will Saddam Hussein go to war?' Bush is different. He doesn't get into global bull sessions; he wants your knowledge."

Bush wants your knowledge even if you disagree with him. Darla St. Martin, an officer of the National Right to Life Committee, who was introduced to Bush in 1988 by Lee Atwater, sees this trait from the vantage of her special interest. "On abortion, his father has one view [pro-life] and his mother has another [pro-choice]. That may be a reason he respects people even if he disagrees with them."

Bush is capable of stirring things up. "He can listen to a roomful of consensus and say no," Mitchell Daniels, of the OMB, says. "He's often roughest when things seem too neat and pre-packaged. He will ask [the opinion of] a person who hasn't spoken up. You better be ready with a point of view." Rice agrees: "He'll say something to provoke." During the war against the Taliban regime in Afghanistan he pressed his advisers relentlessly asking, "If we don't have victory by winter, what do we do?" Ralph Reed says that "some people don't want to hear what they don't want to hear," but Bush is different. "I don't know where it comes from. I've been doing this a long time. I know it's unusual."

The issue of stem-cell research, which came at Bush fast, fueled by the pace of technological innovation, offers a good case study of his open Q&L style. In 1996 Congress passed the Dickey-Wicker Amendment, a pro-life measure that barred the federal government from funding research in which human embryos were destroyed (strict pro-lifers view embryos as persons, just like fetuses, newborns, and the ailing old). In 1999 the Clinton Administration's Department of Health and Human Services interpreted the amendment to mean that the federal government could fund research on embryos as long as private money paid for their destruction. By the time Bush was inaugurated, in January of 2001, scientists were arguing that experiments on embryonic stem-cell tissue could help to find cures for Alzheimer's and Parkinson's diseases. They were joined by a chorus of relatives of the afflicted, including Nancy Reagan, and by many otherwise pro-life Republican lawmakers, who saw such research as an opportunity to do good.

Bush is not a scientist. To address the stem-cell problem, he would have to rely heavily on expert advice. But because he had not had a stem-cell team during the campaign (the issue was not then in play), he had to create one from scratch. Pro-life lobbyists—people like Darla St. Martin—were available. The opinions of Republican senators such as Senators Orrin Hatch and Bill Frist (each of whom supported at least some types of stem-cell research) were out there as political givens; the opinion of an iconic figure like Nancy Reagan would have to be taken into account. Bush also turned to academic pro-life ethicists—for example, Leon Kass, of the University of Chicago.

In August of 2001 Bush revealed his thoughts in a televised speech from Crawford. He announced that he would create a President's Council on Bioethics, headed by Kass. The presidential council or commission is traditionally a place to send awkward decisions and unwelcome responsibilities. But Bush's speech gave the council clear guidelines on stem-cell research.

Bush acknowledged the benefits that researchers sought, and the utilitarian calculations that would allow them to seek those benefits. If frozen embryos "are going to be destroyed anyway," he said, "shouldn't they be used for a greater good?" But he rejected a proposal by Bill Frist that federally funded research be allowed on certain newly destroyed embryos. In Bush's view, embryos fell within the definition of human life—"a sacred gift from our creator." He decided, however, that the federal government could rightly fund research on existing stem-cell lines, "where the life-and-death decision has already been made." Some pro-lifers were not happy with this exception: the National Conference of Catholic Bishops called it "morally unacceptable." But Bush would not try to fix what he viewed as mistakes of the past; he would only try to prevent new ones.

"Many people," Bush said, "are finding that the more they know about stem-cell research, the less certain they are about the right ethical and moral conclusions." The puzzlement that Bush imputed to "many people" clearly reflected his own process of sorting through the issue. He had assembled a team of advisers, from his world but as sophisticated as possible; he had considered their (conflicting) counsel; and he had found a clear, though not universally popular, position. Another President might have ducked the problem by following the emerging consensus of the country, or of his own base. Bush handled it like a manager—staffing it out and then making his own decision.

"Instinct." Almost everyone calls Bush an instinctive decision-maker, including Bush himself. In an interview for *Bush at War*, Bob Woodward's 2002 sketch of the defeat of the Taliban, Bush told Woodward, "I'm not a textbook player. I'm a gut player." Both Bush and his aides tend to exalt instinct; this propensity can seem like a rationalization, a cover for his lack of more obvious qualifications, such as intellect conventionally measured.

Bush's pre-presidential experience was limited in one obvious way: he had no knowledge of the world, though that is an occupational hazard of governors. Unlike Vice Presidents, congressmen, or generals who have fought foreign enemies, governors know their states and Washington, little else. Governors of Texas are more worldly than most, because they must deal with Mexico and Mexican immigrants, and during Bush's presidential campaign his advisers argued, with straight faces, that this was experience enough. It is a limitation that American voters seem to be comfortable with, since three of the past four Presidents—Carter, Reagan, and Clinton—came to the White House from statehouses.

It is easy for Bush supporters to construct a counter-mythology of brainy men who have been bad Presidents and less brainy ones who have been excellent. In the former category fall both Adamses and James Madison; for evidence of the latter they can cite Oliver Wendell Holmes's quip about FDR ("second-class intellect ... first-class temperament") or Aaron Burr's judgment of Washington ("One who could not spell a sentence of common English").

Gingrich cuts through the instinct talk. "Bush has thought systematically about leaders his whole life," he says, "and he has a very wide repertoire of experiences." When Bush encounters new people or situations, Gingrich says, "he cues off things he probably doesn't even remember" from past experiences. Gingrich offers Bush's favorable judgment of Russian President Vladimir Putin as an example of his ability to size someone up rapidly. Better to say that he is not an instinctive decider but a fast one.

Providence. In one debate among Republican hopefuls during the 2000 election cycle the candidates were asked to pick a political philosopher important to their lives. Steve Forbes, who answered first, named John Locke, and explained why he thought Locke was important. Bush, who answered after Forbes, picked Jesus Christ, saying, "He changed my heart." A couple of the remaining Republicans began their answers by testifying that they, too, thought highly of Jesus.

It was a moment made for H. L. Mencken, but it exposed, not for the first time, a truth about Bush: he did not give up drink at age forty by himself; he believes he had the help of Jesus. He continues to believe that life is ruled and sustained by God.

Bush's faith makes "his sense of history very hard for secular intellectuals to understand," according to Gingrich. Given the care with which his associates discuss his beliefs, there must be a lot of secular intellectuals in the Bush Administration. "The great mystery in his decision-making," Frum says, "is the role of religion. When Bush says, 'I'll pray on this,' it's not a figure of speech." Mitchell Daniels believes that faith gives Bush "a certain serenity," as if he trusts that "history will take care of itself if he pursues the right policies." Daniels is "tempted," he says, to call the force that Bush sees guiding history "Providence," but he is reluctant to do so: "I wouldn't want anyone to over-read [the word]," he says. Bush's well-wishers—at least those who are not as aggressive as Gingrich—worry that if they speak bluntly about his faith, it will put people in mind of the culture wars of the 1980s and 1990s. Bush is not a culture warrior like many conservatives of that period, who thanked God for their enemies. But he is blunt, and specific, about his faith. "Providence" might strike him as too indefinite a word, smacking of the gentlemanly theological evasions of the Anglo-American Enlightenment (of John Locke, for instance).

Practically, Bush's faith means that he does not tolerate, or even recognize, ambiguity: there is an all-knowing God who decrees certain behaviors, and leaders must obey. Such beliefs, however much they may alienate him from opinion-makers, are part of his bond with one other leader—the devout Anglican Tony Blair.

Follow-through. One of the most important aspects of making a decision is making sure that it is carried out.

Bush believes in what is known in business as single-point accountability. "He does not want to know that a committee or a consortium is working together to coordinate a solution," Daniels says. "He wants one organization, or one person, to have responsibility; he wants to know who he can call. I can't tell you how alien this is to the federal government, which is marvelous at evading it."

To monitor the people or organizations responsible, Bush keeps track of certain details—ideally, not so many that he becomes a micro-manager, but enough to keep those he is managing alert. From 9/11 until January of 2002 many officials who had no direct connection to the war on terror lost contact with Bush. When he began meeting with them again, he had "a stream of informed questions about the innards of their departments," Daniels recalls. "He makes it his business to know a little bit about everything."

Bush knows that following through can require patience. This is new for him: when he was with the Rangers, and in his father's White House, he was just learning patience. Though he may still see the fundamental issues in black and white, he can now wait to achieve his goals. "He gives things time to work," Rice says. "He understands, probably better than his advisers, that there is a rhythm to things."

Bush's decision to withdraw from the ABM treaty, and the way he put that decision into effect, provide an archetypal example of his relentless follow-through. The treaty was a three-decades-old arrangement designed to ensure the mutual vulnerability of the superpowers during the Cold War. Conservatives had opposed it since the Reagan Administration, because it prevented all but basic research on Star Wars technology. Bush shared their opposition. How would he act on it?

In September of 1999 candidate Bush laid down a personal marker in a speech at the Citadel. He pledged that he would "defend the American people against missiles and terror" and that he would "at the earliest possible date . . . deploy anti-ballistic missile systems . . . to guard against attack and blackmail." He would propose amendments to the ABM treaty to permit this, but if Russia refused them, he would give notice, as the treaty allowed, that the United States would pull out.

Once Bush was elected, he put strong proponents of missile defense in key positions—Rice at the National Security Council, Rumsfeld and Paul Wolfowitz at the Defense Department, John Bolton, as the undersecretary for arms control, at the State Department. He then asked for plans for what should be built and how the decision should be presented to the world. By May of 2001 he was ready with another speech, to the National Defense University, in which he offered Russia a "new cooperative relationship" based on missile defense and smaller nuclear stockpiles in both countries.

Stroking Russia was the key to persuading reluctant Americans and European allies alike that Bush's plans were not cowboy unilateralism. If the Russians did not object, how could anyone else? Through the summer and fall Bush met with President Vladimir Putin. The Russians were surprised at the scope of the testing that the Americans proposed; by December of 2001, when the United States gave notice that it would pull out of the ABM treaty in six months, Russia still had not given its assent. But in May of last year Putin agreed to missile-defense cooperation. The ABM treaty effectively expired the next month, without a whimper. "We thought Russia would throw a tantrum and then get on with it," one congressional staffer told me. "They didn't even throw a tantrum." Bush's soft hard sell—soft in its manner, hard in its persistence—had worked.

Neither Bush's black-and-white view of the world nor his obsession with time makes him hasty. He identified the ABM treaty as a bad thing in the fall of 1999 and spent two and a half years withdrawing from it.

No decision-making style is without its limitations. No President's approach would work for anyone else; no President's approach works perfectly in all cases for him. What are Bush's limitations?

Restricted habitat. Bush may be comfortable with reservations and disagreement, and may probe for them among his advisers. But the disagreements he will encounter are limited by the politics of the advisers he has picked, Republicans who range from moderately liberal to moderately conservative (Colin Powell to Karl Rove). Those people, in turn, reflect the scope of his thoughts and inclinations. Bush may be a free-range animal, but he has a habitat, in which he stays. If he needs to know some facts that his advisers don't know, he can discover them. But if he needs to think some thoughts that they can't, he may have a hard time doing it.

Consider Saudi Arabia. To a moderate liberal like Powell, Saudi Arabia seems to be a non-radical Arab state, possibly a partner in resolving the Israel-Palestine issue. Moderate conservatives like Cheney and Rumsfeld would remember it as a strategic partner during the Cold War and the Gulf War. Texans would think of the Saudis as fellow oilmen. But if the Saudis, in addition to being these things, are breeders of terrorists and bankrollers of anti-American ideology worldwide, how will Bush's advisers help him see that? They generally won't—and generally haven't.

The first member of Bush's circle to break ranks and go public with criticism was the Princeton academic John DiIulio, a Roman Catholic Democrat who had advised Bush on the role of faith-based institutions in welfare. Last October DiIulio sent a 3,400-word letter to Ron Suskind, a reporter for *Esquire*, which was quoted in part in the magazine, and in its entirety in the Drudge Report. DiIulio hadn't at all liked his experience with the Bush White House, which he found to be populated by political hacks ("Mayberry Machiavellis") who needed "more serious policy fiber" in their diet. It is hard, DiIulio wrote, "for policy-minded staff . . . to get much West Wing traction, or even get a non-trivial hearing."

The memo certainly tells us that its author found it hard to get a hearing. DiIulio's picture of White House drones both ignoring and misunderstanding his ideas may well be accurate, however. Ignorance and incomprehension are the norms in every White House. The government and the world are so protean that no polymaths or even whole administrations are capable of entirely filtering the torrent of information and events washing over them. The best a President can hope to do is identify a handful of problems and, by bearing down on them, accomplish a handful of things.

Phantom framework. Bush's strictly defined mental horizons don't necessarily amount to a clearly expressed set of political principles. It is, of course, one of the mantras of his associates that Bush, unlike some other modern Presidents, has such principles. (Richard Nixon was famously indifferent to both the principles and the details of domestic policy: he told the historian Theodore H. White that the country needed a President for foreign affairs, but that the home front could take care of itself.) More specific than Bush's reliance on Providence, his principles supposedly form a framework for the decisions he makes. His "framework" of ideas, Rove says, "colors how he reacts" to problems as they arise. "He lays out the strategic ground," Rice says, as if to say, "Here is the ground on which we're playing."

Bush may indeed have a framework of ideas that guides him. Isn't this all we expect of a decision-maker? Not quite. A leader is most effective when his policy framework is evident to others (Reagan is the recent classic example). Then they know what to expect of him; they better understand what he is saying as he says it. The framework that Rove and Rice allude to is obscured by Bush's unwillingness or inability to theorize. Bush makes his ideas clear about each decision as he faces it, much as Rice described. But in the absence of a need to decide, what does his framework of ideas amount to? One of Bush's failures is instructive here. On December 6 [2002] Bush dismissed Paul O'Neill, his Treasury Secretary (yet another Ford Administration veteran). O'Neill had a penchant for shooting his mouth off, and the economy was in sad shape, suggesting the need for a scapegoat. But O'Neill also fell into a trap unintentionally prepared for him by Bush.

Whereas the first great Treasury Secretaries—Hamilton, Gallatin—created the economic policy of the new nation, today a Treasury Secretary's main job is to act as an advocate for the President's economic policy. Bush's policy has been one of steady tax cuts. After his inauguration he proposed a $1.3 trillion tax cut, spread over ten years. After 9/11 Bush proposed a stimulus package that allowed businesses to write off depreciation of their equipment more quickly. This January he proposed to stop taxing the dividends that stocks pay to individuals. Together these cuts will be the largest since Ronald Reagan's income-tax cuts in 1981. But there is a difference between the two Presidents. Reagan was messianic about tax cuts, campaigning for them, identifying himself with them. Bush cuts taxes—but he has not laid out a systematic, ideological case for what he is up to or how far he intends to go. Bush's reticence set up O'Neill's fatal mistake.

It was the dividend tax cut that did O'Neill in. Last November, O'Neill, traveling in Britain, told the *Financial Times* that his priority was tax simplification. "Far from promising a hefty tax cut," the paper wrote, "he said the reforms that were most likely   were 'minimally controversial and not very costly.'" O'Neill did acknowledge that the ultimate decision was not his: In time "[the President will] decide what he wants to do, and we'll try and get it done," he told the *Financial Times*. But O'Neill did not seem to know that the decision had already been made. Bush had warmed to the idea of abolishing the dividend tax at an economic summit in August at Baylor University, in Waco, where the popular investment broker Charles Schwab had proposed it. When Bush read what O'Neill was saying in Britain, according to one economist who has known Bush since the 1980s, he "went berserk." "Berserk" does not sound right—Bush (unlike Nixon and Clinton) is not a tantrum thrower. But "ticked off" is certainly in the repertoire of his reactions. The man who should have been his advocate was sending contradictory signals. O'Neill would have to go.

But it was not entirely O'Neill's fault that he was out of sync with his chief. Bush's phantom framework must share the blame. O'Neill did not have a sense of where, specifically, Bush was going on tax policy because Bush had not conveyed one during his first two years in office. A ten-year cut in income-tax rates and a break on business expenses do not necessarily predict a dividend-tax cut. If Bush's economic ideas had been clearer, his Treasury Secretary might have been clearer about them.

"Compassionate conservatism" is another example of a phantom framework, a framework that does not frame. Bush has since the early days of his presidential campaign defined himself as a compassionate conservative. This was in part rhetorical positioning—signaling that he was different from Ronald Reagan, whom liberals saw as harsh beneath a smiling face, or Newt Gingrich, whom they saw as harsh beneath a harsh face. In practice compassionate conservatism has meant allowing faith-based organizations to perform certain federally sponsored good works. One program, however, does not define a world view—and even that program has yet to get off the ground.

In the real world compassionate conservatism so far resembles what the historian Forrest McDonald has called good issues, which from a politician's point of view have "little substance" and are "ethically neutral" but can "inflame voters as if [they] were a primal moral cause." (McDonald was referring to the politics of the 1830s and 1840s, when "good issues . . . included protective tariffs and the recharter of the Bank of the United States; emphatically not good issues, because they were genuinely moral and potentially explosive, were slavery and Indian policy.") Perhaps by the end of Bush's Administration we will know what "compassionate conservatism" means; perhaps not.

Lack of imagination? Bush has intelligence, energy, and humility, but does he have imagination? Winston Churchill didn't learn about Adolf Hitler by questioning journalists, or by sizing Hitler up in person. Hitler and Churchill almost met in the summer of 1932, when Hitler was rising to power but still half a year away from achieving it. Churchill, in contrast, was out of office and seemed unlikely ever to return. Churchill was in Germany, touring old battlegrounds for a biography of his ancestor the Duke of Marlborough. Ernst Hanfstängl, a Nazi hanger-on, ran into him in a Munich hotel and tried to set up a meeting with Hitler, but Churchill made a pro-Jewish remark that scotched it. Even without a meeting, Churchill intuited that this German politician was a dynamic and disastrous force. Perhaps he intuited it because he shared Hitler's dynamism, and at least some of his impulses. "I admire men who stand up for their country in defeat," he wrote in his war memoirs, "even though I am on the other side."

Bush thinks in prose. Can he hear music?

No other President has faced anything quite like 9/11. Pearl Harbor was militarily disastrous but not devastating to the economy, or so destructive of civilian life. During the War of 1812 the British captured Washington and burned the White House; the United States, however, had arguably brought that war on itself, out of greed for Canada. But New York City had not been attacked since 1776, when General George Washington was responsible for defending it and failed.

Senator Charles Schumer, of New York, saw Bush make one early decision that quickly became public knowledge. Schumer and other senators from afflicted states met with Bush in the Oval Office on Thursday, September 13. "I told him how emotional it was in the city," Schumer says. "I had not been able to find my daughter, who went to Stuyvesant High School [near Ground Zero], for six hours. I told him about the smell of death in the air." "That is why New York needs twenty billion dollars," Schumer told the President. He says now, "I expected him to say 'Let me get back to you,' or 'Let's start off with three or four billion,' or 'Send me a memo'—the usual political things. 'New York really needs twenty billion?' he said. I said, 'Yes, sir.' He said, 'You got it.'"

In the ensuing tugging and hauling over the $20 billion, Schumer never joined his fellow New York Democrats in charging Bush with betrayal, because he believed that Bush had meant what he said. "He convinced me that he felt the pain I felt and that he had thought it through. Here is a man who, on one minute's reflection, commits to something." Schumer goes on, sounding a bit like Gingrich, "In the parlors they say he's stupid. That's nonsense. He's a bright man. Is he the smartest who has ever been President? No, but he's smart enough."

This article is not a war report. But the war on terrorism has thrown Bush's decision-making style into sharp relief, even as it has raised the stakes. "You are who you are," Rove says, "and you either live up to the moment or you don't." (Rove cites Lincoln's predecessor, James Buchanan, who failed to preserve the Union, as an example of someone who didn't.) But great and terrible events offer great choices. Thomas Gray evoked an Oliver Cromwell "guiltless of his country's blood," slumbering in a rural churchyard because never called to England's stage. One can imagine the lives that great men might have had in the absence of their decisive tests: Abraham Lincoln, railroad lobbyist; Ulysses S. Grant, failed businessman; Winston Churchill, scribbling back-bencher. Sir George Washington, knighted at age sixty as a loyal and industrious subject of the United Provinces, sometimes takes out his militia uniform from the French and Indian War and regrets that he never won a commission in His Majesty's regular army. . . .

The attack called upon Bush's considerable capacity to focus. He rehearsed his September 20 speech to the joint session of Congress three times, the draft mutating with each read-through. For the second rehearsal a piñata of domestic issues had been hung from the text. The logic of that addition harked back to his father's Administration: despite his victory in the Gulf War, the elder Bush lost the country's confidence by failing to attend to domestic issues. George W. Bush's advisers did not want him to repeat the mistake. He looked at the paper through the half glasses he wears for reading and said, "Take it out." Yet on one occasion he relaxed his usual discipline. When he went to New York on September 14 and met privately at the Jacob K. Javits Convention Center with the families of the victims, the clock ran unwatched.

In the first hundred days of the war Bush's decision-making style clearly served him well. Woodward's *Bush at War* is a catalogue of self-serving revelations by members of the Administration, but the vignettes of Bush that emerge are consistent with one another, and with his past. Bush led a team with some divergences of opinion, but not major ones. He had the patience to follow a strategy through ("boots on the ground"—that is, Americans in Afghanistan—before winter) and a sense of urgency that prodded those under him to get their acts together and get it done. He had to take expert advice, since he lacked both the military experience of a Washington or an Eisenhower, and the civilian war-time responsibility of a Churchill (who had been First Lord of the Admiralty in World War I). At the same time, he had to take charge. Two moments stand out. On September 12 Cheney asked Bush if there should be a war cabinet of his principal advisers, to hash out options and present them to him; it might streamline decision-making, he said. Bush replied that he would run important meetings himself: that was a commander in chief's function, not to be delegated. A month later, on October 15, eight days after the American bombing had begun, Bush told the attendees of such a meeting that they were losing their focus. "There's been too much discussion of post-conflict Afghanistan," he is reported to have said. In other words, don't everybody forget to win.

Bush's greatest strength as a wartime leader is strategic and personal clarity. The rapid decisions, forced on him by disaster, that everyone mislabels "instinctual" have created a framework that in this case is solid, not a phantom. He saw, seemingly immediately, that America was in a war, and that fighting it was to be the mission of his life.

He has been mostly well served by his team. Powell, Rice, and Rumsfeld have different approaches and emphases, and Bush turns from one to another like a carpenter going to his toolbox. An acquaintance who has known Bush for twenty years supplied a different metaphor: "Bush knows which senior vice-presidents to send to which meetings."

But has Bush stretched his team and himself far enough? After learning of Pearl Harbor, Churchill remembered a comment by an older politician, Edward Grey, who had compared the United States to "a gigantic boiler." Grey said, "Once the fire is lighted under it there is no limit to the power it can generate." Bush has chosen to tap only a fraction of America's power. We are essentially fighting a war in peacetime; most of our casualties have been civilians. The reason for Bush's relative restraint is obvious. Mobilizing for total war is economically and morally disorienting, a dire course that should be taken only in extreme necessity. We must wait to see if Bush's estimate of the force needed is correct.

Does Bush have the imagination to lead a great war? And even if he does, can he communicate it? The day before Abraham Lincoln's first inauguration, in the thick of the secession crisis, William Seward, who was to be the new Secretary of State, observed that "the President has a curious vein of sentiment running through his thought, which is his most valuable mental attribute." This is one of the shrewdest remarks ever made about Lincoln. That vein of sentiment changed the logician of the 1860 campaign into the visionary who delivered the Gettysburg Address and the Second Inaugural. Seward's remark is also one of the most astonishing ever made about Lincoln, because it came at a time when Lincoln's sentiment had not yet shown itself, and when few people, even among his supporters, had full confidence in him. Lincoln struck most people as a lanky rube, no doubt sharp but quite untried. The next day Charles Francis Adams Jr., the grandson and great-grandson of Presidents, observed the inauguration and wrote afterward that the outgoing President Buchanan was "undeniably . . . more presentable."

Time will judge Bush, as it judged Lincoln. The story of Lincoln's inauguration, like the story of Sam Houston leaving Austin, is hopeful: virtue temporarily unrecognized. But if virtue can be unappreciated, so can mediocrity be overpraised. Bush's approval rating after 9/11 was sky-high, but we must wait for the long run to see how effective his decision-making is. The verdict of history will settle the question of Bush's mind. If he prevails, Americans will want to understand how he did it. If he fails, he and the decisions that misfired will be disgraced and dismissed.

Special K

Jonathan Chait

The New Republic | December 30, 2002

The pro-business orientation of the Bush administration has been widely noted. George W. Bush himself is an ex-oil man and the first president ever to hold a master's degree in business (having graduated from Harvard Business School in 1975), while Vice President Dick Cheney served as chief executive of the Halliburton Corporation, the world's largest oil-field services company, before taking office. Many other admin- istration officials hail from the corporate world, where they worked as executives or lobbyists. These connections have been scrutinized at length by the national media, but no journalist has probed the links between the White House and the business community more deeply than The New Republic's *Jonathan Chait. In this article, Chait—who in the past year also authored a* TNR *article sharply critical of Bush's home- land security efforts, titled "The 9/10 President"—starts with the premise of Ron Suskind's notorious* Esquire *article (see "Why are These Men Laughing?", p. 10), and names the political master the White House is trying so hard to please. His conclu- sion: "The Bush administration's presumptive allegiance in virtually every case is to corporate America.". . .*

When President Bush appointed a successor to Treasury Secretary Paul O'Neill earlier this month, a handful of news outlets (this magazine included) pointed out that the identity of Bush's pick was essentially irrelevant to economic policy-making. The policies that new Treasury Secretary John Snow will be asked to sell to the public—tax cuts, tax cuts, and more tax cuts—have already been crafted without any need for his input, thank you very much. Indeed, the fact that policymakers in the Bush administration have been reduced essentially to an ornamental role was spelled out explicitly in an article by reporter Ron Suskind in the January issue of *Esquire*. In the piece, former administration staffer John DiIulio, along with two anonymous White House officials, alleged that the White House has totally subsumed its policy-making to its political decisions. "There is no precedent in any modern White House for what is going on in this one: a complete lack of a policy apparatus," DiIulio told Suskind. "What you've got is everything—and I mean everything—being run by the political arm." Lest anybody doubt DiIulio's analysis, a column on *National Review Online* by Republican economist Bruce Bartlett affirmed it. "[O]ne cannot dispute [DiIulio's] characterization because it clearly is true. Since the beginning of the Bush administration, insiders have complained to me that the policymaking process was not working," Bartlett wrote. "This vacuum in terms of policy analysis has tended to be filled by those in the White House who look at issues solely in terms of their political implications."

Suskind's explanation for this disturbing and unprecedented state of affairs is straightforward: The power wielded by political adviser Karl Rove (whether you believe he wields it for good or ill) is so great that he simply eclipses any other influence in the administration. "I was still regarding this White House in terms of the long-standing model," Suskind writes, "in which the art of political strategy is carefully balanced against serious policy discussion, in which church-state separations of these two distinct functions are respected, even championed. It seemed that in the person of Karl Rove such distinctions had been blurred."

But the total dominance of politics over policy in the Bush administration is not merely a function of personality; it is a reflection of deeper structural forces. Put simply, the administration is subservient to economic pressure groups to an extent that surpasses any administration in modern history. Whereas the Clinton administration was regularly forced to weigh policy demands from competing interests within the Democratic coalition, the Bush administration's presumptive allegiance in virtually every case is to corporate America. It is simply unnecessary for the White House to generate its own policies because that role has been filled by business lobbyists. Bush has abdicated to K Street the basic functions of domestic governance, not merely in cases where K Street's interests run roughshod over liberal principles, but in cases where they contradict conservative principles as well. Indeed, the simple rule for understanding Bush's economic policy is that in virtually every instance, whether tacking right or left, the president sides with whatever interest group has the strongest stake in the issue at hand. The result is an administration whose domestic actions persistently, almost uniformly, fail to uphold the broader public good.

One might wonder why the Clinton administration was not captive to its economic supporters while the Bush administration is. The answer isn't, as some Clintonites have suggested, that the denizens of the previous White House possessed more moral courage than their successors. It's the deep asymmetry between the two parties' financial support. The Republicans receive support from business or from groups, such as the religious right, that don't oppose business's agenda. (Pat Robertson may not have any special passion for, say, protecting offshore tax havens, but he won't denounce them, either.) Democrats, by contrast, draw financial support from a broader range of interests—from corporate America, too, but also from labor, environmentalists, consumer groups, trial lawyers, and other associations whose agendas regularly conflict with those of business.

One way to think about this dynamic is a political science theory called democratic pluralism. Pluralism was a way of describing, and justifying, the system that emerged after World War II. The most active players in the political system of the 1950s and 1960s were large organizations like the United States Chamber of Commerce and the AFL-CIO. Even though these pressure groups wielded far more influence than everyday citizens, pluralism theory held that most citizens' interests were adequately accounted for anyway, because the various pressure groups represented them by proxy. Political scientists applied this theory to the U.S. political system as a whole, but currently it's a decent model only for the Democratic Party. That is, since Democrats must listen to representatives of business, labor, consumers, and others, the consensus that it reaches is usually a pretty good reflection of the broader good. But Republicans, whose base represents just a narrow elite sliver of the economy, usually fail to take account of the broader interest.

This dynamic does not apply to cultural issues—Republicans are no more subservient to the whims of social conservatives than Democrats are to social liberals. Nor does it apply to foreign policy, where both parties make policy largely free from the influence of organized special interests. And, while it should be noted that the Democratic Party as a whole draws from a variety of economic interests, individual Democratic politicians do not. In the Senate, for instance, New York Democrat Charles Schumer is essentially a tool of the financial industry; Louisiana's John Breaux, the oil and gas industry; Michigan's Carl Levin, the auto industry; and so on. But the diversity of, and lack of agreement between, these interests generally allows a Democratic administration to transcend this sort of parochialism. Conservatives attack the Democrats as beholden to unions and other left-wing special interests. Meanwhile, leftists like Ralph Nader attack it as having sold out its union and liberal allies for the embrace of business. They're both half right: Being beholden to everybody means being beholden to nobody.

This can be seen in the behavior of the Clinton administration. At the time, the president's dogged pursuit of soft money was seen both by liberals and conservatives as the apex of political sleaze. But, in fact, the breadth of Bill Clinton's fund-raising is precisely what insulated his decision-making from undue influence. In 1993, Clinton infuriated his labor allies, but pleased his business backers, by lobbying for and signing NAFTA. In 1995, he delighted trial lawyers, but angered lobbyists for business (especially in the Democrat-friendly technology industry), by vetoing a GOP-backed bill making it more difficult for investors to sue based on misleading financial reports. As surpluses emerged in the last few years of his term, Clinton stymied both the tax-cutting urges of his business allies and the spending urges of his labor allies by insisting on debt reduction. The point is not that Clinton got every policy decision right but that the discordant nature of his support put him in a position where, on most issues, it was at least *possible* for him to make a detached judgment on the merits. That is precisely what Bush cannot do.

The extent of the Bush administration's bond with the lobbyists of K Street is necessarily hidden from public view, since neither party to the relationship has any incentive to publicize it. But a sense of it can be gleaned from stories like the one that appeared in *The Wall Street Journal* last January. "Top administration officials," the *Journal* reported, "led by political adviser Karl Rove, have been meeting with industry lobbyists in recent weeks seeking input on the president's 2002 agenda." The article proceeded to detail the ways in which corporate America's wish list coincided with Bush's agenda for that year.

In fact, if you look at the major economic issues of the Bush presidency, in every instance Bush's position has been identical to that of whichever interest group applied the heaviest political pressure. On behalf of the accounting industry he fought tooth-and-nail against audit reform, until a 99 to zero Senate vote overwhelmed his opposition. (And, after the heat was off, Bush weakened the new auditing oversight board and reneged on his promise to boost the Securities and Exchange Commission's budget.) His energy bill was written in consultation with energy producers and reflected their desires almost perfectly. In signing legislation to overturn workplace ergonomic standards and supporting tougher bankruptcy standards on consumers, he fulfilled longtime corporate demands by using a broad-based corporate coalition. He fought campaign finance reform until opposition grew politically untenable, and even now his appointees to the Federal Election

Commission are helping gut it. His telecommunications position preserved the monopoly status of local cable providers. His positions on prescription drugs and a patients' bill of rights were the positions of the drug industry and HMOs, respectively. He supported the oil companies in their quest to drill in Alaska and the auto companies in their disdain for higher fuel-efficiency standards. When, after the September 11 attacks, private airline security firms enlisted a massive lobbying effort to keep their contracts, Bush supported them (until that, too, became politically unsupportable). In none of these cases did organizations representing those affected by these policies—labor, environment, or consumer organizations—receive any meaningful hearing.

Paradoxically, the only major issue on which Bush exerted any discipline upon K Street was his tax cut. And even that was done in the spirit of mutual interest. Bush decided that if lobbyists loaded up the tax cut with business tax breaks, the entire thing might sink from its own weight. And so, business was persuaded to line up behind a tax cut that left corporate rates untouched—forming a "tax-relief coalition" that raised millions to press for the bill's passage—with the promise that subsequent bills would directly give corporations their long-sought breaks. (To be sure, corporate executives, as highly compensated individuals, would have benefited disproportionately from Bush's income tax cuts even if they hadn't been followed by corporate tax relief.) And indeed, last winter, Bush unsuccessfully pushed for a package of business breaks under the guise of "stimulus," and he is preparing to do so yet again this year.

It is often on the smaller issues, which receive almost no public attention, where the influence of lobbyists can be seen most clearly. There are countless such case studies, but, rather than slogging through all of them, consider just one: the Research and Experimentation Tax Credit. This was created in 1981 in order to reward companies whose product research generated broader scientific benefits. Alas, as Robert S. McIntyre of Citizens for Tax Justice has written, companies quickly claimed the credit for researching products with no merit whatsoever, such as Chicken McNuggets. In 1997, the Clinton Treasury Department imposed a new regulation restricting the credit to actual scientific advances. But, when Bush took office, his Treasury Department quickly rescinded it. Mark Weinberger, Bush's Assistant Secretary of the Treasury for Tax Policy at the time, had served as a tax lobbyist immediately prior to joining the administration. His clients included the R&E Tax Credit Coalition, which represented corporations seeking to preserve this particular scam. Early in his tenure, Weinberger described his goal to the *Journal* thusly: "I want to change the 'us versus them' mentality—the 'us' being government, the 'them' being business."

That line would serve as an appropriate epigram for Bush's governing philosophy. Since he's taken office, government and business have melded together as one big "us." Scores of mid-level appointees, like Weinberger, oversee industries for which they once worked. Deputy Interior Secretary J. Steven Griles is a former coal-bed methane lobbyist. Interior Department Solicitor William Geary Myers III previously lobbied to preserve federal grazing subsidies. Assistant Secretary of Energy for Fossil Energy Carl Michael Smith came to government from the oil industry and told one oil and gas group that his job is to determine "how best to utilize taxpayer dollars to the benefit of industry." The prevalence of such appointees is a stark departure from the previous administration. "Clinton weighed factors other than whether you contributed significantly to his campaign," explains G. Calvin MacKenzie, who studies presidential appointees for the Brookings Institution.

It has become common under Bush not only for appointees to move easily between pleading for industry and adjudicating such pleadings but to do both simultaneously. Republican National Committee (RNC) Chairman Marc Racicot not only comes from K Street (which is hardly unprecedented for either party) but proposed to continue his lobbying work while serving as party chairman. The unpleasant symbolism of this forced Racicot to reverse himself, but the real scandal wasn't that his lobbying would conflict with his chairmanship of the RNC—it was that it wouldn't. Last year, Enron Chairman Kenneth L. Lay privately promised to support keeping the chairman of the Federal Energy Regulatory Commission (FERC) if he would reverse his stance on energy regulation—implying that Lay had veto power over the FERC chairmanship. My colleague Jonathan Cohn reported in these pages last week that two members of the Advisory Committee on Childhood Lead Poisoning Prevention were solicited for their positions not by the Bush administration but by the lead industry itself. That is, lobbyists have in some instances literally taken over the responsibilities of governing.

Bush's defenders would no doubt maintain that it's only natural that a conservative president regularly sides with business, which usually desires less taxation and regulation. It's true that, in most instances, conservative ideology and business self-interest both militate toward the same end. Yet no disinterested conservative ideology would take the form of Bush's actual mix of policies. His energy bill, proposing massive new production subsidies, earned disdain from free-market purists like *National Review* and the Cato Institute. Bush has quietly acquiesced to congressional pork, declining to veto a single spending bill. Meanwhile, he has cut funding for programs—such as recovery of loose radioactive material—that many conservatives support but that lack powerful constituencies. Back in the 1980s, Ronald Reagan's Budget Director David Stockman pledged to attack "weak claims, not weak clients." Bush has done just the opposite.

One of the great perversities of Bush's domestic policy is that, when he does deviate from conservatism, he follows this same pattern—that is, he tacks left not because it is in the broad public interest but because it will please a narrow but powerful special interest. Take, for example, the three domestic policy decisions for which he has taken the most flak from free-market conservatives: support for farm subsidies and for tariffs on steel and textiles. In each case, Bush acquiesced to the demands of a small, organized minority whose interests clearly run contrary to those of the majority. Studies have found that every job saved by tariffs costs consumers $800,000 in higher prices. Farm subsidies are even less justifiable: They artificially deluge the agriculture industry and transfer money to relatively affluent farmers by boosting the price of food, which disproportionately hurts the poor. Note that in all those instances Clinton managed to stand up to the special pleaders, despite the fact that acquiescing would have been more compatible with his ideology than it was with Bush's.

Perhaps the most important common element of Bush's leftward lurches is that they involve adopting positions through which he can win favor with a Democratic-leaning pressure group without running up against business interests. For instance, Bush has embraced scandal-tarred carpenters' union President Douglas McCarron and Teamsters President James P. Hoffa—this despite the fact that GOP opposition to organized labor is frequently explained by aversion to "corrupt union bosses." So why has Bush cozied up to two of the more controversial bosses around? Because, as my colleague John B. Judis has pointed out, whereas most union leaders' top priorities involve winning concessions from employers, both McCarron and Hoffa are equally concerned with having the administration help them with internal issues—in McCarron's case, squelching a court case brought by reformers within the union; in Hoffa's, lifting the Independent Review Board that oversees the union as a result of past transgressions.

The only factor that clearly mitigates Bush's embrace of an agenda set by the business sector is his own sense of political self-preservation. After all, if the administration is publicly discredited as shilling for K Street, then it will be less effective at shilling for K Street. This is where Rove comes in. Sometimes half-measures (say, an industry-friendly prescription-drug plan) must be embraced to stave off more sweeping changes. Other times full retreat (as on airport security) is required in order to avoid a p.r. debacle. Hence Bush approved offshore drilling in politically marginal California but not in politically crucial Florida. This is also the reason that Bush has not endorsed some of the business lobby's more politically unattainable goals, such as complete abolition of the corporate income tax. This caution should not be mistaken for principled independence.

But caution has generally proved to be unnecessary for this White House because the public so rarely has focused upon Bush's domestic agenda. The reason for this lies in another phenomenon of political science: Bad policies can exist when they have concentrated benefits and diffuse costs. For instance, the public should be outraged at steel tariffs, but in fact most people are not because the cost to each individual is very low. The people who care the most about steel tariffs are those who work in the steel industry, and they're all for tariffs. Likewise, few people have any desire to run long-term deficits in order to provide a large tax cut for the affluent. But the people who stand to gain the most from such tax cuts tend to appreciate them a great deal, and they express their appreciation, among other ways, in the form of political donations that can be used to help convince the majority that the tax cuts are actually aimed at them.

On virtually every issue that has come before him, Bush has sided with the intense preferences of the well-organized minority. Judging from his lofty polls and his bulging coffers, the strategy has worked brilliantly. In a democracy, of course, you can never completely discount the possibility that the majority will eventually focus on the fact that it is getting persistently fleeced. From what we've seen of Karl Rove, though, he doesn't appear very worried.

The Ideological Impostor

Robert Kuttner

The American Prospect | June 3, 2002

If there's one thing about Bill Clinton that drove the Republicans crazy, it was his penchant for taking GOP issues like welfare reform and making them his own. And if there's one thing that drives Democrats crazy about George W. Bush, it's his ability to at least sound like he's embracing left-wing values, such as maintaining and strengthening Medicare, Social Security, and other elements of the social safety net. In this essay, Robert Kuttner parses what he feels to be the president's blatantly misleading rhetoric—and asks why the media and the U.S. public continue to let him get away with it. . . .

In the 2000 election, the voters of this country could have been forgiven for sizing up George W. Bush as a cross between a moderate Republican and DLC Democrat. Here are some of the things he said while campaigning:

In a stirring passage in his convention speech, Bush invoked

single moms struggling to feed their kids and pay the rent. Immigrants starting a hard life in a new world. Children without fathers in neighborhoods where gangs seem like friendship. . . .We are their country, too. . . . When these problems aren't confronted, it builds a wall within our nation. On one side are wealth and technology, education and ambition. On the other side of the wall are poverty and prison, addiction and despair. And, my fellow Americans, we must tear down that wall.

One could imagine Bobby Kennedy or Lyndon Johnson—or even Al Gore on a good day—uttering just those words.

"To seniors in this country," Bush earnestly declared, "you earned your benefits, you made your plans, and President George W. Bush will keep the promise of Social Security—no changes, no reductions, no way."

"Medicare," he added, "does more than meet the needs of our elderly; it reflects the values of our society. We will set it on firm financial ground, and make prescription drugs available and affordable for every senior who needs them."

In the third presidential debate, Bush told Gore, "You know I support a national patients' bill of rights, Mr. Vice President. And I want all people covered." He called for grants to the states "so that seniors—poor seniors—don't have to choose between food and medicine."

He pledged to change the tone in Washington, to govern as a bipartisan the way he had done as governor of Texas. "I know it's going to require a different kind of leader to go to Washington and say to both Republicans and Democrats, 'Let's come together,'" he said.

Bush repeatedly promised to balance the budget and insisted that the nation could afford a tax cut without slipping into deficit. He even criticized a House Republican plan to achieve budget savings by cutting the Earned Income Tax Credit: "I don't think they ought to balance their budget on the backs of the poor," he said.

Turning to the environment, Bush regularly suggested that he would be unusually green for a Republican. "To enhance America's long-term energy security," he said, "we must continue developing renewable energy."

On education, he famously promised to "leave no child behind," borrowing not only liberal ideas about universal inclusion but literally plagiarizing the three-decades-old slogan of the Children's Defense Fund (the fund now prints its slogan with a trademark sign).

All of these declarations were, of course, lies. While all recent presidents have periodically gone back on promises and some have told explicit untruths, what's interesting about this president is that his multiple lies are something very rare in politics: They are ideological lies. Worse still, according to *The Washington Post*'s David Broder, Bush seems determined to make compassionate conservatism the centerpiece of the 2002 campaign—the actual substance of his presidency notwithstanding.

Hypocrisy, as La Rochefoucauld observed, is the homage that vice pays to virtue. In the case of Bush, campaign lies are the homage that Republican sloganeering paid to the popularity of Democratic ideology.

Imagine instead that Bush had hit the campaign trail promoting a Social Security shift that increased the system's deficits, requiring cuts in benefits and an increase in the retirement age; that he'd promised a tax cut that cost more than twice Social Security's long-term shortfall. Imagine that his patients' rights bill was advertised as authored by the HMO industry—and as prohibiting patients denied care from suing their insurer; that he'd touted a Medicare plan that would keep ratcheting down payments to hospitals and doctors; that his environmental policy would scrap one protection after another and let industry rewrite the rules; that he'd pledged to demonize Democrats who resisted his policies; that his No Child Left Behind program pledged to freeze funding for Head Start and money for child care—and to go back on a bipartisan deal to increase federal funds for poor public schools in exchange for high-stakes testing.

Campaigning on that set of views, Bush would have been the minority candidate of a minority party. There would have been no cliffhanger in Florida and no narrow Supreme Court resolution of *Bush v. Gore*. Yet that set of views has been his actual program.

More interesting still, Bush has mostly gotten away with it. While a careful reader of the quality press might connect the dots and conclude that Bush's presidency is a double fraud—not only wasn't he really elected, he isn't remotely governing on the program he offered voters—there's been no widespread outrage.

One simply cannot conjure up a systematic presidential deception of comparable cynicism and scale. Bill Clinton, to be sure, lied about his sexual escapades. He often enraged allies both left and center: The DLC and the labor movement agree on just about nothing but they share Monica Lewinsky's assessment that Clinton is a faithless lover. Clinton tacked right on values issues in the 1992 campaign only to embrace gay rights. He assiduously courted the gay community only to back a lame halfway policy of "don't ask, don't tell." Conversely, he initially postured liberal on economic issues only to abandon both universal health insurance and economic stimulus by public investment. Many blacks were so comfortable with Clinton that they considered him the first African-American president. But for all his marquee appointments of black officials, Clinton could embrace a cruel version of welfare reform and abandon old friends such as Lani Guinier.

Yet there was about Clinton a broad ideological consistency. Though he could infuriate his friends on the particulars, these were tactical reversals within a relatively narrow, consistent ideological whole. Clinton was at heart a centrist—a moderate with some liberal leanings who governed as a wily pragmatist and who often fought his conservative adversaries to a draw or better. Jimmy Carter was similar. Bush Senior was essentially a moderate Republican who tried to court his party's right wing, but his heart wasn't really in it. Ronald Reagan was a genuine conservative who never pretended to be anything but. To find a deception of comparable scale to Bush's, you have to go all the way back to Lyndon Johnson, who ran in 1964 as the candidate who would keep us from a wider war in Vietnam and then escalated the conflict. On domestic policy, Johnson gave the country the progressive program he promised and more. Indeed, as Robert Caro's latest installment [of his multi-volume LBJ biography] makes clear, if anyone should feel betrayed by LBJ, it was the Senate's southern bourbons with whom he'd allied himself to become majority leader in the 1950s.

As ideological fraud, then, George W. Bush remains in a class by himself. It's understandable why he does it: Democrats' domestic positions are basically popular. But why does he get away with it? He pulls it off, I think, for several reasons (of which September 11 is fairly far down the list).

First, in his own goofy way he's a political natural, a nice guy. His political style has a chumminess and warm physicality that's disarming. It's easy to detest his policies but not so easy to hate the man. The first time I watched him at close range, he was working a room of Democratic senators (he'd boldly solicited an invitation to a Democratic Caucus retreat and I was an invited speaker). That's when I realized how much his critics had underestimated the man as a politician. Bush was off script and off the record, and he did just fine at the banter. The wisecracks were spontaneous and smart. Indeed, if Clinton alienated because he was too clever by half, Bush endears when it turns out he's not as dumb as you thought. You're waiting for him to stumble and you're charmed when he doesn't.

Second, Bush has absolutely superb handlers and tacticians. His speechwriter, Michael Gerson, is so gifted that he could make a trained monkey sound like Thomas Jefferson. Karl Rove, his political grand strategist, has perfected a game of leaving the Democrats with no popular issues on the table. If Democrats are for Social Security, so is Bush. If they back patients' rights and prescription drugs, so does he. If they embrace kids, he does them one better. Bush then takes away in the fine print everything that he offers in the headlines. Politically, alas, this is mere detail—so much policy wonkery. The betrayal enrages experts and advocates but can be dealt with by creative obfuscation when it comes to the voters. But what does that say about the voters?

Here we have the third and most alarming factor. This is an era in which voters are unusually quiescent. For two decades, expectations about what government can do have been so lowered—and here many Democrats are just as culpable as Republicans—that the broad public doesn't get terribly indignant about betrayals, much less of the ideological kind. The public has come to expect government to jerk people around. When Bush breaches a promise, it only confirms the general suspicion that government can't be trusted anyway. And the fact that the Democratic Party doesn't have a clear opposition ideology makes Bush's task that much easier.

September 11 certainly allowed Bush to change the subject. At the same time, however, voters remain closer to core Democratic views on a broad range of domestic issues. Polls consistently show that voters don't translate Bush's popularity on national-security issues into support for Republican positions on patients' rights, Social Security, and the rest. But politics itself is so debased and devalued that all Bush need do is genuflect to those broad Democratic themes. After all, the guy really does seem to care about poor people, seniors, and kids.

In fairness, voters were well aware that Bush was no liberal—on some issues, at least. He straightforwardly called for a tax cut, and for vouchers as a remedy to "failing schools." He said he wanted to reduce the incidence of abortion, though he was careful not to support overturning *Roe v. Wade*. He embraced private retirement accounts as a complement to Social Security for younger workers, but not at the cost of weakening Social Security itself. And he advocated greater use of religious institutions to carry out social services. But he carefully balanced these views with a sweeping embrace of liberal rhetoric and programs on a host of other issues.

Moreover, a lot of Bush's hard-right program has flown beneath the radar. On the issue of reproductive rights, for example, where Bush has always stopped just short of calling for an end to a woman's right to terminate an unwanted pregnancy, he's done just about everything else to hobble abortion, family planning, and even the therapeutic use of discarded fertilized embryos. An administration plan to eliminate contraception coverage from federal employees' insurance plans was reversed by Congress.

Or consider No Child Left Behind. Bush's grand scheme for children in low-performing schools had three elements: relentlessly test kids, let some parents opt out of such schools with vouchers, and increase public-school funding. But Bush has repeatedly welshed on the funding. Under the newly enacted education law, children as young as eight will be subjected to standardized testing. In inner-city schools, as many as half will fail. These kids will be "left back" as they used to say, but without adequate resources for good remedial education. What then? Will they just keep repeating fourth grade?

Schools carry the burden of society's other deficits. If Bush were serious about leaving no child behind, he would not just throw tests at kids and vouchers at their parents. He would offer kids decent day care while their mothers worked, fully fund Head Start, and get children of low-income families prepared for school with high-quality pre-kindergarten. Decent wages wouldn't hurt, either. He's of course done none of this, and millions of children will be left behind. But with a few eloquent Gerson speeches informed by careful focus groups and some nice photos of himself with poor kids, Bush has seized the rhetorical high ground.

Holding Bush accountable for these deceptions will require more than partisan or journalistic truth squads. The detail is hidden in plain view, courtesy of the Web (for one-stop shopping, try our own www.movingideas.org). However, information without political narrative might as well not exist. So the larger challenge is to re-energize not just liberal politics, but politics as such. Today's characteristic politics lends itself perfectly to slogan, symbol, deception, even systematic prevarication.

As political scientists since Maurice Duverger have pointed out, a disengaged politics is necessarily a conservative politics. Without the counterweight of a mobilized citizenry that has the motivation to pay attention and the institutions that can aggregate and express its concerns, the system defaults to its other source of residual power: concentrated wealth. Institutions like the labor movement, which give ordinary people the mechanisms to effect political change and the motivation to take politics seriously, are diminished. It's no accident that labor did so much of the heavy lifting for Gore—and that it wasn't quite enough. As another political scientist, Kay Lehman Schlozman, has observed, most people of modest means no longer participate vigorously in politics—not only because they don't believe politics make a difference, but also because the institutions that invite their participation are dwindling.

Media are also culpable: Short-attention-span TV and Internet gossip sites function as though politics were not about how a great democracy makes weighty choices; it's just another form of commerce or entertainment. The media loves the gotcha game, but whopping discrepancies in the Medicare budget or global-warming policy are not good gotcha.

These trends, all of which debase politics, have been building for a long time; their full fruit is George W. Bush. Now the Bush charade is due for a revival in this year's campaign. As long as the citizenry is anesthetized, however, even systematic presidential lying is of little consequence. And a polity in which leaders lie and the public shrugs falls short of a democracy. That's the hard truth.

With Signals and Maneuvers, Bush Orchestrates an Ouster

Elisabeth Bumiller

The New York Times | December 21, 2002

If luck is a matter of preparation meeting opportunity, then surely the same can be said about bad luck, too. For the former Senate majority leader Trent Lott of Mississippi, malevolent opportunity appeared in the most deceptive of settings: an elegant lunch honoring the 100th birthday of Strom Thurmond, legendary Senator from South Carolina. For the record, here's what Lott uttered on that afternoon of December 5, 2002, when he stood to toast his colleague: "I want to say this about my state: when Strom Thurmond ran for President, we voted for him. We're proud of it. And if the rest of the country had followed our lead, we wouldn't have had all these problems over all these years, either."

Lott was referring to 1948, when Thurmond (then governor of South Carolina) ran for president on a pro-segregation platform as a candidate of the States Rights Party, known as the Dixiecrats. The room reportedly fell silent at Lott's gaffe. Still, it took the better part of a week before Lott began to take serious fire from the media for his words. By day seven, however, as the press was busily delving into Lott's less-than-stellar record on racial issues, the furor reached the tipping point. That's when the White House weighed in, calling Lott's comments "offensive."

From then on, Lott's days were numbered. It seems (here's where the preparation comes in) that the White House and other GOP members had not been particularly keen on Lott's leadership anyway. What's more, the administration had a perfect substitute already waiting in the wings. New York Times White House correspondent Elisabeth Bumiller describes what happened next, as the vaunted White House political machine swung into action. . . .

As President Bush was cheerily shaking the hands of thousands of guests at glittering White House Christmas parties this week, his advisers and influential Republicans were working overtime to jettison Trent Lott as the Senate Republican leader.

One Republican close to the White House who talked to reporters about the troubles Mr. Lott was bringing upon the party said today that he had been given careful instructions by top White House officials to "stick to the president's words"—meaning that he should take his cues from the president's criticism of Mr. Lott on Dec. 12 in Philadelphia—and to "stay out of the story." That meant critics should remain anonymous when they talked to reporters about Mr. Lott, said this Republican ally of the White House.

By the end of the week, as the White House watched its favorite, Senator Bill Frist of Tennessee, step up to replace Mr. Lott of Mississippi, Washington's political professionals were left awed. They said Mr. Bush and his powerful political adviser, Karl Rove, had stumbled at times but had still managed to depose in eight short days the unanimously elected Senate leader of their own party.

The president, they said, had ruthlessly maneuvered to contain a stain on Republicans that was threatening his own agenda. And he did it without overtly appearing to be behind the effort.

"They've got a skilled surgeon coming in to run the Senate, and they used a surgeon's skill to remove Lott without leaving any fingerprints," said Robert S. Strauss, the former Democratic National Committee chairman who has been a friend of the Bushes for years. "Whether you agree or disagree with this administration on policy, you have to give the White House tremendous credit for coming to town and after two years having this kind of political performance."

In just eight days, influential Republicans said, the White House used a succession of carefully timed public statements and anonymous, damaging leaks to bring about the resignation of Mr. Lott and the ascension of Mr. Frist, while publicly denouncing the leaks and repeatedly expressing the view that the president did not think Mr. Lott should resign.

"It was a clean extraction," said James Carville, the Democratic strategist, who is married to Mary Matalin, a top aide to Vice President Dick Cheney.

It was no less than the president himself who began the destruction of Mr. Lott. Last Thursday in Philadelphia, in a sharp rebuke that was the political equivalent of cutting off Mr. Lott's legs, the president said that comments Mr. Lott made on Dec. 5, applauding Senator Strom Thurmond's presidential run in 1948 "do not reflect the spirit of our country" and that "any suggestion that the segregated past was acceptable or positive is offensive and it is wrong."

Republicans said that the condemnation was the idea of Mr. Bush, not Mr. Rove, and that the president was well aware that his words would set in motion a chain of events that were likely to lead to Mr. Lott's resignation. Mr. Bush—who began his political education at the side of Lee Atwater, the bad-boy strategist of the first President Bush's successful 1988 campaign— then immediately ordered his staff to speak no more on the subject.

At that point, Republicans said, no one at the White House had to say a word. "When the president made his statement in Philadelphia, it signaled the White House's view on Lott's continuing as leader," one Republican said. "And it was a strong, unmistakable signal that it would be extraordinarily difficult for Lott to be effective as leader."

The next day, Mr. Lott held a news conference in Mississippi apologizing for his comments. Mr. Bush, meanwhile, headed for a weekend at Camp David and maintained a determined public silence on Mr. Lott. Although Ari Fleischer, the White House press secretary, said after Mr. Lott's news conference that "the president doesn't think Trent Lott needs to resign" (a line Mr. Fleischer repeated all week), not once did the president offer any public support for Mr. Lott.

By Sunday, as the influential Washington Sunday morning talk shows went into overdrive with the news that Senator Don Nickles of Oklahoma had called for his colleagues to consider replacing Mr. Lott, Mr. Frist's name had already surfaced. It was put forth by Republicans who were in regular contact with the White House.

"In Washington the river grabs an event and the current just takes it," one of those Republicans said. "The White House doesn't have to do much. But we all knew that the White House had a great relationship with Frist and that it was in the interest of the president and the party to start talking him up."

By Monday, the leaking itself went into overdrive as numerous Republicans from across the country told reporters, always anonymously, that Mr. Lott had no chance of remaining as Senate Republican leader and that the White House wanted him out. The next day, as the White House publicly denounced the leakers, the leaking continued. But now Mr. Rove, who was in close contact with crucial Republicans, was described as "monitoring" the situation, but not trying to influence it.

"He's not standing behind the curtain making the smoke come out and when the smoke comes out, some person engineered by him appears," a Republican said then.

It was critical, Republicans said, that the White House not be seen as interfering in the clubby world of the Senate. They said that any perceived attempts to manipulate a vote were likely to backfire.

By Wednesday, Mr. Lott had been fired upon again, this time publicly by two lethal guns. Secretary of State Colin L. Powell said he "deplored'" the sentiments behind Mr. Lott's statement, while Gov. Jeb Bush of Florida, the president's brother, told *The Miami Herald* that "something's going to have to change."

"This can't be the topic of conversation over the next week," he said.

By Thursday, Mr. Lott appeared doomed when Mr. Frist became the first Republican to openly challenge him for his post and earned the support of important Republicans. Mr. Frist's candidacy was a relief for White House officials, who had grown increasingly frustrated as Mr. Lott clung to his job and the headlines veered out of their control. Administration officials insisted they had not encouraged Mr. Frist, and had no interest in the outcome of any Senate vote. But Republicans close to the White House, speaking as always anonymously, said Mr. Frist had long been the president's choice.

This evening, another Republican who spoke to reporters as well as to Mr. Rove most days this week said that Mr. Rove had not instructed him what to say to the press about Mr. Lott. "But I've worked with him enough to know that I shouldn't get ahead of the president," the Republican said, "and yet he knows that I'm helping the White House along with what they want to do."

National Conversation: Debt and Taxes

What Is He Thinking?
Eleanor Clift

Newsweek | February 7, 2003

As we all know by now, the Bush administration's economic policy can be summed up in a phrase: tax cuts. Clearly, the decision makers in the White House are convinced that a significantly lower rate of taxation is the key to the country's long-term health and vitality. Just as clearly, this entails a return to hefty Federal budget deficits, at least for the next few years (this year's deficit is projected to be at least $450 billion). The administration's economic experts insist that this situation will eventually reverse itself, as the predicted economic boom (fueled by these very same tax cuts) causes tax revenues to swell again.

This is essentially supply-side economics—the approach championed by President Reagan, which many economists think largely discredited. Its resurrection by the Bush White House has led many observers to wonder whether the administration truly believes it will work this time—or whether the supply-side rhetoric is actually just a smoke screen for rolling back the taxes of upper-income earners while starving the Federal government to the point where substantial spending cuts will have to be made. In this column, Eleanor Clift interviews a Democratic Senator who says he fears for the future of Medicare and Social Security. . . .

Sticker shock. That's the reaction on Capitol Hill to President George W. Bush's budget. The deficit numbers are staggering, even to Bush loyalists: $307 billion next year, more than a trillion dollars in five years. And that's not counting the looming war with Iraq and the cost of a prolonged occupation. Bush talks plenty about war, but he doesn't tell the country how he plans to pay for it.

His borrow-and-spend budget even shortchanges some of his alleged priorities. Money for medical research is flat-lined, barely keeping up with inflation. Funding for his "No child left behind" education bill is scaled back. Other assistance programs in Africa are raided to pay for Bush's pledge to fight AIDS in Africa. Add to this the states that are looking to Congress for help, and it's a very sobering time for Democrats and Republicans alike. "You don't have to be a deficit hawk to be worried," says a Senate Republican aide.

The first casualty will be Bush's dividend-tax-relief plan, which will be reduced drastically if not killed altogether. Bush reportedly has been warned by Federal Reserve Board Chairman Alan Greenspan to put the brake on tax cuts before gigantic deficits drag down the economy.

President Ronald Reagan, who ran up the government charge account, took a what-me-worry attitude, declaring jovially, "The deficit is big enough to take care of itself." Reagan wasn't hurt politically, but the sea of red ink his administration created caught up with his successor, the first President Bush. Now, the younger Bush has overtaken his father, who previously held the record in deficit spending.

Deficit doves point out that today's deficits represent a smaller percentage of the gross national product than during Reagan's heyday, but that is no consolation to Kent Conrad, ranking Democrat on the Senate Budget Committee. Poring over Bush's budget documents in his Capitol Hill townhouse one evening this week, Conrad couldn't believe what he was seeing: mushrooming deficits that peak just when the baby-boom generation begins to retire. That means government spending on Social Security and Medicare will increase when government debt is at its highest.

"It is nuts, stone-cold nuts," Conrad said in an interview with *Newsweek*. "And they're not nuts, and they're not stupid. They're smart people, and they know what we know, that the deficit will explode when federal expenditures peak. And that's when I had this revelation: the only rationale for what they're doing is that they plan to fundamentally gut Social Security and Medicare."

Republicans are used to Democrats accusing them of heartlessness, of wanting to throw old people out in the snow and deny hungry children a meal. Democrats don't have any new ideas of their own, Republicans say, so they resort to the old, tired charges. But Conrad represents one of the red states that Bush won by a large margin, and he's never been a typical liberal. He was North Dakota's tax commissioner before he was elected to the Senate, and he knows his numbers. His idea of fun is to watch a baseball game and calculate in his head how each player's turn at bat changes his batting average.

Conrad is convinced that the debt Bush is piling up will threaten the country's long-term economic security, and that Social Security and Medicare will not survive. Privately, Republicans say Conrad is right, but with a caveat. Social Security and Medicare cannot survive in their current form. Under the guise of reform, both programs will have to adapt to the budget realities.

Conrad's prediction: That it will be reforming by cutting benefits. He has charts to illustrate the choices government will face if Bush's tax cuts proceed as planned. They range from bad to worse. Record deficit spending means government borrowing crowds out entrepreneurial investment and hurts economic growth. To sustain benefits and keep the social contract as is would require an unprecedented tax increase to 30 percent of GDP (it's now 20 percent). "Or we'll have to eliminate the rest of government as we know it," says Conrad. "This is breathtaking; this is radical, radical stuff."

Unlike the senior Bush, who put his political career on the line to raise taxes and begin the long climb out of the deficit hole, this President Bush has shown no inclination to back down. Just as his foreign policy can be summed up in two words—Get Saddam—his domestic policy is all about tax cuts. First, the administration said tax cuts were needed to spend down the surplus. When the surplus disappeared, tax cuts were needed to get the economy out of recession. Now, tax cuts are billed as the way to balance the budget by growing the economy, an idea the elder Bush once called "voodoo economics."

A decade after Texas billionaire Ross Perot made the deficit a campaign issue against Bush the father, Bush the son has plunged the country back into the red. He's poised to spend billions toppling Saddam while launching a crackdown on eligibility for poor children for federally subsidized meals in school. The Reagan administration tried to classify ketchup as a vegetable and caught hell. But Bush doesn't have to explain or defend his priorities. He has a one-size-fits-all answer that so far has provided him Teflon coating thicker than Reagan's. "The war," says Conrad, "overwhelms everything."

Partisan Lines Harden in Debate Over Tax Cuts

David Francis

Christian Science Monitor | March 31, 2003

In late May of 2003, President Bush signed into law the third-largest tax cut in history—the only larger ones being Reagan's tax cut in 1981, and Bush's own 2001 tax cut. The latest bill reduces income tax rates by 2 to 3 percent, raises the child tax credit from $600 to $1,000, increases the standard deduction for couples filing jointly, and slashes the top tax rate on dividend and capital gains income to 15 percent (from 38.6 and 20 percent, respectively).

One way the Republicans have been able to sell their tax cut proposals—which put much more money into the pockets of wealthy individuals than they give back to middle-class taxpayers, while at the same time requiring large budget cuts in social programs—is by citing the "average" monetary benefits that would accrue to large segments of the population. As David Francis points out in this column (written before the final bill had been drafted), this is essentially a statistical con game—and one that could provide the Democrats with a potent political issue, if the public ever catches on to it.

One other note: Francis refers here to the Senate's $350 billion dollar "cap" on tax cuts—which at first glance appears to be a defeat for Bush, who had asked for much more. In fact, the final bill met this limit through the use of "sunset" provisions, which call for phasing out the child tax credit and joint filing breaks in 2005, and the dividend and capital gains cuts in 2008. If these tax breaks are eventually extended—as the GOP has vowed to do—then the total price tag for the 10-year tax package is estimated to be around $1 trillion. Now that's real money. . . .

Here's a switch: Democrats and liberals are accusing the Republicans of engaging in "class warfare."

Ever since the battle over the $1.4 trillion tax cuts in 2001, President Bush and his supporters have tried to squelch talk of the benefits going mostly to the well-to-do by charging the critics with class warfare.

Now what's gone around is coming around.

On March 21, the House passed a budget resolution with $265 billion in cuts, primarily from programs for low-income families, children, and elderly or disabled people. Also, student loans will be hurt.

"Class warfare turns out to be alive," holds Robert Greenstein, director of the Center on Budget and Policy Priorities. "Deep budget cuts that could harshly affect the poor, the vulnerable, and many middle-class Americans alongside lavish tax cuts for the nation's richest individuals."

Last Wednesday, though, the Senate voted to halve the president's latest proposal, for a $726 billion tax cut over 10 years, to $350 billion. Several moderate Republicans joined Democrats to pass that budget resolution amendment 51 to 48. They disliked the combination of big tax cuts, growing budget deficits, and a $75 billion six-month down payment on the cost of the Iraqi war requested by Bush. The Senate had already voted a $100 billion trim of the Bush tax-cut plan to accommodate war expenditures.

Presumably, the Senate action would allow smaller spending cuts. Republican leaders tried unsuccessfully to enlarge the budget resolution beyond $350 billion. A budget resolution acts, in effect, as a mushy limit on tax cuts and spending.

The Senate and House must agree next month on a resolution number. Final spending and tax-cut votes are months away.

If a large tax-cut, large benefit-cut combination comes out of the congressional mill, and it is possible, Democrats could have a dandy campaign issue in the 2004 elections. It worries moderate Republicans.

You can imagine the Democrats' campaign slogans: The nation's poorest families face slashes in Medicare and childcare so millionaires can pay $90,000 a year less in taxes.

Populism might have a comeback—if better-off voters care about the poor.

Merely dropping the corporate dividend tax cut in Bush's new tax-cut plan would save enough revenue—$396 billion over 10 years—to more than fund the benefit cuts in the House plan.

Partly because dividend-tax relief benefits mostly high-income taxpayers, it is regarded as vulnerable in Congress. About 75 percent of the tax benefits would go to those making $100,000 or more, the top 8 percent of taxpayers, finds economist Brian Roach. They would save $3,000 in taxes per year. Most would be middle-aged and white.

The administration's sales pitch for this tax cut is "misleading," says Mr. Roach, a researcher at Tufts University, Medford, Mass. Contrary to the claim that seniors receive more than half of all dividend income, Census Bureau data indicates they get only one quarter.

The administration holds that the average tax savings for the 7 million seniors receiving dividends would be $936 a year, "money they could spend or reinvest for their retirement."

But that $936, notes Roach, is an average rather than what the "typical" or "median" senior would save. Although not able to come up with a specific median number for seniors, Roach notes that three-quarters of seniors have no dividend income at all. Of those who do, most would realize benefits less than $936 while a relatively small number would save far more.

The Bush administration uses the same statistical tactic in other tax-cut claims. Because incomes in the United States are so skewed to the top, an average often sounds better from a political standpoint than the median. For illustration, if one person saves $3,000 a year in taxes and another $75,000, their average saving comes to $36,000.

Mr. Greenstein accuses administration officials of audacious manipulation of budget numbers: "They are cynical to a degree that I have never witnessed in any other administration, Democratic or Republican."

Since high-end taxpayers would receive the bulk of the benefits from the dividend proposal, it would increase US income inequality, already at a historic high and greater than in any other developed country, notes Roach.

But administration officials argue that all this income-distribution analysis is irrelevant, that the tax cuts will so boost the economy that everyone will benefit from more jobs, more income. The dividend plan alone would add 431,000 jobs over the next 18 months.

It is a trickle-down theory. It maintains that tax savings, especially by small business, would be invested in job-creating activities.

Roach counters that tax cuts aimed more at low-income groups would give the economy a bigger, more immediate boost because they tend to spend nearly all extra income, whereas the prosperous save proportionately more. Business, with a large amount of excess capacity at present, needs more customers far more than it needs new capacity.

Wealthy Choice

Ryan Lizza

The New Republic | January 20, 2003

One of the hardest-to-understand aspects of the 2003 Bush tax cut proposal—for all of us non-economists, anyway—was why the White House placed so much emphasis on eliminating taxation of stock dividends. One explanation is that they've fallen under the sway of conservative tax theorists who believe that reducing taxes on investment income is the key to economic growth. In this column, New Republic *political analyst Ryan Lizza identifies an additional, more political motive behind their thinking: A dividend tax cut now is the Bush administration's best shot at boosting the value of the stock market by next year, when the presidential election rolls around. A higher stock market, in turn, makes people who own stock feel richer and encourages them to spend more. Result: A timely economic upturn, and clear sailing toward a second term for George W. . . .*

On the afternoon of President Bush's economic speech this Tuesday, there was no happier Republican in Washington than Grover Norquist, the president of Americans for Tax Reform, conservative-coalition builder, and the White House's favorite anti-tax radical. Like many conservatives, Norquist has long fought to kill the tax on dividends, and he was giddy that Bush made that the centerpiece of his new tax plan. He had just come from a debate on National Public Radio in which he eviscerated a "midget commie from Massachusetts"—former Clinton administration Labor Secretary Robert Reich—and couldn't wait to square off Thursday on Bill Moyers's PBS show, which he "thinks" is called "Why we should steal everyone's money and give it to bums who won't work." He was looking forward to meetings on Friday with Dick Cheney and Karl Rove, presumably to plot a strategy for getting the new plan passed. Norquist insists the dividend tax-cut debate will be devastating for his opposition. "We are going to cripple the entire Democratic leadership all at once," he predicts. "I'm winning on all fronts."

It wasn't obvious, however, that this was the front the Bush administration wants attacked. In fact, in the pantheon of taxes that conservatives like Norquist have fought to eliminate, the tax paid by shareholders on their dividends has never quite caught on like the "death tax" or "marriage penalty."

First of all, very few people actually pay it; only one-quarter of all tax-filers currently receive dividends. And, for Republicans defensive about tax cuts skewed toward the ultra-wealthy, a crusade against the dividend tax confirms their opponents' worst suspicions: More than 70 percent of the benefits of eliminating it will go to the wealthiest 5 percent of American taxpayers.

Why then has the Bush administration suddenly taken an issue dear to a handful of anti-tax cranks and made it the cornerstone of its economic policy? Partly it's because the administration thinks it can make the politics work. But mainly it's because conservatives inside and outside the White House fervently believe that the key to economic health (and Bush's reelection) is a booming stock market.

Democrats are already calling the tax cut a payoff to Bush's K Street allies. But that analysis doesn't quite hold up. To begin with, the case against the dividend tax is that it is "double taxation"; corporations pay a tax on their profits, and then investors pay a tax when they receive those profits as dividends. If Bush really wanted to reward the business community, he would have proposed eliminating this tax at the corporate end. But, fearing being tarred as too close to corporations, he rejected this approach. The other problem with the simple K Street explanation is that the business community hasn't been clamoring for a dividend tax cut. What corporations really wanted from Bush were new tax incentives for investment—and they didn't get them.

In fact, Bush's embrace of the dividend tax cut is less about campaign contributions than ideology. In the past, liberals and conservatives both discounted the stock market's role in stimulating the economy. But, during the Clinton boom, this view began to change. Most famously, Alan Greenspan warned that overvalued markets could actually cause inflation. Economists call it the "wealth effect," and now Bush and his aides have become its greatest champions. Simply put, the wealth effect is the extra dollar amount a person spends from an increase in wealth. The theory is that the 1990s stock boom dramatically increased the net wealth of many Americans. The stock market soared, investors' portfolios fattened, and—at least on paper—investors' net wealth shot up, leading them to consume more. Even if they didn't have actual extra income, they felt rich and therefore spent more and saved less. That investor-class consumption drove the '90s economy. By making the dividend tax cut the centerpiece of his economic plan, Bush is embracing the idea that the stock market is the most important economic indicator in the United States—in other words, he's embracing the wealth effect.

The most influential work on the wealth effect has been done by Michael Palumbo, a Federal Reserve Board economist. In a recent study, he and another Board economist, Dean Maki, showed for the first time that in the '90s the households that gained the most from the stock-market boom are the same households responsible for the era's plummeting savings rate. Almost all the drops in savings in the late '90s—from about 7 percent of disposable income to about 1 percent—can be attributed to the richest 20 percent of households. The savings rate of the bottom 80 percent—the people least likely to own stocks—barely changed. Another influential paper, by Maki and fellow Board economist Karen Dynan, looked at data from 1983 to 1999 and clearly showed that stock-owning households spend more after stock prices rise, while non-stock-owning households don't.

The most radical part of Palumbo's work is his rejection of the traditional economic view that to stimulate the economy, cash must be pumped into the hands of lower-income Americans—in the form of a quick rebate check or payroll tax holiday, for example—because they are more likely than the wealthy to spend that extra disposable income. For adherents of the wealth effect, the way to boost consumption is to make relatively wealthy investors feel richer by juicing the stock market. One of the main critiques of the wealth effect was that it was impossible that the small slice of shareholding households was responsible for so much extra spending. But Palumbo says that is exactly what happened. "[A]ll of the consumption boom [of the '90s] really can be attributed to the richest groups of households," his paper argues.

You won't hear the White House making this point publicly, but the Bushies believe that returning cash to rich investors is their insurance policy against a bad economy in 2004. While Greenspan worried about the inflationary impact of the wealth effect, that danger has obviously passed. Now the danger is that battered investors will stop consuming. In a recent speech, Bush's top economist and the architect of the new plan, Glenn Hubbard, noted, "One of the key risks obviously now in the economy's recovery are recent equity price declines in the United States. And you know there's something called a wealth effect, an effect on consumer spending and business spending when wealth is destroyed, much as we have seen in the decline in stock-market prices in the United States."

What worries Hubbard and the White House is that more than $7 trillion in value has been wiped out of the stock market over the last three years.

According to the wealth effect, consumption should be plummeting in the wake of the market's decline, and yet consumer spending has continued to hold up the economy. One reason for this is that the enormous decline in the value of stocks has been cushioned by an incredible rise in the value of homes. "Fortunately, the losses in stock wealth to the midpoint of 2002 have been partly offset by gains in real estate wealth in the United States," an analysis from the financial services firm RBC recently noted. But wealth effect advocates also attribute the continued spending to the slow pace at which investors fully adjust to their decreased wealth. In other words, the predicted drop in consumption may well kick in this year.

For the White House, that means stimulating the stock market is more important than ever. Bush's aides argue that the dividend tax cut will bring investors flooding back into the market and raise share prices by 10 percent, which will presumably keep consumption high as shareholders start to feel wealthy again.

This emphasis on the investor class dovetails with the politics of Bush's reelection. He cares about how the economy will look to voters in 2004, not today. If the dividend tax cut has any impact on the markets and consumption, it won't be until next year, when Bush is campaigning. Bush is also trying to appeal to the two-thirds of voters who own stocks. The Democrats failed to capitalize on the bear market in the last election, and Bush wants to put them on the defensive about an issue supposedly dear to investors. "They are all getting locked in as enemies of the investor class," says one Republican strategist. And whereas in the 1970s and 1980s unemployment and inflation were the key indicators of economic performance to the public, the White House has come to believe that the stock market is now the key barometer. "There is a new number, and it is wealth," says Norquist. If the economy cooperates with these politics, the White House will have invested well.

From Baghdad to Iwo Jima

Lawrence Kudlow

National Review Online | April 15, 2003

This column, by veteran Wall Street economist Larry Kudlow, picks up the 2003 tax cut narrative in mid-April: The Republicans in the House are furious at the GOP-controlled Senate's effort to cap the proposed tax cut at $350 billion. Meanwhile, the White House, determined to avoid the economic doldrums that cost the first George Bush his presidency, is continuing to press hard for complete elimination of the dividend tax. Kudlow suggests here that all interested parties might be better off settling for a partial reduction in dividend taxes, arguing that it would be far cheaper than a full reduction, and would still provide a substantial lift to the stock market, thereby relieving the current shortage of capital and stimulating new job creation.

In the end, this is more or less what happened. Whether the strategy will pay off remains to be seen, but Kudlow is indisputably right about one thing: "victory [on tax cuts] is vital to the president's political credibility and his reelection next year.". . .

Twelve years ago, after the first U.S. victory in the Gulf, President George H. W. Bush was unwilling to invest his new political capital in much needed economic stimulus. Instead, he weakly called for a transportation bill—a huge political miscue. What he wound up with was a budget-busting Christmas tree adorned with expensive district-by-district ornaments. What he didn't get was enough pre-election economic growth to counter his misbegotten tax hike of 1990.

President George W. Bush's advisors are well aware of this. They recognize that a capital shortage following the three-year stock market plunge continues to hold back the business capital spending that is vital to new job creation. Therefore, virtually everyone in the White House sees the new tax-cut fight more in terms of a tough military campaign like Iwo Jima than the easy capture of Baghdad. In other words, they will do whatever it takes to win on tax cuts, understanding that such a victory is vital to the president's political credibility and his reelection next year.

In Monday's *Wall Street Journal*, Shailagh Murray suggests that the president's dividend tax cut is dead. But the White House believes otherwise. A senior West Wing staffer told me that the administration wants the whole

package: "It's the number-one priority around here, including the entire dividend piece."

Here's where the tax cut stands. Senate finance chairman Charles Grassley
promised his colleagues Olympia Snowe and George Voinovich that his committee would not pass a tax-cut bill exceeding $350 billion in static costs. The
Iowa senator said the deal was necessary to produce their two votes for a
budget resolution—although last year, under Democratic leadership, the
Senate operated without a resolution.

House leaders are furious at the Grassley deal. Speaker Dennis Hastert
said, "With all due respect to Senator Grassley, he is ultimately irrelevant
because our agreement was made with the Senate leadership and they have
the power to keep it."

More, if the House Ways & Means committee reports out a $550 billion
bill, then the leadership of both Houses, working with the administration,
can craft a compromise that will be closer to the House version.

And here's some strategy. If the budget revenue target is squeezed down,
it might make sense to tax dividends and capital gains at the same 18% or
20% marginal rate. This simple logic would tax all investment income the
same. It would amount to a 50% reduction in the dividend tax, which was
39.6% before President Bush's first tax cut in 2001.

Half a loaf is better than no loaf at all. It would still provide a strong stock
market incentive. And surprisingly, a 20% dividend tax rate would "cost" only
$90 billion over 10 years, compared with $400 billion for the 100% exclusion. Even at 20%, if the cut is made retroactive, investor and corporate
behavior would be significantly altered. The demand for dividend-paying
equity shares would shoot up, corporate deleveraging out of debt would accel-
erate, and corporate governance would become more transparent. Down the
road, future tax bills could even lower the dividend rate to zero.

In addition, after-tax profits declared by a company, but retained on a balance sheet, would still be considered "deemed dividends" to provide a capital-
gains break for investors. This would create a disincentive for corporate tax
evasion and boost the market capitalization of a firm's stock.

In scorekeeping terms, reducing the dividend tax rate will undoubtedly
spur higher share prices and a significant revenue increase from resulting
capital-gains realizations. After the 1997 capital-gains tax cut that lowered
the rate to 20% from 28%, capital-gains-related tax receipts soared to $120
billion from $60 billion. This experience could be used as a precedent to lower
the cost of the dividend tax cut in the current session.

House Majority Leader Tom DeLay remains a strong supporter of the dividend tax cut. He's expected to maintain maximum pressure on Ways and Means chair Bill Thomas to include a dividend piece in the committee markup.

The administration, meanwhile, is considering a presidential address before Congress to underscore the need to pass the entire tax-cut plan as a strong post-war economic growth measure. But a presidential speech—one that goes over the heads of Congress and communicates directly with the public—may be necessary.

Polls today show that prospective voters do not yet see how a dividend-centered tax-cut plan will lead to more jobs and economic growth. But if Bush can make the case that a revival of business and the stock market is necessary for job creation, then Americans who have come to trust him overwhelmingly on foreign policy and national security will be more willing to put their faith in his economic battleplan.

Bushonomics
John Cassidy

The New Yorker | May 12, 2003

In this New Yorker *"Talk of the Town" item, economics writer John Cassidy catches up with the tax cut issue in mid-May, with the Senate on the verge of passing their own down-sized version of the bill, and the president still busy making a public case for his own larger package. Here, Cassidy provides a good overview of the ongoing economic debate over tax cuts and their potential impact on the U.S. economy—tossing in the views of the International Monetary Fund's chief economist for good measure. . . .*

Economics has never been the Bush family's thing. The first President Bush was so bored by financial briefings that he sometimes dozed off during them. The second hasn't been caught napping yet, but it's fair to say that the economy isn't his favorite topic. George W. Bush is well aware, however, of the fate that befell his father after he waged a successful war in the Gulf— "It's the economy, stupid"—so he briefly turned his attention away from foreign policy to defend his controversial tax-cut plan, which is fighting for survival in the Senate.

"With a robust package of at least five hundred and fifty billion dollars in across-the-board tax relief, we will help create more than a million new jobs by the end of 2004," he declared in his weekly radio address. "Some members of Congress support tax relief but say my proposal is too big. Since they already agree that tax relief creates jobs, it doesn't make sense to provide less tax relief and, therefore, create fewer jobs. I believe that we should enact more tax relief so that we can create more jobs, and more Americans can find work and provide for their families."

There is a pressing need for more jobs—another forty-eight thousand vaporized last month—but the link between tax policy and payrolls is a lot murkier than the President made it out to be. If tax cuts automatically created jobs, businesses would be scouring the streets for workers right now, and nobody's twenty-five-year-old children would still have to live at home. Two years ago, after all, President Bush persuaded Congress to pass the biggest tax cuts in a generation. But since then a million and a half jobs have disappeared. By contrast, between 1993 and 2000, President Clinton raised taxes to reduce the budget deficit, and the economy created more than twenty million jobs. Of course, this doesn't mean that higher taxes create jobs, either. The number of people working is determined by the over-all state of the economy, to which fiscal policy is just one contributor. Other things being equal, tax cuts can help the economy by putting more cash in consumers' pockets, but they are an expensive and unreliable way to raise employment, especially when they are aimed at people who tend to save their windfalls rather than spend them.

More than half the President's tax cuts would come in the form of abolishing the taxation of corporate dividends. The primary recipients would be rich people and senior citizens, since they own most of the dividend-yielding stocks. For example, Sanford Weill, the chairman of Citigroup, would get a tax cut of about six million dollars. Based on 2001 figures, Vice-President Dick Cheney would save about a hundred thousand dollars. The dividend plan might persuade yacht builders and assisted-living communities to hire some extra help, but it won't do much for the rest of the nearly nine million unemployed.

In view of this problem, the White House has put forward a more subtle rationale for the dividend-tax cut: It will cause the stock market to rise, which will make consumers and businesses feel more confident. This, in turn, will boost spending, which will generate more hiring. But if any of these links fail to materialize, so will the new jobs.

Even taking the President at his word, each new job would cost the government five hundred and fifty thousand dollars in lost revenues, which is about seventeen times the salary of the average American worker. It would be far cheaper for the federal government to give private firms subsidies to hire more people, or to give money to the states, which are facing their worst financial crisis since the Second World War, and which at this moment are being forced to fire teachers, troopers, and health workers. Parks, museums, and libraries are closing; cultural programs are being cut. College-tuition fees are rising, and scholarships are vanishing. Hundreds of thousands of people stand to lose their state-provided health-care coverage. (Meanwhile, taxpayers will be laying out billions of dollars to reconstruct Iraq.)

None of this factors in the Bush tax plan's impact over the long term. A few years back, the big debate in Washington was what to do with the surplus, which was projected to be five trillion dollars over the coming decade. Now, after the stock-market crash, a prolonged economic downturn, and the 2001 tax cuts, the deficit for this year alone could reach five hundred billion dollars, a figure that even Ronald Reagan and David Stockman failed to match during the last disastrous experiment in "supply-side" economics. And phasing in the tax cuts, which the White House is considering to alleviate the concerns of Republican moderates, will do nothing to reduce their long-term cost. The Center on Budget and Policy Priorities calculates that a dividend-tax cut would deprive the federal government of some seven hundred and fifty billion dollars between 2014 and 2023, just when the baby boomers will be lining up for Medicare and Social Security.

What's more, the President's tax cuts may in the end destroy more jobs than they create. As tax revenues fall and the deficit increases, interest rates will rise, and the higher cost of borrowing will impede business investment and hiring. The reborn supply-side economists who devised the President's plan would dispute this, except that many of them were fired or encouraged to quit in the Administration's recent purge of its financial team. N. Gregory Mankiw, the Harvard professor who was recently nominated as chairman of the Council of Economic Advisers, is more realistic. In his popular textbook *Principles of Economics*, he explains that when a government runs a budget deficit it "pulls resources away from investment in new capital and, thereby, depresses the living standards of future generations." Alan Greenspan, whom the President plans to reappoint for a fifth term as Federal Reserve chairman, said essentially the same thing last week. Kenneth Rogoff, the I.M.F.'s chief economist, went even further. He recently told journalists, "Suppose for a minute that we were talking about a developing country that had gaping current account deficits year after year . . . a budget ink spinning from black into red . . . open-ended security costs, and a real exchange rate that had been inflated by capital inflows. With all that, I think it's fair to say we would be pretty concerned." When I.M.F. types start talking about the United States as if it were a banana republic on a bad day, it's probably time to change course.

The Faces of Budget Cuts
Bob Herbert

The New York Times | May 5, 2003

One major problem with the Bush administration's latest push for tax cuts is that it comes at a time when virtually every state government is facing a looming budget deficit, brought on by a combination of a weak economy, rising Medicaid costs, new Federal mandates for homeland security and election reform, and other factors. (For more on this, see "Govs Under the Gun," p. 92.) Not only do lower Federal tax revenues mean less cash is available to bail out the state governments (the final tax bill did come up with $20 billion in aid for the states, but this covers only a fraction of the shortfall); it also means state revenues will fall even further, since most state income taxes are pegged to the Federal rates. Already, states are cutting back on a wide range of services as a result.

Of course, this number-crunching can all seem pretty abstract—at least until you read the following column by Bob Herbert. . . .

PORTLAND, Ore.—Cheryl Asbell was fidgety, anxious. She compulsively adjusted the soft-brimmed bucket hat that she wore during the interview in her living room. Now she stared at me, her eyes wide.

"I'll tell you what's going to happen," she said. "I'm going to be dead. That's what's going to happen."

Ms. Asbell, tall, thin, and middle-aged, described herself as deeply depressed and paranoid. Her periodic descents into psychosis, she said, are becoming more and more difficult to handle.

She tried to commit suicide in January and ended up in a hospital for 10 days. "I stopped breathing, but they brought me back," she said. "I feel a little better now."

During one psychotic episode she removed the metal plates from all of the switches and outlets in the apartment. "I thought there were cameras in there," she said.

She pointed to a tiny hole in the living room ceiling. "I thought there was a camera in there, too. I thought there were people outside the house watching me. I called the police and they came by and said everything was all right."

Doctors have prescribed a long list of medications to ward off the worst manifestations of Ms. Asbell's illness. But she can't afford them. She has been dumped from a state program that paid for the medication and for sessions of much-needed psychotherapy. Now she gets some medication in the form of samples from doctors' offices. The rest she does without.

Ms. Asbell is one of thousands of Oregon residents who are seriously in need of medical care but are being cut from essential (and even life-saving) programs because of the state's budget meltdown.

Last month *The Oregonian* reported on the case of Douglas Schmidt, a 36-year-old epileptic who lost his prescription drug benefit because of budget cuts. The benefit paid for his anti-seizure medication. Eight to 10 days after his supply of pills ran out, Mr. Schmidt suffered a massive epileptic seizure. He has been in a coma ever since and is not expected to recover.

Last week I interviewed Rose Spears, who is 50, has had thyroid cancer and is disabled from diabetes. She lives alone in a one-bedroom apartment. The table beside her bed is covered with medicine vials.

"I lost my prescription drug coverage," she said, "so I have to pay out of pocket for my 11-odd medications, plus two insulins. I can't afford it. The total bill is $912 per month and my income is $728. Right now I'm surviving off samples my doctor can give me."

Oregon is one of many states caught in a fiscal quagmire. There are many reasons for the budgetary distress, which has spread from coast to coast. They include a lousy national economy, a widespread unwillingness locally and nationally to levy the taxes necessary to support government services, and the refusal of the Bush administration to help state and local governments that are experiencing their worst budget shortfalls since World War II.

In Oregon the situation is getting worse, not better. School financing has been cut so drastically that some districts have had to curtail the school year. And health care cuts that have already hurt thousands of poor and working-poor residents are expected to go much deeper, beginning July 1.

Not too long ago the Oregon health care system was a model that was admired and studied by professionals around the country. Now, because of a lack of funds, it is falling apart.

"It's horrible to see what's happening with some of the very successful things that we did," said Jean Thorne, the state's director of human services.

The drastic cuts in governmental services that are being made in Oregon and other states are eroding the nation's basic defenses against ignorance, disease, and destitution.

Both Rose Spears and Cheryl Asbell are petrified that at some point they won't be able to get doctors' samples and their medication will be cut off entirely.

"I haven't had my blood sugar below 250 since the beginning of the year," said Ms. Spears. "It's the stress. I have to take my medication if I want to stick around. But what if I can't get it? I pray constantly."

"I've lost 45 pounds since my coverage was cut," said Ms. Asbell. "I don't sleep at all, I'm so worried."

She said she is convinced that without her medication she will sink ever more deeply into a depression from which she will not emerge.

Part Two: The State of the Union

Govs Under the Gun

Karen Tumulty

with reporting by Steve Barnes, James Carney, Heidi Marotz, and Margot Roosevelt

Time | May 19, 2003

One of the hallmarks of the United States system of governance has always been a dynamic tension between the central government and the states. During the struggle over civil rights in the 1950s and '60s, this tension sometimes took the form of armed showdowns. More recently, the conflict has tended to center on mandates and money. The Federal government has never been shy about requiring states to carry out programs like Medicaid and election reform—or asking them to help pay for such initiatives. At the same time, almost every state government is required by law to balance its budget. When times are tough, as they have been over the past couple of years, the frequent result is that the states find themselves in a financial bind. But as the following article makes clear, the current situation is something more than that. In fact, if writer Karen Tumulty is correct in her assessment, the current economic squeeze is threatening to turn into a death grip for a number of our nation's governors—who are now beginning to think hard about raising taxes, even as the Federal government is lowering them. . . .

To live in California is to go about your business knowing the earth could move under your feet at any moment. That's pretty much the tectonic nature of California politics too, with voters regularly floating recall petitions to throw out their elected officials and pushing referendums on high-flown social questions like whether a police officer should be allowed to carry a ventriloquist's dummy. So over the past few months, while Governor Gray Davis has battled with the legislature over the state's deepening fiscal crisis, he has paid little heed to the underground rumble of a loosely organized effort to oust him from office.

The ground began to shift last week. Multimillionaire Republican Congressman Darrell Issa announced that he might put up at least $100,000 of his own money toward the recall drive—and pledged to raise in the next week at least half the $1.2 million he thinks the campaign needs. The effort claims

100,000 signatures, and collecting the required 900,000 is a daunting job, but organizers will now have the resources to hire professionals to gather signatures in front of grocery stores and shopping malls across the state. If he succeeds, Issa intends to offer himself as a replacement for Davis. Garry South, Davis' top political adviser, says chances of success are still "less than fifty-fifty, but it's not impossible."

Just a few years ago, Davis was one of the country's more popular Governors. In last year's election, he bucked national trends to lead a Democratic sweep of statewide offices. But now he finds himself with a 24% approval rating, making him the most unpopular Governor in the Field Poll's 55-year history. And he has plenty of company. New York's Republican Governor George Pataki has an approval rating of 43% in the latest Quinnipiac poll, 38 percentage points lower than it was after 9/11. And Pataki is faring better than his neighbors, Democrat James McGreevey of New Jersey (38%) and Republican John Rowland of Connecticut (33%).

What they have in common is that optimistic promises from the fat old days are coming back to haunt them. Democrat Gary Locke pledged to be Washington State's "education Governor," but in January tens of thousands of teachers marched on the state capitol to protest his plan to deny them pay increases, and the Washington Education Association has been running ads accusing him of breaking his word to children. The bleak fiscal situation has also meant no honeymoon for the bumper crop of 24 new Governors elected last year.

The situation is particularly tricky for Republicans, many of whom are now invoking the ultimate GOP heresy—tax hikes. While President Bush held a rally last week near Arkansas' state capitol to drum up support for his tax cuts, a few blocks away, at nearly the same hour, Republican Governor Mike Huckabee was imploring his balky legislature to support a tax raise. "I envy his position of being able to come to Little Rock and preach tax cuts while I preach a tax increase," Huckabee told *Time*. "He has a tool that I do not have, called deficit spending, and can shift—or at least not fix—the Medicaid issue, which is causing most of my heartburn." Medicaid costs in Arkansas have risen from $1.2 billion a decade ago to $2 billion, and Huckabee, like Governors everywhere else, wants Washington to start shouldering more of the burden.

To most Americans, the budget wars in Washington may seem like so much posturing, but what they see close to home is very real. "To the extent that anyone is engaged in public life these days, you're engaged with what's going on at the state level rather than something abstract like the Bush tax cuts," says Democratic pollster Ed Reilly. "It's not an abstraction when your kid's teacher gets laid off."

Governors were the demigods of the flush 1990s—slashing taxes, building schools and prisons, giving raises to teachers and health care to poor children. Times were so good that they even found tens of billions to salt away in "rainy-day funds." Then the rain came, first as a trickle of layoffs and budget cuts last year, and now as a gully washer. With all but Vermont required by law to balance their budgets, the states are working to close a total shortfall of $100 billion between now and the end of fiscal 2004. A dozen state legislatures are in emergency session to deal with their crises. Governors are not just raising taxes but also releasing prisoners and shutting down libraries. Among options that Davis has had to consider: denying prosthetics to amputees who can't afford them and eliminating adult diapers for prostate-cancer patients.

Not the least of the Governors' problems are the new mandates being put on them by Washington—by a President who was once one of their own. Governors must pay increased costs for homeland security in the wake of 9/11 and election reform after the 2000 Florida debacle. And there are billions in added costs connected to meeting the standards imposed on their schools by the President's education reforms. Bush's tax cuts also weigh heavily on their treasuries, because state tax systems are pegged to the federal one. Even the Senate Finance Committee's slimmed-down version of Bush's dividend tax cut, for instance, would cost states as much as $11 billion over the next 10 years, according to an estimate last week by the Center on Budget and Policy Priorities, a liberal Washington think tank.

Governors increasingly blame the Bush Administration for the severity of their situation. "I am a good Republican. I am a good team player," Arkansas' Huckabee said laughingly during an interview. "[But] turn that tape recorder off and I will speak an earful." Aboard Air Force One between Canton and Dayton two weeks ago, Ohio's Governor Bob Taft laid out his predicament to the President. Taft cited his state's high unemployment rate and staggering Medicaid costs and his sinking approval rating. It was, as someone who was there later described it, "a cry for help." Bush sat silently, and all Taft had at the end of the day was a photo op with a President whose popularity he can only envy.

The problems before the Governors are so daunting that solving them sometimes means putting their careers on the line. Idaho Republican Dirk

Kempthorne used to brag that he cut taxes 49 times during his first four years in office. He cruised to re-election in 2002. But now, after the longest legislative session in Idaho history, he has raised sales and cigarette taxes and has announced he will not run for a third term. "I was not going to preside over the dismantling of central services in the state," Kempthorne says. "I've been elected to do what's right."

For California's Davis, things are likely to get even rockier this week, when revised budget numbers are expected to show that the state's $35 billion budget gap has grown by $2 billion. But South, his adviser, grimly notes that before anyone decides to challenge Davis, he or she should consider what would be won: the painful obligation to make ends meet.

The Enron Ponzi Scheme
Jack Beatty

Atlantic Unbound | March 13, 2002

Enron wasn't the only huge U.S. company to sink beneath the weight of its own fraudulent accounting practices in the past two years—think Adelphia, Global Crossing, Tyco, and WorldCom—but it was the first to go under, and it remains the poster child for corporate greed and shady financial practices. As this book went to print, the casualities from the Enron scandal continued to pile up: The Arthur Andersen accounting firm is no more; Enron chief operating office Andrew Fastow has been indicted, along with his wife and a slew of other Enron executives (several of who have already pled guilty); Enron employees have had their retirement savings wiped out; an array of pension funds have also taken multi-million dollar losses; and California is still reeling from the huge hit it took from Enron's manipulation of the state's energy prices. Meanwhile, Enron itself (what's left of it) is now threatening to sue its own bankers, including J.P. Morgan Chase and Citigroup, for giving out bad advice.

In the following article, Jack Beatty explains how Enron used its on-paper wealth to co-opt everyone in sight: the company's own employees, its accountants, its legal advisors, and perhaps most importantly, our country's elected officials—the same folks who were in charge of regulating Enron's business practices. Nice work, if you can get it. . . .

It was Adam Smith who identified what turned out to be the central ethical fault line in Enron. The corporation, he wrote in *The Wealth of Nations*, was an inherently corrupting business form. The problem was the separation of ownership from control. In partnerships and sole proprietorships, the forms he preferred, the owners ran the business. In contrast, managers hired by the owner-stockholders ran the corporation. And the owners were too busy to monitor how their money was spent by the managers. So managers were institutionally liable to what Smith called "negligence" and "profusion." Negligence, because the business was not the consuming dedication of their lives, as it is for partners and sole proprietors; it was merely a job. Profusion, because they could reward themselves by lavishing other people's money, which spends so much easier than our own, on fine dinners, handsome equipages, and all manner of other frippery—and disguise their profusion as business expenses. Smith's distrust of the corporation had empirical backing in the disgraceful behavior of the East India Company, the Enron of his day, a monument to negligence and profusion.

A bankruptcy auction of Enron's gilded London office turned up the following evidence of profusion: an electric train set used to deliver bonuses to high-performing executives; a high-tech gym; a ToneZone for aromatherapy, tanning, and beauty treatments; pricey paintings and sculptures; a 33-foot maple veneer conference table inlaid with solid walnut; and even marble-covered garbage bins, to deposit decorous garbage from the twelve cafés on the premises. As for negligence, the destruction or rather auto-collapse—as no competitor or regulatory change can be considered responsible—of the nation's seventh largest corporation retires the cup. But this was a kind of negligence bound up with profusion. Criminal negligence.

If Enron were a morality play it would be called Conflict of Interest. Conflicts of interest were forbidden in the contracts signed by Enron executives—were even grounds for termination. Yet they were the chief motivational tool at Enron. Let's start inside the company and work outwards, seeking, like Diogenes, to find an honest man or woman. What is a conflict of interest? Consider this example from the Enron petri dish. You are Andrew Fastow, Enron's CFO, and you have this problem. You have set up more than 3,000 partnerships to hide Enron's losses of more than $500,000,000. An Enron comptroller is pressing you on the unsavory details of your scheme. You get him transferred. His replacement you cut in on the deal. He gives you $5,000 to invest in one of the partnerships and two months later gets a $1,000,000 return. Your problem has disappeared. You have snared him in what we might call an Enron. You yourself are mega-Enroned, as overseer and beneficiary of partnerships from which you have gained $30 million dollars.

Bonuses were another way to Enron, to use the verb form. Bonuses were tied to profits and stock price. The purpose of the partnerships was to overstate Enron's profits. The bonuses were a persuasion to silence. Two other Enron executives, according to *The New York Times*, "who were primarily responsible for reviewing the partnership dealings to protect against conflicts of interest also profited by the reports of strong financial performance made possible by those transactions."

A corporation's board of directors, made up of disinterested persons of reputation, represents the stockholder-owners to the manager. The institution is an attempt to deal with the agency problem raised by Adam Smith. At Enron, however, the board was not disinterested but Enroned by means ranging from corporate contributions to the campaign of the senator-husband of one member to sizeable gifts to the favorite charities of another. The board approved the partnerships, and Fastow's conflict of interest in them. Thousands of partners have yet to be named. Will board members turn out to be among them?

The law firm responsible for vetting the legality of the partnerships was Enroned by its desire to keep Enron as a client. Arthur Andersen, Enron's accountant, was Enroned: Andersen's consulting division helped Enron set up the partnerships Andersen's auditing division then reviewed on behalf of investors. Andersen has offered gulled investors a $750,000,000 settlement. The big financial services firms who helped finance the partnerships, on the one hand, while, on the other, analyzing their business potential for a public unaware of this nexus—these great names in finance were Enroned. Enron functioned in a regulatory black hole dug by Enroned politicians. Of the twenty-three senators on one committee questioning Enron figures, only one, Daniel Inouye of Hawaii, had never received contributions from either Enron or Arthur Andersen. Enron was the largest contributor to George W. Bush's political career. Was his vice president Enroned when preparing a Bush energy program favorable to Enron? Karl Rove, Bush's political advisor, held Enron stock while deliberating on the energy program with Enron officials. Was he Enroned? Was the White House counsel, Alberto Gonzales, who received campaign contributions from Enron, Enroned when he found Rove innocent of being Enroned? Did Enroning secure the silence of the Administration officials—the Treasury Secretary, the Commerce Secretary, the President's Chief Economic Advisor, and the President's Chief of Staff—who knew Enron was on the ropes last fall but said nothing to the Securities and Exchange Commission or the public? They said nothing while state pension funds were losing $2.9 billion on a company legitimated by an Enroned board, blessed by Enroned lawyers, pronounced robust by Enroned accountants, and hailed as a "strong buy" right up until the eve of its bankruptcy by Enroned investment bankers.

Enron was not only a financial Ponzi scheme but an ethical one. The whole charade would have ended if one man or woman who knew or suspected the truth had stood up and said no, I will not be Enroned into silence. Even Sherron Watkins, the internal whistle-blower, said she did not go to the board with what she knew for fear of losing her job. She did, however, sell some of her Enron stock, getting off the ship before it sank with nary a whisper to the crew. And she was the best of the lot.

Why did no one stand up? Let's apply moral realism to the question, seeking not to forgive but to understand.

It is hard to stand up: our ethical Occam's Razor need cut no closer than that. How many of us have kept in our seats when the path of right lay up the hill, so clear but so difficult, before us? Unlike physical courage, writes one ethicist, moral courage is "lonely courage." Frank Serpico, the New York City policeman who exposed corruption in the department, was ostracized by his fellow officers, beaten, and nearly killed for his lonely courage.

Another reason people don't blow the whistle is that they would have to blow it on themselves. "The only way you get to know these things," says a social worker who has worked with whistleblowers, "is that you have been in the thick of it." J. Clifford Baxter, the Enron vice president who committed suicide in January, took his concerns about the partnerships to Skilling, was ignored, then, having made his feeble gesture, sold his stock for millions and retired. Whistleblowers, says the social worker, often "take on the guilt of the organization." The weight of Enron's guilt may have been too much for Baxter to bear.

Countervailing ethical demands also keep us from acting ethically. Ibsen's Dr. Stockman, in *Enemy of the People*, stands up to expose a public health scandal—and his righteousness destroys his family. Many of us would be moral lions if we did not have kids.

Then there is the "Everybody does it" defense. At Enron, pretty nearly everybody did do it. Over the last two years, while Enron was collapsing, almost 2,000 of its executives got $432 million in bonuses. One trader, on receiving a paltry $500,000, threw his computer screen across the trading floor. "Well, we've all got to drink the Kool-Aid," a top executive remarked after Lay,

Skilling, and Fastow directed him to do a bogus deal. They got drunk on the Kool-Aid at Enron. It was a milieu of corruption.

It was also a milieu of rules-are-for wimps innovation. Enron was reinventing the energy market. Fleets of Porsches were in the garage and testosterone was in the air. As Marie Brenner reports in a must-read article in the current *Vanity Fair*, one vice president displayed a "hottie board," which ranked the women of Enron on their sexuality. When women complained, they were told, He is making us money. Leave him alone. Care for some Kool-Aid? "Every great business person has been in some way a rule breaker," writes the business historian Richard Tedlow. Yes, but some rules are duties, and some are laws. The ethical compass to tell the difference was broken at Enron. To succeed at business, says Warren Buffet, who should know, you need brains, energy, and character. No wonder Enron failed.

The Smithsonian has begun an Enron collection with two items: a coffee mug and an Enron ethics manual—almost certainly inviolate.

The Evil of Access
Mark Green

The Nation | December 30, 2002

The issue of money buying political influence conjures up Mark Twain's famous crack about the weather: Everyone talks about it, but no one does anything about it. Consider the McCain-Feingold Campaign Reform Bill, passed by Congress in 2002 after a yeoman's effort on the part of its supporters. The law takes the major step of prohibiting corporations, unions, and other organizations from making unlimited donations (known as "soft money") to the national committees of political parties, and sharply curtails the use of "issue ads"—political commercials attacking specific candidates, that are paid for by interest groups rather than the candidates themselves—in the month before a primary and in the two months preceding a general election. The bill also raises the maximum contribution an individual can make to primary and general campaigns from $1,000 to $2,000.

All well and good—but will the new law be deemed constitutional by the courts? This past May, a Federal appeals court struck down several of the bill's key provisions, but ruled that the full law will stay in effect until the Supreme Court rules on it this

fall. At the same time, the Republican and Democratic parties have already begun plan-
ning how to circumvent the soft-money ban by collecting donations on the state level.
*   Here, however, are some reforms that might just work, from New York City mayoral*
candidate Mark Green, the man who in 2001 lost to billionaire Michael Bloomberg in
what turned out to be the most expensive local election in U.S. history. . . .

Among the least-discussed numbers from November 5 is $184 million—the
amount by which Republican national committees out-spent their Democratic equivalents. And with President Bush loudly beating his war drums, who
heard any discussion about the escalating cost of campaigns? Spending in
the New York and Pennsylvania gubernatorial elections, for example, *tripled*
within one election cycle.

The evidence that money shouts is mountainous: Ninety-four percent of
the time, the bigger-spending Congressional candidate wins—and 98 percent
of House incumbents win. The average price of a House seat rose from
$87,000 in 1976 to $840,000 in 2000. It cost Ken Livingstone 80 cents a vote
to win the London mayoralty last year, compared with Michael Bloomberg's
$100 a vote in New York City.

As money metastasizes throughout our political process, the erosion of
our democracy should be evident to left and right alike:

§ *Special Interests Get Special Access and Treatment.* While members publicly
and indignantly deny that big contributions often come with strings attached,
all privately concede the obvious mutual shakedown—or as one Western senator told me, "Senators are human calculators who can weigh how much
money every vote will cost them." Two who violated the usual senatorial
omertà gave dispositions in the federal district court arguments on the
McCain-Feingold law earlier this month. "Who, after all, can seriously con-
tend," said former Senator Alan Simpson, "that a $100,000 donation does
not alter the way one thinks about—and quite possibly votes on—an issue?"
Senator Zell Miller bluntly described the daily conversations from
fundraising cubicles: "I'd remind the agribusinessman I was on the Agriculture
Committee; I'd remind the banker I was on the Banking Committee. . . . Most
large contributors understand only two things: what you can do for them and
what you can do to them. I always left that room feeling like a cheap prostitute who'd had a busy day." The access that money buys, of course, doesn't
guarantee legislative success, but the lack of it probably guarantees failure.

After 9/11, for example, many legislators thought the argument for energy conservation and reduced dependence on Middle Eastern oil was obvious. So Senators John Kerry and John McCain were stunned when their effort to increase fuel-efficiency standards failed 62 to 38—with the average no vote getting $18,000 in donations from auto companies and the average yes vote only $6,000. One senator insisting on anonymity said: "That vote was one of the most politically cowardly things I ever saw in the Senate. We know how to be energy-efficient, and it starts with cars."

§ *Fundraising Is a Time Thief.* Imagine if someone kidnapped all candidates for state and federal office for half of each day. The story would be bigger than Gary Condit, and would surely lead to calls for tougher penalties against political kidnapping.

Well, there is such a culprit. It's the current system of financing political campaigns, which pits each candidate in a spiraling "arms race," not merely to raise enough money but to raise far more than any rival. One Midwestern senator complained, "Senators used to be here Monday through Friday; now we're lucky to be in mid-Tuesday to Thursday, because Mondays and Fridays are for fundraisers. Also, members loathe voting on controversial issues, because it'll be used against you when you're raising money."

Candidates start to feel like Bill Murray in *Groundhog Day*, trapped in a daily, stultifying repetition they can't escape. As a mayoral candidate I made 30,000 phone calls (that is not a misprint) over two years to lists of potential donors and spoke at 205 of my own fundraising events. It's hard to overstate the physical and psychological stamina required in such an effort, and how little time and energy it leaves for all else.

§ *The "Money Primary" Weeds Out Good Candidates.* Potential candidates know they have to succeed in not one but two elections: The first, in which contributors "vote" with their dollars, comes long before constituents have their say. And if you don't win round one financially, you might as well not bother with round two; after all, because incumbency attracts money and money entrenches incumbency, no challenger spending under $850,000 won a House seat in 2000. With odds like those, many talented women and men flinch.

§ *The "Pay to Play" System Especially Hurts Democratic Candidates and Values.* Most Republicans oppose new regulations and taxes out of authentic belief. So they regard the special-interest funding of public elections as a brilliant system: For them, principles and payments go hand in hand. Robert Reich, a former Labor Secretary and recent Massachusetts gubernatorial candidate, believes his party is losing its identity as the champion of the average family "because Democrats became dependent on the rich to finance their campaigns. It is difficult to represent the little fellow when the big fellow pays the tab."

Ever wonder why polls show that so many Americans strongly favor higher minimum wages, prescription drug benefits for Medicare, quality daycare, publicly financed Congressional campaigns and stronger environmental protection, even at the cost of higher taxes—yet the political system can't produce any of these? The pay-to-play system is a circuit breaker between popular will and public policy.

Put yourself in an honest Democrat's shoes: What do you do when a big-business donor privately asks you, "So where do you stand on X?" X being something that hugely helps or hurts his economic interests? You realize not only that your answer could immediately affect a large contribution but that the cost of paying for X will fall on taxpayers who are not listening on the phone.

Or suppose you're in government. Once, as the New York City consumer affairs commissioner, I was considering filing a legal action that could cost a Democratic businessman I knew well millions of dollars. I successfully sued, and he did lose millions, and he wouldn't speak to me for a decade. But this outcome *did* cross my mind as I weighed my decision to prosecute—given the current political money process, how could it not?

§ *Wealth Buys Office.* As more and more multimillionaires run and win—the percentage of them in the Senate has risen to more than one-third, about the same proportion as it was before senators began being elected by popular vote in 1913—more and more experience-rich candidates are grilled by party leaders about how they can possibly run against experience-poor but wealthy candidates. And when a very wealthy candidate inundates TV, radio, and mailboxes with ads portraying him as a young Abe Lincoln and you as the Manchurian Candidate, the pressure to hustle special-interest money becomes even more intense.

Also, as campaign reformer Ellen Miller describes it, "the problem [with] more and more wealthy people running and winning is that then tax policy, healthcare policy, and education policy are seen through the lenses of multimillionaires, people who don't need government services. They are a different class of people and from a different world than most Americans, who sit around the kitchen table calculating their finances."

So although issues like terrorism, healthcare, and pollution absorb far more public attention and concern, the scandal of strings-attached money corrupting politics and government is the most urgent domestic problem in America today—because it makes it harder to solve nearly all our other problems. How can we produce smart defense, environmental, and health policies if arms contractors, oil firms, and HMOs have such a hammerlock on the committees charged with considering reforms? The culprit is not corrupt candidates but a corrupt system that coerces good people to take tainted money.

The old and much-discussed saga of political money may reach a climax between now and 2004 as a result of three epic developments:

First, the corporate scandals of 2001-2 started with questions about corrupt financing practices and then moved to questions about corrupt political practices. Joan Claybrook, head of Public Citizen and a veteran of the campaign finance wars, says, "Political money from the Enrons and others bought loopholes, exemptions, lax law enforcement, underfunded regulatory agencies, and the presumption that corporate officials could buy anything they wanted with the shareholders' money." Once the current war fever abates electorally, will the Enron/Adelphia/Global Crossing/Tyco/WorldCom scandals lead to a shift in our political zeitgeist, as corruption a century ago led to the Progressive Era?

Second, the McCain-Feingold fight re-educated the public about money in politics. Given all the problems of our current system, the McCain-Feingold law is like throwing a ten-foot rope to a drowning swimmer forty feet offshore. But it's necessary to stop huge soft-money federal gifts that enable big interests to make an end run around federal bans on corporate and labor donations.

Third, the Supreme Court will likely rule next spring on the constitutionality of McCain-Feingold's two major provisions: banning soft-money fundraising by the national parties and restricting soft money for sham "issue" ads. This will be the Court's first major consideration of campaign finance since 1976's disastrous *Buckley v. Valeo* ruling, which held that legislatively enacted "expenditure limits" were an unconstitutional infringement on speech. If the Court had reached a different conclusion then, there would be no $2 million House candidates today, no $15 million Senate candidates, no $74 million mayoral candidates.

Moreover, the State of Vermont last year enacted a spending ceiling. The Court of Appeals for the Second Circuit initially upheld the law in August, arguing that evidence of legislators routinely selling access showed the law was a constitutionally permissible way of stopping such corruption. If this case goes to the Supreme Court with McCain-Feingold—and swing Justices Sandra Day O'Connor and Anthony Kennedy agree with the Second Circuit majority—we'll be close to taking the for-sale sign off our democracy.

Meanwhile, can the political process significantly reform not just the soft-money but also the hard-money system?

Most senators and representatives I interviewed thought Congress had exhausted itself in the McCain-Feingold fight and that this Republican Congress had no interest in going further. However, Fred Wertheimer of the campaign-reform group Democracy 21, citing the revolution of rising expectations, believes that "winning McCain-Feingold will open the door to another round," if not in this Republican Congress then in a future one. "And we have put together the best coalition I've ever seen on an issue—from the AARP to the Sierra Club to labor and some businesses."

But 535 campaign finance experts in Congress don't want to change the rules that got them there and have kept them there; and there are hundreds of large interests who invest thousands and reap billions, a rate of return unrivaled since IBM and Microsoft went public—and who like things as they are.

So systemic reform may turn on the 2004 presidential election. If Gore, Kerry, Gephardt, or Daschle runs against the current money game as ardently as McCain did—and wins—our slow-motion decline from democracy to plutocracy could end. Democrats searching for a popular and important message should embrace three fundamental reforms based on the slogan "Don't Let Enron Run Your Democracy."

1. *Public Financing.* The rationale is simple: If, say, twenty special interests give a senator $100,000 each, they own him or her; if instead a million taxpayers give $2 each in public funds, *we* own him or her. Isn't it preferable for elected officials to be responsive to all voters rather than to relatively few donors? "Democratically funded elections" could follow either the New York City or the Arizona model. Under the first, 4-to-1 matching grants are made for all gifts up to $250 from people who can vote for the candidate (so a $25 gift becomes $125); under the second, after a gubernatorial candidate crosses a certain threshold—raising 4,000 contributions of at least $5—he or she receives all subsequent funding up to a specified ceiling from the public treasury, which could be raised by a "democracy surtax" imposed on registered lobbyists, political consultants, and TV advertisers.

Public financing has worked in presidential campaigns and in New York

City, Arizona, and Maine elections. It avoids First Amendment arguments, since it increases speech instead of limiting it, and majorities of 70 percent regularly support it.

Two strategies can help win over even more voters and some legislators to democratically funded elections: Because the current private system of financing costs tens of billions in corporate welfare, pollution, and lost productivity, any public financing system would be inexpensive by comparison. Also, bad policies—for example, privatization of Social Security and weaker fuel-efficiency standards—should be publicly linked to big contributions so voters understand the impact on their health and wallets.

2. *Spending Limits.* Because the financial "alms" race steals time and buys access, Congress and the Supreme Court should approve Vermont-like spending limits, which existed in the 1971 and 1974 federal campaign-finance laws until *Buckley* threw them out. But isn't money protected First Amendment speech, as Senators McConnell, Lott et al. claim? No, money is property, as Justice John Paul Stevens concluded in a recent case, which is why the 1907 Tillman Act has banned corporate contributions for nearly a century. How does it advance First Amendment values to allow a few wealthy interests to spend millions of dollars more and drown out the voices and contributions of millions of average citizens?

3. *Free or Discounted TV.* Because the airwaves belong to the public, we provide broadcasters with federal licenses—for free—on the condition that they agree to serve "the public interest, convenience, and necessity." But they have not lived up to their end of the bargain, perhaps because broadcasters pulled down $1 billion in revenue from political commercials in the 2000 elections. Reducing that revenue would mean cutting into profit margins that average between 30 and 50 percent.

Paul Taylor, executive director of the Alliance for Better Campaigns, a non-partisan group that advocates free airtime, sums up the scam: "Our government gives broadcasters free licenses to operate on the public airwaves. . . . During the campaign season, broadcasters turn around and sell access to these airwaves to candidates at inflated prices." He proposes that candidates who win their parties' nominations receive vouchers for electronic advertising in their general election campaigns. Candidates, particularly from urban areas, who don't find it cost-effective to advertise on television or radio could trade their vouchers to their party in exchange for funds to pay for direct mail or other forms of communication. As historian Arthur Schlesinger Jr. writes, "America is almost alone among the Atlantic democracies in declining to provide political parties free prime time on television during elections." If it did so, it would "do much both to bring inordinate campaign costs under control and revitalize the political parties."

For those who universalize the political moment and doubt we'll ever have public financing, a spending ceiling, or free TV, please remember that you're right if reformers don't try.

The history of America shows a "capacity for self-correction." Even the Supreme Court, given enough time, has reversed itself on such issues as affirmative action, right to counsel, poll taxes, and health and safety regulations.

Only such apologists for the status quo as George Will could believe it's OK for a powerful 0.1 percent of the population to make $1,000 contributions to dictate policy to the other 99.9 percent; for only the rich or the kept to win office; for candidates to spend three-quarters of their time raising money so that the toll-takers known as broadcasters will allow public candidates to speak to the public over our publicly owned airwaves.

"History is like waves lapping at a cliff," wrote French historian Henry See. "For centuries nothing happens. Then the cliff collapses."

For Richer

Paul Krugman

The New York Times Magazine | Oct 20, 2002

Princeton economist Paul Krugman is best known for his twice-weekly op-ed column in The New York Times, *where he has devoted most of his energies to pointing out that, where the Bush administration's stated economic policies are concerned, the emperor is seriously underdressed. In particular, he's been a persistent critic of the White House's tax cut program—attacking, among other things, the shifting rationales for tax cuts (they were needed to whittle down a budget surplus one minute, and to lift us out of recession the next) and the administration's assertion that the tax cuts aren't to blame for the current projected Federal deficits.*

In the following article, Krugman stretches well beyond his usual 750 words to address a much larger issue—the ever-increasing concentration of wealth in the hands of a relatively small group of Americans. "[F]ew people," he writes, "are aware of just how much the gap between the very rich and the rest has widened over a relatively short period of time." This trend, says Krugman, has already turned our country into a very different place than it was in the middle of the last century. . . .

I. The Disappearing Middle

When I was a teenager growing up on Long Island, one of my favorite excursions was a trip to see the great Gilded Age mansions of the North Shore. Those mansions weren't just pieces of architectural history. They were monuments to a bygone social era, one in which the rich could afford the armies of servants needed to maintain a house the size of a European palace. By the time I saw them, of course, that era was long past. Almost none of the Long Island mansions were still private residences. Those that hadn't been turned into museums were occupied by nursing homes or private schools.

For the America I grew up in—the America of the 1950s and 1960s—was a middle-class society, both in reality and in feel. The vast income and wealth inequalities of the Gilded Age had disappeared. Yes, of course, there was the poverty of the underclass—but the conventional wisdom of the time viewed that as a social rather than an economic problem. Yes, of course, some wealthy businessmen and heirs to large fortunes lived far better than the average American. But they weren't rich the way the robber barons who built the mansions had been rich, and there weren't that many of them. The days when plutocrats were a force to be reckoned with in American society, economically or politically, seemed long past.

Daily experience confirmed the sense of a fairly equal society. The economic disparities you were conscious of were quite muted. Highly educated professionals—middle managers, college teachers, even lawyers—often claimed that they earned less than unionized blue-collar workers. Those considered very well off lived in split-levels, had a housecleaner come in once a week and took summer vacations in Europe. But they sent their kids to public schools and drove themselves to work, just like everyone else.

But that was long ago. The middle-class America of my youth was another country.

We are now living in a new Gilded Age, as extravagant as the original. Mansions have made a comeback. Back in 1999 this magazine profiled Thierry Despont, the "eminence of excess," an architect who specializes in designing houses for the superrich. His creations typically range from 20,000 to 60,000 square feet; houses at the upper end of his range are not much smaller than the White House. Needless to say, the armies of servants are back, too. So are the yachts. Still, even J.P. Morgan didn't have a Gulfstream.

As the story about Despont suggests, it's not fair to say that the fact of widening inequality in America has gone unreported. Yet glimpses of the lifestyles of the rich and tasteless don't necessarily add up in people's minds to a clear picture of the tectonic shifts that have taken place in the distribution of income and wealth in this country. My sense is that few people are aware of just how much the gap between the very rich and the rest has widened over a relatively short period of time. In fact, even bringing up the subject exposes you to charges of "class warfare," the "politics of envy" and so on. And very few people indeed are willing to talk about the profound effects—economic, social, and political—of that widening gap.

Yet you can't understand what's happening in America today without understanding the extent, causes, and consequences of the vast increase in inequality that has taken place over the last three decades, and in particular the astonishing concentration of income and wealth in just a few hands. To make sense of the current wave of corporate scandal, you need to understand how the man in the gray flannel suit has been replaced by the imperial C.E.O. The concentration of income at the top is a key reason that the United States, for all its economic achievements, has more poverty and lower life expectancy than any other major advanced nation. Above all, the growing concentration of wealth has reshaped our political system: it is at the root both of a general shift to the right and of an extreme polarization of our politics.

But before we get to all that, let's take a look at who gets what.

II. The New Gilded Age

The Securities and Exchange Commission hath no fury like a woman scorned. The messy divorce proceedings of Jack Welch, the legendary former C.E.O. of General Electric, have had one unintended benefit: they have given us a peek at the perks of the corporate elite, which are normally hidden from public view. For it turns out that when Welch retired, he was granted for life the use of a Manhattan apartment (including food, wine, and laundry), access to corporate jets, and a variety of other in-kind benefits, worth at least $2 million a year. The perks were revealing: they illustrated the extent to which corporate leaders now expect to be treated like *ancien régime* royalty. In monetary terms, however, the perks must have meant little to Welch. In 2000, his last full year running G.E., Welch was paid $123 million, mainly in stock and stock options.

Is it news that C.E.O.s of large American corporations make a lot of money? Actually, it is. They were always well paid compared with the average worker, but there is simply no comparison between what executives got a generation ago and what they are paid today.

Over the past 30 years most people have seen only modest salary increases: the average annual salary in America, expressed in 1998 dollars (that is, adjusted for inflation), rose from $32,522 in 1970 to $35,864 in 1999. That's about a 10 percent increase over 29 years—progress, but not much. Over the same period, however, according to *Fortune* magazine, the average real annual compensation of the top 100 C.E.O.s went from $1.3 million—39 times the pay of an average worker—to $37.5 million, more than 1,000 times the pay of ordinary workers.

The explosion in C.E.O. pay over the past 30 years is an amazing story in its own right, and an important one. But it is only the most spectacular indicator of a broader story, the reconcentration of income and wealth in the U.S. The rich have always been different from you and me, but they are far more different now than they were not long ago—indeed, they are as different now as they were when F. Scott Fitzgerald made his famous remark.

That's a controversial statement, though it shouldn't be. For at least the past 15 years it has been hard to deny the evidence for growing inequality in the United States. Census data clearly show a rising share of income going to the top 20 percent of families, and within that top 20 percent to the top 5 percent, with a declining share going to families in the middle. Nonetheless, denial of that evidence is a sizable, well-financed industry. Conservative think tanks have produced scores of studies that try to discredit the data, the methodology and, not least, the motives of those who report the obvious. Studies that appear to refute claims of increasing inequality receive prominent endorsements on editorial pages and are eagerly cited by right-leaning government officials. Four years ago Alan Greenspan (why did anyone ever think that he was nonpartisan?) gave a keynote speech at the Federal Reserve's annual Jackson Hole conference that amounted to an attempt to deny that there has been any real increase in inequality in America.

The concerted effort to deny that inequality is increasing is itself a symptom of the growing influence of our emerging plutocracy (more on this later). So is the fierce defense of the backup position, that inequality doesn't matter— or maybe even that, to use Martha Stewart's signature phrase, it's a good thing. Meanwhile, politically motivated smoke screens aside, the reality of increasing inequality is not in doubt. In fact, the census data understate the case, because for technical reasons those data tend to undercount very high incomes—for example, it's unlikely that they reflect the explosion in C.E.O. compensation. And other evidence makes it clear not only that inequality is increasing but that the action gets bigger the closer you get to the top. That is, it's not simply that the top 20 percent of families have had bigger percentage gains than families near the middle: the top 5 percent have done better than the next 15, the top 1 percent better than the next 4, and so on up to Bill Gates.

Studies that try to do a better job of tracking high incomes have found startling results. For example, a recent study by the nonpartisan Congressional Budget Office used income tax data and other sources to improve on the census estimates. The C.B.O. study found that between 1979 and 1997, the after-tax incomes of the top 1 percent of families rose 157 percent, compared with only a 10 percent gain for families near the middle of the income distribution. Even more startling results come from a new study by Thomas Piketty, at the French research institute Cepremap, and Emmanuel Saez, who is now at the University of California at Berkeley. Using income tax data, Piketty and Saez have produced estimates of the incomes of the well-to-do, the rich and the very rich back to 1913.

The first point you learn from these new estimates is that the middle-class America of my youth is best thought of not as the normal state of our society, but as an interregnum between Gilded Ages. America before 1930 was a society in which a small number of very rich people controlled a large share of the nation's wealth. We became a middle-class society only after the concentration of income at the top dropped sharply during the New Deal, and especially during World War II. The economic historians Claudia Goldin and Robert Margo have dubbed the narrowing of income gaps during those years the Great Compression. Incomes then stayed fairly equally distributed until the 1970s: the rapid rise in incomes during the first postwar generation was very evenly spread across the population.

Since the 1970s, however, income gaps have been rapidly widening. Piketty and Saez confirm what I suspected: by most measures we are, in fact, back to the days of *The Great Gatsby*. After 30 years in which the income shares of the top 10 percent of taxpayers, the top 1 percent and so on were far below their levels in the 1920s, all are very nearly back where they were.

And the big winners are the very, very rich. One ploy often used to play down growing inequality is to rely on rather coarse statistical breakdowns—dividing the population into five "quintiles," each containing 20 percent of families, or at most 10 "deciles." Indeed, Greenspan's speech at Jackson Hole relied mainly on decile data. From there it's a short step to denying that we're really talking about the rich at all. For example, a conservative commentator might concede, grudgingly, that there has been some increase in the share of national income going to the top 10 percent of taxpayers, but then point out that anyone with an income over $81,000 is in that top 10 percent. So we're just talking about shifts within the middle class, right?

Wrong: the top 10 percent contains a lot of people whom we would still consider middle class, but they weren't the big winners. Most of the gains in the share of the top 10 percent of taxpayers over the past 30 years were actually gains to the top 1 percent, rather than the next 9 percent. In 1998 the top 1 percent started at $230,000. In turn, 60 percent of the gains of that top 1 percent went to the top 0.1 percent, those with incomes of more than $790,000. And almost half of those gains went to a mere 13,000 taxpayers, the top 0.01 percent, who had an income of at least $3.6 million and an average income of $17 million.

A stickler for detail might point out that the Piketty-Saez estimates end in 1998 and that the C.B.O. numbers end a year earlier. Have the trends shown in the data reversed? Almost surely not. In fact, all indications are that the explosion of incomes at the top continued through 2000. Since then the plunge in stock prices must have put some crimp in high incomes—but census data show inequality continuing to increase in 2001, mainly because of the severe effects of the recession on the working poor and near poor. When the recession ends, we can be sure that we will find ourselves a society in which income inequality is even higher than it was in the late '90s.

So claims that we've entered a second Gilded Age aren't exaggerated. In America's middle-class era, the mansion-building, yacht-owning classes had pretty much disappeared. According to Piketty and Saez, in 1970 the top 0.01 percent of taxpayers had 0.7 percent of total income—that is, they earned "only" 70 times as much as the average, not enough to buy or maintain a mega-residence. But in 1998 the top 0.01 percent received more than 3 percent of all income. That meant that the 13,000 richest families in America had almost as much income as the 20 million poorest households; those 13,000 families had incomes 300 times that of average families.

And let me repeat: this transformation has happened very quickly, and it is still going on. You might think that 1987, the year Tom Wolfe published his novel *The Bonfire of the Vanities* and Oliver Stone released his movie *Wall Street*, marked the high tide of America's new money culture. But in 1987 the top 0.01 percent earned only about 40 percent of what they do today, and top executives less than a fifth as much. The America of *Wall Street* and *The Bonfire of the Vanities* was positively egalitarian compared with the country we live in today.

III. Undoing the New Deal

In the middle of the 1980s, as economists became aware that something important was happening to the distribution of income in America, they formulated three main hypotheses about its causes.

The "globalization" hypothesis tied America's changing income distribution to the growth of world trade, and especially the growing imports of manufactured goods from the third world. Its basic message was that blue-collar workers—the sort of people who in my youth often made as much money as college-educated middle managers—were losing ground in the face of competition from low-wage workers in Asia. A result was stagnation or decline in the wages of ordinary people, with a growing share of national income going to the highly educated.

A second hypothesis, "skill-biased technological change," situated the cause of growing inequality not in foreign trade but in domestic innovation. The torrid pace of progress in information technology, so the story went, had increased the demand for the highly skilled and educated. And so the income distribution increasingly favored brains rather than brawn.

Finally, the "superstar" hypothesis—named by the Chicago economist Sherwin Rosen—offered a variant on the technological story. It argued that modern technologies of communication often turn competition into a tournament in which the winner is richly rewarded, while the runners-up get far less. The classic example—which gives the theory its name—is the entertainment business. As Rosen pointed out, in bygone days there were hundreds of comedians making a modest living at live shows in the borscht belt and other places. Now they are mostly gone; what is left is a handful of superstar TV comedians.

The debates among these hypotheses—particularly the debate between those who attributed growing inequality to globalization and those who attributed it to technology—were many and bitter. I was a participant in those debates myself. But I won't dwell on them, because in the last few years there has been a growing sense among economists that none of these hypotheses work.

I don't mean to say that there was nothing to these stories. Yet as more evidence has accumulated, each of the hypotheses has seemed increasingly inadequate. Globalization can explain part of the relative decline in blue-collar wages, but it can't explain the 2,500 percent rise in C.E.O. incomes. Technology may explain why the salary premium associated with a college education has risen, but it's hard to match up with the huge increase in inequality among the college-educated, with little progress for many but gigantic gains at the top. The superstar theory works for Jay Leno, but not for the thousands of people who have become awesomely rich without going on TV.

The Great Compression—the substantial reduction in inequality during the New Deal and the Second World War—also seems hard to understand in terms of the usual theories. During World War II Franklin Roosevelt used government control over wages to compress wage gaps. But if the middle-class society that emerged from the war was an artificial creation, why did it persist for another 30 years?

Some—by no means all—economists trying to understand growing inequality have begun to take seriously a hypothesis that would have been considered irredeemably fuzzy-minded not long ago. This view stresses the role of social norms in setting limits to inequality. According to this view, the New Deal had a more profound impact on American society than even its most ardent admirers have suggested: it imposed norms of relative equality in pay that persisted for more than 30 years, creating the broadly middle-class society we came to take for granted. But those norms began to unravel in the 1970s and have done so at an accelerating pace.

Exhibit A for this view is the story of executive compensation. In the 1960s, America's great corporations behaved more like socialist republics than like cutthroat capitalist enterprises, and top executives behaved more like public-spirited bureaucrats than like captains of industry. I'm not exaggerating. Consider the description of executive behavior offered by John Kenneth Galbraith in his 1967 book, *The New Industrial State*: "Management does not go out ruthlessly to reward itself—a sound management is expected to exercise restraint." Managerial self-dealing was a thing of the past: "With the power of decision goes opportunity for making money. . . . Were everyone to seek to do so . . . the corporation would be a chaos of competitive avarice. But these are not the sort of thing that a good company man does; a remarkably effective code bans such behavior. Group decision-making insures, moreover, that almost everyone's actions and even thoughts are known to others. This acts to enforce the code and, more than incidentally, a high standard of personal honesty as well."

Thirty-five years on, a cover article in *Fortune* is titled "You Bought. They Sold." "All over corporate America," reads the blurb, "top execs were cashing in stocks even as their companies were tanking. Who was left holding the bag? You." As I said, we've become a different country.

Let's leave actual malfeasance on one side for a moment, and ask how the relatively modest salaries of top executives 30 years ago became the gigantic pay packages of today. There are two main stories, both of which emphasize changing norms rather than pure economics. The more optimistic story draws an analogy between the explosion of C.E.O. pay and the explosion of baseball salaries with the introduction of free agency. According to this story, highly paid C.E.O.s really are worth it, because having the right man in that job makes a huge difference. The more pessimistic view—which I find more plausible—is that competition for talent is a minor factor. Yes, a great executive can make a big difference—but those huge pay packages have been going as often as not to executives whose performance is mediocre at best. The key reason executives are paid so much now is that they appoint the members of the corporate board that determines their compensation and control many of the perks that board members count on. So it's not the invisible hand of the market that leads to those monumental executive incomes; it's the invisible handshake in the boardroom.

But then why weren't executives paid lavishly 30 years ago? Again, it's a matter of corporate culture. For a generation after World War II, fear of outrage kept executive salaries in check. Now the outrage is gone. That is, the explosion of executive pay represents a social change rather than the purely economic forces of supply and demand. We should think of it not as a market trend like the rising value of waterfront property, but as something more like the sexual revolution of the 1960s—a relaxation of old strictures, a new permissiveness, but in this case the permissiveness is financial rather than sexual. Sure enough, John Kenneth Galbraith described the honest executive of 1967 as being one who "eschews the lovely, available and even naked woman by whom he is intimately surrounded." By the end of the 1990s, the executive motto might as well have been "If it feels good, do it."

How did this change in corporate culture happen? Economists and management theorists are only beginning to explore that question, but it's easy to suggest a few factors. One was the changing structure of financial markets. In his new book, *Searching for a Corporate Savior*, Rakesh Khurana of Harvard Business School suggests that during the 1980s and 1990s, "managerial capitalism"—the world of the man in the gray flannel suit—was replaced by "investor capitalism." Institutional investors weren't willing to let a C.E.O. choose his own successor from inside the corporation; they wanted heroic leaders, often outsiders, and were willing to pay immense sums to get them. The subtitle of Khurana's book, by the way, is *The Irrational Quest for Charismatic C.E.O.s.*

But fashionable management theorists didn't think it was irrational. Since the 1980s there has been ever more emphasis on the importance of "leadership"—meaning personal, charismatic leadership. When Lee Iacocca of Chrysler became a business celebrity in the early 1980s, he was practically alone: Khurana reports that in 1980 only one issue of *Business Week* featured a C.E.O. on its cover. By 1999 the number was up to 19. And once it was considered normal, even necessary, for a C.E.O. to be famous, it also became easier to make him rich.

Economists also did their bit to legitimize previously unthinkable levels of executive pay. During the 1980s and 1990s a torrent of academic papers—popularized in business magazines and incorporated into consultants' recommendations—argued that Gordon Gekko was right: greed is good; greed works. In order to get the best performance out of executives, these papers argued, it was necessary to align their interests with those of stockholders. And the way to do that was with large grants of stock or stock options.

It's hard to escape the suspicion that these new intellectual justifications for soaring executive pay were as much effect as cause. I'm not suggesting that management theorists and economists were personally corrupt. It would have been a subtle, unconscious process: the ideas that were taken up by business schools, that led to nice speaking and consulting fees, tended to be the ones that ratified an existing trend, and thereby gave it legitimacy.

What economists like Piketty and Saez are now suggesting is that the story of executive compensation is representative of a broader story. Much more than economists and free-market advocates like to imagine, wages—particularly at the top—are determined by social norms. What happened during the 1930s and 1940s was that new norms of equality were established, largely through the political process. What happened in the 1980s and 1990s was that those norms unraveled, replaced by an ethos of "anything goes." And a result was an explosion of income at the top of the scale.

IV. The Price of Inequality

It was one of those revealing moments. Responding to an e-mail message from a Canadian viewer, Robert Novak of *Crossfire* delivered a little speech: "Marg, like most Canadians, you're ill informed and wrong. The U.S. has the longest standard of living—longest life expectancy of any country in the world, including Canada. That's the truth."

But it was Novak who had his facts wrong. Canadians can expect to live about two years longer than Americans. In fact, life expectancy in the U.S. is well below that in Canada, Japan, and every major nation in Western Europe. On average, we can expect lives a bit shorter than those of Greeks, a bit longer than those of Portuguese. Male life expectancy is lower in the U.S. than it is in Costa Rica.

Still, you can understand why Novak assumed that we were No. 1. After all, we really are the richest major nation, with real G.D.P. per capita about 20 percent higher than Canada's. And it has been an article of faith in this country that a rising tide lifts all boats. Doesn't our high and rising national wealth translate into a high standard of living—including good medical care—for all Americans?

Well, no. Although America has higher per capita income than other advanced countries, it turns out that that's mainly because our rich are much richer. And here's a radical thought: if the rich get more, that leaves less for everyone else.

That statement—which is simply a matter of arithmetic—is guaranteed to bring accusations of "class warfare." If the accuser gets more specific, he'll probably offer two reasons that it's foolish to make a fuss over the high incomes of a few people at the top of the income distribution. First, he'll tell you that what the elite get may look like a lot of money, but it's still a small share of the total—that is, when all is said and done the rich aren't getting that big a piece of the pie. Second, he'll tell you that trying to do anything to reduce incomes at the top will hurt, not help, people further down the distribution, because attempts to redistribute income damage incentives.

These arguments for lack of concern are plausible. And they were entirely correct, once upon a time—namely, back when we had a middle-class society. But there's a lot less truth to them now.

First, the share of the rich in total income is no longer trivial. These days 1 percent of families receive about 16 percent of total pretax income, and have about 14 percent of after-tax income. That share has roughly doubled over the past 30 years, and is now about as large as the share of the bottom 40 percent of the population. That's a big shift of income to the top; as a matter of pure arithmetic, it must mean that the incomes of less well off families grew considerably more slowly than average income. And they did. Adjusting for inflation, average family income—total income divided by the number of families—grew 28 percent from 1979 to 1997. But median family income— the income of a family in the middle of the distribution, a better indicator of how typical American families are doing—grew only 10 percent. And the incomes of the bottom fifth of families actually fell slightly.

Let me belabor this point for a bit. We pride ourselves, with considerable justification, on our record of economic growth. But over the last few decades it's remarkable how little of that growth has trickled down to ordinary families. Median family income has risen only about 0.5 percent per year—and as far as we can tell from somewhat unreliable data, just about all of that increase was due to wives working longer hours, with little or no gain in real wages. Furthermore, numbers about income don't reflect the growing riskiness of life for ordinary workers. In the days when General Motors was known in-house as Generous Motors, many workers felt that they had considerable job security—the company wouldn't fire them except in extremis. Many had contracts that guaranteed health insurance, even if they were laid off; they had pension benefits that did not depend on the stock market. Now mass firings from long-established companies are commonplace; losing your job means losing your insurance; and as millions of people have been learning, a 401(k) plan is no guarantee of a comfortable retirement.

Still, many people will say that while the U.S. economic system may generate a lot of inequality, it also generates much higher incomes than any alternative, so that everyone is better off. That was the moral *Business Week* tried to convey in its recent special issue with "25 Ideas for a Changing World." One of those ideas was "the rich get richer, and that's O.K." High incomes at the top, the conventional wisdom declares, are the result of a free-market system that provides huge incentives for performance. And the system delivers that performance, which means that wealth at the top doesn't come at the expense of the rest of us.

A skeptic might point out that the explosion in executive compensation seems at best loosely related to actual performance. Jack Welch was one of the 10 highest-paid executives in the United States in 2000, and you could argue that he earned it. But did Dennis Kozlowski of Tyco, or Gerald Levin of Time Warner, who were also in the top 10? A skeptic might also point out that even during the economic boom of the late 1990s, U.S. productivity growth was no better than it was during the great postwar expansion, which corresponds to the era when America was truly middle class and C.E.O.s were modestly paid technocrats.

But can we produce any direct evidence about the effects of inequality? We can't rerun our own history and ask what would have happened if the social norms of middle-class America had continued to limit incomes at the top, and if government policy had leaned against rising inequality instead of reinforcing it, which is what actually happened. But we can compare ourselves with other advanced countries. And the results are somewhat surprising.

Many Americans assume that because we are the richest country in the world, with real G.D.P. per capita higher than that of other major advanced countries, Americans must be better off across the board—that it's not just our rich who are richer than their counterparts abroad, but that the typical American family is much better off than the typical family elsewhere, and that even our poor are well off by foreign standards.

But it's not true. Let me use the example of Sweden, that great conservative *bête noire*.

A few months ago the conservative cyberpundit Glenn Reynolds made a splash when he pointed out that Sweden's G.D.P. per capita is roughly comparable with that of Mississippi—see, those foolish believers in the welfare state have impoverished themselves! Presumably he assumed that this means that the typical Swede is as poor as the typical resident of Mississippi, and therefore much worse off than the typical American.

But life expectancy in Sweden is about three years higher than that of the U.S. Infant mortality is half the U.S. level, and less than a third the rate in Mississippi. Functional illiteracy is much less common than in the U.S.

How is this possible? One answer is that G.D.P. per capita is in some ways a misleading measure. Swedes take longer vacations than Americans, so they work fewer hours per year. That's a choice, not a failure of economic performance. Real G.D.P. per hour worked is 16 percent lower than in the United States, which makes Swedish productivity about the same as Canada's.

But the main point is that though Sweden may have lower average income than the United States, that's mainly because our rich are so much richer. The median Swedish family has a standard of living roughly comparable with that of the median U.S. family: wages are if anything higher in Sweden, and a higher tax burden is offset by public provision of health care and generally better public services. And as you move further down the income distribution, Swedish living standards are way ahead of those in the U.S. Swedish families with children that are at the 10th percentile — poorer than 90 percent of the population—have incomes 60 percent higher than their U.S. counterparts. And very few people in Sweden experience the deep poverty that is all too common in the United States. One measure: in 1994 only 6 percent of Swedes lived on less than $11 per day, compared with 14 percent in the U.S.

The moral of this comparison is that even if you think that America's high levels of inequality are the price of our high level of national income, it's not at all clear that this price is worth paying. The reason conservatives engage in bouts of Sweden-bashing is that they want to convince us that there is no tradeoff between economic efficiency and equity—that if you try to take from the rich and give to the poor, you actually make everyone worse off. But the comparison between the U.S. and other advanced countries doesn't support this conclusion at all. Yes, we are the richest major nation. But because so much of our national income is concentrated in relatively few hands, large numbers of Americans are worse off economically than their counterparts in other advanced countries.

And we might even offer a challenge from the other side: inequality in the United States has arguably reached levels where it is counterproductive. That is, you can make a case that our society would be richer if its richest members didn't get quite so much.

I could make this argument on historical grounds. The most impressive economic growth in U.S. history coincided with the middle-class interregnum, the post-World War II generation, when incomes were most evenly distributed. But let's focus on a specific case, the extraordinary pay packages of today's top executives. Are these good for the economy?

Until recently it was almost unchallenged conventional wisdom that, whatever else you might say, the new imperial C.E.O.s had delivered results that dwarfed the expense of their compensation. But now that the stock bubble has burst, it has become increasingly clear that there was a price to those big pay packages, after all. In fact, the price paid by shareholders and society at large may have been many times larger than the amount actually paid to the executives.

It's easy to get boggled by the details of corporate scandal—insider loans, stock options, special-purpose entities, mark-to-market, round-tripping. But there's a simple reason that the details are so complicated. All of these schemes were designed to benefit corporate insiders—to inflate the pay of the C.E.O. and his inner circle. That is, they were all about the "chaos of competitive avarice" that, according to John Kenneth Galbraith, had been ruled out in the corporation of the 1960s. But while all restraint has vanished within the American corporation, the outside world—including stockholders—is still prudish, and open looting by executives is still not acceptable. So the looting has to be camouflaged, taking place through complicated schemes that can be rationalized to outsiders as clever corporate strategies.

Economists who study crime tell us that crime is inefficient—that is, the costs of crime to the economy are much larger than the amount stolen. Crime, and the fear of crime, divert resources away from productive uses: criminals spend their time stealing rather than producing, and potential victims spend time and money trying to protect their property. Also, the things people do to avoid becoming victims—like avoiding dangerous districts—have a cost even if they succeed in averting an actual crime.

The same holds true of corporate malfeasance, whether or not it actually involves breaking the law. Executives who devote their time to creating innovative ways to divert shareholder money into their own pockets probably aren't running the real business very well (think Enron, WorldCom, Tyco, Global Crossing, Adelphia . . .). Investments chosen because they create the illusion of profitability while insiders cash in their stock options are a waste of scarce resources. And if the supply of funds from lenders and shareholders dries up because of a lack of trust, the economy as a whole suffers. Just ask Indonesia.

The argument for a system in which some people get very rich has always been that the lure of wealth provides powerful incentives. But the question is, incentives to do what? As we learn more about what has actually been going on in corporate America, it's becoming less and less clear whether those incentives have actually made executives work on behalf of the rest of us.

V. Inequality and Politics

In September the Senate debated a proposed measure that would impose a one-time capital gains tax on Americans who renounce their citizenship in order to avoid paying U.S. taxes. Senator Phil Gramm was not pleased, declaring that the proposal was "right out of Nazi Germany." Pretty strong language, but no stronger than the metaphor Daniel Mitchell of the Heritage Foundation used, in an op-ed article in *The Washington Times*, to describe a bill designed to prevent corporations from rechartering abroad for tax purposes: Mitchell described this legislation as the "Dred Scott tax bill," referring to the infamous 1857 Supreme Court ruling that required free states to return escaped slaves.

Twenty years ago, would a prominent senator have likened those who want wealthy people to pay taxes to Nazis? Would a member of a think tank with close ties to the administration have drawn a parallel between corporate taxation and slavery? I don't think so. The remarks by Gramm and Mitchell, while stronger than usual, were indicators of two huge changes in American politics. One is the growing polarization of our politics—our politicians are less and less inclined to offer even the appearance of moderation. The other is the growing tendency of policy and policy makers to cater to the interests of the wealthy. And I mean the wealthy, not the merely well-off: only someone with a net worth of at least several million dollars is likely to find it worthwhile to become a tax exile.

You don't need a political scientist to tell you that modern American politics is bitterly polarized. But wasn't it always thus? No, it wasn't. From World War II until the 1970s—the same era during which income inequality was historically low—political partisanship was much more muted than it is today. That's not just a subjective assessment. My Princeton political science colleagues Nolan McCarty and Howard Rosenthal, together with Keith Poole at the University of Houston, have done a statistical analysis showing that the voting behavior of a congressman is much better predicted by his party affiliation today than it was 25 years ago. In fact, the division between the parties is sharper now than it has been since the 1920s.

What are the parties divided about? The answer is simple: economics. McCarty, Rosenthal, and Poole write that "voting in Congress is highly ideological—one-dimensional left/right, liberal versus conservative." It may sound simplistic to describe Democrats as the party that wants to tax the rich and help the poor, and Republicans as the party that wants to keep taxes and social spending as low as possible. And during the era of middle-class America that would indeed have been simplistic: politics wasn't defined by economic issues. But that was a different country; as McCarty, Rosenthal, and Poole put it, "If income and wealth are distributed in a fairly equitable way, little is to be gained for politicians to organize politics around nonexistent conflicts." Now the conflicts are real, and our politics is organized around them. In other words, the growing inequality of our incomes probably lies behind the growing divisiveness of our politics.

But the politics of rich and poor hasn't played out the way you might think. Since the incomes of America's wealthy have soared while ordinary families have seen at best small gains, you might have expected politicians to seek votes by proposing to soak the rich. In fact, however, the polarization of politics has occurred because the Republicans have moved to the right, not because the Democrats have moved to the left. And actual economic policy has moved steadily in favor of the wealthy. The major tax cuts of the past 25 years, the Reagan cuts in the 1980s and the recent Bush cuts, were both heavily tilted toward the very well off. (Despite obfuscations, it remains true that more than half the Bush tax cut will eventually go to the top 1 percent of families.) The major tax increase over that period, the increase in payroll taxes in the 1980s, fell most heavily on working-class families.

The most remarkable example of how politics has shifted in favor of the wealthy—an example that helps us understand why economic policy has reinforced, not countered, the movement toward greater inequality—is the drive to repeal the estate tax. The estate tax is, overwhelmingly, a tax on the wealthy. In 1999, only the top 2 percent of estates paid any tax at all, and half the estate tax was paid by only 3,300 estates, 0.16 percent of the total, with a minimum value of $5 million and an average value of $17 million. A quarter of the tax was paid by just 467 estates worth more than $20 million. Tales of family farms and businesses broken up to pay the estate tax are basically rural legends; hardly any real examples have been found, despite diligent searching.

You might have thought that a tax that falls on so few people yet yields a significant amount of revenue would be politically popular; you certainly wouldn't expect widespread opposition. Moreover, there has long been an argument that the estate tax promotes democratic values, precisely because it limits the ability of the wealthy to form dynasties. So why has there been a powerful political drive to repeal the estate tax, and why was such a repeal a centerpiece of the Bush tax cut?

There is an economic argument for repealing the estate tax, but it's hard to believe that many people take it seriously. More significant for members of Congress, surely, is the question of who would benefit from repeal: while those who will actually benefit from estate tax repeal are few in number, they have a lot of money and control even more (corporate C.E.O.s can now count on leaving taxable estates behind). That is, they are the sort of people who command the attention of politicians in search of campaign funds.

But it's not just about campaign contributions: much of the general public has been convinced that the estate tax is a bad thing. If you try talking about the tax to a group of moderately prosperous retirees, you get some interesting reactions. They refer to it as the "death tax"; many of them believe that their estates will face punitive taxation, even though most of them will pay little or nothing; they are convinced that small businesses and family farms bear the brunt of the tax.

These misconceptions don't arise by accident. They have, instead, been deliberately promoted. For example, a Heritage Foundation document titled "Time to Repeal Federal Death Taxes: The Nightmare of the American Dream" emphasizes stories that rarely, if ever, happen in real life: "Small-business owners, particularly minority owners, suffer anxious moments wondering whether the businesses they hope to hand down to their children will be destroyed by the death tax bill . . . Women whose children are grown struggle to find ways to re-enter the work force without upsetting the family's estate tax avoidance plan." And who finances the Heritage Foundation? Why, foundations created by wealthy families, of course.

The point is that it is no accident that strongly conservative views, views that militate against taxes on the rich, have spread even as the rich get richer compared with the rest of us: in addition to directly buying influence, money can be used to shape public perceptions. The liberal group People for the American Way's report on how conservative foundations have deployed vast sums to support think tanks, friendly media, and other institutions that promote right-wing causes is titled "Buying a Movement."

Not to put too fine a point on it: as the rich get richer, they can buy a lot of things besides goods and services. Money buys political influence; used cleverly, it also buys intellectual influence. A result is that growing income disparities in the United States, far from leading to demands to soak the rich, have been accompanied by a growing movement to let them keep more of their earnings and to pass their wealth on to their children.

This obviously raises the possibility of a self-reinforcing process. As the gap between the rich and the rest of the population grows, economic policy increasingly caters to the interests of the elite, while public services for the population at large—above all, public education—are starved of resources.

As policy increasingly favors the interests of the rich and neglects the interests of the general population, income disparities grow even wider.

VI. Plutocracy?

In 1924, the mansions of Long Island's North Shore were still in their full glory, as was the political power of the class that owned them. When Gov. Al Smith of New York proposed building a system of parks on Long Island, the mansion owners were bitterly opposed. One baron—Horace Havemeyer, the "sultan of sugar"—warned that North Shore towns would be "overrun with rabble from the city." "Rabble?" Smith said. "That's me you're talking about." In the end New Yorkers got their parks, but it was close: the interests of a few hundred wealthy families nearly prevailed over those of New York City's middle class.

America in the 1920s wasn't a feudal society. But it was a nation in which vast privilege—often inherited privilege—stood in contrast to vast misery. It was also a nation in which the government, more often than not, served the interests of the privileged and ignored the aspirations of ordinary people.

Those days are past—or are they? Income inequality in America has now returned to the levels of the 1920s. Inherited wealth doesn't yet play a big part in our society, but given time—and the repeal of the estate tax—we will grow ourselves a hereditary elite just as set apart from the concerns of ordinary Americans as old Horace Havemeyer. And the new elite, like the old, will have enormous political power.

Kevin Phillips concludes his book *Wealth and Democracy* with a grim warning: "Either democracy must be renewed, with politics brought back to life, or wealth is likely to cement a new and less democratic regime—plutocracy by some other name." It's a pretty extreme line, but we live in extreme times. Even if the forms of democracy remain, they may become meaningless. It's all too easy to see how we may become a country in which the big rewards are reserved for people with the right connections; in which ordinary people see little hope of advancement; in which political involvement seems pointless, because in the end the interests of the elite always get served.

Am I being too pessimistic? Even my liberal friends tell me not to worry, that our system has great resilience, that the center will hold. I hope they're right, but they may be looking in the rearview mirror. Our optimism about America, our belief that in the end our nation always finds its way, comes from the past—a past in which we were a middle-class society. But that was another country.

Children Left Behind
Stephanie Mencimer

The American Prospect | December 30, 2002

The lack of affordable, accessible and reliable child care for preschoolers is one of the biggest problems facing American parents today, yet it's a topic we hear very little about from our politicians. The issue is not just one of convenience, but economic necessity: More mothers are in the workforce than ever before, and many families now rely on two incomes to get by. But as Stephanie Mencimer points out in this wrenching article, no one is affected more by the scarcity of child-care options than single moms and their children—for whom it can sometimes be a matter of life and death. . . .

In early October, Nakia Burgess had just gotten a job as a transcriber in Atlanta. She had already lost two other jobs because of her inability to secure reliable and affordable child care for her 3-year-old daughter, Asan'te, who had Down syndrome. So when the temp agency she had signed up with sent her out for a new assignment, Burgess was desperate to hang on to the position. But on her second day, her child-care arrangement fell through. She took Asan'te to work with her and left the girl in the car on the company's parking deck. Burgess came out periodically to check on the child, but after only 90 minutes, Asan'te was unconscious. The temperature that day had risen to 85 degrees, and it was even higher inside the car. When Asan'te reached the hospital, her temperature registered 108 and she was pronounced dead from hyperthermia.

The story provoked gasps of horror in the Atlanta area, where Burgess was charged with murder even as she drew sympathy from thousands of working parents who understood her difficulties in finding child care. (The charges against Burgess have been changed from felony murder and cruelty to children to involuntary manslaughter and reckless conduct.) The media treated the story as if it were a freak accident, but the incident was far from unusual. A car is increasingly becoming a child-care arrangement of last resort. In 1998, for instance, a 23-year-old mother in Wisconsin was sentenced to six months in prison after leaving her 2-year-old son in the trunk while she worked because she couldn't afford child care.

In November 2000, Rosmarie Radovan was arrested for locking her 5- and 7-year-old sons in the trunk of her car while she worked. A single parent who was owed at least $41,000 in back child-support payments and who was working two jobs to care for her boys, Radovan argued in court that she could not find affordable child care for the children on the nights and weekends when she worked. California's Santa Clara County, where she lived, had at least 8,000 families on the waiting list for child-care openings at the time, according to news reports. Nonetheless, Radovan was sentenced to three months in jail for child endangerment.

The demand for quality, affordable child care has grown acute. In Georgia, where Burgess lived, more than 16,000 people are on the waiting list for a subsidy that would offset the cost of child care, which can run between $5,000 and $10,000 a year. A similar situation exists throughout much of America. Nineteen states currently have long waiting lists for child-care subsidies. (At the end of 2001, California had 200,000 families waiting, Florida had more than 46,000 and Texas had more than 36,000.) What's more, those families generally spend 50 percent of their incomes on child care.

As Burgess and others have demonstrated, desperate people will do desperate things when they must work but can't find care for their children. With all the talk in this country about caring for children—right down to the fetus— you'd think Nakia Burgess' story would have sparked cries to address the nation's child-care crisis. But you'd be wrong. Instead, the Bush administration, which promises to "leave no child behind," has proposed forcing more women on welfare into the workforce while failing to provide even a cost-of-living increase in the federal child-care budget. Meanwhile, the economic downturn and state budget crises are forcing states to slash spending on all child-care services. Without additional funds, nearly half the states will need to scale back federally funded child-care programs by fiscal 2003, according to the Children's Defense Fund—all indications that stories such as Burgess' are likely to become depressingly more common.

The recent shortage of affordable child care is nothing new. When Marian Wright Edelman of the Children's Defense Fund testified before Congress in 1988 in support of the Act for Better Child Care Services, she told the story of Sandra James, a part-time housekeeper who lived in a community that had 5,000 young children competing for 453 day-care slots. James and her husband both worked and were unable to find care for their two children. One day, James left her 6-year-old son and his friend in the care of her 8-year-old daughter. A fire broke out in their apartment, and James' daughter ran for help, inadvertently locking the two younger children in the apartment. Both died in the fire.

Edelman laid out a host of similar horror stories, including those of substandard day-care centers, and implored Congress to take action to correct the problem. The situation is slightly better today—states are spending a record amount of money trying to improve child care—but progress has been slowed by the increased demand due to the welfare-reform legislation passed in 1996. Since then, employment among low-income single mothers with young children grew from 44 percent to 59 percent in 2000, according to the U.S. Department of Health and Human Services, creating a dire need for affordable child care.

Despite more than a decade's worth of tragedies, though, child care rarely prompts a sense of urgency among elected officials. Certainly it's been a divisive issue in this country because of the "culture wars," as conservatives have objected to women (at least white, middle-class women) moving into the workforce and have fought liberals over expanding child-care availability on the grounds that it only encourages more women to abandon their traditional gender roles in the home. But economics have largely silenced the last two decades' debates over mothers in the workforce. Most reasonable people now agree that work is a necessity for most parents.

The biggest political obstacle to addressing the child-care crisis, according to many on Capitol Hill, is simply the cost. In her recent book, *America's Childcare Problem: A Way Out*, economist Barbara Bergmann estimates that creating a national child-care program that would offer both quality and affordable care would cost about $50 billion annually—$30 billion more than the country spends now through Head Start, Title XX, the federal child-care block grant and state child-care subsidies combined. "It is daunting when you think of the size of the problem," says the Urban Institute's Gina Adams.

Rather than attempt a comprehensive approach that would invariably be tagged as expanding "big government," elected officials have preferred to let parents pick up the hefty tab for what most other industrialized countries consider a public obligation. While child care for young children routinely costs parents or guardians more than public university tuition, the government pays for 77 percent of the cost of higher education, according to the Children's Defense Fund, whereas parents assume 60 percent of child-care costs.

Middle-class parents have rarely squawked about this burden, reflecting a national ambivalence about the government's role in caring for children. "This is a country very focused on parental responsibility," says Adams. While seniors may feel entitled to prescription-drug benefits, parents of young children are reluctant to ask for government support, although most would welcome it. And because children (and their harried parents, often) don't vote, they're a demographic that politicians can ignore without risk.

A "Poverty Program"

The silence of middle-class parents combined with the conservative political climate has left the issue of child care to anti-poverty groups, who rightly see it as inextricable from welfare reform. In fact, the relationship between welfare and child care is not a new one. During World War II, the government set up a network of child-care centers to allow women to contribute to the war effort while men served in the military. When the war ended, much of the industrialized world built on similar child-care infrastructures, developing nonparental centers and preschools that extended public schooling down to 3- and 4-year-olds. The United States, however, disbanded the centers and sent working mothers home. Rather than use child care to address the problem of mothers without husbands, the government created subsidies so that women could stay home and raise children. Those subsidies later became known as "welfare."

In the 1970s, as the conservative argument that welfare laws fueled increases in unwed motherhood gained political traction, Congress and various administrations attempted to "reform" welfare and force mothers into the workforce. But nearly every one of those early reform efforts failed, primarily because they neglected to factor in the need for child care. Congress seemed to have learned that lesson when it passed the 1996 welfare-reform effort and encouraged states to use surplus welfare funds to address the child-care problem. Child-care subsidies have increased since then, from about $4 billion in 1997 to about $8 billion last year, according to the Center for Law and Social Policy. Progressive states, which must match the federal grant, have also used some of their surplus welfare funds to expand the subsidies to cover some working families at risk of going on welfare.

The subsidies, though, are vastly inadequate for the need, and also immensely complicated to procure, as Nakia Burgess discovered when she inquired about them in Georgia. (She was told that the money had run out— and it had—so she never bothered to even apply.) In many states, the subsidies don't actually cover the full cost of providing day care, so many providers won't take kids who use them, as doing so would mean that the providers lose money. "The people who get them are the ones who can navigate the byzantine system to get it," says Ruby Takanishi, president of the Foundation for Child Development. "It's often so bad that people say, 'Forget it, I'm going to leave my kids in the car.'"

Today, only one out of seven eligible children actually gets the subsidies, and the Congressional Budget Office estimates that the program will need an additional $5 billion or so over the next five years just to maintain the current slots. In the recent debate over reauthorizing the welfare-reform law, Senate Democrats lobbied to increase child-care funding by $11 billion over the next half-decade—but ended up with a bill that would increase it by $5.5 billion. House Republicans passed their own version, which would only increase the funding by $1 billion. The whole reauthorization package stalled, and Congress will have to revisit the issue again next year.

The focus on subsidies as a substitute for a larger national debate on the crisis limits child care's prominence as a political issue. "Because subsidies are so narrowly focused, there is no organized constituency except for those particular advocacy groups [for the poor]," says Takanishi. Mustering political support for increased subsidies for welfare recipients is difficult when those being asked to support—and pay for—them are also struggling with their own child-care burdens. "Most people view child care as a private matter, so when it's used as a work support, it's not something that's looked kindly upon," says Takanishi.

Indeed, the issue affects nearly all families with children, regardless of income. The number of married mothers in the workforce with children under 6 has jumped from 11 percent in 1949 to 64 percent in 2001. Fifty-seven percent of women with infants are now in the workforce, while two-thirds of all 3- to 5-year-olds spend at least 35 hours a week being cared for by someone other than a parent, and that care is wildly expensive. Those costs put a significant dent in the average American family's finances.

People such as New York Times columnist Paul Krugman frequently note that the median household income in the United States has barely budged in the past 20 years, and that it's fallen for families in the bottom one-fifth of the income scale. What those numbers don't reflect is that most of the increases occurred not because salaries went up but because women went to work. To do so, they had to pay someone else to look after their kids. Today, the median income for a family of four—about $62,000 in 2000—may have increased 10 percent since 1979, but it doesn't account for the cost of child care, which could eat up nearly half of a second wage earner's salary. As a result, a family of four is probably getting by on far less than it did 20 years ago.

Yet advocacy groups have largely neglected these folks in their quest for more government child-care support, on the not-so-unreasonable grounds that whatever aid they can wrest from Congress—which isn't likely to be much—should go to those most in need. While the approach is well-intentioned, it neglects to enlist the critical support of the middle class, whose political heft might add some urgency to the issue. As a result, child care is now viewed as a "poverty program," and it gets treated as such.

In 2001, President George W. Bush actually proposed cutting $200 million from the Child Care and Development Block Grant to help pay for his massive tax cut for the rich. And this year, the administration advanced a version of welfare-reform reauthorization that would have forced even more mothers into the workforce without providing any new money to care for their children. The prospects for meaningful progress in the next Congress are grim. "We're in a deficit and we're at war. We don't have the money. No one is going to take money out of security. It's going to be a bad year for kids," says a Senate staffer whose boss is involved in the debate.

It's not yet clear whether congressional Democrats—now in the minority—will demand funding for such broad-based initiatives as universal preschool and after-school programs, which would also relieve some of the burden shouldered by middle-class parents. While Al Gore initially campaigned on the issue of universal preschool in 2000, it has all but disappeared since September 11. And infant care is expensive and in chronically short supply, not to mention of extremely poor quality.

California has already demonstrated that such programs are tremendously popular with voters who are now largely ignored by political campaigns. The state recently passed the first paid parental-leave law in the country—a measure that national polls show 82 percent of women and 75 percent of men support. California voters also overwhelmingly approved Arnold Schwarzenegger's ballot initiative to provide universal after-school care for the state's children so they wouldn't continue to be sent home to empty houses.

Fixing child care is likely to be expensive, but $50 billion a year is pocket change compared with what the nation is paying to cover last year's tax cuts, which will amount to more than $200 billion annually. And there is little doubt that a significant government expenditure for child-care programs would actually serve the public interest by helping to nurture and educate the future workforce—at all income levels. Universal all-day preschool, in fact, could have saved the life of 3-year-old Asan'te Burgess. Sadly, while Georgia is the only state in the country that offers universal, free preschool for 4-year-olds, the state has been unable to come up with the money to expand the program to include 3-year-olds and to make it all-day. If the federal government had filled in the gap, Asan'te would likely still be alive and playing with her new public-school classmates rather than having met an untimely death in the backseat of her mother's car.

The Media: An Ongoing Non-Debate
Ralph Nader

from *Crashing the Party*

There are a lot of bitter Democrats who still blame Ralph Nader for siphoning off the votes that might have allowed Al Gore to defeat George Bush in the 2000 presidential election. But Nader himself has consistently shrugged off this criticism, sticking to his view that there's essentially very little difference between the two major political parties and their candidates—and that he would have done even better in the election if the system hadn't been rigged against him. He expands on this last point in the following excerpt from his recent book, Crashing the Party, *in which he discusses one of the biggest challenges facing any third-party candidate: Getting coverage from the national media. . . .*

There is a major problem for anyone who runs for president, especially a third-party candidate. No matter how long or extensively you campaign in every state of the union, no matter how large your audiences become, you cannot reach in direct personal communication even 1 percent of the eligible voters. In essence, you don't run for president directly; you ask the media to run you for president or, if you have the money, you also pay the media for exposure.

Reaching the voters relies almost entirely on how the media chooses to perceive you and your campaign. In short, this "virtual reality" *is* the reality.

Since the media controls access to 99 percent-plus of your audience, it is not shocking that 99 percent of most candidates' strategies is born and bred for media play. The media is the message. When George W. Bush nuzzles next to two little schoolchildren, his handlers make sure that the AP and other photographers on his campaign have good positioning. When Al Gore stands near some national park in his L. L. Bean attire, his handlers know they succeeded only if the image and a few choice words are played throughout the country. There are very few rallies anymore. Instead there are carefully orchestrated photo opportunities that often leave some locals resentful, feeling they have been used. And, of course, they have been used, just as the candidates use journalism for their poses, or try to, and just as journalism uses them.

There can be, though, alternatives to such contrivances. The people could have their own media, a point I made repeatedly at my press conferences. The people own the airwaves. "The people are the landlords," I would say, "and the radio and television stations are the tenants. They pay us no rent to our real estate agents, the Federal Communications Commission (FCC), yet they control who says what and who doesn't, for twenty-four hours a day. What is needed are our own stations, well equipped, our own audience network, both controlled and funded by viewers. A portion of the rent that should be charged for this vast public asset, which since day one we have given away, would amplify the viewers' stations." The camera crews and attendant reporters first would appear curious, then amused, knowing that this was one long sound bite that would never make it onto the evening news. Neither did my words reach the newspaper columns. The media itself was never viewed as an issue in the campaign. A few years ago I asked a candidate why not? His reply stuck in my memory: "The media represents that part of my voice that gets through to the people. I'm not going after my voice."

There is another, much older and inexpensive way to reach people. Once under way, word of mouth is the most credible, quickest, and most lasting medium of all. It goes from friend to friend, neighbor to neighbor, worker to worker, relative to relative—between people who afford each other longtime credibility. Word of mouth goes on all the time, but it is very hard to escalate to high levels of velocity or intensity. It would take a veritable cultural revolution of civic interest, awareness, and engagement to change the tide. We are far from that nexus as a society, except for a few hot-button issues such as abortion and gun control, which possess their own intense grapevines.

In an age of deepening concentration of conglomerate media corporations, their executives have their own interests to defend and expand. More and more, newspapers, magazines, and television and radio stations are caught up in larger megacorporate strategic objectives, which shape the nature of campaign coverage. During the summer, on the television in my hotel room, I saw Sumner Redstone, boss of Viacom, which bought CBS, being interviewed about his reportedly strained relationship with CBS boss Mel Karmazin. "Nothing to it," replied Redstone. "Mel and I are both driven by our stock price." Shades of Herbert Hoover and Edward R. Murrow, who saw the public airwaves as a public trust. That being Redstone's yardstick means that hypercommercialism becomes ever more the governing standard. This results in downgrading respect for the public service requirement of the 1934 Communications Act and its famous provision for licensees to reflect "the public interest, convenience, and necessity."

When they are not merging or joint venturing, these mass communications giants are in a frantic race down the sensuality ladder, filling the airwaves with what John Nichols and Robert McChesney call the "trivial, sensational and salacious." These authors published a little paperback in the middle of the presidential campaign titled *It's the Media, Stupid*, where they illuminated the connection between "media reform and democratic renewal." This little volume is a factually immersed brief for their thesis, best expressed by their own words:

> The flow of information that is the lifeblood of democracy is being choked by a media system that every day ignores a world of injustices and inequality, and the growing resistance to it. No, the media system is not the sole cause of our political crisis, nor even the primary cause, but it reinforces every factor contributing to the crisis, and it fosters a climate in which the implementation of innovative democratic solutions is rendered all but impossible.
>
> The closer a story gets to examining corporate power the less reliable our corporate media system is as a source of information that is useful to citizens of a democracy. Commercial indoctrination of children is crucial to corporate America.

It is at least permissible to assume that corporations such as Disney, AOL-Time Warner, Rupert Murdoch's News Corporation, Viacom, Seagram (Universal), Sony, Liberty (AT&T), and General Electric, which rely heavily on corporate advertising revenue for their expenses and profits, are not likely to go out of their way to cover candidates who are critics of their major advertisers who are big contributors to both the Republican and Democratic parties. It's just simple business sense.

As these media giants become ever more global, along with global advertisers, their self-importance and impact become almost unreal. On the occasion of announcing Time Warner's merger with AOL, Time Warner CEO Gerald Levin declared exuberantly that the global media is "fast becoming the predominant business of the twenty-first century" and is "more important than government, it's more important than educational institutions and nonprofits."

Even with fewer and fewer key individuals controlling more and more print and broadcast media properties (one company now owns eleven hundred radio stations), much of their power to frame the agendas and confine the issues is the result of a two-party default. Twenty-one years ago, the especially perceptive Duke historian James David Barber wrote about the "emergence" of mass communication

> to fill virtually the whole gap in the electoral process left by the default of other independent elites who used to help manage the choice. Their power is all the stronger because it looks, to the casual observer, like no power at all. Much as the old party bosses used to pass themselves off as mere "coordinators" and powerless arrangers, so some modern-day titans of journalism want themselves thought of as mere scorekeepers and messenger boys. Yet the signs of journalists' key role as the major advancers and retarders of presidential ambitions are all around us.

In Barber's view, the political parties failed because "their giant ossified structures, like those of the dinosaurs, could no longer adapt to the pace of political change. Journalism could adapt . . . journalism took over where the parties left off."

Well, maybe some Democrats and Republicans were reading Barber, because they decided to take back from the media the management of choice in one area of crucial importance to any political challengers to them: the presidential debates. Until the late eighties, the League of Women Voters sponsored these debates. In 1980, they allowed independent candidate Congressman John Anderson to join Jimmy Carter and Ronald Reagan, which helped Anderson considerably in national recognition and the polls. At one point he scored 21 percent in the polls, and he ended up with 7 percent on Election Day. The two parties did not like the League—a nonpartisan civic group—setting the rules and running the debates. So a private corporation was formed, given the official-sounding title of the Commission on Presidential Debates (CPD) and headed by co-chairs who were the former chairmen of the Republican and Democratic National Committees. Its phony purpose was voter education. The debates cost money, so the CPD found corporations to write big checks. These firms have included Anheuser-Busch, Philip Morris, Ford Motor Co., and other companies that also gave soft money to the parties' national committees.

In 1992, Ross Perot came on the scene, and his wealth and widespread polling support led to his being allowed to join the debates. His polls went up, too. He received nineteen million votes, shaking the political establishment with his Reform Party and his paid televised lectures. Never again, vowed the two parties. Fully ninety-two million Americans saw the debate among Perot, Clinton, and Bush, more than double the average of the three 2000 debates. Too destabilizing for the duopoly. Perot was barred in 1996 by a series of vague criteria based on interviews with columnists, pollsters, and consultants who concurred that he could not win. He was also barred by the national television networks from buying the same kind of thirty-minute time slots that brought his message of deficit reduction and political reform into the living rooms of millions of households.

Speaking with him after the election, I said, "Ross, at least you've proved that the big boys can keep even a megabillionaire off the air."

In the year 2000, the CPD revised its criterion for third-party candidates: 15 percent or more as measured by the average of five private polling organizations (which just happened to be owned by several major newspaper and television conglomerates). So if their parent companies did not cover the third-party candidate, the polls would not likely move up. Without moving up, there would be little media, and so a catch-22 was built in the CPD's entry barrier. How can a private company get away with this? By virtue of the mass media default, of course. There's absolutely nothing stopping the major networks and newspapers from sponsoring their own debates.

The televised debates are the only way presidential candidates can reach tens of millions of voters. Several polls during 2000 showed a majority of the voters wanted Pat Buchanan and me at the debates, regardless of folks' voting preferences. Larger audiences and ratings would almost certainly follow. People want a wide variety of subjects, viewpoints, forthrightness, and candidates. They do not see the presidential debates as a cure for insomnia. However, the great default is now on the shoulders of the media moguls, and the major parties are back in charge of the ticket for admission to the public.

This is all about giving small starts a chance to have a chance. This does not mean that there be only three debates. It doesn't mean there are no criteria. An Appleseed Foundation project suggested in a report for campaign 2000 that candidates be included who meet one of two tests: (1) the polls show that a majority want the candidate included; and/or (2) the candidate has at least 5 percent support in the polls (the statutory minimum for receiving federal matching funds) and is on enough state ballots to theoretically be able to win a majority in the electoral college. Law professor David Kairys, who advised us on the debate matter, wrote in the *Washington Post*:

> The nation's broadcast media have so far been accomplices in this charade. CPD debates should at least be accurately labeled as Republican-Democratic campaign events, rather than as "presidential debates." . . . [T]he rules of the debates should not be left to the major parties or their handpicked representatives, who have a history of excluding candidates and ideas the public wants—and deserves—to hear.

We did not take the CPD's autocratic exclusionary mission passively. Throughout the spring, summer, and early fall of the campaign, I denounced the CPD to one rally or audience after another. We encouraged citizens to communicate with the CPD, as we did, and demand the opening of its doors to competition. I sent letters to the major networks asking them to sponsor their own multicandidate debates. Two replied sympathetically but to no result. In September, I wrote the heads of the major industrial unions in the critical, close states of the Midwest urging that they cosponsor presidential debates with special emphasis on neglected labor agendas. No one from the Steelworkers, the Machinists, the Teamsters, or the United Auto Workers responded. I urged national civil rights organizations, including the major Hispanic civil rights association in Southern California, but to no avail. Granted, they had their reasons—the CPD debates were already scheduled, logistics, and the risk of being turned down and viewed as powerless. Now, with plenty of time until 2004, I call on people and institutions who want robust and diverse debates to join together and form a People's Debate Commission.

The newspapers take elections more seriously, comparatively speaking, than the broadcast media. Television and radio have many ready-made excuses for their shrinking coverage. A twenty-two-minute national television news program, excluding advertising time, is not sprung from holy writ. The format of the local television news, with its nine minutes of ads, with several leadoff accounts from the police crime blotter, four minutes of sports, four minutes of weather, one minute of chitchat, and the prescribed animal and medical journal health story, is not carved in stone. Apart from public radio and the few nonprofit community radio stations, commercial radio and television devote about 90 percent of airtime around the clock to entertainment and advertisements. News is sparse, abbreviated, and very repetitious. When radio is not singing or selling, it is traffic, weather, and sports with headline news spots. The number of reporters and editors has been cut to the bone. No more are there FCC requirements for ascertaining the news needs of the community. Gone are the Fairness Doctrine and the Right of Reply. In 1996 there was near silence on the tube regarding the congressional fight to block the giveaway of $70 billion worth of the new spectrum to the television stations—a giveaway opposed even by the Republican candidate that year, Robert Dole. The notorious Telecommunications Act of 1996 received the cold shoulder, notwithstanding its paving the way for a massive binge of mergers and further concentration of media power. In 2000 the FCC, under its chairman, William Kennard, started granting community radio licenses to nonprofit neighborhood associations. The formidable media lobby, led by the National Association of Broadcasters, descended on Congress. They pummeled into line a majority of Congress—Democrats and Republicans—to pass legislation, which Clinton reluctantly signed, that blocked the FCC from licensing these little stations, which could accept no paid advertising. A minor Hollywood celebrity's DUI received more television and radio coverage than did the FCC's attempt to give people a radio voice of a few miles' radius.

After dealing with reporters, editors, producers, and media honchos for nearly forty years, and being a reporter and columnist myself, I had few illusions about the difficulties in obtaining a fair quantity and quality of coverage for our campaign. Making any challenge to the existing two-party hegemony is akin to climbing a sheer cliff with a slippery rope. No other democracy in the world erects so many barriers and is so uncongenial to small political starts. From the starting gate, the major parties radiate the message to all the media that no one but them has a chance to make it a contest, much less to win. This easily convinces the media powers that a small-party candidate doesn't merit coverage because he or she can't possibly win. This produces the most insurmountable obstacle of all, which is the virtual lock enjoyed by the two major parties on coverage in the national media. We are left with the old chicken-egg routine. Waiting for poll risings to receive coverage means no poll activity due to little coverage.

We were quite aware of conventional media mind-sets and routines. There was, even among the more competent and experienced news reporters and columnists, what people inside the fourth estate have called "blackbird journalism." One blackbird takes off and the rest follow. This phenomenon is hardly counteracted by the smaller, community media or magazines like *The Nation* or *The Progressive,* which are so often ahead of the news curve. It is entrenched through horizontal peer dynamics. The *Washington Post* looks over the shoulder of the *New York Times* and vice versa, and the national networks read both papers every morning to see what is deemed significant. I came across a nearly perfect passage from James Barber's *The Pulse of Politics: Electing Presidents in the Media Age* that speaks to all of this:

> Journalism's strength is not theory but fact. . . . A war over the facts, every four years, could help journalism break out of its losing preoccupation with the nuances of hypothetical opinion, symbolic epistemology, electoral bookie work, and the tired search for someone to quote, and do what it does best: get relevant information, quickly and accurately. Citizens, now woefully mis- and un- and under-informed on the way things work, . . . might begin to see through the fog of rhetoric to the shape of reality. The drama of revelation might grip the public imagination a good deal more firmly than do the campaign gossip and ideological chit-chat that now drone through so many eminently forgettable paragraphs.

That is the point, isn't it? Journalism should give at least equal attention to the messages as it does to the carrier, if not more. Abraham Lincoln once said that if brought the "real facts," the people "can be depended upon to meet any national crisis."

Take a simple numerical hypothetical. Suppose a first-time candidate for the presidency, running as an independent, marshaled ten thousand super-energetic volunteers to work on one objective: registering at least two hundred thousand voters a week, week after week. The candidate didn't show in the polls, had no track record of successful advocacy, and never held public office. Should the media give that candidate regular coverage? Surely, the difficulty of getting any significant number of the one hundred million people who stay home from the polls has puzzled everyone. This candidate seemed to be achieving something that has eluded very experienced and well-funded people and candidacies for decades. In so doing, dozens of interesting stories about this amazing performance were there for reporters to gather. Thinking outside the box may happen in some classes in journalism school but rarely at the news and editorial desks of the news business.

This is not to say that the major media organizations failed to cover our campaign. They did. But they consistently viewed it as an occasional feature story—a modestly colorful narrative dispatch from the trail with a marginal candidate—rather than a news story about our agenda. During the months when I was traveling throughout the fifty states, the local press usually reported on the visits. In contrast, the national print and electronic media was capricious. It would parachute in a reporter to travel with us for a day or two and file a profile that focused on the so-called spoiler issue. We were never a news beat, even when the margins narrowed between Al Gore and George W. Bush during the last month and made our voters very consequential. So much so that a radio reporter in Washington, D.C., about a week before the election preposterously asked, "How does it feel to be the most powerful politician in America?" I demurred and returned to our fourteen-seat van for reporters, which was more than half empty.

In April, the first poll (Zogby) came out and put us at over 5 percent nationwide. Our audiences were growing and we had an exhaustive agenda—much of which we had worked on for years—that was of compelling concern to millions of Americans. These were topics that, over the years, many news outlets had reported on, investigated, and editorialized about. Bush and Gore were either dismissing us or taking positions opposite ours. Their poor respective records gave further credibility to our agenda. We had a long track record, and we weren't offering easy rhetoric. And, as the weeks unfolded, the Nader-LaDuke ticket was qualifying on forty-three state ballots and the District of Columbia, far exceeding any potential electoral college majority.

I paid a visit in May to Jim Roberts, the political editor of the mighty *New York Times*. Unlike some reporters and editors at the *Times*, Roberts appeared genuinely open to our requests for more regular coverage. I asked him whether the *Times* had any overall newsworthiness criteria for covering significant third-party candidates. He allowed that there were no specific standards, implying that *Times* editors made judgment calls as events unfolded. When I asked, for example, what would qualify as a newsworthy event in our case, he replied, "If you do anything with Pat Buchanan, or when you campaign in California, I'd be interested." At the time, California was considered a must-win state for Gore's campaign and favorable territory for our candidacy.

I often asked newspaper editorial boards across the country what I had to do to be more newsworthy. The responses were either noncommittal or related to our effect on the Gore-Bush competition. One would think that merely to escape the tedium, the press would declare itself some holidays from the horse-race question. Imagine their business reporters interviewing the CEO of a corporate start-up like RealNetworks' Robert Glaser in competition with Microsoft with the query, "Mr. Glaser, aren't you worried about taking dollars away from Bill Gates and Microsoft?"

The media handlers for Bush and Gore knew that politics is theater and entertainment, and their candidate had to get on the late-night comic shows and some of the more sane daytime talk shows. So both Bush and Gore got on, at least once and sometimes twice, the Jay Leno and David Letterman shows, where they could deliver their well-rehearsed jokes or Top Tens. In mid-September, both Gore and Bush appeared on *Oprah*. Bush won that round among the pundits by greeting Oprah with a kiss and discussing his giving up alcohol at age forty. He told the audience that he was not "running on Daddy's name." And he showed tears in eyes when he discussed the joyous birth of his twin daughters. That was the point of appearing on these shows—laughs, emotion, a little self-deprecation, and very little on the issues. In previous presidential campaigns, invitations by Phil Donahue meant tough questioning by the host and by members of the audience if they so chose. Today, the main challenge is to be funny, to appear congenial, and to confess a little as if you are the interviewed celebrity on the cover of *Parade* magazine.

Well, I decided to make the trek and asked these shows to have me on. First was Bill Maher of *Politically Incorrect*, which Gore and Bush steered away from. I mean, could you imagine either of them exposing himself to Bill and three other wildcat guests? Bill is very perceptive—he voted for me.

Then I went on Jay Leno, who does go into the green room with the guests to chat, and David Letterman, who does not. Probably the latter approach makes for more spontaneity—at least it did for me. Both appearances went well. Then there was *Saturday Night Live,* my fourth visit since 1977, where I did my five-minute sketch about being excluded from the debates, with Rob Lowe and the show's originator, Canadian Lorne Michaels. The impersonations of Bush and Gore by Will Ferrell and Darrell Hammond were side-splitters and deserved the media's—and the candidates'—attention.

After learning that Bush and Gore were invited on *Oprah,* with its large afternoon following, our press office asked if there was a chance for me to go on too. After all, when Oprah was a lonely talk-show host in Baltimore, well before she made the big time in Chicago, I gladly appeared on her small program. So we tried to penetrate the show's iron curtain. Like most of today's daytime television shows, just getting through to a live person, much less getting a response, is next to impossible. Oprah's people were no exception. Calls, letters—it didn't matter how or who—there was not the courtesy of a reply. Disappointing but not surprising. Oprah never replied after I wrote and spoke in her defense when she was frivolously sued by Texas beef businesses for her famous show on the negative side of eating meat.

A new entry to daytime television, the *Queen Latifah Show* in New York City, offered greater promise. The staff was responsive, courteous, and professional. With the added delight of being joined by Susan Sarandon and Phil Donahue, we had a serious and enjoyable half hour with Queen Latifah.

The *Charlie Rose Show*—one of the last serious national television interview programs—told us in May that they wanted me for a full hour. When we finally found a date of mutual convenience, they promised thirty minutes. When I got to the studio, it was reduced to fifteen minutes. Charlie loves to interview actors, actresses, prominent authors, diplomats, and corporate executives, but he doesn't much like talking about corporate domination of society. Once when I prevailed on him to have Jim Hightower, William Greider, and me—corporate critics all—on the show, he put us all together for fifteen minutes sandwiched between two new novelists whose works he probably could no longer remember three years later. There was a great response to our segment the following day. The show's producer, in a message inadvertently sent to us, told her associates that viewer reactions were probably orchestrated. Sometimes you can't win.

Cleaning the Pool
Matt Taibbi

New York Press | March 12, 2003

In the wickedly witty commentary he writes for the New York Press, Matt Taibbi often picks up on political angles that more mainstream publications have overlooked. In this column, he zeroes in on a doozy: A blatantly stage-managed presidential "press conference," in which George W. Bush and the White House press corps play out a new form of kabuki theater. . . .

After watching George W. Bush's press conference last Thursday night, I'm more convinced than ever: The entire White House press corps should be herded into a cargo plane, flown to an altitude of 30,000 feet, and pushed out, kicking and screaming, over the North Atlantic.

Any remaining staff at the Washington bureaus should be rounded up for summary justice. The Russians used to use bakery trucks, big gray panel trucks marked "Bread" on the sides; victims would be rounded up in the middle of the night and taken for one last ride through the darkened streets.

The war would almost be worth it just to see Wolf Blitzer pounding away at the inside of a Pepperidge Farm truck, tearfully confessing and vowing to "take it all back."

The Bush press conference to me was like a mini-Alamo for American journalism, a final announcement that the press no longer performs anything akin to a real function. Particularly revolting was the spectacle of the cream of the national press corps submitting politely to the indignity of obviously pre-approved questions, with Bush not even bothering to conceal that the affair was scripted.

Abandoning the time-honored pretense of spontaneity, Bush chose the order of questioners not by scanning the room and picking out raised hands, but by looking down and reading from a predetermined list. Reporters, nonetheless, raised their hands in between questions—as though hoping to suddenly catch the president's attention.

In other words, not only were reporters going out of their way to make sure their softballs were pre-approved, but they even went so far as to *act* on Bush's behalf, raising their hands and jockeying in their seats in order to better give the appearance of a spontaneous news conference.

Even Bush couldn't ignore the absurdity of it all. In a remarkable exchange that somehow managed to avoid being commented upon in news accounts the next day, Bush chided CNN political correspondent John King when the latter overacted his part, too enthusiastically waving his hand when it apparently was, according to the script, his turn anyway.

KING: "Mr. President."

BUSH: "We'll be there in a minute. King, John King. This is a scripted..."

A ripple of nervous laughter shot through the East Room. Moments later, the camera angle of the conference shifted to a side shot, revealing a ring of potted plants around the presidential podium. It would be hard to imagine an image that more perfectly describes American political journalism today: George Bush, surrounded by a row of potted plants, in turn surrounded by the White House press corps.

Newspapers the next day ignored the scripted-question issue completely. (King himself, incidentally, left it out of his *CNN.com* report.) Of the major news services and dailies, only one—the *Washington Post*—even parenthetically addressed the issue. Far down in Dana Milbank and Mike Allen's conference summary, the paper euphemistically commented:

"The president followed a script of names in choosing which reporters could ask him a question, and he received *generally friendly questioning*." [Emphasis mine] "Generally friendly questioning" is an understatement if there ever was one. Take this offering by April Ryan of the American Urban Radio Networks:

"Mr. President, as the nation is at odds over war, with many organizations like the Congressional Black Caucus pushing for continued diplomacy through the U.N., how is your faith guiding you?"

Great. In Bush's first press conference since his decision to support a rollback of affirmative action, the first black reporter to get a crack at him—and this is what she comes up with? The journalistic equivalent of "Mr. President, you look great today. What's your secret?"

Newspapers across North America scrambled to roll the highlight tape of Bush knocking Ryan's question out of the park. The *Boston Globe*: "As Bush stood calmly at the presidential lectern, tears welled in his eyes when he was asked how his faith was guiding him . . ." The *Globe and Mail*: "With tears welling in his eyes, Mr. Bush said he prayed daily that war can be averted . . ."

Even worse were the qualitative assessments in the major dailies of Bush's performance. As I watched the conference, I was sure I was witnessing, live, an historic political catastrophe. In his best moments Bush was deranged and uncommunicative, and in his worst moments, which were most of the press conference, he was swaying side to side like a punch-drunk fighter, at times slurring his words and seemingly clinging for dear life to the verbal oases of phrases like "total disarmament," "regime change," and "mass destruction."

He repeatedly declined to answer direct questions. At one point, when a reporter twice asked if Bush could consider the war a success if Saddam Hussein were not captured or killed, Bush answered: "Uh, we will be changing the regime of Iraq, for the good of the Iraqi people."

Yet the closest thing to a negative characterization of Bush's performance in the major outlets was in David Sanger and Felicity Barringer's *New York Times* report, which called Bush "sedate": "Mr. Bush, sounding sedate at a rare prime-time news conference, portrayed himself as the protector of the country . . ."

Apparently even this absurdly oblique description, which ran on the *Times* website hours after the press conference, was too much for the paper's editors. Here is how that passage read by the time the papers hit the streets the next morning:

"Mr. Bush, at a rare prime-time press conference, portrayed himself as the protector of the country . . ."

Meanwhile, those aspects of Bush's performance that the White House was clearly anxious to call attention to were reported enthusiastically. It was obvious that Bush had been coached to dispense with two of his favorite public speaking tricks—his perma-smirk and his finger-waving cowboy one-liners. Bush's somber new "war is hell" act was much commented upon, without irony, in the post-mortems.

Appearing on *Hardball* after the press conference, *Newsweek*'s Howard Fineman (one of the worst monsters of the business) gushed when asked if the Bush we'd just seen was really a "cowboy":

"If he's a cowboy he's the reluctant warrior, he's Shane . . . because he has to, to protect his family."

Newsweek thinks Bush is Shane?

This was just Bush's eighth press conference since taking office, and each one of them has been a travesty. In his first presser, on Feb. 22, 2001, a month after his controversial inauguration, he was not asked a single question about the election, Al Gore, or the Supreme Court. On the other hand, he was asked five questions about Bill Clinton's pardons.

Reporters argue that they have no choice. They'll say they can't protest or boycott the staged format, because they risk being stripped of their seat in the press pool. For the same reason, they say they can't write anything too negative. They can't write, for instance, "President Bush, looking like a demented retard on the eve of war . . ." That leaves them with the sole option of "working within the system" and, as they like to say, "trying to take our shots when we can."

But the White House press corps' idea of "taking a shot" is David Sanger asking Bush what he thinks of British foreign minister Jack Straw saying that regime change was not necessarily a war goal. And then meekly sitting his ass back down when Bush ignores the question.

They can't write what they think, and can't ask real questions. What the hell *are* they doing there? If the answer is "their jobs," it's about time we started wondering what that means.

The Most Dangerous Branch?
Simon Lazarus

The Atlantic Monthly | June 2002

Trying to divine the philosophical drift of the Supreme Court is high sport in Washington's legal circles. Typically, the analysis breaks down along the lines of conservative vs. liberal. According to this perspective, Chief Justice William Rehnquist, Antonin Scalia, and Clarence Thomas make up the conservative team, while the liberal squad consists of Stephen Breyer, Ruth Bader Ginsburg, David Souter, and John Paul Stevens. Sandra Day O'Connor and Anthony Kennedy are the swing votes, though more often or not they can be expected to side with the conservatives (as they did in Bush v. Gore*).*

In this essay, however, lawyer and former Carter administration staffer Simon Lazarus offers a more unorthodox take on the long-range aims of the Court's "conservative" wing. The conclusion he comes to is startling: In Lazarus's view, the ultimate project of Rehnquist, et al., is not merely to roll back the liberal activism of earlier Courts, but to sharply limit the powers of the Federal government itself. . . .

In Saturday, December 9, 2000, literally minutes before the United States Supreme Court issued its startling 5-4 decision to stay the Florida presidential-ballot recount, I happened to be chatting about the case after tennis with a senior Clinton Administration legal official. Without hesitation my tennis partner, a canny political insider and a seasoned Supreme Court litigator, forecast victory for Gore. The Florida court, he assured a rapt locker-room audience, had "bullet-proofed" its opinion with an elaborate exegesis of the state's complex electoral statutes; no way would conservative justices, whose deference to state prerogatives was well known, second-guess a state supreme court's painstaking interpretation of its own state's laws.

My friend turned out to be wrong, of course—and he wasn't alone. Nearly all mainstream legal experts were blindsided by *Bush v. Gore*.

The decision should not have come as a surprise. For several years now judicial conservatives have been marching to a new and very different drummer, but to date only a tiny, mostly academic cadre of astute Court watchers has grasped the content and the implications of the Supreme Court majority's agenda. To be sure, the intense partisan struggle over President Bush's judicial nominees has not gone unnoticed. But the media and most politicians simply assume that they're witnessing a recycling of the high-decibel constitutional controversies and judicial-nomination struggles of the 1970s and 1980s. Indeed, President Bush has constantly reiterated his goal of naming "strict constructionists" to the federal bench, and has cited Supreme Court Justices Antonin Scalia and Clarence Thomas as model nominees. In fact, however, Scalia, Thomas, and their ideological followers on and off the Court have a very different view of their judicial philosophy. "I am not a strict constructionist," Scalia has written, "and no one ought to be."

Most observers surmise that the President has in mind candidates who would overturn *Roe v. Wade*, the landmark 1973 decision that made abortion a constitutional right, and other bold Bill of Rights interpretations of that era. But the architects of *Bush v. Gore* have a radically different set of priorities. Their focus is not on dismantling the edifice of "rights" built by "activist" liberal judges when Earl Warren and Warren Burger presided over the Supreme Court—indeed, this majority has often defended free-speech, privacy, and due-process safeguards against the claims of aggressive legis-latures and prosecutors. Rather, their focus is on the scope of government power. Brandishing a starkly devolutionist concept of federalism, these new conservatives question decisions as far back as the 1930s that legitimated the New Deal and the Great Society, and that empower Congress to legislate on essentially any matter of national concern. The new credo differs sharply from the judicial restraint practiced by conservative justices such as Burger and Lewis Powell and articulated by the late Yale professor Alexander M. Bickel in his landmark treatise, *The Least Dangerous Branch* (1962).

Clarence Thomas is almost invariably allied with Scalia in expounding and extending this new federalist agenda. Joining in nearly as frequently, but with independent views, is Chief Justice William Rehnquist. More often than not this trio brings Justices Anthony Kennedy and Sandra Day O'Connor with it—though both sometimes balk at the philosophical claims and practical objectives of their colleagues. Off the Court the majority's themes resonate in the rulings of certain federal appellate judges, in conferences and publi-cations of the conservative lawyers' Federalist Society, and in voluminous pub-lished works of conservative scholars at think tanks and universities.

Broad attention to the ideas propounded in these quarters is overdue. If those ideas are substantially realized, they will threaten the viability of major programs in fields as diverse as civil rights, environmental protection, health, and education—in particular the national testing requirements that form the core of President Bush's new No Child Left Behind law. Equally at risk are pending or likely proposals for federal action on such pressing national con-cerns as cloning and homeland security.

Champions of this new federalism first proclaimed its far-reaching scope and signaled their intense commitment to its principles in two 1995 cases—neither of which stirred significant public attention at the time. In *United States v. Lopez* the 5-4 majority that went on to decide *Bush v. Gore* ruled that Congress's constitutional power to regulate interstate commerce did not jus-tify the Gun Free School Zones Act of 1990, which banned possession of a firearm within a thousand feet of a school. The specific holding of this case was narrow enough to permit Congress to salvage the law with minor tech-nical changes. Nevertheless, the decision provoked an impassioned intramural debate on the Court, spanning six opinions and ninety-five pages in the *United States Supreme Court Reports*. Writing for the majority, Rehnquist dwelt only briefly on the gun ban itself; his real concern, he made clear, was to ensure that this federal remedy for school violence not set a precedent for "direct" federal regulation of the "educational process," such as a "mandate[d] federal curriculum for local elementary and secondary schools."

In dissent, Justice Stephen Breyer argued that Congress could readily find a "direct economic link between basic education and industrial productivity." (And indeed, six years after *Lopez*, precisely because of the widely perceived link between education standards and economic productivity, Bush proposed and Congress enacted mandatory national testing requirements to upgrade public school performance.) But to Rehnquist, it was simply irrelevant that Congress might rationally conclude that education materially affects the economy. In terms calculated to reverberate through decades of opinions to come, he wrote, "We start with first principles. The Constitution creates a Federal Government of enumerated powers." The enumerated powers do not include non-economic subjects, such as the regulation of local school curricula, over which the states "historically have been sovereign," and which "the States may regulate but Congress may not."

Rehnquist's zeal to wall off traditional state responsibilities from federal authority was reinforced by Thomas in a dissent to a second 1995 decision, *U.S. Term Limits, Inc. v. Thornton*. In this case a 5-4 majority—in which Kennedy voted with the four "liberal" members of the Court—barred states from imposing term limits on their congressional representatives. In his opinion, which was joined by Scalia, Rehnquist, and O'Connor, Thomas wrote that the concept of exclusive state jurisdiction, described by Rehnquist in *Lopez*, extends, "either expressly or by necessary implication," to all areas that the original Framers of the Constitution neglected to name. Elaborating, he asserted that "the notion of popular sovereignty that undergirds the Constitution does not erase state boundaries, but rather tracks them." In other words, when the Framers wrote "We the People," they meant not we the people of a unified nation but we the people of each state. This theory reduces "We the People" to a meaningless rhetorical flourish; the Constitution and the federal government it creates are not instruments of the American people but creatures exclusively of—and hence decidedly junior to—the states and their governments.

Although eye-catching, such attempts to recast the theoretical limits of federal power are less significant than the operational question of who—Congress or the Court—should decide what those limits are. If there is, to use Rehnquist's term, a "first principle" of the post-New Deal concept of constitutional governance, surely it is that the people's elected representatives, not life-tenured judicial appointees, should determine what problems the federal government will address and where in the federal system to assign responsibility.

For the first third of the twentieth century a conservative Supreme Court enforced a laissez-faire ideology by blocking federal regulatory initiatives on federalist grounds. But in 1937, under pressure from President Franklin Roosevelt, the Court changed its tune. Since that time the nation has engaged in innumerable debates about the proper allocation of power between federal and state governments. These debates have spanned virtually all areas of domestic policy—health, education, environmental protection, discrimination, law enforcement, and, currently, euthanasia, abortion, and cloning. But the debates have never been about whether Congress *can* impose national standards; they have been about whether it *should*. All sides have assumed that Congress has the constitutional authority to address any problem of national importance.

This was the bedrock assumption that the *Lopez* majority challenged as a violation of constitutional "first principles." It is a challenge that has brought the nation close to a point where Congress could find itself virtually unable to pass laws regulating any non-economic matters. The majority opinion in *Lopez* indicated that such matters are inherently those that "States may regulate but Congress may not." Combine that with the February 2001 decision in *Board of Trustees of the University of Alabama v. Garrett*, which barred application of the Americans With Disabilities Act to state employees, and which ruled that even meticulously documented default by state governments will not necessarily permit federal intrusion on state sovereignty to enforce the Fourteenth Amendment. Add the notion—sometimes invoked by the Court majority and frequently repeated by advocates of federalism on the lower federal courts and elsewhere—that control of areas such as education and law enforcement is the states' "sovereign" prerogative. The result could be that non-economic regulatory laws such as the ADA and the Endangered Species Act become flatly unconstitutional.

As the Yale scholar Bruce Ackerman has shown, the United States has several times cast aside one working model of the Constitution and replaced it with another, each time through a highly political process that has involved Congress, the presidency, and elections as well as the Supreme Court. The most recent makeover occurred in the late 1930s and the 1940s, when the Supreme Court was driven to accommodate the New Deal.

The nation may have arrived at a new constitutional watershed. The question of the moment is whether the confirmation process for Bush's judicial nominees will spark a vigorous debate on the merits of the new conservative jurisprudence. The issue is not achieving "balance" on the courts between "liberal" and "conservative" judges, as some Democratic senators and liberal professors have suggested. If Americans elect Republican Presidents, they can expect Republican judges. The issue is the specific agenda of this particular genre of judicial conservatives. Their predecessors were more hard-nosed about the Bill of Rights than their liberal counterparts, but they preached deference to the political branches, and they worked within the post-New Deal constitutional regime. Rehnquist, Scalia, Thomas, and their allies consider themselves outside the consensus that supports that regime. They are working to change it.

At some point groups across the political spectrum will be forced to recalibrate their interest in this debate as they grasp their stakes in such questions as Is the United States a unified democratic nation or, as the Federalist Society claims, a "Federal Republic," in which autonomous state governments are the sole forum for addressing a wide range of issues? Can the electorate discipline the federal establishment, or is active Court intervention necessary, as the libertarian Cato Institute contends, to "constrain government growth"? Is it unrealistic to retain James Madison's belief, expressed in *The Federalist* No. 46, that in allocating federal and state functions the people should be free to give "most of their confidence where they may discover it to be most due"? May Congress determine that effective education requires national testing standards, or that anti-terrorist measures require background checks by local police departments on arrestees, gun buyers, or other groups? Do the states need the courts to protect them from congressional overreaching?

Ultimately, this debate is about democracy—about what the defining elements of our constitutional scheme are and, in particular, what place democracy occupies in it. In a recent speech at New York University, Justice Breyer suggested that the Constitution should be understood primarily as an engine for promoting "democratic self-government." The Constitution itself (and, implicitly, a Court administering it), Breyer said, "does not resolve, and was not intended to resolve, society's problems" but rather "provides a *framework* for the creation of *democratically determined solutions* [italics added]."

Many observers may wonder, What's the big deal? Isn't this obvious? But one suspects that Breyer felt compelled to make this statement because three of his colleagues on the Court disagree and two others are not sure where they stand.

As the New York University professor Larry Kramer has noted, activist conservatives argue that it is *exclusively* the province of the judiciary—not of Congress, the President, or the states—to say what the Constitution means. They do not view federal lawmaking as a process in which the various interests, including state governments and agencies, arrive at "democratically determined solutions." On the contrary, they view Congress through the lens of economic libertarianism and its cousin, "public-choice theory," which cast legislatures as irredeemably warped by the parochial machinations of interest groups and self-seeking officials. New federalists treat the legislative process as merely a first step toward giving the courts the final word on what the law is.

How far will the Court pursue its federalist project? Will it ultimately align the law with the conservative Northwestern law professor Gary Lawson's view that "the post-New Deal administrative state is unconstitutional"? Will the velocity of change increase if the current, shaky 5-4 majority becomes a rock-solid 6-3 or 7-2? Or will Justice O'Connor or Justice Kennedy team with pragmatic conservative appointees and centrists in the current minority to shape a moderate, "mend it, don't end it" approach to federal regulatory excess? The bet here is that the new federalists will continue on their way without missing a beat absent engagement in the issue by the President or Congress. And if *Bush v. Gore* taught us anything, it is that when Justices Rehnquist, Scalia, and Thomas know their destination, they will not worry about breaking doctrinal china to get there.

One Big Happy Prison

Michael Moore

from *Stupid White Men*

Michael Moore is best-known for his film documentaries, including the recent Oscar-winning Bowling for Columbine. *But the self-styled working-class muckraker also topped the literary best-seller list last year with his book* Stupid White Men...and Other Sorry Excuses for the State of the Nation! *In the following excerpt, Moore cites some shocking examples of how our nation's judicial system tends to railroad the poor—a process he calls "ethnic cleansing, American style."* . . .

It was a few minutes after 10:00 P.M. on October 4, 2000, one month before the presidential election. The previous night, the first of three debates between Al Gore and George W. Bush had taken place.

On this balmy October evening in Lebanon, Tennessee, John Adams, sixty-four, had just sat down in his favorite tan recliner to watch the evening news. His cane, the result of a stroke a few years earlier, rested beside him. A well-respected member of Lebanon's African-American community, Adams was now on disability after working for years at the Precision Rubber plant.

The anchors on TV were dishing out their postmortems on the debate. Adams and his wife, Lorine, were discussing their intention to vote for Al Gore when there was a knock at the door. Mrs. Adams left the room, came to the door, and asked who was there. Two men demanded that she open the door and let them in. She asked again who they were, but they refused to identify themselves. She again refused to open the door.

At that moment, two unidentified officers from the Lebanon Police Department's drug task force broke down the door, grabbed Mrs. Adams, and immediately handcuffed her. Seven other officers burst into the house. Two of them ran around the corner into the back room, guns drawn, and pumped several bullets into John Adams. Three hours later, he was pronounced dead at Vanderbilt University Medical Center.

The raid on the Adams house had been ordered after an undercover informant purchased drugs in the house at 1120 Joseph Street. Lebanon's narcotics unit, funded along with thousands of others around the country as part of the Clinton administration's "War on Drugs," obtained warrants from a local judge to arrest the occupants of the house.

The only problem: the Adamses live at 70 Joseph Street. The drug-war police had the wrong house.

A few miles down the road in Nashville, as John Adams was being accidentally executed, scores of paid and volunteer staff bustled about inside Al Gore's national campaign headquarters. Their main concern that night was damage control, as they tried to distract voters from the spectacle of their candidate sighing through Bush's responses the previous night. Phones were lighting up, shipments of bumper stickers and yard signs were being rerouted, strategists were huddling to plan the next day's campaign stops. On the table sat copies of Gore's anticrime proposals, including more funding for additional police and more money to fight the Drug War. None of them knew that their out-of-control efforts to eradicate drugs had just cost them a potential vote—that of an elderly black man across town.

Killing off your voters is no way to win an election.

This was just one of too many incidents in recent years where innocent people have been shot by local or federal drug police who thought they "had their man."

Worse still is the way so many citizens have been locked up in the past decade thanks to Clinton/Gore policies. At the beginning of the nineties, there were about a million people in prison in the United States. By the end of the Clinton/Gore years, that number had grown to TWO MILLION. The bulk of this increase was the result of new laws being enforced against drug *users*, not pushers. Eighty percent of those who go to prison for drugs are in there for possession, not dealing. The penalties for crack use are three times as high as those for cocaine use.

It doesn't take much to figure out why the drug of choice in the white community is treated with so much more leniency than the drug that constitutes the only affordable high in the poor black and Hispanic community. For eight years there was an intense, aggressive move to lock up as many of these minority citizens as possible. Instead of providing the treatment their condition demands, we dealt with the problem by sending them to rot inside a prison cell.

But forget for a moment about helping the less fortunate. Who was the genius in the Clinton/Gore administration who said, "Hey, I've got an idea— why don't we go after the black and Hispanic community—plenty of drug users there! Lock 'em up in record numbers, decimating the voting power of a group that votes for our side nine to one!"

It doesn't make sense, does it? What kind of campaign would purposely destroy its own voting base? You don't see Republicans sitting around trying to plot ways to incarcerate corporate executives and NRA members. Trust me, you won't see Karl Rove convening a White House meeting to figure out a way to lock up and strip the voting rights from a million members of the Christian Coalition.

In fact, just the opposite. The Bush people are committed to seeing that none of their supporters ever enjoys the hospitality of a prison shower room. Much was made after Clinton left office of the pardons he granted to dubious fat cats like Marc Rich. The entire country was up in arms over the absolution given to a fugitive who got away without paying his taxes. A rich person who got away without paying taxes! We were shocked—SHOCKED!

And yet no attention at all was paid to the "pardons" of David Lamp, Vincent Mietlicki, John Wadsworth, or James Weathers Jr. And no one called for a congressional investigation of why criminal charges were dropped against Koch Industries, the largest privately held oil company in America, whose CEO and vice president are the brothers Charles and David Koch. Why was this?

Because *those* "pardons" came during the reign of George W. Bush.

In September 2000, the federal government brought a 97-count indictment against Koch Industries and its four employees—Lamp, Mietlicki, Wadsworth, and Weathers, who were Koch's environmental and plant managers—for *knowingly* releasing 91 metric tons of benzene, a cancer-causing agent, into the air and water, and for covering up the deadly release from federal regulators.

This wasn't Koch's first run-in with the law; it wasn't even their first *that year*. Earlier in 2000, Koch had been fined $35 million for illegal pollution in six states.

But with George W. Bush's election "decided," Koch's fortunes suddenly changed. Koch executives had just contributed some $800,000 to Bush's presidential campaign and other Republican candidates and causes. In January, as John Ashcroft waited in the wings, the government dropped the charges first from 97 to 11 and then to a mere nine.

Koch Industries, however, still faced fines totaling $352 million. Bush's new administration, now firmly in place, quickly fixed that. In March, they dropped two more charges. Then, two days before the case was to go to court, Ashcroft's Justice Department settled the case.

Koch Industries pled guilty to a new charge of falsifying documents, and the government dropped all environmental charges against the company, including all felony counts against their four employees.

Following hard on the heels of their generosity, the Koch executives facing possible prison terms were freed from any prosecution. The company itself had all 90 of the serious counts against it dismissed and in the end paid a fine that wiped out the 7 remaining counts. According to the *Houston Chronicle*, "Koch executives celebrated the conclusion of the case," company spokesman Jay Rosser crowing about how the dropping of charges was proof of Koch's "vindication."

I won't defend the actions of Marc Rich, but correct me if I'm wrong: I believe the willful spewing into the air and water of a deadly chemical that causes cancer (and will surely contribute to who knows how many people's deaths) is a little more serious than skipping out on Rudy Giuliani to go on an eighteen-year ski trip to Switzerland. Yet I'm sure none of you have heard of the pardons granted to Charles and David Koch and their oil company and its executives. Why should you? It was just business as usual, under a national press that's thoroughly asleep at the wheel.

It's too bad that Anthony Lemar Taylor forgot to send in his contribution to the Bush campaign. Taylor was another repeat offender—a petty thief who decided one day in 1999 to pretend he was golf superstar Tiger Woods.

Though Taylor looked nothing at all like Woods (but, hey, they all look alike, don't they?), he was able to use a fake driver's license and credit cards identifying him as Tiger Woods to purchase a 70-inch TV, a few stereos, and a used luxury car.

Then somebody finally figured out he wasn't Tiger Woods, and he was arrested and tried for theft and perjury.

His sentence? TWO HUNDRED YEARS TO LIFE!

You read it right. Two hundred years to life, thanks to California's "three-strikes" law, which says that upon a third criminal conviction, you're put away for life. To date, no corporate executive has been sent away for life after being caught three times polluting a river or ripping off its customers. In America, we reserve that special treatment for those who happen to be poor or African-American or fail to contribute to one of our fine political parties.

Of course, sometimes the justice system, ever the steamroller, is so hell-bent on punishing the have-nots it doesn't care who it locks up, guilty or not.

Kerry Sanders, the youngest child of nine, suffered from paranoid schizophrenia. By the age of twenty-seven he had fought the demons in his mind for over seven years and had been in and out of mental institutions for much of that time. Sometimes, when he went off his medication, he would end up on the streets of Los Angeles, as he did one day in October 1993.

While sleeping on a bench outside the USC Medical Center, Kerry was arrested for trespassing. But Kerry's luck turned worse when a routine warrant check showed that one Robert Sanders, a career criminal, had escaped five weeks earlier from a New York State prison, where he was serving time for attempting to kill a man over cocaine in 1990.

Of course, Kerry Sanders of California wasn't Robert Sanders of New York. But I guess "Kerry" and "Robert" are close enough, and California and New York . . . well, um, they're both BIG STATES, after all. . . .

Unfortunately for Kerry, what he *did* share with Robert was a birthday.

That was enough for the L.A. cop, even though the same computerized warrant search showed that *Kerry* Sanders had been stopped for jaywalking on a Los Angeles street in July 1993—while *Robert* Sanders was still in his New York prison.

No matter: Kerry Sanders was sent to New York to serve out Robert Sanders's sentence. He remained in the New York penitentiary for *two years*, while his mother searched all over Los Angeles for him. Somehow the L.A. cops failed to compare the two records—which would have revealed that their guy had the wrong fingerprints.

Kerry had only one person in the whole process who was supposed to help him—the public defender appointed to protect his interests. But this thirty-year veteran PD encouraged him *not* to fight extradition. The PD explained to Kerry that fighting back would only prolong his stay in the L.A. county jail before being returned to New York anyway. Apparently the PD didn't even notice that Kerry was "slow," much less suffering from severe mental illness. Or would it have even mattered?

The PD failed to ask basic questions. He failed to spend more than a brief few minutes with a helpless client. He never looked into whether Kerry had any family who might be contacted to assist in his defense.

The PD also failed to check the system for any pending cases, or a prior record, or his client's financial status. He didn't even take the time to match the description on the warrant with Kerry, much less demand a fingerprint or booking photo comparison. *So what*, you say? After all, both men were black; they were both the same age—they even shared a birthdate! Isn't that good enough?

It gets worse. During the hearing to waive Kerry Sanders's right to fight the New York extradition, he was asked to sign a form. The form read: "I, *Robert* Sanders, do hereby freely and voluntarily state that I am the identical Robert Sanders"—and then Kerry signed it "Kerry Sanders."

He also drew doodles all over one copy of the waiver.

No bells? No red flags? Not for this public defender!

Finally given his chance to appear before a judge, Kerry was asked if he had read the document he had signed. He said he had not. The judge stopped the extradition proceeding.

"Did *you* sign it?" asked the judge.

"Yeah," Kerry replied.

"Why did you sign it?"

"Because they told me to sign it," Kerry Sanders answered.

Kerry's public defender was ordered by the judge to review the form again with his client. Within minutes the judge was satisfied, and both the court and the public defender moved on to the next case.

After Kerry Sanders was sold down the river by his L.A. public defender, he was shipped across the country to spend the next two years in Green Haven maximum-security prison, sixty miles north of New York City, where he was sexually assaulted by other inmates.

In October 1995, after federal agents in Cleveland arrested the *real* Robert Sanders, Kerry Sanders was reunited with his mother, Mary Sanders Lee. Had it not been for the chance arrest of Robert Sanders, Kerry Sanders would still be in prison today.

Kerry was sent home from Green Haven with $48.13, a plastic bag with some medicine, a soda, and a pack of cigarettes. He told his sister, Roberta: "They took me to New York. It was so cold there. They put me in this little room."

This is not a rare case of the system making a horrible mistake. In a sense, it is not even a mistake. It is the natural result of a society that recklessly locks up anyone who *may* be a criminal, even if they *aren't* a criminal, because it's better to be safe than right. Our courts are nothing but a haphazard assembly line for the poor to be routed *away* from us, out of sight—out of my damn way!

Well, this is America, and I guess if it's good enough to remove thousands of innocent black men from the voting rolls in Florida, it should be good enough to railroad an innocent black man in Los Angeles.

In this assembly-line system of justice, the one thing that mucks up the wholesale delivery of the accused to jail is the jury trial. Why? Because jury trials are shit-disturbers. They force everyone to do their job. The judges, prosecutors, and public defenders do everything in their power to coerce the defendant into accepting a guilty plea to AVOID THE BRUTAL PRISON SEN-TENCE WE WILL GIVE YOU IF YOU DEMAND A JURY TRIAL. If they can get the defendant not only to plead guilty but also to sign a waiver of his right to appeal, then they've hit a home run—and everyone can laugh about it later at the country club.

My sister, Anne, was a public defender in California. She insisted on defending her clients, and getting them a jury trial if that's what they wanted. For that, she was subjected to incredible harassment from the other PDs in the office. In 1998 the public defender's office in her county allowed only one felony client *out of almost nine hundred defendants* to have a jury trial.

Obviously, that didn't mean every single one of the other 899 accused were guilty. They were just coerced into pleading that way, with many of them ending up in prison, perhaps for crimes they didn't commit. But we'll never know, because their Sixth Amendment right to a trial by a jury of their peers was taken from them.

With this standardized railroading of the poor going on daily in every city in America, our justice system has nothing to do with justice. Our judges and lawyers are more like glorified garbage men, rounding up and disposing of society's refuse—ethnic cleansing, American style.

What happens when this fast-track chute sends innocent people to their death? It took only one college class full of kids at Northwestern University in Evanston, Illinois, to uncover and prove that five individuals on Illinois's death row were, in fact, innocent. Those students and their professor saved the lives of five people.

If one college class could do that, how many other hundreds of innocent people on death rows across the country are also sitting there awaiting their permanent disposal?

Thirty-eight states have the death penalty. So does the federal government and the U.S. military. Twelve states, plus the District of Columbia (that little piece of swampland with a majority of African-Americans and those offensive license plates), do not.

Since 1976, there have been over seven hundred executions in the United States.

The top execution-happy states are:

Texas (248 executions—nearly one-third of all U.S. executions since 1976)
Virginia (82)
Florida (51)

Missouri (50)
Oklahoma (43)
Louisiana (26)
South Carolina (25)
Arkansas (24)
Alabama (23)
Arizona (22)
North Carolina (17)
Delaware (13)
Illinois (12)
California (9)
Nevada (9)
Indiana (8)
Utah (6)

A shocking recent death penalty study of 4,578 cases in a twenty-three-year period (1973–1995) concluded that the courts found serious, reversible error in nearly 7 of every 10 capital sentence cases that were fully reviewed during the period. It also found that death sentences were being overturned in 2 out of 3 appeals. The overall prejudicial review error rate was 68 percent.

Since 1973, some ninety-five death row inmates have been *fully exonerated* by the courts—that is, found innocent of the crimes for which they were sentenced to die. Ninety-six persons have been released as a result of DNA testing.

And what were the most common errors?

1. Egregiously incompetent defense lawyers who didn't even look for, or missed important evidence that would have proved innocence or demonstrated that their client didn't deserve to die.
2. Police or prosecutors who *did* discover that kind of evidence but *suppressed* it, actively derailing the judicial process.

In half the years studied, including the most recent one, the error rate was over 60 percent. High error rates exist across the country. In 85 percent of death penalty cases the error rates are 60 percent or higher. Three-fifths have error rates of 70 percent or higher.

Catching these errors takes time—a national average of nine years from death sentence to execution. In most cases, death row inmates wait years for the lengthy review procedures needed to uncover all these errors—whereupon their death sentences are very often reversed. This imposes a terrible cost on taxpayers, victims' families, the judicial system, and the wrongly condemned.

Among the inmates involved in the study who had their death verdicts overturned, nearly all were given a sentence less than death (82 percent), and many were found innocent on retrial (7 percent).

The number of errors has risen since 1996, when President Clinton made it tougher for death row inmates to prove their innocence by signing into law a one-year limit on the time inmates have to appeal to federal courts after exhausting their appeals in state courts. In light of the study that proved how many of these inmates are either innocent or not legally deserving of the death penalty, this attempt to curb their appeals was simply outrageous.

We are one of the few countries in the world that puts to death *both* the mentally retarded and juvenile offenders. The United States is among only six countries that impose the death penalty on juveniles. The others are Iran, Nigeria, Pakistan, Saudi Arabia, and Yemen.

The United States is also the only country besides Somalia that has not signed the United Nations Convention on the Rights of the Child. Why? Because it contains a provision prohibiting the execution of children under eighteen, and we want to remain free to execute our children.

No other industrialized nation executes its children.

Even China prohibits the death penalty for those under eighteen—this from a country that has shown an intolerable lack of respect for human rights.

Currently the total number of death row inmates in the United States tops 3,700. Seventy of those death row inmates are minors (or were when they committed their crime).

But our Supreme Court doesn't find it cruel and unusual punishment (in the terms of the Eighth Amendment to the U.S. Constitution) to execute those who were sixteen years old when they committed a capital crime. This despite the fact that same court has ruled that sixteen-year-olds do not have "the maturity or judgment" to sign *contracts*.

Odd, isn't it, that a child's diminished capacity for signing contracts is viewed as a legal barrier to enforcing a contract, but when it comes to the right to be executed, a child's capacity is equal to that of an adult?

Eighteen states allow juvenile offenders as young as sixteen to be executed. Five others allow the execution of those who were seventeen or older when they committed their crime. In 1999 Oklahoma executed Sean Sellers, who was sixteen at the time of the murders he was found guilty of committing. Sellers's multiple personality disorder wasn't revealed to the jury that convicted him. A federal appeals court found that Sellers might have been "factually innocent" because of his mental disorder, but that "innocence alone is not sufficient to grant federal relief." Unbelievable.

The American public is not stupid, and now that the truth has been coming out about the innocent people who have been sent to death row, they are at least responding with a sense of shame. Just a few years ago public opinion polls showed that upwards of 80 percent of the American people supported the death penalty. But now, with the truth out, a recent *Washington Post/ABC News* poll found that public approval of capital punishment has declined, while the proportion of Americans who favor replacing the death penalty with life in prison has increased. Fifty-one percent favored halting all executions until a commission is established to determine whether the death penalty is being administered fairly.

Sixty-eight percent said the death penalty is unfair because innocent people are sometimes executed. Recent Gallup Polls have shown that support for the death penalty is at a nineteen-year low. Sixty-five percent agreed that a poor person is more likely than a person of average or above-average income to receive the death penalty for the same crime. Fifty percent agreed that a black person is more likely than a white person to receive the death penalty for the same crime. Even in the killing machine known as the state of Texas, the *Houston Chronicle* reported that 59 percent of Texans surveyed believed that their state *has executed an innocent person!*, while 72 percent favor changing state law to include the sentencing option of life without parole, and 60 percent are now opposed to the state executing an inmate who is mentally retarded.

What we have done, in this great country, is to wage a war *not* on crime *but on the poor we feel comfortable blaming for it*. Somewhere along the way we forgot about people's rights, because we didn't want to spend the money.

We live in a society that rewards and honors corporate gangsters—corporate leaders who directly and indirectly plunder the earth's resources and look out for the shareholders' profits above all else—while subjecting the poor to a random and brutal system of "justice."

But the public is starting to realize this is wrong.

We need to reorder society so that every person within it is seen as precious, sacred, and valuable, and that NO man is above the law, no matter how many candidates he buys off. Until this changes, we can utter the words "with liberty and justice for all" only with shame.

National Conversation:
Affirmative Action

Affirmative Action: Goal vs. Issue

William Raspberry

The Washington Post | January 27, 2003

In April of this year, the Supreme Court heard a pair of cases that could decide the future of affirmative action in our nation's colleges and grad schools. The University of Michigan was the defendant in the two cases, in which rejected white applicants challenged the race-based admissions policies of its undergraduate program and its law school, respectively. One of the most astonishing aspects of the hearing was the large number of amicus curae (friend of the court) briefs filed in support of the university's position by some 65 corporations, representatives of the armed forces, and many prominent political figures. They were all sending the same message: Racial and ethnic diversity is essential to our country's well-being.

In June of 2002, the Court upheld the law school's affirmative-action program by a 5–4 vote, while rejecting the undergraduate program, 6–3. Still, the underlying dilemma of affirmative action remains unsolved. The problem, as columnist William Raspberry observes, is that while the goal of diversity has wide support, the debate over how to achieve it is a source of endless disagreement. . . .

How can a concept such as affirmative action split Americans into so many warring factions—separating conservative from liberal, black from white, Condoleezza Rice from Colin Powell, and even George W. Bush from George W. Bush?

Is it that some of us are optimistic about racial progress and others pessimistic? That some are sympathetic to the plight of minorities and others indifferent? That some see a fight for racial justice and others a struggle for group advantage?

My own conclusion—perhaps because it reflects the pulls and tugs of my own mind—is that virtually all of us are both for and against affirmative action. How we argue about it publicly depends very much on whether we see diversity as a goal—or only as an issue.

Leave aside the special situation of the University of Michigan (special because it is that university's affirmative action system on which the U.S. Supreme Court will be ruling) and consider other examples.

It's likely that the Supreme Court itself will never again consist of nine white men—not because it will never be the case that white males happen to be the best-qualified candidates for the court. The court will remain diverse because presidents now and into the future will consider such diversity to be good for America, a way of maximizing public acceptance of the court's judgments even when we disagree with them.

That, even if Clarence Thomas and Sandra Day O'Connor won't acknowledge it, is affirmative action.

Think of post-apartheid South Africa, where blacks are finally as free as whites to attend the country's prestigious universities. If it happens that nearly all of the highest-scoring applicants are white (mainly because blacks, having suffered an inferior education, are generally less prepared to do well on admissions tests), should a top university admit an all-white class?

Or is it reasonable to argue that South Africa's survival will depend on the trained intelligence of all its citizens and that the best of the black applicants ought to be admitted to the top places of learning—provided they demonstrate the ability to perform the work?

A lawyer I know says he once asked a senior partner what his firm would do if it happened one year that all of its top applicants were black. Would they all be hired? The candid, if somewhat embarrassed, reply: No. The explanation may have dealt with client confidence, public perception, etc. But the attitude was: affirmative action—this time for whites.

Most of America's highly selective universities—and most of its top businesses—practice some measure of affirmative action for minorities. They want to continue doing so, as evidenced by the alternatives they come up with when a court order ends affirmative action. They want diversity—for the appearance of racial fairness, for public relations and good will, to help America become a more just society, to enhance the academic experience for all their students.

It's almost fair to say that *everybody* favors affirmative action.

But no one wants quotas, or "reverse discrimination" or too obvious a thumb on the scale. That's why Rice and Powell can look at the same situation and apparently see two different things. My guess is that they simply see two sides of the same coin.

Powell, who has spoken and written favorably about how affirmative action boosted his illustrious military career, sees diversity as a goal. Rice, who may have had some similar experiences, was responding to a president who sees diversity as an issue.

Issues, by their very nature, divide. They force us to choose sides, to work against one another, to produce winners and losers. That is their political purpose.

Goals, on the other hand, can be shared—even when we embrace different means for reaching them. There is, of course, no *one* way of producing the goal of diversity—no way, including Michigan's, that is utterly without flaws. But doing nothing is an option only for those who think the goal isn't very important.

That's the trouble with the president's recent remarks on the Michigan case. He wants to be seen as embracing the goal while doing nothing to bring it nearer. He wants flowers without sowing seeds.

A Policy That Depends on Segregation
Benjamin Forest

The New York Times | March 29, 2003

One of the ironies of the affirmative action debate is that the people who oppose what they perceive to be a quota system for admitting minorities to colleges and grad schools are often the same folks who turn a blind eye to the preferential admission of alumni children to these same schools (surely the purest form of affirmative action), and who support some degree of racial profiling on the grounds of public safety or national security.

Equally disingenuous is the widely-hailed method that's been employed by the Texas state university system in recent years as a way to achieve ethnic diversity in its schools without taking race per se into account. This approach requires state-funded colleges to admit any Texas child who graduates in the top ten percent of his or her high school class. As Benjamin Forest, an assistant professor of geography at Dartmouth, points out, such a policy actually depends on racial segregation in order to have its desired effect. . . .

HANOVER, N.H.—Can there be racial diversity on campus without racial consciousness in admissions? That is the question raised by challenges to the University of Michigan's admissions policies.

Those opposed to Michigan's policy, which considers race as one factor among many in the admissions process, have proposed several alternatives. Foremost among them is the so-called Texas plan, which guarantees admission to the top 10 percent of students in every accredited high school in the state. Florida and California now use versions of the Texas plan as well. Advocates say such plans provide historically disadvantaged groups (including low-income whites) with unprecedented access to elite state universities and produce a diverse student body.

This claim ignores a forgotten reality of the Texas plan: access and diversity in universities will come at the price of continued segregation in high schools. Racial integration in primary and secondary schools was once a national priority; now segregation is a prerequisite for a new kind of politically correct "affirmative action."

The political genius of the Texas plan is that it sidesteps the powerful rhetorical positions for and against affirmative action. Opponents of plans like Michigan's argue that the justification for racial diversity ultimately rests on the classification of applicants by race, and gives an unfair advantage to a limited set of chosen minority groups. Supporters counter that race is merely one of many considerations used in admissions, and that there is educational value in culturally diverse classrooms.

The Texas plan is an attractive compromise: it "rewards" individuals who have excelled in their given circumstances. Because high schools are generally segregated by race, ethnicity, and income, students admitted to college will represent a reasonable cross-section of historically underrepresented groups, regardless of statewide differences in test scores.

But this rosy picture simply replaces race consciousness in admissions with the race consciousness of segregation. The plan glosses over the fact that even within the same high schools, there are differences in average test scores and grades between white and minority students.

For example, African-Americans made up just under 12 percent of those who graduated from high school in Texas in 1998. Yet they were just over 6 percent of graduating students in the top 10 percent of their high school classes. Similarly, Hispanic students were nearly 30 percent of graduates, but less than 22 percent of top 10 percent of students. Whites and Asians have higher representation among the top students.

Whatever the ultimate cause of these differences, in practice it means that only highly segregated high schools will have a significant number of minority students among their top 10 percent. Under typical circumstances, minorities will be only about one-third of the top students in a school that is 50 percent minority. Even in highly segregated schools (90 percent minority), just over 80 percent of the top group will be minority. "Geographic diversity" is a flawed proxy for racial diversity.

To be fair, the Texas plan does not intend to create universities that are demographic mirrors of the state population. At the same time, it will also not produce a student body devoid of minorities.

Nonetheless, the implication of this analysis is clear. Texas-style plans achieve significant diversity only if high schools are highly segregated. It is disingenuous to claim that these plans are not racially conscious. They may prevent universities from considering race in individual cases, but they accept—indeed, they rely on—the racially driven processes that produce and maintain segregation.

Don't Do Me Any Favors
John McWhorter

American Enterprise Magazine | April/May 2003

John McWhorter, an associate professor at the University of California, Berkeley, has gained a reputation for being something of a contrarian on racial issues, thanks to the publication in 2000 of his book, Losing the Race. *In it, he accuses African-Americans of succumbing to what he calls "victimology." The following essay takes up this theme again, arguing that the emphasis on achieving diversity through racial preferences in college admissions is essentially an expression of white guilt—and that it has led to a lowering of academic standards for African-American students, while at the same time contributing to a "black separatist ideology" on our nation's campuses. . . .*

I am an African-American linguistics professor at the University of California at Berkeley, and students often come by my office for mentoring. One such student, a Chinese American, had heard that I'd been on the radio discussing affirmative action. "How do you feel about it?" she asked. "Well," I said, "I think in universities it's obsolete." "Aren't you in favor of diversity?" was her immediate response, as it is for most students exposed to the issue largely through the college newspaper's editorial page and angry speeches by student activists.

"Diversity" only made its way into the affirmative action debate a few decades ago, and through the back door at that. It started with one man. In 1973 and again in 1974, Allan Bakke was denied admission to the University of California at Davis's medical school despite an A- grade-point average and an MCAT score within the top tenth of the nation. Given that black students were regularly admitted with GPAs in the C range and MCATs in the bottom third, Bakke charged the university with discrimination.

In the Supreme Court decision in 1978, Justice Lewis Powell concurred with four other justices that quota systems like Davis's were un-Constitutional. He submitted however that it was nonetheless appropriate for schools to base admissions decisions on a quest for a "diverse student body."

This argument seems innocent enough on its face, but universities quickly seized it as a cover for admitting black students with significantly lower qualifications than white or Asian students. Ever since, university administrators have disguised their two-tier admissions policies by hiding behind "diversity."

Lately, courts have begun calling these policies un-Constitutional distortions of the Bakke decision, with judgments entered recently against the University of Texas, the University of Georgia, and the University of Michigan Law School. I dearly hope that the Supreme Court will invalidate Powell's "diversity" opinion once and for all. Yes, I am in favor of "diversity"—among equals. The Bakke decision has taught a generation of young Americans that black students are more important for their presence in pictures in promotional brochures than for their scholastic qualifications. Ultimately, this perpetuates the very underperformance that has made the "diversity" fig leaf necessary.

White guilt is a dangerous and addictive drug. For nearly three decades the Bakke decision has supported education administrators in this habit. The ideas these people have promoted are untruthful, destructive, and antithetical to both black excellence and racial harmony. And they are racist.

The very term "diversity" is a crafty evasion. Mormons, paraplegics, and poor whites exert little pull on the heartstrings of admissions committees supposedly committed to making college campuses "look like America." In the late 1960s, college administrators assumed that the low representation of blacks on campuses was due to discrimination. The good-thinking white chancellor saw the task ahead as one of door opening, providing some remedial assistance where necessary. But efforts to bring qualified blacks to campuses ran up against the uncomfortably small number of such people in an

America just past legalized segregation. For those who were admitted, professors proved unable to undo years of lacking basic learning skills.

Meanwhile, a black separatist ideology had led to the idea that scholastic achievement was a "white" endeavor rather than a human one. Black kids started teasing other black kids who liked school for "acting white." This has become a central trope of black teen culture, and it continues to decrease the numbers of black students qualified for top schools.

The simple fact is that any group's rise from the bottom is not instantaneous but gradual. The "diversity" construction is a benevolently intended back-door strategy employed by guilty whites to hurry along the utopian vision of a multihued college, even if it requires rounding some corners. What the diversity crusade has done in practice is to spark brute quota systems and a reconception of the very purpose of higher education.

Many people are under the impression that the "diversity" imperative plays out simply as a light "thumb on the scale," choosing the brown-skinned candidate in cases where his qualifications are equal to a white one's. Hence they consider opposition to such harmless racial preferences "racist." It's an easy misunderstanding to fall into, as college administrators minimize their distortions of admissions procedures in their public statements.

But it was almost impossible to maintain this illusion in places like Rutgers University in the mid '80s, where I earned my bachelor's degree. Within my first year, it was painfully clear to me that the black students were by and large a rung below the white students in general preparation and performance. Certainly there were plenty of white slackers and excellent black students. But they were exceptions rather than the rule, and the overall white-black discrepancy stood out in sharp relief. Even as a teenager with little interest in politics or admissions procedures, I spontaneously perceived after just a few semesters that black students were admitted under some sort of numbers system.

The Rutgers top brass had long maintained that race was used as just "one of many factors," as the Bakke decision had counseled. But a few years after I graduated, a student working in the admissions office blew the whistle, revealing that black students were regularly gathered into a special pool and admitted with grade-point averages and standardized test scores significantly lower than those of other students. Nor was Rutgers unique. Similar revelations were made on campus after campus.

Before racial preferences were banned at the University of California at Berkeley in the mid '90s, its quota system had been obvious. A white man who worked as a remedial tutor confided in me that he had worked with so many minority students hopelessly unprepared for work at the college level that he had found himself questioning the wisdom of racial preference policies despite his leftist politics. I have heard similar testimonials from professors across the country.

In *America in Black and White,* Stephan and Abigail Thernstrom note that black Berkeley students who enrolled in 1988 had an average SAT score below 1,000; the white average was over 1,300. The highest quarter of black SAT scores in this class clustered at the bottom quarter of the entire student body. Comparable gaps in SAT scores exist between black and white entrants at Princeton (150 points), Stanford (171), Dartmouth (218), and Rice (271).

Graduation rates reflect these gulfs in preparation. The Thernstroms document that of the black students admitted to Berkeley in 1988, 41 percent did not graduate, compared to only 16 percent of whites. At 28 top universities, William Bowen and Derek Bok, authors of *The Shape of the River,* show, black students in the class of 1989 were about three times more likely to drop out than white students.

Some suppose that bending admissions rules for "diversity" fosters interracial fellowship on campuses. I myself tried to hold to this idea for years. But college campuses, in all of their "diversity," are now among the most racially balkanized settings in America.

Separate black fraternities and sororities thrive. Universities often host separate black graduation ceremonies. Classes in African American Studies often foster hatred of The White Man. At Stanford, where I earned my doctorate, I was a teaching assistant in a predominantly black class on Black English. The class discussion devolved so often into visceral dismissals of whites that one white student complained to the professor that he felt any opinions he ventured beyond genuflections to black victimhood were unwelcome. He was right.

There is a general atmosphere on campuses in which black students are tacitly taught that black "authenticity" means hunkering down behind a barricade glaring hatefully at the white "hegemony." Black students typically cluster in their own section of the dining hall, throw their own parties, live in separate dorms, and are generally ushered into a separatist ideology most did not subscribe to before they came to college.

In John Bunzel's *Race Relations on Campus,* black Stanford students in the early 1990s report being expected to "talk black, dress black, think black, and certainly date black." During my graduate years there, black students disinclined to toe this line frequently ended up in heated debates with other black students who questioned their "blackness."

A black acquaintance once told me that any occasional racist experiences she had during her college years were dwarfed by the overriding hostility from black students scornful of her white friendships and activities. Tragically, many blacks now leave college less interested in interracial outreach than when they were freshmen.

Many of those so furiously committed to "diversity" are not interested in a colorblind America. Their goal is to keep the fires of reflexive black alienation burning. In her book *Why Are All the Blacks Sitting Together in the Cafeteria?* black psychologist Beverly Daniel Tatum cheers that this is due to black students' "anger and resentment" at the "systemic exclusion of black people from full participation in U.S. society." That claim is a bit tricky to accommodate with a black Secretary of State and national security adviser in Washington. But it's an effective way of building the separatist movement that Tatum and others prefer to interracial harmony.

Promoters of "diversity" prattle endlessly that "exposure" to other groups is a crucial component of a college education in a multiethnic America. Given that the origin of "diversity," the Bakke case, concerned medical school, it's not clear how being black would improve the discussions about surgical incisions and metabolic pathways.

On campuses where black students are let in under the bar, there reigns a deathless lie: that most black students come from disadvantaged circumstances. According to this view, even an average performance by a minority student is a miracle.

Yet at selective colleges, black students from inner-city schools are vanishingly rare. (In the late 1960s some universities experimented briefly with actually admitting such students. But even the administrators had to concede that these students lacked the necessary preparation for top universities, with social tumult and resentment being the main result.) In the last class admitted to Berkeley under the racial preference regime, more than 65 percent came from households earning at least $40,000 a year, while the parents of about 40 percent earned at least $60,000 a year. Of the black students admitted in 1989 to 28 selective universities surveyed by Bowen and Bok, only 14 percent came from homes earning $22,000 a year or less.

But white guilt finds ways to turn even firmly middle-class blacks into victims. In a tortured 1998 essay professor Ronald Dworkin argued that even middle-class black students should be admitted under the bar—because they embody a lesson for whites that the stereotypes of "poor blacks" are inappropriate. Would Dworkin care to have his own children admitted under a quota system in order to serve as museum exhibits for gentiles? And precisely what traits do middle-class black students display that are so unique and unexpected that white students must be exposed to them?

Even if significant numbers of black students at top schools did come from ghetto neighborhoods, just how would "learning about" their cultural traits be vital to white students' educational experience? In African-American Studies courses on those very same campuses, blacks are taught to decry stereotyping of poor blacks. Wouldn't a four year tutorial in the vibrancy of ghetto life reinforce those very stereotypes?

Every college administrator knows that "diversity" is code for "at least 5 percent black faces with a goodly sprinkling of Latinos." They also know that this is only achievable through quota systems euphemized by artful terminology, chronic doubletalk, and outright lies. Nor do any of them miss the fact, as black students dutifully erupt in furious protest every second spring over manufactured instances of "racism," that in practice campus "diversity" means that black students are carefully taught that they are eternal victims in their own country.

But the most tragic result of racial preferences is their effect on their supposed beneficiaries. Extended disenfranchisement often leaves a group ill-equipped to compete at the highest level, even when the doors to success are wide open. These realities are not pretty. But what they mean is that a crucial component in a group's rise to the top is learning tricks to a new trade, as disadvantaged groups in America have done for centuries. There comes a point, during any previously reviled group's climb to the top, where that group can reach the same level as the ruling group only if the safety net is withdrawn. Sometimes a group must refashion its entire self concept in order to move ahead.

Lowered standards are directly antithetical to these endeavors. A person can only hit the highest note when he has the incentive to do so: This is a fundamental tenet of economics and psychology alike. Black Americans are not exempt from this fact of the human condition.

My opposition to racial preferences is based on a purely logical conviction: They dumb black people down. The injustices that blacks have suffered in America in the past are obvious. But the fact remains: Students growing up in a system whose message is "You only have to do pretty well to get into a top school" will rarely drive themselves to the top. Enshrining "diversity" over true excellence condemns black students to mediocrity. This is the inevitable result of denying them, and their parents, high school teachers, and guidance counselors, the one thing that elicits the best in anyone—the path of individual perseverance. That's not "politics"; it's common sense.

The claim that racial preferences are necessary to compensate for past horrors creates "tit for tat" applications of racial preferences that certainly won't solve this country's racial dilemma. It may make whites feel better, but it won't give black students the tools they need to truly excel. You can only learn to ride a bicycle by mastering the subtle muscular demands on your own. As long as the training wheels are on, you're not truly riding a bike. Birds learn to fly by being nudged out of the nest. People gain fluent command of a foreign language by living for an extended period in a setting where it is impossible to use their native language for any length of time. Black students will achieve their highest potential in school only by being required to do so.

Short of tough demands, top-rate black students will continue to constitute only a tiny coterie—with children of recent Caribbean and African immigrants heavily overrepresented. Asian students never had any illusion that there was a way to the top other than through hard work, which is why they have succeeded in such large numbers. A culture in which black students are denied the stimulus of high demands is, quite simply, a racist one. What are we to make of university administrators' apparent conviction that black people are the only ones in American history who cannot triumph over historical obstacles?

The truth is, after California voters eliminated racial preferences at state colleges in 1996, black admissions fell at only two campuses—UCLA and Berkeley. They rose at several of the other University of California campuses. This is evidence that blacks will eventually work their way up the status ladder. Already, black admission rates at Berkeley have risen every year since the initial drop when admissions first were made colorblind.

In any case, it's not as if students who don't make it into Berkeley or UCLA are doomed to lives of destitution. Over the past few years many black students who would have been accepted at Berkeley under its previous quota system are now attending UC Santa Cruz, UC Davis, and other solid schools where they are much more likely to thrive and succeed. On these campuses black students learn through everyday, concrete successes that they are as qualified as their classmates, rather than having to assert it on the basis of empty, tribalist rhetoric. Armed with this true confidence, black students will be less likely to retreat to their own sides of the cafeteria to compensate for private feelings of inferiority.

As for the claim that sorting out black students meritocratically is somehow unjust, remember that the majority of the students at these second-rank schools are white and Asian. The demise of racial preferences in the UC system has simply brought black students to the places that their current levels of skill, initiative, and preparation allow—as has long been the lot of white college applicants.

There is also the oft-heard claim that blacks must be admitted to top schools despite inadequate qualifications, because the prestige of these schools, and the resulting social connections, are crucial to success after graduation. But as James Fallows has noted, the top universities are sparse among the résumés of members of Congress, Nobel laureates, industrial leaders, even U.S. Presidents.

Among black Americans specifically, the Thernstroms report that of today's African-American congressmen, army officers, recent Ph.D. earners, and top business leaders, none but a sliver attended elite colleges. Thus "diversity" serves no better to foster black excellence beyond college than within it.

On today's college campuses, all students are indoctrinated with the piety that racism is at the root of any and all racial discrepancies, with the inevitable result that furiously self-righteous people are constantly clamoring for increased black presence by any means available. No one could be appointed a university president today without supporting racial preferences in one guise or another. And while the diversity argument hasn't done much for black students, it has been very useful to white administrators.

University of Michigan president Lee Bollinger became a media darling by criticizing the court decision against the use of race preferences at his university's law school. It's telling that Bollinger was selected as president of Columbia University shortly after his defense of preferences, while his law school dean Jeffrey Lehman, equally vehement in defending Michigan's quotas in recent months, has just been picked to head Cornell University.

"Aren't you in favor of diversity?" is code for "Don't you like black people?" And nothing chills white Americans more than the notion that they might be considered racist. So admitting black people under the bar becomes imperative. Meanwhile many blacks cheer, under the misimpression that racism is the only possible cause of unequal performance.

But the unequal performance of black students doesn't evaporate once they hit college. Racial preferences do not, as so often thought, "correct" a "raw deal" that black students have been saddled with. Instead, racial preferences merely sanction and perpetuate the separation of blacks from high academic performance.

It is high time we relegated preference by skin color to the dustbin of history.

Mongrel America
Gregory Rodriguez

The Atlantic Monthly | January/February 2003

The U.S. government has officially confirmed that Hispanic-Americans now out-number African-Americans as the nation's largest ethnic minority. In this widely noted article, however, Gregory Rodriguez points out an even more significant demographic trend: At the rate Americans of different ethnic backgrounds are intermarrying, the number of people claiming a mixed racial heritage will outnumber any single minority group by the end of this century. Our country is fast reaching the point, in other words, when racial categories will become meaningless. . . .

Are racial categories still an important—or even a valid—tool of government policy? In recent years the debate in America has been between those who think that race is paramount and those who think it is increasingly irrelevant, and in the next election cycle this debate will surely intensify around a California ballot initiative that would all but prohibit the state from asking its citizens what their racial backgrounds are. But the ensuing polemics will only obscure the more fundamental question: What, when each generation is more racially and ethnically mixed than its predecessor, does race even mean anymore? If your mother is Asian and your father is African-American, what, racially speaking, are you? (And if your spouse is half Mexican and half Russian Jewish, what are your children?)

Five decades after the end of legal segregation, and only thirty-six years after the Supreme Court struck down anti-miscegenation laws, young African-Americans are considerably more likely than their elders to claim mixed heritage. A study by the Population Research Center, in Portland, Oregon, projects that the black intermarriage rate will climb dramatically in this century, to a point at which 37 percent of African-Americans will claim mixed ancestry by 2100. By then more than 40 percent of Asian-Americans will be mixed. Most remarkable, however, by century's end the number of Latinos claiming mixed ancestry will be more than two times the number claiming a single background.

Not surprisingly, intermarriage rates for all groups are highest in the states that serve as immigration gateways. By 1990 Los Angeles County had an intermarriage rate five times the national average. Latinos and Asians, the groups that have made up three quarters of immigrants over the past forty years, have helped to create a climate in which ethnic or racial intermarriage is more accepted today than ever before. Nationally, whereas only eight percent of foreign-born Latinos marry non-Latinos, 32 percent of second-generation and 57 percent of third-generation Latinos marry outside their ethnic group. Similarly, whereas only 13 percent of foreign-born Asians marry non-Asians, 34 percent of second-generation and 54 percent of third-generation Asian-Americans do.

Meanwhile, as everyone knows, Latinos are now the largest minority group in the nation. Two thirds of Latinos, in turn, are of Mexican heritage. This is significant in itself, because their sheer numbers have helped Mexican-Americans do more than any other group to alter the country's old racial thinking. For instance, Texas and California, where Mexican-Americans are the largest minority, were the first two states to abolish affirmative action: when the collective "minority" populations in those states began to outnumber whites, the racial balance that had made affirmative action politically viable was subverted.

Many Mexican-Americans now live in cities or regions where they are a majority, changing the very idea of what it means to be a member of a "minority" group. Because of such demographic changes, a number of the policies designed to integrate nonwhites into the mainstream—affirmative action in college admissions, racial set-asides in government contracting—

have been rendered more complicated or even counterproductive in recent years. In California cities where whites have become a minority, it is no longer clear what "diversity" means or what the goals of integration policies should be. The selective magnet-school program of the Los Angeles Unified School District, for example, was originally developed as an alternative to forced busing—a way to integrate ethnic minority students by encouraging them to look beyond their neighborhoods. Today, however, the school district is 71 percent Latino, and Latinos' majority status actually puts them at a disadvantage when applying to magnet schools.

But it is not merely their growing numbers (they will soon be the majority in both California and Texas, and they are already the single largest contemporary immigrant group nationwide) that make Mexican-Americans a leading indicator of the country's racial future; rather, it's what they represent. They have always been a complicating element in the American racial system, which depends on an oversimplified classification scheme. Under the pre-civil-rights formulation, for example, if you had "one drop" of African blood, you were fully black. The scheme couldn't accommodate people who were part one thing and part another. Mexicans, who are a product of intermingling—both cultural and genetic—between the Spanish and the many indigenous peoples of North and Central America, have a history of tolerating and even reveling in such ambiguity. Since the conquest of Mexico, in the sixteenth century, they have practiced *mestizaje*—racial and cultural synthesis—both in their own country and as they came north. Unlike the English-speaking settlers of the western frontier, the Spaniards were willing everywhere they went to allow racial and cultural mixing to blur the lines between themselves and the natives. The fact that Latin America is far more heavily populated by people of mixed ancestry than Anglo America is the clearest sign of the difference between the two outlooks on race.

Nativists once deplored the Mexican tendency toward hybridity. In the mid-nineteenth century, at the time of the conquest of the Southwest, Secretary of State James Buchanan feared granting citizenship to a "mongrel race." And in the late 1920s Representative John C. Box, of Texas, warned his colleagues on the House Immigration and Naturalization Committee that the continued influx of Mexican immigrants could lead to the "distressing process of mongrelization" in America. He argued that because Mexicans were the products of mixing, they harbored a relaxed attitude toward interracial unions and were likely to mingle freely with other races in the United States.

Box was right. The typical cultural isolation of immigrants notwithstanding, those immigrants' children and grandchildren are strongly oriented toward the American melting pot. Today two thirds of multiracial and multi-ethnic births in California involve a Latino parent. *Mexicanidad*, or "Mexi-canness," is becoming the catalyst for a new American cultural synthesis.

In the same way that the rise in the number of multi-racial Americans muddles U.S. racial statistics, the growth of the Mexican-American mestizo population has begun to challenge the Anglo-American binary view of race. In the 1920 census Mexicans were counted as whites. Ten years later they were reassigned to a separate Mexican "racial" category. In 1940 they were officially reclassified as white. Today almost half the Latinos in California, which is home to a third of the nation's Latinos (most of them of Mexican descent), check "other" as their race. In the first half of the twentieth century Mexican-American advocates fought hard for the privileges that came with being white in America. But since the 1960s activists have sought to reap the benefits of being nonwhite minorities. Having spent so long trying to fit into one side or the other of the binary system, Mexican-Americans have become numerous and confident enough to simply claim their brownness—their mixture. This is a harbinger of America's future.

The original melting-pot concept was incomplete: it applied only to white ethnics (Irish, Italians, Poles, and so forth), not to blacks and other nonwhites. Israel Zangwill, the playwright whose 1908 drama *The Melting Pot* popularized the concept, even wrote that whites were justified in avoiding inter-marriage with blacks. In fact, multiculturalism—the ideology that promotes the permanent coexistence of separate but equal cultures in one place—can be seen as a by-product of America's exclusion of African-Americans from the melting pot; those whom assimilation rejected came to reject assimilation. Although the multicultural movement has always encompassed other groups, blacks gave it its moral impetus.

But the immigrants of recent decades are helping to forge a new American identity, something more complex than either a melting pot or a confederation of separate but equal groups. And this identity is emerging not as a result of politics or any specific public policies but because of powerful underlying cultural forces. To be sure, the civil-rights movement was instrumental in the initial assault on racial barriers. And immigration policies since 1965 have tended to favor those immigrant groups—Asians and Latinos—who are most open to intermarriage. But in recent years the government's major contribution to the country's growing multiracialism has been—as it should continue to be—a retreat from dictating limits on interracial intimacy and from exalting (through such policies as racial set-asides and affirmative action) race as the most important American category of being. As a result, Americans cross racial lines more often than ever before in choosing whom to sleep with, marry, or raise children with.

Unlike the advances of the civil-rights movement, the future of racial identity in America is unlikely to be determined by politics or the courts or public policy. Indeed, at this point perhaps the best thing the government can do is to acknowledge changes in the meaning of race in America and then get out of the way. The Census Bureau's decision to allow Americans to check more than one box in the "race" section of the 2000 Census was an important step in this direction. No longer forced to choose a single racial identity, Americans are now free to identify themselves as mestizos—and with this newfound freedom we may begin to endow racial issues with the complexity and nuance they deserve.

Part Three: Marching to War

Next Stop Baghdad?
Kenneth Pollack

from *Foreign Affairs* | March/April 2002

One of the most interesting aspects of the Iraq war was the long and very public buildup it received. The Bush administration began leaking hints about an invasion early in 2002, and the pro-war reports steadily intensified through the summer and fall. Still, two stubborn questions continued to linger: "Why invade?" and, "Why invade now?"

The answer to the second question clearly had a lot to do with the shift in public mood following the 9/11 strikes. If ever the nation was ready to embrace a military action, this was the time. The answer to the first question, however, was tougher to get a handle on. The White House put forward various rationales, all obviously designed for the consumption of their domestic audience, and all containing obvious flaws: If Saddam Hussein was indeed developing weapons of mass destruction, it wasn't apparent that they posed any direct threat to the U.S.; likewise, the intelligence community had failed to establish that there were any direct links between the Iraq regime and Al Qaeda, other than the fact that the presence of American troops in Saudi Arabia (stationed there after the first Gulf War to dissuade Hussein from invading his neighbors) were a primary motivation for Osama Bin Laden's terrorist activities.

Like many foreign policy issues, the real reasons for invading were almost certainly more complex and nuanced than the explanations given to the public. Hussein's attempts to build nuclear weapons unquestionably represented a serious and ongoing threat to the stability of the oil-rich Middle East, and his belligerent regime also remained an impediment to any resolution of the political problems facing Israel and the Arab nations of the region. Even more to the point, the policy of containing Hussein was seen as being increasingly ineffective.

Why Bush didn't try to make this case (which seems more sensible than the administration's other justifications for war) is an open question. At any rate, one of the best expositions of this line of reasoning can be found in the following, widely-noted article by ex-CIA analyst and Iraq specialist Ken Pollack (later expanded into a best-selling book, The Threatening Storm*). The fact that Pollack wasn't a Republican partisan, having served under the Clinton administration, further bolstered the credibility of his argument—namely, that invading Iraq was really America's only remaining option. . . .*

Cutting the Gordian Knot

As the conflict in Afghanistan winds down, the question of what the United States should do about Iraq has risen to the forefront of American foreign policy. Hawks argue that toppling Saddam Hussein should be "phase two" in the war on terrorism. They see Iraq's development of unconventional weapons as a critical threat to U.S. national interests and want to parlay the success of the Afghan campaign into a similar operation further west. Those who pass for doves in the mainstream debate point to the difficulty of such an undertaking and the lack of any evidence tying Saddam to the recent attacks on the United States. They argue that the goal of America's Iraq policy should be to revive U.N. weapons inspections and re-energize containment. Both camps have it partly right—and partly wrong.

Thanks to Washington's own missed opportunities and others' shameful cynicism, there are no longer any good policy options toward Iraq. The hawks are wrong to think the problem is desperately urgent or connected to terrorism, but they are right to see the prospect of a nuclear-armed Saddam as so worrisome that it requires drastic action. The doves, meanwhile, are right about Iraq's not being a good candidate for a replay of Operation Enduring Freedom, but they are wrong to think that inspections and deterrence are adequate responses to Iraq's weapons of mass destruction (WMD) programs.

After the more immediate danger posed by Osama bin Laden's al Qaeda network has been dealt with, the Bush administration should indeed turn its attention to Baghdad. What it should do at that point, however, is pursue the one strategy that offers a way out of the impasse. The United States should invade Iraq, eliminate the present regime, and pave the way for a successor prepared to abide by its international commitments and live in peace with its neighbors.

The Trouble With Containment

The reasons for contemplating such dramatic action have little to do with the events of September 11 and the subsequent crisis and much to do with the course of U.S. policy toward Iraq since 1991. After Iraq's defeat in the Persian Gulf War, the first Bush administration hoped Saddam would fall from power. It had no clear strategy for how to make that happen, however, and so settled for keeping him isolated and defanged until the lucky day eventually arrived. For lack of a better alternative the Clinton administration continued the same policy, as has the current administration.

The central goal of containment over the past decade has been to prevent Saddam—a serial aggressor—from rebuilding Iraq's military power, including its weapons of mass destruction. The United States and its allies did not want to have to deter, repel, or reverse another Iraqi invasion; they wanted to deny Saddam the wherewithal to mount a threat to his neighbors in the first place. So they put in place, under U.N. auspices, a combination of economic, military, and diplomatic constraints that prevented Saddam from once again destabilizing one of the world's most strategically important regions, while simultaneously allowing humanitarian exemptions so Iraq could meet the nonmilitary needs of its population. Despite the criticism it often received, this policy was a sensible approach to a situation in which there were few attractive options. It served its purposes well, and far longer than most thought possible.

Over the last few years, however, containment has started to unravel. Serious inspections of Saddam's WMD programs stopped long ago. Fewer and fewer nations respect the U.N.-mandated constraints, and more and more are tired of constantly battling with Saddam to force him to comply. Ludicrous Iraqi propaganda about how the economic sanctions are responsible for the deaths of more than a million people since 1991 is now accepted at face value the world over. A dozen or more nations have flown commercial airliners into Iraq to flout the ban on air travel to and from the country—a ban they now claim never existed, but one that was a well-respected fact just a few years ago. Smuggled Iraqi oil flows via Jordan, Syria, Turkey, and the Persian Gulf states at a rate more than double what it was in 1998. Iraq is increasingly able to get its hands on prohibited items such as spare parts for its tanks and planes and equipment for its crippled logistical system. Most stunning of all, the Chinese were recently caught building a nationwide fiberoptic communications network for Saddam's regime; the key nodes of this system were destroyed by U.S. airstrikes in January 2001. If respect for the sanctions has already eroded to the point where the Chinese are willing to sell Iraq such critical technology, how long will it be before someone proves willing to sell tanks? Or missiles? Or fissile material?

Repeated calls to resuscitate the anti-Saddam coalition and strengthen containment are correct about the problem but naive in thinking it can be solved easily. Comprehensive sanctions of the type imposed on Iraq are of necessity a multilateral effort, and at this point there are simply too many important countries willing to subvert them for the scheme to be effective. The current administration's unhappy experience in trying to sell "smart sanctions" to the international community shows just how bad the situation is. The administration's proposed reforms would lift most of the economic constraints on Iraq in return for tighter controls over what comes into the country—a perfectly reasonable idea for anyone actually interested in helping the Iraqi people while keeping Saddam's military in check. But France, Russia, China, and others have opposed the plan because Baghdad fears, correctly, that if it were accepted some form of international military and financial controls might be prolonged.

Ironically, in practice the smart sanctions probably would not do much more than briefly stave off containment's collapse. Right now the U.N. uses its control over Iraq's contracts to determine what goes into and out of the country legally. The system is policed through U.N. (read U.S.) scrutiny of every Iraqi contract—a cumbersome and glacially slow process that still fails to stop Saddam's massive smuggling activities. The Bush administration's proposal would shift the enforcement burden away from the U.N. and onto Iraq's neighbors and try to shut down illegal trade by buying the cooperation of those states through which it would have to pass—Jordan, Syria, Turkey, Iran, and the members of the Gulf Cooperation Council (Bahrain, Kuwait, Oman, Qatar, Saudi Arabia, and the United Arab Emirates). The problem is that all these countries profit from the smuggling, all have populations opposed to enforcing the sanctions, and all except the GCC and Iran are now highly vulnerable to Iraqi economic pressure. So no matter what they may say publicly, none of them is likely to help much in blocking the flow of oil, money, and contraband.

At this point, restoring a serious and sustainable containment regime would require an entirely new set of arrangements. General economic sanctions would have to be lifted and the current U.N. contracting system virtually eliminated, while the core military embargo and financial controls would have to be left in place, harsh penalties instituted for violators, and preauthorization arranged for the use of force by the United States to compel compliance. Such a deal is unimaginable in the U.N. Security Council today, where many of the members compete to see who can appease Iraq most. And although in theory similar reforms could be imposed by the United States unilaterally, any attempt to do so would soon run into passionate international opposition, crippling U.S. diplomacy long before it had much effect on Saddam. Reforming containment enough to make it viable, therefore, is simply not in the offing.

The Trouble With Deterrence

In response to the problems of containment, some have argued that the United States should fall back on a strategy of deterrence—or rather, containment as it was actually practiced against the Soviet Union during the Cold War (as opposed to the supersized version applied to Iraq in the 1990s). This would mean allowing the post-Gulf War constraints to slip away altogether and relying solely on the threat of U.S. intervention to dissuade Saddam from future aggression. Such an approach would be generally welcome outside the United States. But it would involve running a terrible risk, for it is not at all clear that Saddam can be deterred successfully for very long.

This is not to argue that Saddam is irrational. There is considerable evidence that he weighs costs and benefits, follows a crude logic in determining how best to achieve his goals, understands deterrence, and has been deterred in the past. Few knowledgeable observers doubt that Saddam refrained from using WMD when he attacked Israel during the Gulf War because he feared Israeli nuclear retaliation, and he seems to have been deterred from using WMD against Saudi Arabia and coalition forces because he feared U.S. retaliation.

Nevertheless, Saddam has a number of pathologies that make deterring him unusually difficult. He is an inveterate gambler and risk-taker who regularly twists his calculation of the odds to suit his preferred course of action. He bases his calculations on assumptions that outsiders often find bizarre and has little understanding of the larger world. He is a solitary decision-maker who relies little on advice from others. And he has poor sources of information about matters outside Iraq, along with intelligence services that generally tell him what they believe he wants to hear. These pathologies lie behind the many terrible miscalculations Saddam has made over the years that flew in the face of deterrence—including the invasion of Iran in 1980, the invasion of Kuwait in 1990, the decision to fight for Kuwait in 1990-91, and the decision to threaten Kuwait again in 1994.

It is thus impossible to predict the kind of calculations he would make about the willingness of the United States to challenge him once he had the ability to incinerate Riyadh, Tel Aviv, or the Saudi oil fields. He might well make another grab for Kuwait, for example, and once in possession dare the United States to evict him and risk a nuclear exchange. During the Cold War, U.S. strategists used to fret that once the Soviet Union reached strategic parity, Moscow would feel free to employ its conventional forces as it saw fit because the United States would be too scared of escalation to respond. Such fears were plausible in the abstract but seem to have been groundless because

Soviet leaders were fundamentally conservative decision-makers. Saddam, in contrast, is fundamentally aggressive and risk-acceptant. Leaving him free to acquire nuclear weapons and then hoping that in spite of his track record he can be deterred this time around is not the kind of social science experiment the United States government should be willing to run.

Phase Two?

With containment collapsing and deterrence too risky, some form of regime change is steadily becoming the only answer to the Iraqi conundrum. In the wake of the September 11 attacks, in fact, supporters of one particular approach to regime change—using the Iraqi opposition to do the job, in conjunction with U.S. air power—have repackaged their ideas to fit the times and gained substantial momentum. The position of these hawks was captured succinctly in a September 20 "open letter" to President Bush from three dozen luminaries, who argued that

> any strategy aiming at the eradication of terrorism and its sponsors must include a determined effort to remove Saddam Hussein from power in Iraq. Failure to undertake such an effort will constitute an early and perhaps decisive surrender in the war on international terrorism. The United States must therefore provide full military and financial support to the Iraqi opposition. American military force should be used to provide a "safe zone" in Iraq from which the opposition can operate.

Once the military operations in Afghanistan succeeded, they were widely touted by such hawks as a model for a future campaign against Saddam.

The hawks are right on two big points: that a nuclear-armed Saddam would be a disaster waiting to happen and that at this point it would be easier to get rid of him than to stop him from reconstituting his weapons programs. Unfortunately, most of them are wrong on key details, such as how regime change should be accomplished. Trying to topple Saddam by using the same limited military approach the United States used in Afghanistan—air power, special forces, and support for local opposition groups—would be trying to do the job on the cheap, and like all such efforts would run a real risk of disaster. . . .

The Case For Invasion

Saddam Hussein must be dealt with. But thinking about Iraq in the context of the war on terrorism or the operations in Afghanistan obscures more than it clarifies. Given the specific features of the Iraqi situation, trying to topple Saddam with an Afghan-style campaign would be risky and ill advised. It might just work, but there is no reason to chance it, especially since adding a major ground component—that is, replaying the Gulf War rather than the Afghan campaign—would not cost much more while making success a near certainty. Even without committing its own ground forces, the United States would still be responsible for Iraq's political and military reconstruction. Using a standoff approach to regime change, however, would limit American ability to control events while opening the door to mischief-makers who would try to turn Saddam's fall to their own advantage. Because of the human, diplomatic, and financial costs involved, invasion should always be a last resort. Unfortunately in this case, since all the other options are worse, it is a necessary one.

The strategic logic for invasion is compelling. It would eliminate the possibility that Saddam might rebuild his military or acquire nuclear weapons and thus threaten the security of the world's supply of oil. It would allow the United States to redeploy most of its forces away from the region afterward, or at the very least return to its pre-Gulf War "over the horizon" presence—something long sought by locals and the United States alike. And by facilitating the reconstruction of Iraq and its re-entry into regional politics it would remove a major irritant from U.S. relations with the Muslim world in general.

The military aspects of an invasion, meanwhile, although hardly painless, would be straightforward and well within U.S. capabilities. In 1991, U.S. forces ran roughshod over their Iraqi counterparts, and in the ten years since then the gap in capabilities between the two sides has widened. At this point, the United States could probably smash Iraq's ground forces with a single corps composed of two heavy divisions and an armored cavalry regiment. To be on the safe side and to handle other missions, however, it would make sense to plan for a force twice that size. Some light infantry will be required in case Saddam's loyalists fight in Iraq's cities. Airmobile forces will be needed to seize Iraq's oil fields at the start of hostilities and to occupy the sites from which Saddam could launch missiles against Israel or Saudi Arabia. And troops will have to be available for occupation duties once the fighting is over. All told, the force should total roughly 200,000-300,000 people: for the invasion, between four and six divisions plus supporting units, and for the air campaign, 700-1,000 aircraft and anywhere from one to five carrier battle groups (depending on what sort of access to bases turned out to be possible). Building up such a force in the Persian Gulf would take three to five months, but the campaign itself would probably take about a month, including the opening air operations.

The casualties incurred during such an operation might well be greater than during the Afghan or Gulf Wars, but they are unlikely to be catastrophic. Two factors that could increase the toll would be the willingness of Iraqi forces to fight tenaciously for their cities and a decision by Saddam to employ unconventional weapons during the crisis. On the other hand, it is possible that the mere presence of such American forces on Iraq's doorstep could produce a coup that would topple Saddam without significant combat.

The military aspects of an invasion, actually, are likely to be the easiest part of the deal. The diplomatic fallout will probably be more difficult, with its severity directly related to the length of the campaign and the certainty of its outcome. Just as in Afghanistan, the longer it drags on and the more uncertain it looks, the more dissent will be heard, both at home and abroad—whereas the quicker and more decisive the victory, the more palatable it will be for all concerned.

The only country whose support would be absolutely necessary for an invasion is Kuwait. The task would be made dramatically easier if the Saudis helped, however, both because of the excellent bases on their territory and because the GCC and Jordan would undoubtedly follow the Saudi lead. Although both the Saudis and the Kuwaitis have said they do not want the United States to attack Iraq, the consensus among those who know those countries' leaders well is that they would grudgingly consent if the United States could convince them it was willing to use the full range of its military capabilities to ensure a swift, successful campaign.

Egyptian permission would be required to move ships through the Suez Canal and planes across its airspace, but given the importance of U.S. economic and military assistance to Egypt that should not be a problem. Turkey's support would also be useful, in particular because it would make it much easier to defend the Kurds in northern Iraq from an Iraqi counteroffensive. Other regional states would have an incentive to come on board because they would want to have a say in the postinvasion political arrangements in Baghdad. The French, the Russians, and the Chinese would object strongly to the whole concept and might try to kill it by raising a diplomatic firestorm. Still, they could not stop a U.S. invasion were the administration truly set on one, and they might eventually jump on board once it went ahead if only to retain political and economic influence in Iraq later on.

The biggest headaches for the United States are likely to stem not from the invasion itself but from its aftermath. Once the country has been con-quered and Saddam's regime driven from power, the United States would be left "owning" a country of 22 million people ravaged by more than two decades of war, totalitarian misrule, and severe deprivation. The invaders would get to decide the composition and form of a future Iraqi government—both an opportunity and a burden. Some form of unitary but federalized state would probably best suit the bewildering array of local and foreign interests involved, but ideally this decision would be a collective one: as in Afghanistan, the United States should try to turn the question of future Iraqi political arrange-ments over to the U.N., or possibly the Arab League, thus shedding and spreading some responsibility for the outcome. Alternatively, it might bring in those countries most directly affected by the outcome—the Saudis, Kuwaitis, Jordanians, and Turks—both to co-opt them and as an incentive for their diplomatic support. In the end, of course, it would be up to the United States to make sure that a post-Saddam Iraq did not slip into chaos like Lebanon in the 1980s or Afghanistan in the 1990s, creating spillover effects in the region and raising the possibility of a new terrorist haven.

Because it will be important to ensure that Iraq does not fall apart after-ward, the United States will also need to repair much of the damage done to the Iraqi economy since Saddam's accession. It could undoubtedly raise substantial funds for this purpose from the GCC and perhaps some Euro-pean and East Asian allies dependent on Persian Gulf oil. And as soon as Iraq's oil started flowing again, the country could contribute to its own future. Cur-rent estimates of the cost of rebuilding Iraq's economy, however, range from $50 billion to $150 billion, and that does not include repairing the damage from yet another major war. The United States should thus be prepared to contribute several billion dollars per year for as much as a decade to rebuild the country.

If Not Now, When?

It is one thing to recognize that because of the unique features of this case—the scale of the interests involved, Saddam's unparalleled record of aggres-sion and violence, and the problems with other options—an invasion of Iraq is the least bad course of action available. It is another to figure out just when such an invasion should be launched. Despite what many hawks now argue, it is a mistake to think of operations against Iraq as part of the war on ter-rorism. The dilemma the United States must now grapple with, in fact, is that attacking Iraq could jeopardize the success of that war, but the longer it waits before attacking the harder it will be and the greater the risk that Saddam's strength will increase.

Toppling Saddam is not a necessary component of the war on terrorism, and by itself Iraq's support for terrorism would not justify the heavy costs of an invasion. Iraq is indeed a state sponsor of terrorism, but on the grand roll of such sponsors it is well behind Iran, Syria, Pakistan, Sudan, Lebanon, North Korea, Libya, and several others. If the only problem the United States had with Iraq were its support for terrorism, it would be a relatively minor concern. Conversely, if one were to list Saddam Hussein's crimes against humanity in order of their importance, his support for terrorism would rank low.

The reason for even contemplating all the costs that an invasion would entail is the risk that a nuclear-armed Saddam might wreak havoc in his region and beyond, together with the certainty that he will acquire such weapons eventually if left unchecked. Nevertheless, there is no indication that he is about to get them within weeks or months. Containment may be dying, but it is not dead yet, and a determined U.S. effort could keep it alive for some time longer. Iraq represents an emerging threat, but bin Laden and his accomplices constitute an immediate one.

Al Qaeda has demonstrated both the ability and the willingness to reach into the American homeland and slaughter thousands, and it now has the motive of revenge to add to its general ideological hostility. Breaking the network's back in Afghanistan and elsewhere should therefore be the Bush administration's top national security priority, and this cannot be done without the active cooperation of scores of U.S. allies around the world—for intelligence gathering, police work, and financial cooperation, all on top of any military or diplomatic help that might be required.

So far the administration's efforts in this area are paying off, largely because others have supported them. Should that trend continue, it is likely that within anywhere from six months to two years the United States and its partners will have disrupted al Qaeda's communications, recruitment, financing, and planning so much that what is left of the network will be largely innocuous. Until this point has been reached, it would be a mistake to jeopardize success by risking a major break with U.S. allies—something that a serious campaign against Iraq might well make necessary. And besides, laying the appropriate military, political, diplomatic, and economic groundwork for an invasion will take considerable time and effort.

Nevertheless, those calling for an immediate attack on Iraq make a legitimate point. Too much delay could be as problematic as too little, because it would risk the momentum gained from the victory over Afghanistan. Today the shock of the September 11 attacks is still fresh and the U.S. government and public are ready to make sacrifices—while the rest of the world recognizes American anger and may be leery of getting on the wrong side of it. The longer the wait before an invasion, the harder it will be to muster domestic and international support for it, even though the reason for invading would have little or nothing to do with Iraq's connection to terrorism. And over time the effort to take down al Qaeda could actually exacerbate the problems with containment, since some of America's partners in that effort want to loosen rather than tighten the noose on the Iraqi regime and may try to use the leverage of their cooperation with us to stall any bold moves. The United States can afford to wait a little while before turning to Saddam, in other words, but not indefinitely.

Even when a policy cannot be sustained forever, it often makes sense to spin out its final stages for as long as possible. This is not the case with the containment of Iraq today. The last two years have witnessed a dramatic erosion of the constraints on the Iraqi regime. The Bush administration's initial solution to this problem, the smart sanctions plan, would be little more than a Band-Aid and even so could not find general acceptance. If no more serious action is taken, the United States and the world at large may soon confront a nuclear-armed Saddam. At that point the danger would be obvious to all, but it would be infinitely more difficult to confront. Taking down al Qaeda should indeed be the priority of the moment, and using half-measures, such as the Afghan approach, against Saddam would be a mistake. But these should not become permanent excuses for inaction. We may tarry, but Saddam will not.

Bush at War
Bob Woodward

from *Bush at War*

It came as no surprise when Bob Woodward's book, Bush at War, *became a national best-seller upon its publication last year. As always, Woodward's work—which is mainly devoted to the Bush team's war against the Taliban in Afghanistan—relies on a large number of in-depth interviews with key players in the administration and elsewhere, and it offers an unmatched portrait of the inner workings of government. One of the criticisms of Woodward is that he invariably makes his sources look good—perhaps too good. Then again, this reputation is probably a major reason why he has such unparalleled access to Washington's heavy hitters. Our reading of the book, especially the interview with George W. Bush that makes up the last part of this selection, is that Woodward provides an even-handed and often quite candid picture of the people who are currently shaping our country's policy.*

The following excerpt is taken from the book's epilogue, which covers the period in mid-2002 when the Afghanistan conflict was winding down and the issue of Iraq was beginning to take center stage. We pick up the narrative at the point where Colin Powell is commencing his campaign to persuade President Bush of the importance of working through the United Nations on the Iraq problem, at least for the time being. . . .

The Iraq issue heated up substantially. It was going to be the next real—and perhaps the greatest—test of Bush's leadership and the role of the United States in the world.

Iraq carried lots of baggage. When Rice first signed up to be Bush's foreign policy adviser before the 2000 presidential campaign, she had raised the issue with him. Bush told her he disagreed with those who thought that his father had ended the war against Saddam in 1991 too quickly. At the time, Bush senior, Secretary of Defense Cheney, and Chairman of the Joint Chiefs of Staff Powell had all agreed to end the war after achieving the stated goal of the U.N. resolution: evicting Saddam's armies from Kuwait. The U.S. would not drive to Baghdad to oust Saddam. Chasing down the retreating Iraqi army might look like a massacre. Half of Saddam's army was destroyed. He had suffered one of the most humiliating military defeats in modern history. Surely he was finished. The CIA and various Arab leaders predicted that he would soon be deposed, that some Iraqi Army colonel or general would put a bullet in him or lead a coup.

Saddam survived and Bush's father was defeated for reelection in 1992 by Clinton. In 1998 when Saddam shut down U.N. inspections of facilities suspected of making weapons of mass destruction, Clinton ordered Operation Desert Fox. Some 650 bomber and missile sorties were launched at Iraq over a three-day period, but Saddam would still not allow the U.N. inspectors back in.

Still Bush defended his father and his advisers. "They did the right thing at the time," he told Rice. His father was limited by the U.N. resolution authorizing the use of force only to get Saddam out of Kuwait. She agreed and noted that often in history leaders had blundered by letting a short-term tactical success change their strategic goals. Going to Baghdad to force Saddam from power might have been an entirely different matter. Because something seemed militarily easy was not a reason to do it, she said.

After Bush's initial decision not to attack Iraq immediately following the September 11 terrorist attacks, the issue had continued to percolate in the war cabinet—actively for Cheney and Rumsfeld, passively for Powell, who was not spoiling for another war.

When the president delivered his first State of the Union address on January 29, 2002, the big headline was his declaration that Iraq, Iran, and North Korea were "an axis of evil." But he had said that the real peril and potential catastrophe was the growing availability of weapons of mass destruction to terrorists or these regimes.

Bush had considered raising this danger in his speech to Congress nine days after the terrorist attacks but he postponed, thinking such candor might be too much for the public at that time.

"I will not wait on events," he said in the State of the Union address, hinting that he would act preemptively—a strategy that he later articulated more directly.

As one of the first steps against Saddam, the president soon signed a new intelligence order significantly expanding the CIA covert operation to oust Saddam. He allocated $100 million to $200 million in new covert money— vastly more than the $70 million the CIA spent in Afghanistan. He increased support to the Iraqi opposition, stepped up intelligence gathering inside Iraq, and prepared for possible deployment of CIA paramilitary teams and U.S. Special Forces similar to those used in Afghanistan.

Iraq is not Afghanistan, Tenet warned the president. The Iraqi opposition was much weaker, and Saddam ran a police state. He was hard to locate, and he used decoy look-alikes. Without companion military action and other pressure, Tenet told the president, the CIA had only a 10 to 20 percent chance of succeeding.

Bush, nonetheless, concluded that a larger covert operation would help prepare for a military strike by vastly increasing the flow of intelligence and contacts that might be needed later.

In April, the president began publicly declaring a policy of regime change in Iraq. In June he formally declared that he would launch preemptive attacks against countries believed to be a serious threat to the United States.

Powell still had not squared his relationship with the president. During the first half of 2002, Armitage had received reliable reports that Rumsfeld was requesting and having periodic private meetings with Bush. Powell was not particularly worried, because he could usually find out what had transpired through Rice, though she had had some difficulties initially finding out herself.

"It seems to me that you ought to be requesting some time with the president," Armitage suggested to Powell. Face time was critical, and it was a relationship that Powell had not mastered.

Powell said he recalled his time as national security adviser for Reagan when everyone was always trying to see the president. He didn't want to intrude. If Bush wanted to see him, any time or any place, he was, of course, available. He saw Bush all the time at meetings, and he was able to convey his views.

"You've got to start doing it," Armitage said. He was the fucking secretary of state. It wouldn't be an imposition. Better relations would help in all the battles, would help the department across the board.

In the late spring of 2002—some 16 months into the Bush presidency—Powell started requesting private time with Bush. He did it through Rice, who sat in on the meetings which took place about once a week for about 20 to 30 minutes. It seemed to help, but it was like his experience in the Middle East, no big breakthroughs.

During the summer, Powell was over at the White House one day with time to kill before a meeting with Rice. The president spotted him and invited him into the Oval Office. They talked alone for about 30 minutes. They shot the breeze and relaxed. The conversation was about everything and nothing.

"I think we're really making some headway in the relationship," Powell reported to Armitage afterward. The chasm seemed to be closing. "I know we really connected."

In early August, Powell made the diplomatic rounds in Indonesia and the Philippines and, as always, kept in touch with what was happening at home. Iraq was continuing to bubble. Brent Scowcroft, the mild-mannered national security adviser to Bush's father during the Gulf War, had declared on a Sunday morning talk show on August 4 that an attack on Iraq could turn the Middle East into a "cauldron and thus destroy the war on terrorism."

Blunt talk, but Powell basically agreed. He had not made clear his own analysis and conclusions to the president and realized he needed to do so. On the long flight back, from nearly halfway around the world, he jotted down some notes. Virtually all the Iraq discussions in the NSC had been about war plans—how to attack, when, with what force levels, military strike scenario this and military strike scenario that. It was clear to him now that the context was being lost, the attitudes and views of the rest of the world which he knew and lived with. His notes filled three or four pages.

During the Gulf War, when he had been chairman of the Joint Chiefs of Staff, Powell had played the role of reluctant warrior, arguing to the first President Bush, perhaps too mildly, that containing Iraq might work, that war might not be necessary. But as the principal military adviser, he hadn't pressed his arguments that forcefully because they were less military than political. Now as secretary of state, his account was politics—the politics of the world. He decided he had to come down very hard, state his convictions and conclusions so there would be no doubt as to where he stood. The president had been hearing plenty from Cheney and Rumsfeld, a kind of A-team inside the war cabinet. Powell wanted to present the B-team, the alternative view that he believed had not been aired. He owed the president more than PowerPoint briefings.

In Washington, he told Rice that he wanted to see the president. Bush invited the two to the residence on the evening of Monday, August 5. The meeting expanded into dinner and then moved to the president's office in the residence.

Powell told Bush that as he was getting his head around the Iraq question, he needed to think about the broader issues, all the consequences of war.

With his notes by his side, a double-spaced outline on loose-leaf paper, Powell said the president had to consider what a military operation against Iraq would do in the Arab world. Cauldron was the right word. He dealt with the leaders and foreign ministers in these countries as secretary of state. The entire region could be destabilized—friendly regimes in Saudi Arabia, Egypt, and Jordan could be put in jeopardy or overthrown. Anger and frustration at America abounded. War could change everything in the Middle East.

It would suck the oxygen out of just about everything else the United States was doing, not only in the war on terrorism, but all other diplomatic, defense, and intelligence relationships, Powell said. The economic implications could be staggering, potentially driving the supply and price of oil in directions that were as yet unimagined. All this in a time of an international economic slump. The cost of occupying Iraq after a victory would be expensive. The economic impact on the region, the world, and the United States domestically had to be considered.

Following victory, and they would surely prevail Powell believed, the day-after implications were giant. What of the image of an American general running an Arab country for some length of time? he asked. A General MacArthur in Baghdad? This would be a big event within Iraq, the region, and the world. How long would it be? No one could know. How would success be defined?

"It's nice to say we can do it unilaterally," Powell told the president bluntly, "except you can't." A successful military plan would require access to bases and facilities in the region, overflight rights. They would need allies. This would not be the Gulf War, a nice two-hour trip from a fully cooperative Saudi Arabia over to Kuwait City—the target of liberation just some 40 miles away. Now the geography would be formidable. Baghdad was a couple of hundred miles across Mesopotamia.

The Middle East crisis was still ever-present. That was the issue that the Arab and Muslim world wanted addressed. A war on Iraq would open Israel to attack by Saddam, who had launched Scud missiles at it during the Gulf War.

Saddam was crazy, a menace, a real threat, unpredictable, but he had been largely contained and deterred since the Gulf War. A new war could unleash precisely what they wanted to prevent—Saddam on a rampage, a last desperate stand, perhaps using his weapons of mass destruction.

On the intelligence side, as the president knew, the problem was also immense, Powell said. They had not been able to find bin Laden, Mullah Omar, and other al Qaeda and Taliban leaders in Afghanistan. They didn't know where Saddam was. Saddam had all kinds of tricks and deceptions. He had an entire state at his disposal to hide in. They did not need another possibly fruitless manhunt.

Powell's presentation was an outpouring of both analysis and emotion that encompassed his entire experience—35 years in the military, former national security adviser, and now chief diplomat. The president seemed intrigued as he listened and asked questions but did not push back that much.

And Powell realized that his arguments begged the question of well, what do you do? He knew that Bush liked, in fact insisted on, solutions, and he wanted to take his views all the way down the trail. "You can still make a pitch for a coalition or U.N. action to do what needs to be done," he said. International support had to be garnered. The U.N. was only one way. But some way had to be found to recruit allies. A war with Iraq could be much more complicated and bloody than the war in Afghanistan, which was Exhibit A demonstrating the necessity of a coalition.

The president said he preferred to have an international coalition, and he loved building one for the war in Afghanistan.

Powell responded that he believed the pitch could still be made to the international community to build support.

What did he think the incentives and motives might be of some of the critical players such as the Russians or the French, the president asked. What would they do?

As a matter of diplomacy, Powell said he thought the president and the administration could bring most countries along.

The secretary felt the discussion became tense several times as he pressed, but in the end he believed that he had left nothing unsaid.

The president thanked him. It had been two hours—nothing of Clintonesque, late-night-at-the-dorm proportions, but extraordinary for this president and Powell. And Powell felt he had stripped his argument down to the essentials. The private meeting with just Bush and Rice had meant that there was not a lot of static coming in from other quarters—Cheney and Rumsfeld.

Rice thought the headline was, "Powell Makes Case for Coalition as Only Way to Assure Success."

"That was terrific," Rice said the next day in a phone call to Powell, "and we need to do more of those."

The tip-off about the potential importance of the evening was when [White House chief of staff Andrew] Card called Powell the next day and asked him to come over and give him the same presentation, notes and all.

The dinner was a home run, Powell felt.

Bush left for his Crawford vacation the next afternoon, as Iraq continued to play to a packed house in the news media. There was little other news, and speculation about Iraq filled the void. Every living former national security adviser or former secretary of state who could lift pen to paper was on the street with his or her views.

On Wednesday, August 14, the principals met in Washington without the president.

Powell said they needed to think about getting a coalition for action against Iraq, some kind of international cover at least. The Brits were with us, he noted, but their support was fragile in the absence of some international coalition or cover. They needed something. Most of Europe was the same way, he reported, as was all of Arabia, especially the U.S. friends in the Gulf who would be most essential for war. And Turkey, which shared a 100-mile border with Iraq.

The first opportunity the president would have after his vacation to address formally the subject of Iraq was a scheduled speech to the United Nations General Assembly on September 12, Powell pointed out. There had been some talk about making the speech about American values or talking about the Middle East. But Iraq was topic A. "I can't imagine him going there and not speaking about this," Powell said.

Rice agreed. In the atmosphere of continuing media discussion, not to talk about Iraq might suggest that the administration was not serious about Saddam's threat, or that it was operating in total secrecy. And Bush liked to explain to the public at least the general outlines of where his policy was heading.

They discussed how they would face an endless process of debate and compromise and delay once they started down the U.N. road—words not action.

"I think the speech at the U.N. ought to be about Iraq," Cheney agreed. But the U.N. ought to be made the issue. It should be challenged and criticized. "Go tell them it's not about us. It's about you. You are not important." The U.N. was not enforcing more than a decade of resolutions ordering Saddam to destroy his weapons of mass destruction and allow weapons inspectors inside Iraq. The U.N. was running the risk of becoming irrelevant and would be the loser if it did not do what was necessary.

Rice agreed. The U.N. had become too much like the post–World War I League of Nations—a debating society with no teeth.

They all agreed that the president should not go to the U.N. to ask for a declaration of war. That was quickly off the table. They all agreed that a speech about Iraq made sense. Given the importance of the issue, it had to be addressed. But there was no agreement about what the president should say.

Two days later, Friday, August 16, the NSC met, with the president attending by secure video from Crawford. The sole purpose of the meeting was for Powell to make his pitch about going to the U.N. to seek support or a coalition in some form. Unilateral war would be tough, close to impossible, Powell said. At least they ought to try to reach out and ask other countries to join them.

The president went around the table asking for comments, and there was general support for giving the U.N. a shot—even from Cheney and Rumsfeld.

Fine, Bush finally said. He approved of the approach—a speech to the U.N. about Iraq. And it couldn't be too shrill, he cautioned them, or put too high a standard so that it would be obvious to all that they weren't serious. He wanted to give the U.N. a chance.

Powell walked out feeling they had a deal, and he went off for a vacation in the Hamptons on Long Island, New York.

It was four days later when I went to Crawford, Texas, for my final interview with President Bush on August 20, 2002. A number of his closest aides had suggested I interview him in Crawford, the place he feels most comfortable. It was 11 months after the terrorist attacks. He and Laura Bush had built a beautiful, small, one-story home in a secluded corner of their 1,600-acre ranch. Their home overlooks a man-made lake. It was his vacation, and the president was dressed in jeans, a short-sleeved shirt, and heavy, working cowboy boots. He seemed relaxed and focused.

Most of my questions dealt with the war in Afghanistan and the broader war on terrorism. His answers are fully reflected in this book. But he made a number of points worth contemplating now.

I asked the president whether he and the country had done enough for the war on terror. The possibility of another major attack still loomed. But the absence of an attack reenforced the sense of normalcy. Washington and New York City 2002 could not have been further from London 1940 or

America after December 7, 1941. He had not put the country on a war footing, demanded sacrifices from large numbers of citizens, or taken what for him would be the unthinkable and draconian step of raising taxes or repealing his 2001 tax cut. Was it not possible that he had undermobilized given the threat and the devastation of September 11?

"If we get hit soon again," I asked him, "big, spectacular—people are going to look back and say, we did a lot but we didn't do enough?"

"The answer to your question is, Where do you mobilize? We're mobilizing in the sense that we're spending," Bush said. He mentioned big budget increases for the FBI, CIA, firefighters, and others, the first responders to terrorist attacks.

I said that someone had mentioned to me that there were only about 11,000 FBI agents but nearly 180,000 United States Marines. Could not some of those Marines, some of whom are excellent intelligence officers and security experts, be assigned to airports and other vulnerable, potential targets? He was spending most of his time on the issues of the war and homeland security. Rice was spending probably 80 percent of hers. Where was the rest of the government?

"It's an interesting question," he replied. "The answer is, if they hit us hard, the answer is no"—that he did not do enough. "If they don't hit us hard, the answer is, we did it right."

I said that I had talked with Karl Rove who said that ultimately the war would be measured by the outcome. "Everything will be measured by results," Rove had said. "The victor is always right. History ascribes to the victor qualities that may or may not actually have been there. And similarly to the defeated."

Bush agreed but he said the problem was that the war had turned into a kind of international manhunt. The terrorists had to be chased one by one. It was not just to satisfy what he called "a public blood lust." At the same time, he knew the importance of getting bin Laden—"decapitating" the al Qaeda leadership.

He was of the view that there was no convincing evidence of whether bin Laden was alive or dead. He wondered about the absence of communication from him, not a single taped message. "All I know is that he is a megalomaniac," Bush said. "Is he that disciplined that he can be quiet for now nine months?"

"Why have they not struck again?" I asked.

"Maybe we're pretty good at what we're doing," Bush said. But maybe not. The investigators had established that the September 11 attacks had been at least two years in the planning. Perhaps, he suggested, he had underestimated the other side, that they spent more time on their long-range efforts, that what might happen right now had been in the works much longer.

The president raised a more chilling prospect. It was the gravest worry of the FBI, that members of al Qaeda, "cold, calculating killers" he called them, had buried themselves into American society, hanging out in garden apartments or anywhere else, waiting for their prearranged moment to strike. "Maybe there's a planning cycle of four years," he said.

I wanted to attempt to understand the president's overall approach or philosophy to foreign affairs and war policy. The Taliban had been deposed, but possibly bin Laden and certainly many in his al Qaeda network had escaped. Other terrorist attacks were expected. The United States now had some 7,000 troops on the ground in Afghanistan, which was still a dangerous, unstable place. [Afghan president Hamid] Karzai was in continual jeopardy even with American Special Forces acting as his bodyguards.

The theoretical pronouncements Bush had made about not nation building have been discarded almost wholesale in the face of the need to keep Afghanistan together. He was at times acting like the Afghan budget director and bill collector.

"If I have asked once, I have asked 20 times, I want to see the cash flow projections of the Afghan government," Bush said. "Who owes money? I wrote a letter the other day dunning these people over in Europe for money." He learned it only costs $500 a year to pay a trained Afghan soldier. "I said it makes no sense to train people for a military and then not pay them."

Until that day in Crawford, I had not heard the sweeping aspirations Bush has for his presidency and the United States. Most presidents have high hopes. Some have grandiose visions of what they will achieve, and he was firmly in that camp.

"I will seize the opportunity to achieve big goals," Bush told me as we sat in a large room in his home with the breeze comfortably blowing through the screens. "There is nothing bigger than to achieve world peace."

Action was not just for strategic purposes or defensive purposes, he said. "You see, it's like Iraq," he said. "Condi didn't want me to talk about it." He and Rice, who was sitting with us during the interview, laughed. "But wait a minute," he continued. "Just as an aside, and we'll see whether this bears out. Clearly, there will be a strategic implication to a regime change in Iraq, if we go forward. But there's something beneath that, as far as I'm concerned, and that is, there is immense suffering."

Bush glanced at Rice. "Or North Korea," he quickly added. "Let me talk about North Korea." But he seemed to mean Iraq also. Iraq, North Korea, and Iran were the "axis of evil" he had identified in his State of the Union speech.

The president sat forward in his chair. I thought he might jump up he became so emotional as he spoke about the North Korean leader.

"I loathe Kim Jong Il!" Bush shouted, waving his finger in the air. "I've got a visceral reaction to this guy, because he is starving his people. And I have seen intelligence of these prison camps—they're huge—that he uses to break up families, and to torture people. I am appalled at the . . ."

I asked if he had seen the overhead satellite photography of the prison camps provided by the U.S. intelligence agencies?

"Yes, it appalls me." He wondered how the civilized world could stand by and coddle the North Korean president as he starves his people. "It is visceral. Maybe it's my religion, maybe it's my—but I feel passionate about this." He said he also realized that the North Koreans had massive military might poised to overrun the U.S. ally South Korea.

"I'm not foolish," the president continued. "They tell me, we don't need to move too fast, because the financial burdens on people will be so immense if we try to—if this guy were to topple. Who would take care of—I just don't buy that. Either you believe in freedom, and want to—and worry about the human condition, or you don't."

In case I didn't get the message, he added, "And I feel that way about the people of Iraq, by the way." He said that Saddam was starving his people in the outlying Shiite areas. "There is a human condition that we must worry about.

"As we think through Iraq, we may or may not attack. I have no idea, yet. But it will be for the objective of making the world more peaceful."

In Afghanistan, he said, "I wanted us to be viewed as the liberator."

I asked him specifically about the time in late October 2001 when he had told his war cabinet that a coalition was held together not by consultations as much as by strong American leadership that would force the rest of the world to adjust.

"Well," the president said, "you can't talk your way to a solution to a problem. And the United States is in a unique position right now. We are the leader. And a leader must combine the ability to listen to others, along with action.

"I believe in results. If I said it once, I said, I know the world is watching carefully, would be impressed and will be impressed with results achieved. It's like earning capital in many ways. It is a way for us to earn capital in a coalition that can be fragile. And the reason it will be fragile is that there is resentment toward us.

"I mean, you know, if you want to hear resentment, just listen to the word unilateralism. I mean, that's resentment. If somebody wants to try to say something ugly about us, 'Bush is a unilateralist, America is unilateral.' You know, which I find amusing. But I'm also—I've been to meetings where there's a kind of 'we must not act until we're all in agreement.'"

Bush said he didn't think agreement was the issue, and I was surprised at the sweep of his next statement.

"Well, we're never going to get people all in agreement about force and use of force," he declared, suggesting that an international coalition or the United Nations were probably not viable ways to deal with dangerous, rogue states. "But action—confident action that will yield positive results provides kind of a slipstream into which reluctant nations and leaders can get behind and show themselves that there has been—you know, something positive has happened toward peace."

Bush said a president deals with lots of tactical, day-to-day battles on budgets and congressional resolutions, but he sees his job and responsibilities as much larger. His father had with some regularity derided the notion of a "vision" or "the vision thing" as unhelpful. So I was also surprised when the younger Bush said, "The job is—the vision thing matters. That's another lesson I learned. "

His vision clearly includes an ambitious reordering of the world through preemptive and, if necessary, unilateral action to reduce suffering and bring peace.

During the interview, the president spoke a dozen times about his "instincts" or his "instinctive" reactions, including his statement, "I'm not a textbook player, I'm a gut player." It's pretty clear that Bush's role as politician, president, and commander in chief is driven by a secular faith in his instincts—his natural and spontaneous conclusions and judgments. His instincts are almost his second religion.

When I specifically asked about Powell's contributions, the president offered a tepid response. "Powell is a diplomat," Bush responded. "And you've got to have a diplomat. I kind of picture myself as a pretty good diplomat, but nobody else does. You know, particularly, I wouldn't call me a diplomat. But, nevertheless, he is a diplomatic person who has got war experience."

Did Powell want private meetings? I asked.

"He doesn't pick up the phone and say, I need to come and see you," Bush said. He confirmed that he did have private meetings with Powell which Rice also attended. "Let me think about Powell. I got one. He was very good with [Pakistani president Pervez] Musharraf. He single-handedly got Musharraf on board. He was very good about that. He saw the notion of the need to put a coalition together."

A Decade of Deception and Defiance
President George W. Bush's Address to the United Nations General Assembly | September 12, 2002

President George W. Bush's address to the U.N. General Assembly on Sept. 12, 2002 (a year and a day after the 9/11 attacks on New York and Washington) is widely agreed to be one of the best and most effective speeches of his presidency. Going into the speech, the onus was clearly on Bush to justify his aggressive stance on Iraq, and to explain why the current policy of containment was no longer sufficient. In his address, however, Bush turned the tables on the international community, taking the generally accepted view within his administration—that Hussein was already in violation of a long string of U.N. resolutions, and showed no signs of changing his behavior—and sharpening this into a pointed attack on the U.N. itself. In a nutshell, he argued that if the U.N. is unwilling to enforce its own mandates, then it is openly admitting its own uselessness.

The bottom line is, the speech worked. Shortly afterwards, the U.N. Security Council unanimously passed Resolution 1441, sending weapons inspectors back into Iraq and also (though some countries later denied this) laying the legal groundwork for a U.S.-led invasion, in the event that Iraq failed to comply. . . .

Mr. Secretary General, Mr. President, distinguished delegates, and ladies and gentlemen: We meet one year and one day after a terrorist attack brought grief to my country, and brought grief to many citizens of our world. Yesterday, we remembered the innocent lives taken that terrible morning. Today, we turn to the urgent duty of protecting other lives, without illusion and without fear.

We've accomplished much in the last year—in Afghanistan and beyond. We have much yet to do—in Afghanistan and beyond. Many nations represented here have joined in the fight against global terror, and the people of the United States are grateful.

The United Nations was born in the hope that survived a world war—the hope of a world moving toward justice, escaping old patterns of conflict and fear. The founding members resolved that the peace of the world must never again be destroyed by the will and wickedness of any man. We created the United Nations Security Council, so that, unlike the League of Nations, our deliberations would be more than talk, our resolutions would be more than wishes. After generations of deceitful dictators and broken treaties and squandered lives, we dedicated ourselves to standards of human dignity shared by all, and to a system of security defended by all.

Today, these standards, and this security, are challenged. Our commitment to human dignity is challenged by persistent poverty and raging disease. The suffering is great, and our responsibilities are clear. The United States is joining with the world to supply aid where it reaches people and lifts up lives, to extend trade and the prosperity it brings, and to bring medical care where it is desperately needed.

As a symbol of our commitment to human dignity, the United States will return to UNESCO. This organization has been reformed and America will participate fully in its mission to advance human rights and tolerance and learning.

Our common security is challenged by regional conflicts—ethnic and religious strife that is ancient, but not inevitable. In the Middle East, there can be no peace for either side without freedom for both sides. America stands committed to an independent and democratic Palestine, living side by side with Israel in peace and security. Like all other people, Palestinians deserve a government that serves their interests and listens to their voices. My nation will continue to encourage all parties to step up to their responsibilities as we seek a just and comprehensive settlement to the conflict.

Above all, our principles and our security are challenged today by outlaw groups and regimes that accept no law of morality and have no limit to their violent ambitions. In the attacks on America a year ago, we saw the destructive intentions of our enemies. This threat hides within many nations, including my own. In cells and camps, terrorists are plotting further destruction, and building new bases for their war against civilization. And our greatest fear is that terrorists will find a shortcut to their mad ambitions when an outlaw regime supplies them with the technologies to kill on a massive scale.

In one place—in one regime—we find all these dangers, in their most lethal and aggressive forms, exactly the kind of aggressive threat the United Nations was born to confront.

Twelve years ago, Iraq invaded Kuwait without provocation. And the regime's forces were poised to continue their march to seize other countries and their resources. Had Saddam Hussein been appeased instead of stopped, he would have endangered the peace and stability of the world. Yet this aggression was stopped—by the might of coalition forces and the will of the United Nations.

To suspend hostilities, to spare himself, Iraq's dictator accepted a series of commitments. The terms were clear, to him and to all. And he agreed to prove he is complying with every one of those obligations.

He has proven instead only his contempt for the United Nations, and for all his pledges. By breaking every pledge—by his deceptions, and by his cruelties—Saddam Hussein has made the case against himself.

In 1991, Security Council Resolution 688 demanded that the Iraqi regime cease at once the repression of its own people, including the systematic repression of minorities—which, the Council said, threatened international peace and security in the region. This demand goes ignored.

Last year, the U.N. Commission on Human Rights found that Iraq continues to commit extremely grave violations of human rights, and that the regime's repression is all pervasive. Tens of thousands of political opponents and ordinary citizens have been subjected to arbitrary arrest and imprisonment, summary execution, and torture by beating and burning, electric shock, starvation, mutilation, and rape. Wives are tortured in front of their husbands, children in the presence of their parents—and all of these horrors concealed from the world by the apparatus of a totalitarian state.

In 1991, the U.N. Security Council, through Resolutions 686 and 687, demanded that Iraq return all prisoners from Kuwait and other lands. Iraq's regime agreed. It broke its promise. Last year the Secretary General's high-level coordinator for this issue reported that Kuwaiti, Saudi, Indian, Syrian, Lebanese, Iranian, Egyptian, Bahraini, and Omani nationals remain unaccounted for—more than 600 people. One American pilot is among them.

In 1991, the U.N. Security Council, through Resolution 687, demanded that Iraq renounce all involvement with terrorism, and permit no terrorist organizations to operate in Iraq. Iraq's regime agreed. It broke this promise. In violation of Security Council Resolution 1373, Iraq continues to shelter and support terrorist organizations that direct violence against Iran, Israel, and Western governments. Iraqi dissidents abroad are targeted for murder. In 1993, Iraq attempted to assassinate the Emir of Kuwait and a former American President. Iraq's government openly praised the attacks of September the 11th. And al Qaeda terrorists escaped from Afghanistan and are known to be in Iraq.

In 1991, the Iraqi regime agreed to destroy and stop developing all weapons of mass destruction and long-range missiles, and to prove to the world it has done so by complying with rigorous inspections. Iraq has broken every aspect of this fundamental pledge.

From 1991 to 1995, the Iraqi regime said it had no biological weapons. After a senior official in its weapons program defected and exposed this lie, the regime admitted to producing tens of thousands of liters of anthrax and other deadly biological agents for use with Scud warheads, aerial bombs, and aircraft spray tanks. U.N. inspectors believe Iraq has produced two to four times the amount of biological agents it declared, and has failed to account for more than three metric tons of material that could be used to produce biological weapons. Right now, Iraq is expanding and improving facilities that were used for the production of biological weapons.

United Nations' inspections also revealed that Iraq likely maintains stockpiles of VX, mustard, and other chemical agents, and that the regime is rebuilding and expanding facilities capable of producing chemical weapons.

And in 1995, after four years of deception, Iraq finally admitted it had a crash nuclear weapons program prior to the Gulf War. We know now, were it not for that war, the regime in Iraq would likely have possessed a nuclear weapon no later than 1993.

Today, Iraq continues to withhold important information about its nuclear program—weapons design, procurement logs, experiment data, an accounting of nuclear materials, and documentation of foreign assistance. Iraq employs capable nuclear scientists and technicians. It retains physical infrastructure needed to build a nuclear weapon. Iraq has made several attempts to buy high-strength aluminum tubes used to enrich uranium for a nuclear weapon. Should Iraq acquire fissile material, it would be able to build a nuclear weapon within a year. And Iraq's state-controlled media has reported numerous meetings between Saddam Hussein and his nuclear scientists, leaving little doubt about his continued appetite for these weapons.

Iraq also possesses a force of Scud-type missiles with ranges beyond the 150 kilometers permitted by the U.N. Work at testing and production facilities shows that Iraq is building more long-range missiles that can inflict mass death throughout the region.

In 1990, after Iraq's invasion of Kuwait, the world imposed economic sanctions on Iraq. Those sanctions were maintained after the war to compel the regime's compliance with Security Council resolutions. In time, Iraq was allowed to use oil revenues to buy food. Saddam Hussein has subverted this program, working around the sanctions to buy missile technology and military materials. He blames the suffering of Iraq's people on the United Nations, even as he uses his oil wealth to build lavish palaces for himself, and to buy arms for his country. By refusing to comply with his own agreements, he bears full guilt for the hunger and misery of innocent Iraqi citizens.

In 1991, Iraq promised U.N. inspectors immediate and unrestricted access to verify Iraq's commitment to rid itself of weapons of mass destruction and long-range missiles. Iraq broke this promise, spending seven years deceiving, evading, and harassing U.N. inspectors before ceasing cooperation entirely. Just months after the 1991 cease-fire, the Security Council twice renewed its demand that the Iraqi regime cooperate fully with inspectors, condemning Iraq's serious violations of its obligations. The Security Council again renewed that demand in 1994, and twice more in 1996, deploring Iraq's clear violations of its obligations. The Security Council renewed its demand three more times in 1997, citing flagrant violations; and three more times in 1998, calling Iraq's behavior totally unacceptable. And in 1999, the demand was renewed yet again.

As we meet today, it's been almost four years since the last U.N. inspectors set foot in Iraq, four years for the Iraqi regime to plan, and to build, and to test behind the cloak of secrecy.

We know that Saddam Hussein pursued weapons of mass murder even when inspectors were in his country. Are we to assume that he stopped when they left? The history, the logic, and the facts lead to one conclusion: Saddam Hussein's regime is a grave and gathering danger. To suggest otherwise is to hope against the evidence. To assume this regime's good faith is to bet the lives of millions and the peace of the world in a reckless gamble. And this is a risk we must not take.

Delegates to the General Assembly, we have been more than patient. We've tried sanctions. We've tried the carrot of oil for food, and the stick of coalition military strikes. But Saddam Hussein has defied all these efforts and continues to develop weapons of mass destruction. The first time we may be completely certain he has nuclear weapons is when, God forbids, he uses one. We owe it to all our citizens to do everything in our power to prevent that day from coming.

The conduct of the Iraqi regime is a threat to the authority of the United Nations, and a threat to peace. Iraq has answered a decade of U.N. demands with a decade of defiance. All the world now faces a test, and the United Nations a difficult and defining moment. Are Security Council resolutions to be honored and enforced, or cast aside without consequence? Will the United Nations serve the purpose of its founding, or will it be irrelevant?

The United States helped found the United Nations. We want the United Nations to be effective, and respectful, and successful. We want the resolutions of the world's most important multilateral body to be enforced. And right now those resolutions are being unilaterally subverted by the Iraqi regime. Our partnership of nations can meet the test before us, by making clear what we now expect of the Iraqi regime.

If the Iraqi regime wishes peace, it will immediately and unconditionally forswear, disclose, and remove or destroy all weapons of mass destruction, long-range missiles, and all related material.

If the Iraqi regime wishes peace, it will immediately end all support for terrorism and act to suppress it, as all states are required to do by U.N. Security Council resolutions.

If the Iraqi regime wishes peace, it will cease persecution of its civilian population, including Shi'a, Sunnis, Kurds, Turkomans, and others, again as required by Security Council resolutions.

If the Iraqi regime wishes peace, it will release or account for all Gulf War personnel whose fate is still unknown. It will return the remains of any who are deceased, return stolen property, accept liability for losses resulting from the invasion of Kuwait, and fully cooperate with international efforts to resolve these issues, as required by Security Council resolutions.

If the Iraqi regime wishes peace, it will immediately end all illicit trade outside the oil-for-food program. It will accept U.N. administration of funds from that program, to ensure that the money is used fairly and promptly for the benefit of the Iraqi people.

If all these steps are taken, it will signal a new openness and accountability in Iraq. And it could open the prospect of the United Nations helping to build a government that represents all Iraqis—a government based

on respect for human rights, economic liberty, and internationally super-
vised elections.

• • •

The United States has no quarrel with the Iraqi people; they've suffered too
long in silent captivity. Liberty for the Iraqi people is a great moral cause,
and a great strategic goal. The people of Iraq deserve it; the security of all
nations requires it. Free societies do not intimidate through cruelty and conquest, and open societies do not threaten the world with mass murder. The
United States supports political and economic liberty in a unified Iraq.

We can harbor no illusions—and that's important today to remember.
Saddam Hussein attacked Iran in 1980 and Kuwait in 1990. He's fired
ballistic missiles at Iran and Saudi Arabia, Bahrain, and Israel. His regime
once ordered the killing of every person between the ages of 15 and 70 in certain Kurdish villages in northern Iraq. He has gassed many Iranians, and 40
Iraqi villages.

My nation will work with the U.N. Security Council to meet our common
challenge. If Iraq's regime defies us again, the world must move deliberately,
decisively to hold Iraq to account. We will work with the U.N. Security Council
for the necessary resolutions. But the purposes of the United States should
not be doubted. The Security Council resolutions will be enforced—the just
demands of peace and security will be met—or action will be unavoidable.
And a regime that has lost its legitimacy will also lose its power.

Events can turn in one of two ways: If we fail to act in the face of danger,
the people of Iraq will continue to live in brutal submission. The regime will
have new power to bully and dominate and conquer its neighbors, condemning the Middle East to more years of bloodshed and fear. The regime
will remain unstable—the region will remain unstable, with little hope of
freedom, and isolated from the progress of our times. With every step the
Iraqi regime takes toward gaining and deploying the most terrible weapons,
our own options to confront that regime will narrow. And if an emboldened
regime were to supply these weapons to terrorist allies, then the attacks of
September the 11th would be a prelude to far greater horrors.

If we meet our responsibilities, if we overcome this danger, we can arrive
at a very different future. The people of Iraq can shake off their captivity. They
can one day join a democratic Afghanistan and a democratic Palestine, inspiring
reforms throughout the Muslim world. These nations can show by their example
that honest government, and respect for women, and the great Islamic tradi-

tion of learning can triumph in the Middle East and beyond. And we will show that the promise of the United Nations can be fulfilled in our time.

Neither of these outcomes is certain. Both have been set before us. We must choose between a world of fear and a world of progress. We cannot stand by and do nothing while dangers gather. We must stand up for our security, and for the permanent rights and the hopes of mankind. By heritage and by choice, the United States of America will make that stand. And, delegates to the United Nations, you have the power to make that stand, as well.

Thank you very much.

Cause for Dissent
Lewis Lapham

Harper's Magazine | April 2003

One reason many Democrats have viewed the plans for invading Iraq with suspicion—even as they've acknowledged Saddam Hussein's regime to be an evil and dangerous one, that the world would be well rid of—is the political advantage that accrues to President Bush in his role as wartime leader. Not only is it a part that Bush excels at, but it also gives him a club with which to silence any and all domestic opposition. In this essay, Harper's *editor Lewis Lapham raises a voice against the chorus of pro-war rhetoric, and in doing so, reminds us that a willingness to speak out in dissent is the very life-blood of our democracy. . . .*

> *The dissenter is every human being at those moments of his life*
> *when he resigns momentarily from the herd and thinks for himself.*
> —Archibald MacLeish

As a director of the government's ministry of propaganda during World War II, Archibald MacLeish knew that dissent seldom walks on stage to the sound of warm and welcoming applause. As a poet and later the librarian of Congress, he also knew that liberty has ambitious enemies, and that the survival of the American democracy depends less on the size of its armies than on the capacity of its individual citizens to rely, if only momentarily, on the strength of their own thought. We can't know what we're about, or whether we're telling ourselves too many lies, unless we can see or hear one another think out loud. Tyranny never has much trouble drumming up the smiles of prompt agreement, but a democracy stands in need of as many questions as its citizens can ask of their own stupidity and fear. Voiced in the first-person singular and synonymous with the courage of a mind that a former editor of this magazine once described as "unorganized, unrecognized, unorthodox and unterrified," dissent is what rescues the democracy from a slow death behind closed doors.

Unpopular during even the happiest of stock-market booms, in time of war dissent attracts the attention of the police. The parade marshals regard any wandering away from the line of march as unpatriotic and disloyal; the unlicensed forms of speech come to be confused with treason and registered as crimes, and in the skyboxes of the news media august personages reaffirm America's long-standing alliance with God and the Statue of Liberty. Counting through the list of the country's exemplary virtues—a just cause, an invincible air force, a noble truth—they find no reasons for dissent. On the threshold of a war in Iraq, I can think of ten:

1. Agitprop

I don't know how else to characterize the Bush Administration's effort to convince the public of the need for an immediate American assault on the land of Mordor. Whether expressed in the language of religious exorcism by President Bush in his annual message to Congress or chopped into nourishing sound bites by National Security Adviser Condoleezza Rice for the fans of CNN's *Larry King Live,* the government's relentless ad campaign rests on the principle announced nearly a year ago by Secretary of Defense Donald Rumsfeld at a press conference in Brussels. Asked by a crowd of European journalists for proof of the assertion that weapons of mass destruction confronted the United States with a clear and present danger, Rumsfeld said, "The absence of evidence is not evidence of absence."

Secretary of State Colin Powell didn't come up with a substantially different explanation in early February when he presented the United Nations Security Council with a slide show meant to serve as a trailer for the forthcoming action movie soon to be filmed in the deserts of Mesopotamia. The surveillance photographs of Iraqi trucks demanded the kind of arcane exposition that New York art critics attach to exhibitions of abstract painting. By way of adding drama to the performance, Powell held up a vial of white powder (meant to be seen as anthrax but probably closer in its chemistry to granulated sugar) and rolled tape of two satellite telephone intercepts of Iraqi military officers screaming at one another in Arabic, but he didn't provide an answer to the question, Why does America attack Iraq when Iraq hasn't attacked America? In lieu of demonstrable provocations Mr. Powell offered disturbing signs and evil portents, and when the voice of Osama bin Laden turned up a week later on an audiotape broadcast from Qatar, the secretary seized upon the occasion to discover a "partnership" between Al Qaeda and the government of Iraq. No such conclusion could be drawn from even a careless reading of the transcript, but to Mr. Powell the sending of a message (any message) proved that Osama bin Laden and Saddam Hussein somehow had morphed into the same enemy.

The secretary's power points didn't add to the sum of a convincing argument, but then neither did the advertising copy for the Spanish-American War or the sales promotions for the war in Vietnam, and if the agitprop failed to persuade the French, Russian, or Chinese representatives to the Security Council, it was more than good enough for the emissaries from the major American news media. Our television networks and large-circulation newspapers trade in the same commodity. They identify themselves as instruments of the American government rather than as witnesses beholden to the American people, and they bring to their work the talents and the haircuts of expensive corporate lobbyists. All but unanimous in their infatuation with President Bush (a Churchillian figure, sometimes Lincolnesque), they've been packing their safari hats ever since the navy sent the carriers to the Persian Gulf. In Secretary Powell's remarks to the U.N. the editors of the *Wall Street Journal* discovered echoes of Talleyrand and Metternich.

2. The Korean Exception

The Bush Administration makes a boast of its "moral clarity" and principled resolve, also of its willingness to "exercise power without conquest" and "sacrifice for the liberty of strangers." Why then no imbecile invasion of North Korea?

Although cold in the winter, the country abounds in unfortunate strangers, and unlike the reports being brought back to New York in February by Hans Blix and International Atomic Energy Agency director general Mohamed ElBaradei the news from Pyongyang that month amounted to something more than a threatening hypothesis. A Communist despotism controlled by a heartless dictator easily the peer of Saddam Hussein had resumed its manufacture of enriched uranium and expelled the U.N. inspectors assigned to monitor its Yongbyon nuclear reactor complex. Three bombs were thought to exist, several others were said to be within a few months of production; the civilian population had been reduced to near starvation, and the army, believed to number a million soldiers, heavily armed and fanatic in its devotion to "the Dear Leader," was stationed within artillery range of the 30,000 American troops just south of the demilitarized zone. The North Korean threat was both plainly visible and alarmingly present, but it was not one against which the United States cared to launch the wrath of eagles. Confronted with Kim Jong Il's blunt demand for ransom money (payment acceptable in trade agreements, bank credit, or bags of rice), the Bush Administration referred the unpleasantness to the United Nations— the same United Nations that Secretary Rumsfeld had deemed "irresponsible" and on "a path of ridicule" because of its reluctance to endorse an American expedition to Baghdad. The referral dimmed the lamp of moral clarity, and the cautious retreat to the policy of containment that President Bush had declared obsolete clarified the distinction between threats both real and apparent and those cleverly hidden by illusory enemies who also happen to command small armies and govern countries rich with oil.

3. "We refuse to live in fear."

President Bush presented the statement to an audience in Cincinnati on October 7, [2002] and of all lies told by the government's faith healers and gun salesmen, I know of none as cowardly. Where else does the Bush Administration ask the American people to live except in fear? On what other ground does it justify its deconstruction of the nation's civil liberties?

Ever since the September 11 attacks on New York and Washington, no week has passed in which the government has failed to issue warnings of a sequel. Sometimes it's the director of the FBI, sometimes the attorney general or an unnamed source in the CIA or the Department of Homeland Security, but always it's the same message: suspect your neighbor and watch the sky; buy duct tape, avoid the Washington Monument, hide the children.

Let too many citizens begin to ask impertinent questions about the shambles of the federal budget or the disappearance of a forest in Montana and the government sends another law-enforcement officer to a microphone with a story about a missing tube of aluminum or a newly discovered nerve gas.

4. Somnambulism

Washington these days suffers no shortage of visionary geopoliticians touting the wonders of an American empire imposing, by act of conscience and force of arms, peace on earth and good will toward men. The prophets enjoy the patronage of power, some of them White House privy counselors, others advisers to the Pentagon, all of them utopian anarchists. They envision a slum-clearance project for the whole of the Islamic Middle East, Iraq the first in a series of model democracies soon to be erected in Syria, Iran, Libya, Egypt, and Saudi Arabia, and when reading their articles in the policy journals, I remember a remark I once came across in a novelist's description of four Marxist assassins seated at a café table in Paris in the 1920s: "They believe everything they can prove, and they can prove everything they believe."

The Bush Administration employs a good many ideologues afflicted with a similarly messianic turn of mind and who take for granted the stupefaction of an electorate too lazy to open its mail. Assuming a general state of political somnambulism not much different from their own, the authors of the government's press releases count on an audience that thinks of politics as trivial entertainment. The supposition isn't entirely wrong.

The successful operation of a democracy relies on acts of government by no means easy to perform, and for the last twenty years we have been unwilling to do the work. Choosing to believe that the public good comes to us at the discretion of private wealth, all politicians therefore as interchangeable as hotel bartenders, we don't bother to vote, don't read through the list of budget appropriations, content ourselves with the opinions advertised on prime-time television by talk-show guests holding up little vials of important news—sometimes anthrax, usually sugar. Our prosperity finances the habits of indolence. We leave the small print for the lawyers to clean and maybe press, and in place of an energetic politics we get by with nostalgic sentiment and the public-spirited postcards sent by PBS—elections a cascade of balloons, liberty a trust fund, and America the land in which the money never dies.

5. The Insolence of Office

In a recent and best-selling book, *Bush at War,* Bob Woodward presents a portrait of the president so flattering that had it been rendered in oil on canvas, the curator of the White House art collection might wish to hang it in the Blue Room. One of the bons mots that Woodward attributes to his subject could as easily have been attributed to Louis XIV: "That's the interesting thing about being the President. Maybe somebody needs to explain to me why they say something, but I don't feel like I owe anybody an explanation."

The administration's senior ministers share the view. Often petulant and openly contemptuous of opinions not their own, they listen to opposing argument with impatience and disdain. At the United Nations last winter, when the French and German statesmen raised pointed questions about both the necessity and the timing of a police raid on Iraq, Mr. Rumsfeld received the skepticism as an insult. France and Germany, he said, spoke for an "old Europe" long ago reduced to a harmless tourist attraction, France a country famous for its vanity and pride; Germany stubborn and wrongheaded.

At the higher altitudes of Washington officialdom, the tone of condescension is traditional. Dean Acheson, secretary of state in the Truman Administration, understood as long ago as 1947 that if America wished to do as it pleased in the world, it would be necessary to come up with a slogan that could serve as both a reason and an explanation for high-handed, unilateral decision. Knowing that the American people might balk at the prospect of the Cold War if they thought the strategy open to discussion, Acheson explained to his associates in the State Department that the country's foreign policy must be presented as "nonpartisan," that any and all political argument "stops at the water's edge."

"If we can make them believe that," Acheson said, "we're off to the races."

Over the next two generations the word "nonpartisan" proved invaluable to a succession of presidents bent on waging declared and undeclared wars in Korea, Vietnam, Guatemala, Grenada, Panama, Cambodia, Lebanon, Nicaragua, Angola, and the Persian Gulf. Replace the once magic word "nonpartisan" with the phrase "never-ending war on terrorism," and we arrive at the policy of Rumsfeld the Implacable and the wisdom of Cheney the Unseen.

6. Negligence

The destruction of the World Trade Center evoked an immense surge of pro-American feeling everywhere in the world—in Cairo and Amman as well as in London and Paris. Within the brief span of nineteen months our government has managed to squander almost the whole of the asset. Mocked by its failure to find Osama bin Laden, the Bush Administration has bullied our allies, scorned the United Nations, subverted the principle of international law, recruited an angry host of new enemies, and exchanged the hard currency of our inherent idealism for the counterfeit coin of a hair-brained cynicism.

In return for what? A "regime change" in Afghanistan. The horsedrawn and all but helpless Taliban put to rout at a cost of more than $15 billion, Kabul remanded to the custody of a freedom-loving warlord, and tranquillity along the border of Pakistan achieved with a $1 billion bribe paid to the military dictatorship of General Pervez Musharraf.

7. Our Staunchest Ally

When I look at the handsomely detailed maps with which the Pentagon marks out the road to glory in Iraq, I'm sure that I miss a good many of the military fine points, but I never doubt that the maps must gladden the heart of Osama bin Laden. Who but Osama stands to pluck so rich a prize from the fires of holy crusade? Fresh recruits for Al Qaeda, the Western democracies at odds with one another (and their intelligence agencies therefore less cooperative), the scourge of civil war conceivably spread across the whole of the Middle East, the Saudi Arabian monarchy maybe overthrown, and Israel possibly forced onto the reefs of destruction.

As utopian an anarchist as the Washington apostles of American empire, Osama preaches a parallel vision of a world transformed, justice restored, and the desert cleansed of its impurities. President Bush knows that the work of pious destruction is blessed by the God of Abraham and that liberty is the gift of heaven and not the work of men. Allah the all-merciful sends Osama an American army bringing the torches and the mops.

8. Barbed Wire

Unable to erect a secure perimeter around the whole life and landscape of a free society, the government bureaus of public safety solve the technical problems by seeing to it that the society becomes less free. The USA Patriot Act has been reinforced so many times since it was first passed by Congress in October 2001 that by now the country's law-enforcement agencies have been equipped with as many powers as they choose to exercise—random search, unwarranted seizure, arbitrary arrest.

Every month brings with it some new proof of the frightened and punitive states of mind that inform the imposition of additional rules, more efficient procedures, further restrictions. My notes from the last week in January through the second week in February mention the dropping of a blue curtain over a tapestry of Pablo Picasso's *Guernica* outside the Security Council chambers (to preserve Secretary Powell from the embarrassment of having to pose for photographs in front of a work of art depicting the horrors of war), Laura Bush canceling a poetry symposium at the White House when told that one or more of the poets might read an anti-war poem, the New York Police Department forbidding an antiwar march in front of the United Nations, a consortium of scientific journals (among them *Nature* and *The New England Journal of Medicine*) agreeing to censor any articles that might compromise national security, and then, most unequivocally, in January the Department of Transportation proposing to establish a system of records classifying any and all commercial airline passengers as suspected terrorists and thus subject to background investigations that might otherwise require a court order.

9. Sloth

The question most often asked of the American mission to Iraq can be reduced to two words: "Why now?" I've listened to numerous explanations—the weather, America's credibility at stake, Saddam about to poison Israel's reservoirs—but I suspect that the best answer is the simplest. War is easier than peace. The government elects to punish an enemy it perceives as weak because it's easier to send the aircraft carriers to the Persian Gulf than to attempt the harder task of making an American society not so wretchedly defaced by its hungry children, its crowded prisons, and its corporate thieves.

The Bush Administration owes its existence to our apathy and sloth; if we have allowed the American political argument to degenerate into mindless catchphrase and the fifteen-second sound bite, how can we not expect our government to think in the same language, to depend for its authority on the easy and patriotic lie, and whenever it doesn't know what else to do, to arrest mysterious strangers and bomb Iraq?

10. Candor

The energy of our democracy springs from the willingness of its citizens to speak and think in their own voices, and among all the American political virtues, candor is probably the one most necessary to the health of our mutual estate. Not meant to be either popular or fun, the dissenting view on first hearing usually strikes the audience as impolite, treasonable, or plain wrong. Prior to the public demonstrations that took place on February 15 in more than 600 cities in all twenty-four of the world's time zones (at least 200,000 people in New York, 750,000 in London, 1.3 million in Barcelona), the major American news media were busy discounting objections to the invasion of Iraq as words of no worth and little consequence—the work of aging flower children, overly liberal college professors, and B-list celebrities. Three days after the crowds showed up in the streets, President Bush compared the event to the assembling of an ad agency's hired focus group, the expression of non-serious and uninformed opinion and certainly not one that he would allow to affect his judgment, alter his course of action, or in any way violate the temple of his own enlightenment.

Every society can always count on the parties of reaction crying up the wish to make time stand still, seeking to protect themselves against the storm of the world with impregnable bureaucracies and choruses of adoring praise. Democracy proceeds from a more adventurous premise, its structure akin to a suspension bridge rather than to an Egyptian pyramid, its strength dependent upon the complicity of its citizens in a shared work of the political imagination. The enterprise collapses into either anarchy or tyranny unless the countervailing stresses oppose one another with equal weight, unless enough people possess enough courage to sustain the dialectic between the government and the governed, between city and town, capital and labor, men and women, matter and mind.

Defined as a ceaseless process of change, democracy assumes the pain of contradiction and new discovery not only as the normal but also as the necessary condition of existence. As has been said, a hard act to perform, and one that failed and was abandoned by nearly every country in Europe in the generation between the First and Second World Wars. In place of truthful and therefore possibly unpleasant argument, the Bush Administration offers warm and welcome lies, advising us to lay aside the tool of thought and rest safely on the pillows of glorious and world-encircling empire. We accept the invitation at our peril.

What if They Gave a War and Nobody Cared?

James Wolcott

Vanity Fair | March 2003

As the Iraq war drew inevitably closer, one question raised in a number of quarters was, Why is there no anti-war movement to speak of? Yes, there were a few weekends of protest marches, which drew a sizeable turnout in the U.S. and abroad—but overall the public's reaction has been remarkably muted. As James Wolcott notes in the following essay, "Those in power can't be accused of thwarting the will of the people, because the people seem to have lost their will . . ."

In his essay, Wolcott also mentions a New York Times Magazine *article by George Packer titled "The Liberal Quandary Over Iraq," in which Packer argues that many American liberals have effectively been turned into hawks by the recent interventions in Bosnia and Kosovo. Wolcott himself offers another explanation for the silence on the left— suggesting that, similar to its new preemptive foreign policy, the right wing has also developed a preemptive strategy for marginalizing the anti-war crowd. Rather than demonize them, the preferred approach now is to cast anti-war types as strictly fringe characters, to be viewed not so much with disdain as with amused contempt. . . .*

Near the end of his latest bill of indictment, *Dreaming War: Blood for Oil and the Cheney-Bush Junta,* Gore Vidal envisions a sad finish for the political fortunes of George W. Bush and his ministry of fear. "Mark my words. He will leave office the most unpopular president in history. The junta has done too much wreckage."

Gore, ever the cockeyed optimist. His faith in the slow-burn wrath of the American people is touching, considering how little we have done to earn it. Never before have so many put up with so much from so few. Despite corporate robbery, a trampling of civil liberties that makes the Red scare look like a dress rehearsal, a rapist urge to ram a paved road or oil pipeline through every nature preserve, a Tony Soprano foreign policy that fingers which dirtbag country we're going to whack next, an unaccountable vice president who pops out of his groundhog hole only to raise money for the Republican Party or play bad cop on *Meet the Press,* and the corny spectacle of the president himself imploring us to visit a shut-in and say, "I love you" (and they accused Clinton of being Empath in Chief!), despite all this, the huddled, befuddled masses have been as quiet as church mice. Those in power can't be accused of thwarting the will of the people, because the people seem to have lost their will, or traded it in for Powerball tickets. Most puzzling is the quiet resignation, the iceberg drift of collective apathy (apart from a few well-attended marches), which has marked the escalation of the prospect of war against Iraq.

This mass sleepwalk isn't confined to America. Suspended animation seems to have seized hold of our staunchest (only?) ally, England. "You might have imagined that the country would be riven by argument and debate," Jackie Ashley wrote in *The Guardian* of this pre-war lull. "So far, there's been a great national shrug." Perhaps England's indifference is based on the knowledge that it will be taking only a lesser role in the actual fighting, but what's our lame excuse? The U.S. will be shouldering the lion's share of blood and hardware, and our shrug has been even more pronounced.

"So where are the antiwarriors?" asked George Packer in the pages of *The New York Times Magazine* in December. The anti-war marches that caterpillared down the streets of a few major cities have underwhelmed Packer. "Speakers at the demonstrations voice unnuanced slogans like 'No Sanctions, No Bombing' and 'No Blood for Oil.' As for what should be done to keep this mass murderer and his weapons in check, they have nothing to say at all." (By "mass murderer," Packer is presumably referring to Saddam Hussein and not the current occupant of the Oval Office.) In *The Washington Post*, reporter David Montgomery previewed an anti-war rally and deemed the protesters an amusing menagerie of human flotsam that time forgot. "Don't forget the suburban seniors fixing to march on the White House in spite of arthritis and titanium kneecaps, women wearing pink keeping vigil in the cold, Quakers in the basement debating slogans that are too long and nuanced to fit on a bumper sticker . . ." No, and let's not forget that a contingent of Quakers who were arrested during the 1967 anti-war march on the Pentagon refused to eat, drink, or wear prison uniforms, and were thrown into the Hole of the D.C. jail. "There they lived in cells so small that not all could lie down at once to sleep," Norman Mailer wrote in *The Armies of the Night*, ". . . —these naked Quakers on the cold floor of a dark isolation cell in D.C. jail, wandering down the hours in the fever of dehydration." In the current climate, however, Quakers are considered quaint.

So here we have two supposed liberal bastions, *The New York Times* and *The Washington Post*, chiming that (a) there is no peace movement, and (b) well, there is one, sorta, but it's a motley parade of fringe lefties, college kids, and historical retreads stretching their legs in an exercise in futility. Policy debate is best left to the manly professionals, such as the East Coast "liberal hawks" Packer cites for approval. Liberal doves should just stay in their cages and coo.

We have been down this slope before. The drumbeat of war traditionally drowns out dissent. Patriotism is employed as a silencer, a cattle call to get the herd chugging in the same direction. "Once the war is on," wrote the progressive intellectual Randolph Bourne at the outbreak of World War I, "the conviction spreads that individual thought is helpless, that the only way one can count is as a cog in the great wheel. We are told to dry our unnoticed and ineffective tears and plunge into the great work." Big thinkers and ordinary citizens alike are urged to jettison their Jiminy Cricket consciences and get with the program. "Be with us, they call, or be negligible, irrelevant. Dissenters are . . . excommunicated." Under this barrage, many of those harboring doubts cast them aside and persuade themselves that, war being inevitable, the wiser, more pragmatic course is to accept harsh reality. "The realist thinks he at least can control events by linking himself to the forces that are moving," Bourne observed, anticipating the rationale of those liberal Democrats who rubber-stamped a resolution for Bush to pursue war with Iraq rather than risk being called the party of weak knees and appeasement. But, as Bourne also warned, linking yourself to the forces in motion offers no guarantee of influence. War is a rogue elephant that may not whoa, whether you're riding its back or standing on the ground waving like a traffic cop. It took years before reluctant supporters acknowledged that the Vietnam War was a runaway nightmare.

What's unique this time is the pro-war camp didn't wait for American troops to pour across the borders before it began stigmatizing and sidelining dissent at home and abroad. As befits a pre-emptive war, the hawks and their media pigeons launched a pre-emptive strike on the anti-war camp while it was taking its first baby steps. Opposition has been discounted in advance with a knowing sneer. According to the new rules of disengagement, the following are disqualified from having their opinions signify as America prepares to climb into the ring with the Axis of Evil.

A-list celebrities. In December of 2002, Sean Penn visited Baghdad. Earlier, the actor and director had paid for a full-page ad in *The Washington Post* to publish an open letter to the president, urging him to leash the dogs of war and rethink the consequences of invasion. The letter was stilted and ingenuous in parts, but was written in a respectful tone and reflected a serious moral concern; it wasn't a fiery salvo from a Hollywood hothead. Penn's visit to Baghdad demonstrated a similar brooding modesty. He toured hospitals, spoke to Iraqis, snapped photographs, and avoided posturing before the news cameras and microphones; in fact, he was so concerned about being used as a propaganda device by the Hussein regime that he immediately issued a disavowal after an Iraqi press report attributed quotes to him saying Iraq was squeaky-clean of weapons of mass destruction.

None of the pains Penn took spared him the inevitable sliming. He was branded a traitor and bracketed with Jane Fonda, "Baghdad Sean" to her "Hanoi Jane." In a column in *The Wall Street Journal*, Clifford D. May, a gratingly familiar cable-news guest and president of the Foundation for the Defense of Democracies (one of those bogus-sounding right-wing think tanks where no one needs to think, because their minds have been made up ever since they first gazed upon Reagan resplendent), reached deep into the fish barrel:

> Lenin, father of the Soviet Union, had a name for people like Mr. Penn: "Useful idiots." Lenin's successor, Stalin, was even able to dupe Walter Duranty, the *New York Times* correspondent in Moscow whose Pulitzer Prize—winning reporting helped convince the world that no government-orchestrated famine was occurring in the Ukraine.
>
> Similarly, during World War II, the Nazis took representatives of the Red Cross to the model concentration camp at Thereisenstadt, where they established to the Red Cross's satisfaction that those nasty rumors about Hitler's mistreatment of the Jews were unfounded and really quite outrageous.

In this amazing guilt-by-disassociation glissade, May managed to lump Penn, who has never uttered word one in favor of Saddam Hussein, with a long line of Commie sympathizers and Nazi apologists. Words were not enough to convey the contempt felt by some of May's brethren on the right. After mentioning Penn's shutter-bug activities in Baghdad, *The Weekly Standard* mused, "We must admit, we were kind of hoping that some poor Iraqi citizen, mindful of his privacy, would make like stateside Sean Penn and punch him in the face."

B-list celebrities. Also in December, 100 lesser Hollywood celebrities lent their names to another quixotic open letter to Bush, publicized at a press conference attended by signatories Martin Sheen, Mike Farrell, and Tony Shalhoub among others. Unlike Penn, "the Hollywood 100"—a deliberate allusion to the blacklisted Hollywood 10?—weren't roasted as useful idiots, but derided as attention-hungry has-beens hoping for guest spots on a gala *Love Boat* reunion. Grilled by cable-news hosts doing their populist shtick—among them MSNBC's Jerry Nachman, whose anachronistic set is decorated like a dumpy newspaper editor's office out of a Mickey Spillane novel (he begins each show, "Let's go to press," as if magic elves were about to put out the next edition)— the hapless celebrity reps were barely able to defend their position, they were so busy being fitted for dunce caps. Nachman sneered to an unflappably cool Janeane Garofalo that most celebrities were dopes "whose knowledge of the subject seems to be informed by a bumper sticker and not much else." A-list or B-list, the message is the same: Clam up and leave the political discussion to the serious and well informed. You know, top-notch minds like Ollie North and Jerry Falwell.

Un-Americans. The quickest way to dismiss a dissenter is to label him un-American, a worm-from-within who stresses what's wrong with the U.S.A. instead of what's right, or plays a devious game of "moral equivalence." Typical of this tack is the recent George Will column in which he chides, "The left, its anti-capitalism transmogrified into anti-Americanism expressed in the argot of anti-globalization, will repeat that of course Iraq and North Korea are dangerous, but so are McDonald's and Microsoft." Those vegetarian, open-code bastards! Combating such nattering nabobs of negativism has become a cottage industry for busy beavers like William J. Bennett (*Why We Fight*) and Dinesh D'Souza (*What's So Great About America*). Also flying the red, white, and blue are cable-news hosts Sean Hannity and Chris Matthews, whose inspirational books (*Let Freedom Ring* and *American*, respectively) plaster the grinning author on the cover posed with an American flag. Apple-pie pride beams from every airbrushed pore. As long as such patriots strut the ramparts, the best-seller list will be safe for democracy.

The greatest hotbeds of anti-American bad-mouthing are sheltered behind the ivy walls of our over-endowed universities. According to legend, former '60s radicals—now affluent, middle-aged, saggy NPR listeners whose gray ponytails flop limp against their wattled necks—remain nostalgic for the

revolutionaries they might have been, and have indoctrinated a new generation of misguided idealists and snot-nosed brats to loathe corporate logos
and make excuses for Osama bin Laden. Why, if they had their druthers, these
tenured Pied Pipers would hand out a Molotov cocktail with each diploma.
Happily, help is on the way. Classroom gurus who formerly polluted the dim
skulls of students by slandering their own country are being put under hairy
surveillance. Daniel Pipes, the Mideast expert with a sardonic beard like Rex
Harrison's in *The Ghost and Mrs. Muir*, presides over something called Campus
Watch, which keeps tabs on college professors antagonistic to Israel and the
U.S. (or, as he called them in a *New York Post* op-ed piece, "Profs Who Hate
America"). Pipes's ideological bunkmate David Horowitz, another fiery,
bearded prophet who has never found a burning issue he couldn't bugger
senseless, fronts the Take Back Our Campuses campaign, which, like Pipes's
operation, lists and excoriates left-wing hypnotists in the college classrooms.
(A donation at Horowitz's Web site will "Help David Expose The Leftist Plot
to Control America's Young Minds.") And then there is a blandly titled organization, the American Council of Trustees and Alumni, co-founded by
Lynne Cheney and Senator Joseph Lieberman through some satanic pact,
which issued a post-9/11 report criticizing educators and other chrome domes
for failing to prop up Western civ. "When a nation's intellectuals are unwilling
to defend its civilization, they give comfort to its adversaries," the report
stated, listing more than 100 examples of unpatriotic utterances by academics.
Giving comfort to the enemy is one of the rough definitions of what constitutes treason. Raising that McCarthyite specter is one way of putting the fear
of the state into the faculty. What's next, loyalty oaths?

Arab-Americans. Judging from the media, they don't exist. Apart from a few
public-service spots, we never see any on TV, either in prime-time entertainment or cable news, and the op-ed pages seldom blaze with their views.
The threat of detention and deportation that hangs over Arab communities
(not idle threats, either: hundreds of Muslims were arrested in Los Angeles
after voluntarily registering with the Immigration and Naturalization Service) has put them on probation for the endless duration of the War on Terror.
If they achieve any visibility in the months ahead, it will be as a painted backdrop, bearing mute witness to the unfolding drama.

Non-Americans. After expressing sympathy and solidarity with America post-9/11, foreigners seem to have gotten uppity again. How dare they criticize the policies of this country? Especially those pampered, effete, ungrateful, deodorant-averse European wussies. Don't they remember how we bailed them out of two World Wars? God knows we remind them of it often enough. We drag it out of the trunk every time they make a minor objection to, oh, say, plans to orbit a Death Star satellite. "Europeans are the ultimate free-riders on American power," Charles Krauthammer snipped in *The Washington Post*, and hawks like him have had it with their backseat driving. After German chancellor Gerhard Schroeder said, Include me out of a pre-emptive whack at Iraq, Donald Rumsfeld not only snubbed Germany's defense minister at a NATO meeting but taped a nasty note to his hall locker. What was different this time was that the hostility in conservative journals and Web sites wasn't limited to German officials but was lavished on Germany and the Germans themselves, who were scolded for being whiners and ingrates harboring a snake pit of renascent anti-Semitism. Entire nations were now being written off as unworthy—as bad as France! Even our geographically closest ally wasn't spared. Jonah Goldberg, trying too hard to be the new P. J. O'Rourke, ventured north to do a cover story for *National Review*, which branded the word WIMPS! across a photograph of Royal Canadian Mounties. The article itself, cheekily titled "Bomb Canada: The Case for War," argued that carpet bombing might be the best thing for this socialistic, soft-on-terrorism, politically correct snowland. It would shake them out of their smug lethargy and learn 'em not to lecture the U.S. and call our president a "moron." Even as a Swiftian modest proposal, "Bomb Canada" makes for unhappy irony, given that four Canadian soldiers were killed in Afghanistan in a "friendly fire" incident when American pilots, allegedly cranked up on amphetamine, fired a laser-guided missile at their position. Many Canadians were already understandably sore with the U.S. over the government's weak apology for the incident, and then Goldberg opens his big trap.

The backlash didn't deter Goldberg's colleague John Derbyshire from daydreaming about how much good a few kabooms might do another of our wayward allies, South Korea. Derbyshire, the journalistic charmer who once wished for the murder of Chelsea Clinton (otherwise, "the vile genetic inheritance of Bill and Hillary Clinton may live on to plague us in the future"), said that, since the longtime ally had tilted anti-U.S., perhaps it wouldn't be such a bad thing if a hard rain fell below the 48th parallel. "It would be a shame, of course, if a few dozen of those glittering malls, luxury apartment blocks, fast-food franchises, Hyundai showrooms, and Ikea outlets were to be smashed up by North Korean missiles." However, "given that the South Korean people keep electing leaders who sound like Walter Mondale, and register positively Parisian levels of anti-Americanism when polled, it's hard to see why we Americans [Derbyshire, an Englishman, received his citizenship in 2002] should mind if their nice prosperous little country gets knocked about a bit." That there would be thousands of human beings who would perish during this up-scale property damage was a pesky detail he skirted.

This is more than a matter of funning. The cartoon devastation advocated by Goldberg, Derbyshire, and cohorts is a trickle-down expression of the deadly serious might-makes-right policies of the neo-imperialists inside the administration—Richard Perle, Paul Wolfowitz, Condoleezza Rice, et al. In the '60s and '70s militant lefties (parroting Mao) would spout, "Political power grows out of the barrel of a gun." What pikers they were. For righties, geopolitical power flows out of the bomb-bay doors: Seoul or Baghdad, friend or foe, wherever the payload hits the road.

Liberals. I know, I know: what liberals? Way back in 1973, Wilfrid Sheed wrote, "Although I myself have not met a self-confessed liberal since the late fifties . . . , hardly a day passes that I don't read another attack on the 'typical liberal'—as it might be announcing a pest of dinosaurs or a plague of unicorns." To suspicious minds, liberals still remain dangerously at large, Out There somewhere gnawing on the social fabric, undermining our moral defenses. Conservative viper vixen Ann Coulter is publishing a five-alarm wake-up call this summer titled *Treason: Liberal Treachery from the Cold War to the War on Terrorism*, unmasking the traitors and no-goodniks in our midst. Even a bold exaggerator like Coulter may have bitten off more than she could vomit. If liberalism translates as treason and Democrats are overwhelmingly liberal, then a lot of Al Gore voters have some explaining to do, and even Attorney General John Ashcroft might have a tough time rounding up that many suspects. (It would be like the episode of *The Andy Griffith Show* where Sheriff Andy returned to a deserted Mayberry—in his absence, Barney Fife had jailed the entire town.)

Lastly, smokers. I include them among the dispossessed because they are the guinea pigs for every new social experiment in group ostracism, harassment, and regulation. The fearless journalist Oriana Fallaci told the *Financial Times* that "persecution of the people who smoke is fascist." Fallaci currently lives in New York, whose mayor has taken a page out of the Bush playbook. He orders; we obey. He's the one who gets to decide.

National Conversation:
The Iraq Conflict

We Stand Passively Mute

U.S. Senator Robert Byrd, on the floor of the United States Senate |
  February 12, 2003

*On October 11, 2002, the two chambers of Congress officially authorized President
Bush to use force against Iraq in the event that Saddam Hussein failed to comply
with U.N. weapons inspectors. The vote was 296-133 in the House and 77-23 in the
Senate, with the Republicans virtually unanimous in their support and the Democrats
sharply divided. One of the most vociferous opponents of the resolution was Senator
Robert Byrd of West Virginia, who attempted to filibuster the resolution but was voted
down. Four months later, with American troops poised to invade Iraq, a still-angry
Byrd stood in the well of the Senate and delivered this speech. In the days that followed, his words spread across the nation via e-mail and quickly became a rallying
cry for those opposed to the war. . . .*

We stand passively mute in the United States Senate, paralyzed by our own
uncertainty, seemingly stunned by the sheer turmoil of events. Only on the
editorial pages of our newspapers is there much substantive discussion of
the prudence or imprudence of engaging in this particular war.

And this is no small conflagration we contemplate. This is no simple
attempt to defang a villain. No. This coming battle, if it materializes, represents a turning point in U.S. foreign policy and possibly a turning point in
the recent history of the world.

This nation is about to embark upon the first test of a revolutionary doctrine applied in an extraordinary way at an unfortunate time. The doctrine
of preemption—the idea that the United States or any other nation can legit-
imately attack a nation that is not imminently threatening but may be threatening in the future—is a radical new twist on the traditional idea of self
defense. It appears to be in contravention of international law and the U.N.
Charter. And it is being tested at a time of world-wide terrorism, making many
countries around the globe wonder if they will soon be on our—or some other
nation's—hit list.

High level Administration figures recently refused to take nuclear weapons
off of the table when discussing a possible attack against Iraq. What could be
more destabilizing and unwise than this type of uncertainty, particularly in a
world where globalism has tied the vital economic and security interests of many

nations so closely together? There are huge cracks emerging in our time-honored alliances, and U.S. intentions are suddenly subject to damaging world-wide speculation. Anti-Americanism based on mistrust, misinformation, suspicion, and alarming rhetoric from U.S. leaders is fracturing the once solid alliance against global terrorism which existed after September 11.

Here at home, people are warned of imminent terrorist attacks with little guidance as to when or where such attacks might occur. Family members are being called to active military duty, with no idea of the duration of their stay or what horrors they may face. Communities are being left with less than adequate police and fire protection. Other essential services are also short-staffed. The mood of the nation is grim. The economy is stumbling. Fuel prices are rising and may soon spike higher.

This Administration, now in power for a little over two years, must be judged on its record. I believe that that record is dismal.

In that scant two years, this Administration has squandered a large projected surplus of some $5.6 trillion over the next decade and taken us to projected deficits as far as the eye can see. This Administration's domestic policy has put many of our states in dire financial condition, under-funding scores of essential programs for our people. This Administration has fostered policies which have slowed economic growth. This Administration has ignored urgent matters such as the crisis in health care for our elderly. This Administration has been slow to provide adequate funding for homeland security. This Administration has been reluctant to better protect our long and porous borders.

In foreign policy, this Administration has failed to find Osama bin Laden. In fact, just yesterday we heard from him again marshaling his forces and urging them to kill. This Administration has split traditional alliances, possibly crippling, for all time, international order-keeping entities like the United Nations and NATO. This Administration has called into question the traditional worldwide perception of the United States as well-intentioned peace-keeper. This Administration has turned the patient art of diplomacy into threats, labeling, and name calling of the sort that reflects quite poorly on the intelligence and sensitivity of our leaders, and which will have consequences for years to come.

Calling heads of state pygmies, labeling whole countries as evil, denigrating powerful European allies as irrelevant—these types of crude insensitivities can do our great nation no good. We may have massive military might, but we cannot fight a global war on terrorism alone. We need the cooperation and friendship of our time-honored allies as well as the newer found friends whom we can attract with our wealth. Our awesome military machine will do us little good if we suffer another devastating attack on our homeland which severely damages our economy. Our military manpower is already stretched thin and we will need the augmenting support of those nations who can supply troop strength, not just sign letters cheering us on.

The war in Afghanistan has cost us $37 billion so far, yet there is evidence that terrorism may already be starting to regain its hold in that region. We have not found bin Laden, and unless we secure the peace in Afghanistan, the dark dens of terrorism may yet again flourish in that remote and devastated land.

Pakistan as well is at risk of destabilizing forces. This Administration has not finished the first war against terrorism and yet it is eager to embark on another conflict with perils much greater than those in Afghanistan. Is our attention span that short? Have we not learned that after winning the war one must always secure the peace?

And yet we hear little about the aftermath of war in Iraq. In the absence of plans, speculation abroad is rife. Will we seize Iraq's oil fields, becoming an occupying power which controls the price and supply of that nation's oil for the foreseeable future? To whom do we propose to hand the reigns of power after Saddam Hussein?

Will our war inflame the Muslim world resulting in devastating attacks on Israel? Will Israel retaliate with its own nuclear arsenal? Will the Jordanian and Saudi Arabian governments be toppled by radicals, bolstered by Iran which has much closer ties to terrorism than Iraq?

Could a disruption of the world's oil supply lead to a world-wide recession? Has our senselessly bellicose language and our callous disregard of the interests and opinions of other nations increased the global race to join the nuclear club and made proliferation an even more lucrative practice for nations which need the income?

In only the space of two short years this reckless and arrogant Administration has initiated policies which may reap disastrous consequences for years.

One can understand the anger and shock of any President after the savage attacks of September 11. One can appreciate the frustration of having only a shadow to chase and an amorphous, fleeting enemy on which it is nearly impossible to exact retribution.

But to turn one's frustration and anger into the kind of extremely destabilizing and dangerous foreign policy debacle that the world is currently witnessing is inexcusable from any Administration charged with the awesome power and responsibility of guiding the destiny of the greatest superpower on the planet. Frankly many of the pronouncements made by this Administration are outrageous. There is no other word.

Yet this chamber is hauntingly silent. On what is possibly the eve of horrific infliction of death and destruction on the population of the nation of Iraq—a population, I might add, of which over 50% is under age 15—this chamber is silent. On what is possibly only days before we send thousands of our own citizens to face unimagined horrors of chemical and biological warfare—this chamber is silent. On the eve of what could possibly be a vicious terrorist attack in retaliation for our attack on Iraq, it is business as usual in the United States Senate.

We are truly "sleepwalking through history." In my heart of hearts I pray that this great nation and its good and trusting citizens are not in for a rudest of awakenings.

To engage in war is always to pick a wild card. And war must always be a last resort, not a first choice. I truly must question the judgment of any President who can say that a massive unprovoked military attack on a nation which is over 50% children is "in the highest moral traditions of our country." This war is not necessary at this time. Pressure appears to be having a good result in Iraq. Our mistake was to put ourselves in a corner so quickly. Our challenge is to now find a graceful way out of a box of our own making. Perhaps there is still a way if we allow more time.

War and Consequences

Christopher Hitchens

Slate.com | March 17, 2003

Christopher Hitchens, long considered to be an irascible but dependable upholder of left-ish positions, has strayed noticeably toward the center vis a vis America's recent foreign policy—a shift prompted, he acknowledges, by his visceral disgust at the attempt by liberals to blame the mass murder of September 11, 2001 on the United States' own shortcomings.

In this column, Hitchens takes aim at left-wing critics of the war, including former president Jimmy Carter, for their contention that a future without Saddam Hussein at the helm in Iraq would somehow be worse than one in which he still held power. . . .

There has been a certain eeriness to the whole Iraq debate, from the moment of its current inception after Sept. 11, 2001, right through the phony period of protracted legalism that has just drawn to a close. It was never really agreed, between the ostensibly contending parties, what the argument was "about." (Nor had it been in the preceding case of Kuwait in 1991: You may remember Secretary of State James Baker on that occasion exclaiming that the justification could be summarized in the one word "jobs.") Nobody has yet proposed that this is a job-creating war—though it may turn out to be—nor has anyone argued that it will be a job-losing one (though it might turn out to be that, too). The president bears his share of responsibility for this, for having made first one case and then another. So do the "anti-war" types, for picking up and discarding a series of straw arguments.

Conspicuous among the latter, and very popular recently, is the assertion that proponents of regime change have been too consistent. On every hand, I hear it darkly pointed out that several neoconservative theorists have wanted to get rid of Saddam Hussein for a very long time. Even before Sept. 11! Even before the invasion of Kuwait! It's easy to look up the official papers and public essays in which Paul Wolfowitz, for example, has stressed the menace of Saddam Hussein since as far back as 1978. He has never deviated from this conviction. What could possibly be more sinister?

The consistency with which a view is held is of course no guarantee of that view's integrity. But it seems odd to blame Wolfowitz for having in effect been right all along. Nor, by his repeated hospitality and generosity to gangsters from Abu Nidal to Islamic Jihad and al-Qaida (in the latter instance most obviously after Sept. 11, 2001), has Saddam Hussein done much to prove him wrong. So, the removal of this multifarious menace to his own population, to his neighbors, and to targets further afield would certainly be an "intended consequence" of a policy long-meditated at least on some peoples' part.

Back to the Future

What of the "unintended" consequences? By some bizarre convention, only those who favor action to resolve this long-running conflict are expected to foresee, or to take responsibility for, the future. But there's no evading the responsibility here, on either side. (I wouldn't want, for example, the responsibility of having argued for prolonging the life of a fascist regime.) But who can be expected to predict the future? The impossibility doesn't stop people from trying. Jimmy Carter, in 1991, wrote a public letter to Arab heads of state urging them to oppose the forcible eviction of Saddam Hussein from Kuwait. An American-led counterattack would, he instructed them, lead at once to massive rioting and disorder across the Islamic world. It would cause untold numbers of casualties. And it would lead to an increase in terrorism. Carter said all this again recently in a much-noticed op-ed piece. He could even be right this time, but not for any reason or reasoning that he's been able to demonstrate.

As an experiment, let's take a Carter policy. As president, he encouraged Saddam Hussein to invade Iran in 1979 and assured him that the Khomeini regime would crumble swiftly. The long resulting war took at least a million and a half lives, setting what is perhaps a record for Baptist-based foreign policy and severely testing Carter's proclaimed view that war is a last resort. However, of these awful casualties, an enormous number were fervent Iranian "revolutionary guards," who were flung into battle as human waves. Not only did this rob Shiite fundamentalism of its most devoted volunteers, but it left Iran with a birth deficit.

The ayatollahs then announced a policy of replenishment, financing Iranian mothers with special inducements and privileges if they would have large families. The resulting baby-boom generation is now entering its 20s and has, to all outward intents and purposes, rejected the idea of clerical rule. The "Iranian street" is, if anything, rather pro-American. How's that for an unintended or unforeseen consequence?

Unforeseen Consequences

Or take another thought-experiment, this time from one of Carter's lugubrious warnings. There are many smart people who have come to believe that the first bombing of the World Trade Center, in 1993, was in fact a terrorist revenge for Kuwait on Saddam Hussein's part. Ramzi Yusef, generally if boringly described as the "mastermind" of that and related plots—and the nephew of the recently apprehended Khalid Sheikh Mohammed of al-Qaida—may have been an Iraqi agent operating with a Kuwaiti identity forged for him during Saddam's occupation of that country. One cannot be sure.

But suppose that this was a terrorist counterstroke of the sort that is now so widely predicted to be in our future rather than our past. Would it have been better to have let Saddam Hussein keep Kuwait and continue work on what was (then) his nuclear capacity? That seems to be the insinuation of those who now argue that a proactive policy only makes our enemies more cross.

If consequences and consistency are to count in this argument, then they must count both ways. One cannot know the future, but one can make a reasoned judgment about the evident danger and instability of the status quo. Odd that the left should think that the status quo, in this area of all areas, is so worthy of preservation.

The Sounds of Silence
Anna Quindlen

Newsweek | April 21, 2003

In this column, Anna Quindlen ponders the grim fate of the anti-war movement's First Couple, Susan Sarandon and Tim Robbins, and what it says about the condition of American democracy. . . .

Last month a United Way chapter in Florida disinvited the actress Susan Sarandon from a fund-raising luncheon at which she'd agreed to speak. This was scarcely surprising. Many charities are happy to use celebrities to attract donors to their events, but they like them to be as decorative and inoffensive as the flower centerpieces. And with war looming, the Oscar-winning actress, who has been outspokenly liberal on a variety of social issues and consistently critical of the invasion of Iraq, must have suddenly seemed akin to a cactus.

It was an early salvo in the difficult and painful war here at home. The rules of engagement were clear. If you had early doubts about the use of American power in Iraq, you should sit down and shut up because you might imperil the eventual result. If you continued to have doubts about our foreign policy while the war was ongoing, you should sit down and shut up because you were giving aid and comfort to the enemy.

And, trust me, if you still have doubts about the wisdom of unilateral action now, you should sit down and shut up because we won.

Never mind if you are asking yourself why a nation we were told was lousy with chemical and biological weapons never used them during a punishing bombardment. Never mind if you are asking yourself why the oft-invoked but never factually supported ties between Saddam and Al Qaeda didn't lead to the predicted terrorist attacks in the United States.

Sit down, you're rocking the boat.

The bright side of this is that it offers a valuable lesson in American history. Each time the United States becomes imperial it betrays the very keystone upon which its greatness rests. It suppresses dissent and suggests that national interest is more important than free speech. In the wake of its primacy after World War II, this became so pernicious that lives were ruined, not only by Communist Party membership, but also by thirdhand suggestions of it. Only a decade that put the lid on discourse as tightly as the '50s did could have exploded into the free association of the '60s.

The division between those who support the Iraqi war and those who do not has become an unbridgeable ravine of accusation and name-calling, as fraught an issue as this country has had since it first discovered abortion. The greatness of America is almost unrecognizable in the resulting maelstrom. Its most basic principles are mangled, when, in places like Albany, N.Y., a man is arrested at a mall for wearing a T shirt with the Biblical legend PEACE ON EARTH on the front and the musical legend GIVE PEACE A CHANCE on the back. (The mall has a policy that bans patrons from wearing clothing "with slogans that may incite a disturbance." Let's hope no one ever comes in with a shirt that reads FREE BEER IN THE FOOD COURT.)

The all-purpose accusation against dissenters is that they are "unpatriotic," which is deeply ironic since those first patriots are celebrated for rebelling against government policies they considered wrong. Children learn of the greatness of those who spoke out against the policies of George III, then hear vilified those who do not agree with George W. How confusing. Almost as confusing as seeing your parents glued to "Access Hollywood" and then hearing them complain they can't understand why celebrities believe anyone would pay attention to anything they have to say.

If the free exchange of ideas is temporarily suspended in the interest of "supporting our troops" (as though all soldiers are also of one mind about foreign policy), then what is the gift we bring to the Iraqi people? Old Navy fleece? Stuffed-crust pizza? Much of what we have to export as a nation is similarly transient, except for this: the right to elect leaders, to watch what they do through the vehicle of a free press, and then, if we choose, to damn them for doing it, in coffeehouses, at home, from the steps of the courthouse or the statehouse, in private and in public, too. If there is any justification for an imperial America, it is because this is the jewel in its crown.

Last week the war at home continued unabated; the president of the National Baseball Hall of Fame, a former Reagan assistant press secretary, canceled an anniversary screening of the film "Bull Durham" because it stars Sarandon and her equally uncompliant companion, Tim Robbins. In a letter, he made the incendiary, baseless, and, given his past life, clearly partisan accusation that the failure of the two actors to go along with a policy they cannot support puts American soldiers in harm's way.

"May we never confuse honest dissent with disloyal subversion." A line from Robbins's irate reply to the baseball guy? Nah, it's Eisenhower at a time when the Constitution was mutilated by McCarthy and his minions, and dissent and subversion were constantly confused. And so it is in our time. If, in the shadow of the unilateralist power niche the United States will occupy in the foreseeable future, its citizens are pressured by their government, their communities, and their neighbors to speak with one cautious voice, we will have saved Iraq and damned ourselves. In a democratic society, the only treason is silence.

Befuddled in Baghdad

John Leo

U.S. News & World Report | April 21, 2003

Is George W. Bush really a bigger villain than Saddam Hussein? In this column, John Leo mulls the ethical pitfalls of pacifism. . . .

Mr. Answer Man, I notice that R. W. Apple, chief front-page analyst of the *New York Times*, got caught again predicting another quagmire, though he had the wit to avoid the exact word this time. Why does he keep doing this?

A: Quagmireology is not an exact science. Perhaps he was using outdated tea leaves or defunct chicken bones. Maybe he got the brutal Afghan winter confused with the brutal Iraqi summer. All we know is that from now on, every general hoping for victory anywhere in the world will crave one of Apple's dire predictions. It's the only sure way to know you're going to win.

Q: I also noticed that the *Times* said President Bush sat by as Defense Secretary Rumsfeld and Vice President Cheney watched the toppling of Saddam's statue and "barely disguised their glee." Aren't Republican officials allowed to feel joy and satisfaction when a tyrant falls?

A: No.

Q: When it came time to explain why Jessica Lynch and her brother wanted to join the Army, both print and TV reporters paddled over quickly to a purely economic motive—there aren't many other jobs around these days in West Virginia. Would it have been too much to say that the Lynches appear to be a close-knit, traditional family with a strong sense of patriotism and high respect for the military?

A: Yes.

Q: As you know, both the BBC and National Public Radio have been criticized for their heavy-handed antiwar tilt. The coalition victory must be a terrible disappointment. How will they cope?

A: The possible re-emergence of Gulf War syndrome may revive their spirits. Some analysts want to talk about the war's possible damage to crops in the Fertile Crescent. That could be kicked around awhile. There are lots of negative things to feature—troubling developments and understandable Arab turmoil as the United States strives to impose its imperial will on an ancient land, and so forth. They could keep saying it was obvious the allies would win, then add a lot of "but" clauses about things that could well go wrong. If any looters get shot, correspondents can always produce stories on how the Nazi occupation troops shot civilians in France and the Netherlands. There's plenty of room here for creativity.

Q: Didn't a lot of celebrity war critics make concern for Iraqi kids a center-piece of their opposition to war? I notice they didn't say much about the horrific mutilation of Kurdish kids in Saddam's gas attacks. Now it turns out that Saddam had a children's jail. Some kids were in there for years for refusing to join the Baath Party's children's group, an Iraqi version of Hitler Youth. They came out signaling with both hands together to show that their wrists had been bound. Do you think the stars will comment and perhaps give the allies some credit for freeing the children?

A: You ask a lot. These are difficult days at Hollywood's Foreign Desk. Vicious cable reporters are digging up old TV clips of entertainers talking nonsense about Iraq. The reporters are showing this stuff on the air, thus creating the impression that these stars are ignorant fools! Next thing you know, people will not want to watch Susan Sarandon, Janeane Garofalo, and Rosie, thus violating the First Amendment and re-establishing the McCarthyite era in America. What was your question again? Was it something about children?

Q: Never mind. Well, if Hollywood hasn't got much to say, what about feminists? Saddam had state-run rape teams and sent videotapes of the rapes to families. He had gender-specific tortures for women, and his son Uday had more than 200 women beheaded. He hung the heads on the doors of the women's homes. Surely feminists said something about all this.

A: I'm afraid not. The leadership of the women's movement is deep into postcolonial relativism and not inclined to say much about Third World despots. Besides, men are bad everywhere. National Organization for Women President Kim Gandy put Saddam and Bush on the same moral plane: "This has become an issue of one dictator vs. another."

Q: Isn't there something simpleminded about that? How many women has Bush tortured and beheaded?

A: I guess you would have to ask Kim Gandy to check her figures.

Q: Well, what about Amnesty International? Surely they must be relieved by Saddam's overthrow.

A: If so, they are keeping their relief to themselves. Actually, Amnesty was very strong in indicting Saddam up until 9/11. But since then it has basically shut up and looked the other way. Apparently it didn't want to keep making a case against Iraq that the West might act on. It issued only two complaints about the current war, both against the allies.

Q: You mean nothing on the horrors of Saddam during the war—fake surrenders, shooting civilians, the revelations of jailed children, and all the rest?

A: Not yet. Apparently they're thinking about it.

Q: Do you sometimes think we need an entire new left side of our political spectrum?

A: Not my call. I report. You decide.

The Power of One
Michael Kinsley

Time | April 14, 2003

In this column, former Slate *editor Michael Kinsley crystallizes an emerging truth about President George W. Bush: For better or worse, he is one of that rare breed— a natural leader. . . .*

The "great man" theory of history has been out of fashion for decades. Historians trying to explain the course of human events point to geography or climate or technology. They explore the everyday life of ordinary people and the tides of change that sweep through whole populations. When they write about individual historical actors, the emphasis tends to be on psychology. Kings and Queens, Presidents and Prime Ministers may affect events at the margins, but the notion that history happens because someone decided it should happen is regarded as unenlightening if not simply wrong.

About Gulf War II and its consequences (whatever they may be), though, the "great man" theory is correct, and the great man is President George W. Bush. Great in this context does not necessarily mean good or wise. It does usually suggest a certain largeness of character or presence on the stage, which Bush does not possess. Whatever gods gave him this role were casting against type. But the role is his. This was George W. Bush's war. It was the result of one man's deliberate, sudden and unforced decision. Yes, Saddam Hussein deserves the ultimate moral blame, but Bush pushed the button.

Bush's decision to make war on Iraq may have been visionary and courageous or reckless and tragic or anything in between, but one thing it wasn't was urgently necessary. For Bush, this war was optional. Events did not impose it on him. Few public voices were egging him on. He hadn't made an issue of the need for "regime change" during the presidential campaign or made it a priority in the early months of his Administration. If he had completely ignored Iraq through the 2004 election, the price would have been a few disappointed Administration hawks and one or two grumpy op-eds. But something or someone put this bee in his bonnet, and from a standing start, history took off. Thousands died, millions were freed from tyranny (we hope), billions were spent, a region was shaken to its core, alliances ruptured, and the entire world watched it all on TV.

Compare America's other wars of the past 60 years. All of them had, if not inevitability, at least a bit of propulsion from forces larger than one man's desire. Gulf War I was provoked by an actual event: Iraq's occupation of Kuwait. George the Elder didn't have to make war, but he had to do something. Vietnam, famously, was never an explicit decision. Even the parody war in Grenada had a few captive American medical students to force its way onto the agenda. Some people believe that Franklin Roosevelt personally, deliberately and even dishonestly maneuvered a reluctant America into World War II. But World War II was history boiling over and impossible to avoid one way or another.

Why did Bush want this war? His ostensible reasons were unconvincing. Whatever we may find now in the rubble of Baghdad, he never offered any good evidence of a close link between Iraq and al-Qaeda or of weapons of mass destruction that could threaten the U.S. His desire to liberate a nation from tyranny undoubtedly was sincere, but there are other tyrants in the world. Why this one? On the other hand, the ulterior motives attributed to

Bush by critics are even more implausible. He didn't start a war to serve his re-election campaign or avenge his father or enrich his oil buddies or help Israel. The mystery of Bush's true motives adds to the impression of a wizard arbitrarily waving his wand over history.

War on Iraq was optional for George W. Bush in another sense too. He could have easily chosen not to have it, in which case it wouldn't have happened, but when he decided to have it, that was it: we had it. The President's ability to decide when and where to use America's military power is now absolute. Congress cannot stop him. That's not what the Constitution says, and it's not what the War Powers Act says, but that's how it works in practice. The U.N. cannot stop him. That's not what the U.N. Charter says, but who cares? And who cares what America's allies think either?

Even more amazing than the President's pragmatic power over military resources is his apparent spiritual power over so many minds. Bush is not the only one who decided rather suddenly that disempowering Saddam had to be the world's top priority. When Bush decided this, so did almost every congressional Republican, conservative TV pundit, and British Prime Minister. In polls, a large majority of Americans agreed with Bush that Saddam was a terrible threat and had to go, even though there had been no popular passion for this idea before Bush brought it up. You could call this many things, but one of them is leadership. If real leadership means leading people where they don't want to go, George W. Bush has shown himself to be a real leader. And he now owns a bit of history to prove it.

Bush Family Values

Michael Wolff

New York magazine | March 10, 2003

> *When indulging in political analysis, it's all too easy to overlook the basic human element. In the following essay, Michael Wolff considers the Iraq question through the prism of the Bush family subtext, and suggests that the best tool for understanding the whole affair might be that old psychological saw—"like father, like son.". . .*

I never know if I'll be thinking, as I read the *Times* at breakfast, that reasonable men have reasonable disagreements—maybe it *is* a good idea to "free" Iraq— or that all reason has discreetly departed. Or, perhaps, that we have entered one of those surreal historical moments that reasonable men simply don't have the language for.

The *Times* has assumed its most official kind of voice. Its Pentagon reporters command the front page. Other reporters are in war training. The tone is sober, meticulous, striving to be nonjudgmental—intent on ignoring all the various elephants in the room.

When the *Times* has General Tommy Franks discussing the intricacies of mobilization, everything seems serious and competent. But then as soon as you get to the numbers and the costs, everything becomes dreamlike and obtuse. The New York *Post* business pages might be better at handling these numbers than the *Times* front page—we need a War-Cost-o-Meter.

And then we're paying Turkey $15 billion to be our ally? Huh? But the *Times*, more or less pointedly, hasn't used the almost-unavoidable phrase *checkbook diplomacy* once. (Has anyone thought to offer a similarly sized retirement package to Saddam?)

And there's Wolfowitz, whom the *Times* alternately treats as Strangelovian and charming (there was a recent story in which the *Times* had Wolfowitz squirming about never having been in the Army himself—but as he squirmed, he seemed, in the *Times'* respectful going-to-war tone, cuddly, too).

And then, complementing the *Times* coverage, there was that full-page ad from the Department of Homeland Security urging *Times* readers to get their duct-tape family terror kit ready. Certainly surreal. (Do Homeland Security staff really have their kits all made up at home? Does Howell Raines have a kit in his house?)

Tonally, television tends to make more sense than the *Times*—possibly because it doesn't *try* to make sense. It's just all about countdown (MSNBC replaced Phil Donahue with *Countdown: Iraq*) and pictures of equipment, stylized soldiers, and big planes taking off.

But then there was Dan Rather's interview with Saddam, and that was certainly off-the-charts surreal.

Dan Rather, of course, is always a little surreal. And here he was with the most wanted man in the world, warmly grasping his hand in his own.

And Saddam himself: He looked good. I liked his suit. He seemed substantially more reasonable (and less interesting) than Michael Jackson (and Dan Rather was no Martin Bashir) and less monstrous than Robert Chambers ("Am I a monster? No"), whose interview followed Saddam's on CBS.

But the weirdest thing to me was Dan doing this *again*. Dan back in Baghdad, just like in 1990, getting his "get." The whole thing elaborately repeating itself—without any kind of humor or self-consciousness at all.

The Democrats, too, of course, are in a tonal black hole. Somehow the Bush people seem canny and in control—the *Times* certainly takes their lists of rationalizations and possible smoking guns seriously—whereas the Democrats seem rather silly and contemptible for their earnestness.

Nobody is quite acknowledging—not the *Times*, or Dan Rather, or the Democrats, and certainly not the White House—that it's plainly odd to be back here on the eve of war with Iraq. (It's not just Dan's interview that's a rerun.) Or possibly the oddness is just written into the story—we're accustomed to the elephants by now.

Certainly, the fixation has been squarely up-front—there's been practically no effort at hiding it at all. Let's state the obvious: Those lost, halcyon days of the first Gulf War are the ever-present background to doing this all once more. How could they not be? Who doesn't want to return to his—or his father's—finest moment?

Arguably, we haven't seen, among respectable nations, such a derring-do determination to go to war since, well, possibly before 1914. It's a breach of modern norms: One is never supposed to want to go to war; one is supposed to be *dragged* into war. It seems like an odd strategic mess-up, too: Don't begin by saying you want to be at war and then seek justifications; rather, look for ways to avoid war, and then have your hand forced.

But the Bushies have been nothing less than open about it: They're desperate to do Iraq; they *need* to do it; they will do it.

There have been, though, no cable-news talk shows debating the nature of neurotic obsession—the son's dealing with the father's issues. (Obviously, though, given his repeated delineation of Bush the Father and Bush the Son, this is on Saddam's mind.) Nor even has there been much discussion of the possibly cynical nature of all this: that it worked so well once before, so why not do it again? (Elisabeth Bumiller did refer the other day in the *Times* to the "political capital from a war," with "victory a turnkey to legislative success.") There's been scant wag-the-dog talk here—not like with the Clinton adventures, when you could make that reference and suggest a large and conspiratorial subtext and have lots of people eager to believe it. There have been few *Strangelove* references, either (even about Wolfowitz).

We've been assiduously treating this Iraq war as normal—at least as far as wars go—rather than unique to the Bushes.

The argument is in many ways rather quaintly old-fashioned: hawk versus dove. Hawks argue for the efficiency of war (the *Times*, notably, often seems to accept this argument), and doves argue about its vast and grievous hurtfulness.

Even the millions of protesters seem to regard the prospect of war as a basic moral or strategic disagreement—MR. PRESIDENT, LET THE INSPECTIONS WORK, read a particularly forlorn set of placards. Or some revert to the oil view—which, however mendacious, would still be a straightforward reason to go to war. Even the most extreme and creative lefties seem to have no real language for distinguishing the Bush motivation from any other kind of aggression.

And yet the question lurks. Sometimes it's phrased as "Why now?" But that's still strategic and moral, when perhaps it should be larger, more theatrical: "What's the character motivation? What's the emotional payoff?"

There is, weirdly, the grandness of it all. The operatic quality. The zeal. The demonizing. The ever-greater building of the tension. The duct tape.

Surely, too, it's out of balance to have staked everything on Iraq—the economy, the world order, the favorability rating of the president himself.

Then to have made it so entirely us against almost everybody else—to have, at almost every point, emphasized our dead-set determination in contrast to all the more moderate voices (in diplomacy, you always try to align with the moderate voices)—is hardly textbook politics.

And to have let it go on for so long is, in any conventional political-operations manual, crazy.

It is all so counterintuitive that it can only mean there is another really big idea here. It isn't just happenstance or a mistake. Rather, this is being craftily managed. Stage-managed, if you will.

Everybody may just be too polite or cowed or impressed with the whole operation (or afraid of it) to bring up with any insistence the history-repeating-itself-as-farce thing.

In some sense, there may even be a tendency to think that history will repeat itself verbatim. Even improve upon the first time around.

There was, after all, negative opinion then—but it reversed itself almost immediately. Fascination just took over. It was great television. (In the initial hours, it was most of all CNN that was being rooted for.) It was irresistible.

As U.S. forces and a potpourri of allied friends began to move across the desert—unstopped, unstoppable—the enthusiasm got even greater. There was the sudden, unexpected supremacy of the American fighting man over the desert (the first time we had seen the American fighting man decked out in new military techno-garb—in fact, the first time we'd seen the American fighting man in action mode since Vietnam). And then there was this joke army fighting us—and the burnt-out carcasses of the machinery it left behind. (This was the moment: Everywhere in the world, from Berlin to Moscow to Prague to Bucharest to Kuwait, when you pushed back against the bully, he fell.)

The president was swept up—however fleetingly—in as much popularity and good feeling as, arguably, an American president has ever known. The man was really reinvented. All that inarticulateness and Wasp awkwardness, and those poor media skills, were suddenly transformed into authenticity and decisiveness and pluck. For a minute there, he must have felt that he was who he believed he was. The man in the mirror matched the man on television. I know that I certainly thought, *What a guy!*

But then, of course, it all got messed up. They didn't play it through (didn't get Saddam). Didn't hold onto it.

But here we are again.

And if it's too much—certainly it's hokey, not to mention dangerous—that the same guys are trying to do the same thing once more, I think the smart money believes they're going to pull it off.

That, shortly, a screaming will come across the sky with a destructive virtuosity heretofore unimagined. Never before in the history of warfare, the smart money assumes, will there have been an attack so choreographed and one-sided.

So it's not going to really matter that the whole deal was something of a put-up job—a forced construct—because when it works even better than it worked twelve years ago (after all, we've really improved all this stuff), when we roll in like nobody's business, when the Iraqi Army runs for its life, this victory, like all victories, is going to be irresistible, too (the White House and Pentagon are so confident of this that, for the first time in a generation, they're getting ready to bring reporters to the front). The American media will swoon—and the American people will be glued to their sets, cheering the winner, who is us.

And, of course, the French and the Germans will, in a New York minute, be on the side of the victors, too. You'll never find a frog or Kraut who doubted the president. Everyone—Iraqis, lefties, Euros—will acquiesce (and fawn), and George Bush will be acclaimed some really marvelous man of the moment. Strong, steadfast, determined, invincible—ready to stand up to all manner of tyrants and yellow-bellied world opinion.

And this time the Bushies no doubt believe they won't blow it.

The End of the Beginning
William Kristol

The Weekly Standard | May 12, 2003

If anyone can be described as a Republican "opinion leader," it's Bill Kristol, long-time editor of the conservative Weekly Standard, *and a fixture on the political talk-show circuit. He has also been one of the most vocal advocates of intervention in Iraq. The following editorial was written as the Iraq war was drawing to a successful close. As Kristol makes clear, however, he views Hussein's overthrow as simply one important battle in a larger (and still unfinished) war. . . .*

*"Now this is not the end. It is not even the beginning of the end.
But it is, perhaps, the end of the beginning."*
Winston Churchill, November 10, 1942, after the
British defeat of the German Afrika Korps in Egypt

The war on terror is not World War II, and George W. Bush is not Winston Churchill. Still, the war in which we are presently engaged is a fundamental challenge for the United States and the civilized world. It is a defining moment for America and American foreign policy. The victory in what the president called Thursday night "the battle of Iraq" is, perhaps, the end of the beginning of this larger war.

President Bush understands that we are engaged in a larger war. His opponents, on the whole, do not, and this accounts in large measure for the yawning gulf between the supporters and critics of the Bush Doctrine.

It is unclear, to say the least, what actual policies most of Bush's critics would follow. Different opponents would presumably embrace differing combinations of the sporadic use of American force, wishful exercises in appeasement, and endless negotiations at the United Nations and elsewhere. But what Bush's opponents have in common is a refusal to come to grips with the fundamental character of the war on terror: the fact that it is a *war*, of which Afghanistan and Iraq, as the president said, are merely battles. Thus they refuse to embrace the president's ambitious agenda, eloquently reiterated aboard the USS *Abraham Lincoln,* of targeting all terrorist groups and the states that support them, of confronting outlaw regimes that seek weapons of mass destruction, and of standing with the friends of freedom around the world.

When the president laid out his principles on Thursday, one formulation was particularly interesting: "Anyone in the world, including the Arab world, who works and sacrifices for freedom has a loyal friend in the United States." Why "including the Arab world"? Because that world—or better, perhaps, the Middle East or the Islamic world—is the heart of the problem. North Korea is a danger, to be sure. But it probably can be contained—and the global threat it poses is primarily in proliferating its deadly weapons to terrorists and terrorist states. Almost all of these are in the Middle East.

The liberation of Iraq was the first great battle for the future of the Middle East. The creation of a free Iraq is now of fundamental importance, and we must do what it takes to make a decent, democratic Iraq a reality. But the next great battle—not, we hope, a military battle—will be for Iran. We are already in a death struggle with Iran over the future of Iraq. The theocrats ruling Iran understand that the stakes are now double or nothing. They can stay in power by disrupting efforts to create a pluralistic, non-theocratic, Shia-majority state next door—or they can fall, as success in Iraq sounds the death knell for the Iranian revolution.

So we must help our friends and allies in Iraq block Iranian-backed sub-version. And we must also take the fight to Iran, with measures ranging from public diplomacy to covert operations. Iran is the tipping point in the war on proliferation, the war on terror, and the effort to reshape the Middle East. If Iran goes pro-Western and anti-terror, positive changes in Syria and Saudi Arabia will follow much more easily. And the chances for an Israeli-Palestinian settlement will greatly improve.

The president said on Thursday night, "Any outlaw regime that has ties to terrorist groups, and seeks or possesses weapons of mass destruction, is a grave danger to the civilized world, and will be confronted." That is Iran, above all. On the outcome of the confrontation with Tehran, more than any other, rests the future of the Bush Doctrine—and, quite possibly, the Bush presidency—and prospects for a safer world.

As Churchill also said in his speech of November 10, 1942, "We have not entered this war for profit or expansion, but only for honor and to do our duty in defending the right." All honor to Bush for confronting the challenge of our day in the same spirit, and with the same confidence. There will be setbacks and difficulties ahead. But surely we can, as we must, prevail.

Part Four: America and the World

The Burden
Michael Ignatieff

The New York Times Magazine | January 5, 2003

Our section on the United States and its role in international politics begins with an essay by Michael Ignatieff, director of the Carr Center of Human Rights Policy at Harvard's Kennedy School of Government. In this article, Ignatieff examines the responsibilities and dangers that America faces as the world's sole superpower. His premise is that the U.S. is already well on the way to establishing a global empire, even if we prefer not to admit it. The big question, in his view, is how this new imperial agenda will shape our future as a democratic republic. . . .

I.

In a speech to graduating cadets at West Point in June, President Bush declared, "America has no empire to extend or utopia to establish." When he spoke to veterans assembled at the White House in November, he said: America has "no territorial ambitions. We don't seek an empire. Our nation is committed to freedom for ourselves and for others."

Ever since George Washington warned his countrymen against foreign entanglements, empire abroad has been seen as the republic's permanent temptation and its potential nemesis. Yet what word but "empire" describes the awesome thing that America is becoming? It is the only nation that polices the world through five global military commands; maintains more than a million men and women at arms on four continents; deploys carrier battle groups on watch in every ocean; guarantees the survival of countries from Israel to South Korea; drives the wheels of global trade and commerce; and fills the hearts and minds of an entire planet with its dreams and desires.

A historian once remarked that Britain acquired its empire in "a fit of absence of mind." If Americans have an empire, they have acquired it in a state of deep denial. But September 11 was an awakening, a moment of reckoning with the extent of American power and the avenging hatreds it arouses. Americans may not have thought of the World Trade Center or the Pentagon as the symbolic headquarters of a world empire, but the men with the box cutters certainly did, and so do numberless millions who cheered their terrifying exercise in the propaganda of the deed.

Being an imperial power, however, is more than being the most powerful nation or just the most hated one. It means enforcing such order as there is in the world and doing so in the American interest. It means laying down the rules America wants (on everything from markets to weapons of mass destruction) while exempting itself from other rules (the Kyoto Protocol on climate change and the International Criminal Court) that go against its interest. It also means carrying out imperial functions in places America has inherited from the failed empires of the 20th century—Ottoman, British, and Soviet. In the 21st century, America rules alone, struggling to manage the insurgent zones—Palestine and the northwest frontier of Pakistan, to name but two—that have proved to be the nemeses of empires past.

Iraq lays bare the realities of America's new role. Iraq itself is an imperial fiction, cobbled together at the Versailles Peace Conference in 1919 by the French and British and held together by force and violence since independence. Now an expansionist rights violator holds it together with terror. The United Nations lay dozing like a dog before the fire, happy to ignore Saddam, until an American president seized it by the scruff of the neck and made it bark. Multilateral solutions to the world's problems are all very well, but they have no teeth unless America bares its fangs.

America's empire is not like empires of times past, built on colonies, conquest, and the white man's burden. We are no longer in the era of the United Fruit Company, when American corporations needed the Marines to secure their investments overseas. The 21st century imperium is a new invention in the annals of political science, an empire lite, a global hegemony whose grace notes are free markets, human rights, and democracy, enforced by the most awesome military power the world has ever known. It is the imperialism of a people who remember that their country secured its independence by revolt against an empire, and who like to think of themselves as the friend of freedom everywhere. It is an empire without consciousness of itself as such, constantly shocked that its good intentions arouse resentment abroad. But that does not make it any less of an empire, with a conviction that it alone, in Herman Melville's words, bears "the ark of the liberties of the world."

In this vein, the president's National Security Strategy, announced in September, commits America to lead other nations toward "the single sustainable model for national success," by which he meant free markets and liberal democracy. This is strange rhetoric for a Texas politician who ran for office opposing nation-building abroad and calling for a more humble America overseas. But Sept. 11 changed everyone, including a laconic and anti-rhetorical president. His messianic note may be new to him, but it is not new to his office. It has been present in the American vocabulary at least since Woodrow Wilson went to Versailles in 1919 and told the world that he wanted to make it safe for democracy.

Ever since Wilson, presidents have sounded the same redemptive note while "frantically avoiding recognition of the imperialism that we in fact exercise," as the theologian Reinhold Niebuhr said in 1960. Even now, as President Bush appears to be maneuvering the country toward war with Iraq, the deepest implication of what is happening has not been fully faced: that Iraq is an imperial operation that would commit a reluctant republic to become the guarantor of peace, stability, democratization, and oil supplies in a combustible region of Islamic peoples stretching from Egypt to Afghanistan. A role once played by the Ottoman Empire, then by the French and the British, will now be played by a nation that has to ask whether in becoming an empire it risks losing its soul as a republic.

As the United States faces this moment of truth, John Quincy Adams's warning of 1821 remains stark and pertinent: if America were tempted to "become the dictatress of the world, she would be no longer the ruler of her own spirit." What empires lavish abroad, they cannot spend on good republican government at home: on hospitals or roads or schools. A distended military budget only aggravates America's continuing failure to keep its egalitarian promise to itself. And these are not the only costs of empire. Detaining two American citizens without charge or access to counsel in military brigs, maintaining illegal combatants on a foreign island in a legal limbo, keeping lawful aliens under permanent surveillance while deporting others after secret hearings: these are not the actions of a republic that lives by the rule of law but of an imperial power reluctant to trust its own liberties. Such actions may still be a long way short of Roosevelt's internment of the Japanese, but that may mean only that the worst—following, say, another large attack on United States citizens that produces mass casualties—is yet to come.

The impending operation in Iraq is thus a defining moment in America's long debate with itself about whether its overseas role as an empire threatens or strengthens its existence as a republic. The American electorate, while still supporting the president, wonders whether his proclamation of a war without end against terrorists and tyrants may only increase its vulnerability while endangering its liberties and its economic health at home. A nation that rarely counts the cost of what it really values now must ask what the "liberation" of Iraq is worth. A republic that has paid a tiny burden to maintain its empire—no more than about 4 percent of its gross domestic product—now contemplates a bill that is altogether steeper. Even if victory is rapid, a war in Iraq and a postwar occupation may cost anywhere from $120 billion to $200 billion.

What every schoolchild also knows about empires is that they eventually face nemeses. To call America the new Rome is at once to recall Rome's glory and its eventual fate at the hands of the barbarians. A confident and care-free republic—the city on a hill, whose people have always believed they are immune from history's harms—now has to confront not just an unending imperial destiny but also a remote possibility that seems to haunt the history of empire: hubris followed by defeat.

II.

Even at this late date, it is still possible to ask: Why should a republic take on the risks of empire? Won't it run a chance of endangering its identity as a free people? The problem is that this implies innocent options that in the case of Iraq may no longer exist. Iraq is not just about whether the United States can retain its republican virtue in a wicked world. Virtuous disengagement is no longer a possibility. Since Sept. 11, it has been about whether the republic can survive in safety at home without imperial policing abroad. Face to face with "evil empires" of the past, the republic reluctantly accepted a division of the world based on mutually assured destruction. But now it faces much less stable and reliable opponents—rogue states like Iraq and North Korea with the potential to supply weapons of mass destruction to a terrorist internationale. Iraq represents the first in a series of struggles to contain the proliferation of weapons of mass destruction, the first attempt to shut off the potential supply of lethal technologies to a global terrorist network.

Containment rather than war would be the better course, but the Bush administration seems to have concluded that containment has reached its limits—and the conclusion is not unreasonable. Containment is not designed to stop production of sarin, VX nerve gas, anthrax, and nuclear weapons. Threatened retaliation might deter Saddam from using these weapons, but his continued development of them increases his capacity to intimidate and deter others, including the United States. Already his weapons have sharply raised the cost of any invasion, and as time goes by this could become prohibitive. The possibility that North Korea might quickly develop weapons of mass destruction makes regime change on the Korean peninsula all but unthinkable. Weapons of mass destruction would render Saddam the master of a region that, because it has so much of the world's proven oil reserves, makes it what a military strategist would call the empire's center of gravity.

Iraq may claim to have ceased manufacturing these weapons after 1991, but these claims remain unconvincing, because inspectors found evidence of activity after that date. So what to do? Efforts to embargo and sanction the regime have hurt only the Iraqi people. What is left? An inspections program, even a permanent one, might slow the dictator's weapons programs down, but inspections are easily evaded. That leaves us, but only as a reluctant last resort, with regime change.

Regime change is an imperial task par excellence, since it assumes that the empire's interest has a right to trump the sovereignty of a state. The Bush administration would ask, What moral authority rests with a sovereign who murders and ethnically cleanses his own people, has twice invaded neighboring countries, and usurps his people's wealth in order to build palaces and lethal weapons? And the administration is not alone. Not even Kofi Annan, the secretary general, charged with defending the United Nations Charter, says that sovereignty confers impunity for such crimes, though he has made it clear he would prefer to leave a disarmed Saddam in power rather than risk the conflagration of war to unseat him.

Regime change also raises the difficult question for Americans of whether their own freedom entails a duty to defend the freedom of others beyond their borders. The precedents here are inconclusive. Just because Wilson and Roosevelt sent Americans to fight and die for freedom in Europe and Asia doesn't mean their successors are committed to this duty everywhere and forever. The war in Vietnam was sold to a skeptical American public as another battle for freedom, and it led the republic into defeat and disgrace.

Yet it remains a fact—as disagreeable to those left wingers who regard American imperialism as the root of all evil as it is to the right-wing isolationists, who believe that the world beyond our shores is none of our business—that there are many peoples who owe their freedom to an exercise of American military power. It's not just the Japanese and the Germans, who became democrats under the watchful eye of Generals MacArthur and Clay. There are the Bosnians, whose nation survived because American air power and diplomacy forced an end to a war the Europeans couldn't stop. There are the Kosovars, who would still be imprisoned in Serbia if not for Gen. Wesley Clark and the Air Force. The list of people whose freedom depends on American air and ground power also includes the Afghans and, most inconveniently of all, the Iraqis.

The moral evaluation of empire gets complicated when one of its benefits might be freedom for the oppressed. Iraqi exiles are adamant: even if the Iraqi people might be the immediate victims of an American attack, they would also be its ultimate beneficiaries. It would make the case for military intervention easier, of course, if the Iraqi exiles cut a more impressive figure. They feud and squabble and hate one another nearly as much as they hate Saddam. But what else is to be expected from a political culture pulverized by 40 years of state terror?

If only invasion, and not containment, can build democracy in Iraq, then the question becomes whether the Bush administration actually has any real intention of doing so. The exiles fear that a mere change of regime, a coup in which one Baathist thug replaces another, would suit American interests just as well, provided the thug complied with the interests of the Pentagon and American oil companies. Whenever it has exerted power overseas, America has never been sure whether it values stability—which means not only political stability but also the steady, profitable flow of goods and raw materials—more than it values its own rhetoric about democracy. Where the two values have collided, American power has come down heavily on the side of stability, for example, toppling democratically elected leaders from Mossadegh in Iran to Allende in Chile. Iraq is yet another test of this choice. Next door in Iran, from the 1950s to the 1970s, America backed stability over democracy, propping up the autocratic rule of the shah, only to reap the whirlwind of an Islamic fundamentalist revolution in 1979 that delivered neither stability nor real democracy. Does the same fate await an American operation in Iraq?

International human rights groups, like Amnesty International, are dismayed at the way both the British government of Tony Blair and the Bush administration are citing the human rights abuses of Saddam to defend the idea of regime change. Certainly the British and the American governments maintained a complicit and dishonorable silence when Saddam gassed the Kurds in 1988. Yet now that the two governments are taking decisive action, human rights groups seem more outraged by the prospect of action than they are by the abuses they once denounced. The fact that states are both late and hypocritical in their adoption of human rights does not deprive them of the right to use force to defend them.

The disagreeable reality for those who believe in human rights is that there are some occasions—and Iraq may be one of them—when war is the only real remedy for regimes that live by terror. This does not mean the choice is morally unproblematic. The choice is one between two evils, between containing and leaving a tyrant in place and the targeted use of force, which will kill people but free a nation from the tyrant's grip.

III.

Still, the claim that a free republic may sense a duty to help other people attain their freedom does not answer the prudential question of whether the republic should run such risks. For the risks are huge, and they are imperial. Order, let alone democracy, will take a decade to consolidate in Iraq. The Iraqi opposition's blueprints for a democratic and secular federation of Iraq's component peoples—Shiites, Sunnis, Kurds, Turkomans, and others—are noble documents, but they are just paper unless American and then international troops, under United Nations mandate, remain to keep the peace until Iraqis trust one another sufficiently to police themselves. Like all imperial exercises in creating order, it will work only if the puppets the Americans install cease to be puppets and build independent political legitimacy of their own.

If America takes on Iraq, it takes on the reordering of the whole region. It will have to stick at it through many successive administrations. The burden of empire is of long duration, and democracies are impatient with long-lasting burdens—none more so than America. These burdens include opening up a dialogue with the Iranians, who appear to be in a political upsurge themselves, so that they do not feel threatened by a United States-led democracy on their border. The Turks will have to be reassured, and the Kurds will have to be instructed that the real aim of United States policy is not the creation of a Kurdish state that goes on to dismember Turkey. The Syrians will have to be coaxed into abandoning their claims against the Israelis and making peace. The Saudis, once democracy takes root next door in Iraq, will have to be coaxed into embracing democratic change themselves.

All this is possible, but there is a larger challenge still. Unseating an Arab government in Iraq while leaving the Palestinians to face Israeli tanks and helicopter gunships is a virtual guarantee of unending Islamic wrath against the United States. The chief danger in the whole Iraqi gamble lies here—in supposing that victory over Saddam, in the absence of a Palestinian-Israeli settlement, would leave the United States with a stable hegemony over the Middle East. Absent a Middle East peace, victory in Iraq would still leave the Palestinians face to face with the Israelis in a conflict in which they would destroy not only each other but American authority in the Islamic world as well.

The Americans have played imperial guarantor in the region since

Roosevelt met with Ibn Saud in 1945 and Truman recognized Ben-Gurion's Israel in 1948. But it paid little or no price for its imperial pre-eminence until the rise of an armed Palestinian resistance after 1987. Now, with every day that American power appears complicit in Israeli attacks that kill civilians in the West Bank and in Gaza, and with the Arab nations giving their tacit support to Palestinian suicide bombers, the imperial guarantor finds itself dragged into a regional conflict that is one long hemorrhage of its diplomatic and military authority.

Properly understood, then, the operation in Iraq entails a commitment, so far unstated, to enforce a peace on the Palestinians and Israelis. Such a peace must, at a minimum, give the Palestinians a viable, contiguous state capable of providing land and employment for three million people. It must include a commitment to rebuild their shattered government infrastructure, possibly through a United Nations transitional administration, with U.N.-mandated peacekeepers to provide security for Israelis and Palestinians. This is an awesomely tall order, but if America cannot find the will to enforce this minimum of justice, neither it nor Israel will have any safety from terror. This remains true even if you accept that there are terrorists in the Arab world who will never be content unless Israel is driven into the sea. A successful American political strategy against terror depends on providing enough peace for both Israelis and Palestinians that extremists on either side begin to lose the support that keeps violence alive.

Paradoxically, reducing the size of the task does not reduce the risks. If an invasion of Iraq is delinked from Middle East peace, then all America will gain for victory in Iraq is more terror cells in the Muslim world. If America goes on to help the Palestinians achieve a state, the result will not win over those, like Osama bin Laden, who hate America for what it is. But at least it would address the rage of those who hate it for what it does.

This is finally what makes an invasion of Iraq an imperial act: for it to succeed, it will have to build freedom, not just for the Iraqis but also for the Palestinians, along with a greater sense of security for Israel. Again, the paradox of the Iraq operation is that half measures are more dangerous than whole measures. Imperial powers do not have the luxury of timidity, for timidity is not prudence; it is a confession of weakness.

IV.

The question, then, is not whether America is too powerful but whether it is powerful enough. Does it have what it takes to be grandmaster of what Colin Powell has called the chessboard of the world's most inflammable region?

America has been more successful than most great powers in understanding its strengths as well as its limitations. It has become adept at using what is called soft power—influence, example, and persuasion—in preference to hard power. Adepts of soft power understand that even the most powerful country in the world can't get its way all the time. Even client states have to be deferred to. When an ally like Saudi Arabia asks the United States to avoid flying over its country when bombing Afghanistan, America complies. When America seeks to use Turkey as a base for hostilities in Iraq, it must accept Turkish preconditions. Being an empire doesn't mean being omnipotent.

Nowhere is this clearer than in America's relations with Israel. America's ally is anything but a client state. Its prime minister has refused direct orders from the president of the United States in the past, and he can be counted on to do so again. An Iraq operation requires the United States not merely to prevent Israel from entering the fray but to make peace with a bitter enemy. Since 1948, American and Israeli security interests have been at one. But as the death struggle in Palestine continues, it exposes the United States to global hatreds that make it impossible for it to align its interests with those Israelis who are opposed to any settlement with the Palestinians that does not amount, in effect, to Palestinian capitulation. The issue is not whether the United States should continue to support the state of Israel, but which state, with which borders and which set of relations with its neighbors, it is willing to risk its imperial authority to secure. The apocalyptic violence of one side and the justified refusal to negotiate under fire on the other side leave precious little time to salvage a two-state solution for the Middle East. But this, even more than rescuing Iraq, is the supreme task—and test—of American leadership.

V.

What assets does American leadership have at its disposal? At a time when an imperial peace in the Middle East requires diplomats, aid workers, and civilians with all the skills in rebuilding shattered societies, American power projection in the area overwhelmingly wears a military uniform. "Every great power, whatever its ideology," Arthur Schlesinger Jr. once wrote, "has its warrior caste." Without realizing the consequences of what they were doing, successive American presidents have turned the projection of American power to the warrior caste, according to the findings of research by Robert J. Lieber of Georgetown University. In President Kennedy's time, Lieber has found, the United States spent 1 percent of its G.D.P. on the nonmilitary aspects of promoting its influence overseas—State Department, foreign aid, the United Nations, information programs. Under Bush's presidency, the number has declined to just 0.2 percent.

Special Forces are more in evidence in the world's developing nations than Peace Corps volunteers and USAID food experts. As Dana Priest demonstrates in *The Mission*, a soon-to-be-published study of the American military, the Pentagon's regional commanders exercise more overseas diplomatic and political leverage than the State Department's ambassadors. Even if you accept that generals can make good diplomats and Special Forces captains can make friends for the United States, it still remains true that the American presence overseas is increasingly armed, in uniform, and behind barbed wire and high walls. With every American Embassy now hardened against terrorist attack, the empire's overseas outposts look increasingly like Fort Apache. American power is visible to the world in carrier battle groups patrolling offshore and F-16s whistling overhead. In southern Afghanistan, it is the 82nd Airborne, bulked up in body armor, helmets, and weapons, that Pashtun peasants see, not American aid workers and water engineers. Each month the United States spends an estimated $1 billion on military operations in Afghanistan and only $25 million on aid.

This sort of projection of power, hunkered down against attack, can earn the United States fear and respect, but not admiration and affection. America's very strength—in military power—cannot conceal its weakness in the areas that really matter: the elements of power that do not subdue by force of arms but inspire by force of example.

VI.

It is unsurprising that force projection overseas should awaken resentment among America's enemies. More troubling is the hostility it arouses among friends, those whose security is guaranteed by American power. Nowhere is this more obvious than in Europe. At a moment when the costs of empire are mounting for America, her rich European allies matter financially. But in America's emerging global strategy, they have been demoted to reluctant junior partners. This makes them resentful and unwilling allies, less and less able to understand the nation that liberated them in 1945.

For 50 years, Europe rebuilt itself economically while passing on the costs of its defense to the United States. This was a matter of more than just reducing its armed forces and the proportion of national income spent on the military. All Western European countries reduced the martial elements in their national identities. In the process, European identity (with the possible exception of Britain) became postmilitary and postnational. This opened a widening gap with the United States. It remained a nation in which flag, sacrifice, and martial honor are central to national identity. Europeans who had once invented the idea of the martial nation-state now looked at American patriotism, the last example of the form, and no longer recognized it as anything but flag-waving extremism. The world's only empire was isolated, not just because it was the biggest power but also because it was the West's last military nation-state.

Sept. 11 rubbed in the lesson that global power is still measured by military capability. The Europeans discovered that they lacked the military instruments to be taken seriously and that their erstwhile defenders, the Americans, regarded them, in a moment of crisis, with suspicious contempt.

Yet the Americans cannot afford to create a global order all on their own. European participation in peacekeeping, nation-building, and humanitarian reconstruction is so important that the Americans are required, even when they are unwilling to do so, to include Europeans in the governance of their evolving imperial project. The Americans essentially dictate Europe's place in this new grand design. The United States is multilateral when it wants to be, unilateral when it must be; and it enforces a new division of labor in which America does the fighting, the French, British, and Germans do the police patrols in the border zones and the Dutch, Swiss, and Scandinavians provide the humanitarian aid.

This is a very different picture of the world than the one entertained by liberal international lawyers and human rights activists who had hoped to see American power integrated into a transnational legal and economic order organized around the United Nations, the World Trade Organization, the International Criminal Court, and other international human rights and environmental institutions and mechanisms. Successive American administrations have signed on to those pieces of the transnational legal order that suit their purposes (the World Trade Organization, for example) while ignoring or even sabotaging those parts (the International Criminal Court or the Kyoto Protocol) that do not. A new international order is emerging, but it is designed to suit American imperial objectives. America's allies want a multilateral order that will essentially constrain American power. But the empire will not be tied down like Gulliver with a thousand legal strings.

VII.

On the new imperial frontier, in places like Afghanistan, Bosnia, and Kosovo, American military power, together with European money and humanitarian motives, is producing a form of imperial rule for a postimperial age. If this sounds contradictory, it is because the impulses that have gone into this new exercise of power are contradictory. On the one hand, the semiofficial ideology of the Western world—human rights—sustains the principle of self-determination, the right of each people to rule themselves free of outside interference. This was the ethical principle that inspired the decolonization of Asia and Africa after World War II. Now we are living through the collapse of many of these former colonial states. Into the resulting vacuum of chaos and massacre a new imperialism has reluctantly stepped—reluctantly because these places are dangerous and because they seemed, at least until Sept. 11, to be marginal to the interests of the powers concerned. But, gradually, this reluctance has been replaced by an understanding of why order needs to be brought to these places.

Nowhere, after all, could have been more distant than Afghanistan, yet that remote and desperate place was where the attacks of Sept. 11 were prepared. Terror has collapsed distance, and with this collapse has come a sharpened American focus on the necessity of bringing order to the frontier zones. Bringing order is the paradigmatic imperial task, but it is essential, for reasons of both economy and principle, to do so without denying local peoples their rights to some degree of self-determination.

The old European imperialism justified itself as a mission to civilize, to prepare tribes and so-called lesser breeds in the habits of self-discipline necessary for the exercise of self-rule. Self-rule did not necessarily have to happen soon—the imperial administrators hoped to enjoy the sunset as long as possible—but it was held out as a distant incentive, and the incentive was crucial in co-opting local elites and preventing them from passing into open rebellion. In the new imperialism, this promise of self-rule cannot be kept so distant, for local elites are all creations of modern nationalism, and modern nationalism's primary ethical content is self-determination. If there is an invasion of Iraq, local elites must be "empowered" to take over as soon as the American imperial forces have restored order and the European humanitarians have rebuilt the roads, schools, and houses. Nation-building seeks to reconcile imperial power and local self-determination through the medium of an exit strategy. This is imperialism in a hurry: to spend money, to get results, to turn the place back to the locals and get out. But it is similar to the old imperialism in the sense that real power in these zones—Kosovo, Bosnia, Afghanistan, and soon, perhaps, Iraq—will remain in Washington.

VIII.

At the beginning of the first volume of *The Decline and Fall of the Roman Empire*, published in 1776, Edward Gibbon remarked that empires endure only so long as their rulers take care not to overextend their borders. Augustus bequeathed his successors an empire "within those limits which nature seemed to have placed as its permanent bulwarks and boundaries: on the west the Atlantic Ocean; the Rhine and Danube on the north; the Euphrates on the east; and towards the south the sandy deserts of Arabia and Africa." Beyond these boundaries lay the barbarians. But the "vanity or ignorance" of the Romans, Gibbon went on, led them to "despise and sometimes to forget the outlying countries that had been left in the enjoyment of a barbarous independence." As a result, the proud Romans were lulled into making the fatal mistake of "confounding the Roman monarchy with the globe of the earth."

This characteristic delusion of imperial power is to confuse global power with global domination. The Americans may have the former, but they do not have the latter. They cannot rebuild each failed state or appease each anti-American hatred, and the more they try, the more they expose themselves to the overreach that eventually undermined the classical empires of old.

The secretary of defense may be right when he warns the North Koreans that America is capable of fighting on two fronts—in Korea and Iraq—simultaneously, but Americans at home cannot be overjoyed at such a prospect, and if two fronts are possible at once, a much larger number of fronts is not. If conflict in Iraq, North Korea, or both becomes a possibility, Al Qaeda can be counted on to seek to strike a busy and overextended empire in the back. What this suggests is not just that overwhelming power never confers the security it promises but also that even the overwhelmingly powerful need friends and allies. In the cold war, the road to the North Korean capital, Pyongyang, led through Moscow and Beijing. Now America needs its old cold war adversaries more than ever to control the breakaway, bankrupt Communist rogue that is threatening America and her clients from Tokyo to Seoul.

Empires survive when they understand that diplomacy, backed by force, is always to be preferred to force alone. Looking into the still more distant future, say a generation ahead, resurgent Russia and China will demand recognition both as world powers and as regional hegemons. As the North Korean case shows, America needs to share the policing of nonproliferation and other threats with these powers, and if it tries, as the current National Security Strategy suggests, to prevent the emergence of any competitor to American global dominance, it risks everything that Gibbon predicted: overextension followed by defeat.

America will also remain vulnerable, despite its overwhelming military power, because its primary enemy, Iraq and North Korea notwithstanding, is not a state, susceptible to deterrence, influence, and coercion, but a shadowy cell of fanatics who have proved that they cannot be deterred and coerced and who have hijacked a global ideology—Islam—that gives them a bottomless supply of recruits and allies in a war, a war not just against America but against her client regimes in the Islamic world. In many countries in that part of the world, America is caught in the middle of a civil war raging between incompetent and authoritarian regimes and the Islamic revolutionaries who want to return the Arab world to the time of the prophet. It is a civil war between the politics of pure reaction and the politics of the impossible, with America unfortunately aligned on the side of reaction. On Sept. 11, the American empire discovered that in the Middle East its local pillars were literally built on sand.

Until Sept. 11, successive United States administrations treated their Middle Eastern clients like gas stations. This was part of a larger pattern. After 1991 and the collapse of the Soviet empire, American presidents thought they could have imperial domination on the cheap, ruling the world without putting in place any new imperial architecture—new military alliances, new legal institutions, new international development organisms—for a postcolonial, post-Soviet world.

The Greeks taught the Romans to call this failure hubris. It was also, in the 1990s, a general failure of the historical imagination, an inability of the post-cold-war West to grasp that the emerging crisis of state order in so many overlapping zones of the world—from Egypt to Afghanistan—would eventually become a security threat at home. Radical Islam would never have succeeded in winning adherents if the Muslim countries that won independence from the European empires had been able to convert dreams of self-determination into the reality of competent, rule-abiding states. America has inherited this crisis of self-determination from the empires of the past. Its solution—to create democracy in Iraq, then hopefully roll out the same happy experiment throughout the Middle East—is both noble and dangerous: noble because, if successful, it will finally give these peoples the self-determination they vainly fought for against the empires of the past; dangerous because, if it fails, there will be nobody left to blame but the Americans.

The dual nemeses of empire in the 20th century were nationalism, the desire of peoples to rule themselves free of alien domination, and narcissism, the incurable delusion of imperial rulers that the "lesser breeds" aspired only to be versions of themselves. Both nationalism and narcissism have threatened the American reassertion of global power since Sept. 11.

IX.

As the Iraqi operation looms, it is worth keeping Vietnam in mind. Vietnam was a titanic clash between two nation-building strategies, the Americans in support of the South Vietnamese versus the Communists in the north. Yet it proved impossible for foreigners to build stability in a divided country against resistance from a Communist elite fighting in the name of the Vietnamese nation. Vietnam is now one country, its civil war over and its long-term stability assured. An American operation in Iraq will not face a competing nationalist project, but across the Islamic world it will rouse the nationalist passions of people who want to rule themselves and worship as they please. As Vietnam shows, empire is no match, long-term, for nationalism.

America's success in the 20th century owed a great deal to the shrewd understanding that America's interest lay in aligning itself with freedom. Franklin Roosevelt, for example, told his advisers at Yalta in 1945, when he was dividing up the postwar world with Churchill and Stalin, that there were more than a billion "brown people" living in Asia, "ruled by a handful of whites." They resent it, the president mused aloud. America's goal, he said, "must be to help them achieve independence—1,100,000,000 enemies are dangerous."

The core beliefs of our time are the creations of the anticolonial revolt against empire: the idea that all human beings are equal and that each human group has a right to rule itself free of foreign interference. It is at least ironic that American believers in these ideas have ended up supporting the creation of a new form of temporary colonial tutelage for Bosnians, Kosovars, and Afghans—and could for Iraqis. The reason is simply that, however right these principles may be, the political form in which they are realized—the nationalist nation-building project—so often delivers liberated colonies straight to tyranny, as in the case of Baath Party rule in Iraq, or straight to chaos, as in Bosnia or Afghanistan. For every nationalist struggle that succeeds in giving its people self-determination and dignity, there are more that deliver their people only up to slaughter or terror or both. For every Vietnam brought about by nationalist struggle, there is a Palestinian struggle trapped in a downward spiral of terror and military oppression.

The age of empire ought to have been succeeded by an age of independent, equal and self-governing nation-states. But that has not come to pass. America has inherited a world scarred not just by the failures of empires past but also by the failure of nationalist movements to create and secure free states—and now, suddenly, by the desire of Islamists to build theocratic tyrannies on the ruins of failed nationalist dreams.

Those who want America to remain a republic rather than become an empire imagine rightly, but they have not factored in what tyranny or chaos can do to vital American interests. The case for empire is that it has become, in a place like Iraq, the last hope for democracy and stability alike. Even so, empires survive only by understanding their limits. Sept. 11 pitched the Islamic world into the beginning of a long and bloody struggle to determine how it will be ruled and by whom: the authoritarians, the Islamists, or perhaps the democrats. America can help repress and contain the struggle, but even though its own security depends on the outcome, it cannot ultimately control it. Only a very deluded imperialist would believe otherwise.

Bush and Iraq
Anthony Lewis

The New York Review of Books | November 7, 2002

Although Anthony Lewis gave up his long-running op-ed column in The New York Times *a couple of years ago, he continues to write about foreign affairs periodically (and with his usual keen insight) for* The New York Review of Books. *In this article, he examines the Bush administration's newly unveiled doctrine of preemptive military action, and its implications for the future of U.S. foreign policy. . . .*

What is President Bush's ultimate objective in Iraq? Is it to make sure that Saddam Hussein does not have weapons of mass destruction? Or is it to remove Saddam by force and remake the politics of Iraq? And if the latter, would it be the first step toward a new American imperium?

Weeks of Bush administration rhetoric concentrated relentlessly on Iraq have left the answers to those questions in doubt and confusion. Thus on

October 1 [2002] Secretary of State Colin Powell seemed to say that the United States was following the path of United Nations inspections. He held a press briefing to explain that, as inspectors planned a return to Iraq, American policy was to give them "new instructions, strong instructions, and the strongest support possible from the Security Council. . . ." But on the same day President Bush's press secretary, Ari Fleischer, said, "The policy is regime change, and that remains the American position." Mr. Fleischer went on to suggest that an efficient means to that end would be the murder of Saddam in a coup. He said:

> The cost of a one-way ticket is substantially less than [that of an invasion]. The cost of one bullet, if the Iraqi people take it on themselves, is substantially less than that.

President Bush himself has sent sharply conflicting signals. At West Point last June he introduced the idea of preemption. The cold war strategies of deterrence and containment were no longer adequate, he said. "We must take the battle to the enemy, disrupt his plans, and confront the worst threats before they emerge." In September, when he began his drumbeat about the Iraqi threat and the need for "regime change," he was generally thought to be planning a preemptive military attack.

Then, on September 12, Mr. Bush spoke in a very different way to the U.N. General Assembly. His emphasis was on the need for action by the Security Council to enforce its own past resolutions. "We want the United Nations to be effective, and respectful, and successful," he said. "We want the resolutions of the world's most important multilateral body to be enforced." The speech disarmed many of his critics, at home and overseas. They saw it as a step away from war as a first choice, a recognition of the inspection process as the right way to deal with the weapons threat in Iraq.

But on September 20 the administration published its lengthy paper, "The National Security Strategy of the United States." Much of it was a thoughtful analysis of changed realities in the world. It said, for example, that "America is now threatened less by conquering states than we are by failing ones." But what attracted attention was an explicit, formal statement of the preemption doctrine. "The greater the threat," the document said,

> the greater is the risk of inaction—and the more compelling the case for taking anticipatory action to defend ourselves, even if uncertainty

remains as to the time and place of the enemy's attack. To forestall or prevent such hostile acts by our adversaries, the United States will, if necessary, act preemptively.

Senator Edward Kennedy pointed out that the national security document elided the historic distinction between preemption and preventive war. The former is a military attack on an enemy who is known to be about to strike; the classic example was Israel's attack on Egypt as the Egyptians were marshaling their forces to strike in 1967. The latter is a war brought when there is no certainty of the time or even the likelihood of an enemy strike. Senator Kennedy noted that in the Cuban Missile Crisis in 1962 President Kennedy had been urged to strike without warning at the missiles the Soviet Union had placed in Cuba in what would have been a preventive war; he declined, instead going openly to the U.N. Security Council and imposing a blockade on Cuba until the missiles were removed.

The national security document also declared an intention to maintain the United States' overwhelming edge in military power. "Our forces will be strong enough," it said, "to dissuade potential adversaries from pursuing a military buildup in hopes of surpassing or equaling the power of the US."

On October 7, speaking in Cincinnati, the President sought to reassure Americans that war on Iraq was not his first resort. The resolution he had put before Congress, he said, "does not mean that military action is imminent or unavoidable." But he painted the menace of Saddam in dark terms, and he left no doubt that he would attack if Saddam did not meet a long list of demands.

If President Bush's purpose was really just to see to it that Saddam Hussein has no chemical, biological, or nuclear weapons, he greatly complicated his problem by his aggressive rhetoric. If from the beginning he had adopted the tone of his General Assembly speech, if he had concentrated on getting a genuinely enforceable inspection system, if he had reached out to the hesitant permanent members of the Security Council—China, Russia, France—I believe they would more readily have supported his effort and the necessary council resolution. They knew that Saddam Hussein was a monster in whose hands weapons of mass destruction would be extremely dangerous. But they needed to be convinced that George W. Bush would make a good-faith effort to avoid war.

The countries whose support the President needed could hardly have been reassured by the arrogant tone of so much that he and his associates said, their insistence on America's right and duty to act alone. Nor could they have been impressed by the gangster talk of Ari Fleischer about having an enemy rubbed out. If Mr. Bush was serious about working through the United Nations, his tactics were extraordinarily inept.

But I find it increasingly hard to believe that Mr. Bush's objective is limited to seeing that Saddam Hussein has no weapons of mass destruction. The history and the theology of the men whose advice now dominates Mr. Bush's thinking point to much larger purposes. I think this president wants to overthrow the rules that have governed international life for the last fifty years.

Ten years ago Dick Cheney, then the secretary of defense, and Paul Wolfowitz, his undersecretary for policy, began assembling the doctrine of a world ruled from Washington. They are still at it now. But instead of the first President Bush, who was steeped in the post–World War II philosophy of alliances and multilateralism, they are advising a President Bush with no experience in that postwar world and, by all signs, with an instinct for the unilateral.

One fundamental that would be overthrown is the commitment that the United States and all other members have made in the United Nations Charter: to eschew attacks across international frontiers except in response to armed aggression. The idea of preemptive strikes in violation of that provision has worried even some conservatives who would like to move against Saddam Hussein but are concerned about the precedent an attack would set for others—India, say.

But the danger of the Bush doctrine is really broader than that. The reach of the doctrine, and its dangers, were well described in an article in *Foreign Affairs* by Professor G. John Ikenberry of Georgetown University. The grand strategy, he wrote, "is a general depreciation of international rules, treaties, and security partnerships."* Yet it was those very relationships that have so benefited this country since World War II. "The secret of the United States' long brilliant run as the world's leading state," Professor Ikenberry wrote,

> was its ability and willingness to exercise power within alliance and multinational frameworks, which made its power and agenda more acceptable to allies and other key states around the world.

*See *Foreign Affairs*, September–October 2002.

He warned that

unchecked U.S. power, shorn of legitimacy and disentangled from the postwar norms and institutions of the international order, will usher in a more hostile international system, making it far harder to achieve American interests.

What we may be seeing in the Iraq strategy, then, is the rejection of the old American view that, as Professor Ikenberry put it,

a rule-based international order, especially one in which the United States uses its political weight to derive congenial rules, will most fully protect American interests, conserve its power, and extend its influence.

The key phrase in that formulation is "rule-based." For President Bush has shown, across the board, an unwillingness for his country or himself to be bound by the rules.

A dramatic example of this resistance to rules is the administration's obsessive effort to destroy the new International Criminal Court, created under the leadership of our closest European allies to prosecute those suspected of genocide and crimes against humanity. Another is the avoidance of the Geneva Conventions governing the treatment of prisoners of war; rather than comply with the rules that have bound us and the world for decades, the administration unilaterally described the Afghanistan captives it is holding at Guantánamo Bay, Cuba, as "unlawful combatants." The conventions say that questions about the status of prisoners should be referred to a "competent tribunal." The administration has declined to do that. It might have argued that al-Qaeda fighters were so obviously unlawful that international law would not requite the useless gesture of reference to a tribunal. But the Bush administration did not even bother to make the argument; it was not interested in the law. (In any event, it is hard to see how the Geneva process could be avoided in the case of Taliban prisoners; they were soldiers in the army of a government that controlled nearly all of Afghanistan.)

That same rejection of the rules—of the law—can be found at home. One example is the President's order of November 2001 that noncitizens charged with terrorism or with "harboring" terrorists be tried by military tribunals. That order appeared to violate the holding of the Supreme Court in the great post–Civil War case of *Ex parte Milligan* that there can be no criminal trials by military tribunal in this country while the civil courts remain open. An even more astonishing assertion of presidential power is President Bush's claim of a right to hold any American citizen whom he designates as an "enemy combatant" in military prison indefinitely, without trial and without the right to speak with a lawyer. Two men are now being held in military prisons, in Virginia and South Carolina, under that theory, forbidden to speak to a lawyer. Government lawyers argue that no court can examine the lawfulness of their detention.

Respect for the rule of law has been an essential element from the beginning in the survival and success of this vast, disputatious country—and a reason for other people's admiration of American society. But George W. Bush, whatever else his qualities, seems to have no feeling for the law. That was evident when he was governor of Texas, in the cruel casualness of his handling of death penalty cases.

It might be regarded as surprising that a president who came to office with such dubious legitimacy would undertake so radical a transformation of America's world policy. But Mr. Bush acquired legitimacy with the terrorist attack of September 11, 2001. He was president, and he understood that the country looked to him for leadership in the response to terror.

He and his aides have tried hard to make Iraq part of "the war on terrorism," but their propositions have been unconvincing. There is, so far, no clear evidence of collaboration between Saddam Hussein and al-Qaeda. Secretary of Defense Donald Rumsfeld, Deputy Secretary Wolfowitz, and Condoleezza Rice, the president's national security adviser, have all said that connections have been found between al-Qaeda and Iraq. But their statements have been so vague that they have had little credibility. Moreover, the two parties are the opposite of natural collaborators. Al-Qaeda detests secular regimes in Muslim countries, of which Saddam's is a prime example.

A war on Saddam Hussein might in fact distract our attention from the still urgent need for concern about terrorism. Al-Qaeda is in all likelihood a far greater threat to Americans than Saddam Hussein. Our defenses against that kind of terrorism, carried out by a handful of suicidal fanatics from inside this country, remain primitive.

One puzzle about the cry for war in Iraq is its timing. Why now? Why with such urgency? The President himself asked rhetorically, in his October 7 speech, "Why be concerned now?" His main answer was that the danger of terror weapons in Saddam's hands was clear, and "the longer we wait, the stronger and bolder Saddam Hussein will become."

President Bush had little or nothing to say about Iraq in the first year and more of his administration. (But a lengthy article in *USA Today* this September said that President Bush had secretly begun moving to a policy of ousting Saddam by force soon after September 11, 2001. Rumsfeld and Wolfowitz urged that course, the article reported, at a Camp David meeting with the President on September 15; and Bernard Lewis, the Middle East historian, was invited to meetings with Vice President Cheney and other officials, where he said it was time to act for the sake of the oppressed people of Iraq.) Suddenly, as of about September 1, [2002,] virtually his entire agenda became Iraq. Andrew H. Card Jr., the White House chief of staff, explained to the *Times* last month why the rhetorical campaign on Iraq started suddenly in September. His comment left many thinking that the timing had to do with politics. "From a marketing point of view," he said, "you don't introduce new products in August."

From the marketing point of view, the key fact is that there is a mid-term election on November 5, with control of both houses of Congress at stake: a matter of the greatest importance to President Bush. Republicans are running as supporters of a war president, and it is much more effective for them to do that than to rest on Mr. Bush's record. It is, in truth, the most dismal record of any president in memory. That is especially so on the issue that usually counts most with the voters, the economy. Millions of Americans have lost a good part of their savings in the falling stock market. The federal budget, which showed a fat surplus when Mr. Bush took over, is now deeply in the red—and heading for more deficits. Iraq also takes attention away from the shenanigans of corporate executives and questions about connections between the wrongdoers and President Bush, Vice President Cheney, and others.

Protection of the environment, another meaningful subject for many, has taken a terrible beating at the hands of the Bush administration. The integrity of our surroundings has repeatedly been sacrificed to the financial interests of a few. My favorite example is the cancellation of the Clinton administration's rules limiting the use of snowmobiles in national parks, thus inflicting their noise and fumes on the many for the sake of a handful of snowmobile manufacturers. But there have been more profound retreats, such as the stripping of protection from the national forests.

Also suggestive of politics has been the violent reaction to criticism of President Bush on Iraq. When former vice-president Al Gore made a critical speech on September 23, Michael Kelly, a columnist whose obsession used to be hatred of Bill Clinton, called the speech "dishonest, cheap, low . . . hollow . . . wretched . . . vile, contemptible" and full of "embarrassingly obvious lies." When Brent Scowcroft, who was national security adviser to the first President Bush, questioned the case for war on Iraq, he was excoriated by *The Weekly Standard* and *The Wall Street Journal*.

The chief ideological designer of the case for war on Iraq, Deputy Defense Secretary Wolfowitz, has a different motive. An illuminating piece on Wolfowitz, "The Sunshine Warrior" by Bill Keller, appeared in *The New York Times Magazine* on September 22 [2002]. It gave a sympathetic view of his belief that the assertion of American power can turn Iraq into a democracy and help transform the entire Middle East. I was moved by his optimism as I read, but I kept thinking of one thing: Vietnam. Here, as in Vietnam, the advocates are sure that American power can prevail—and sure that the result will be a happy one. But here, as in Vietnam, so many things could go wrong. Iraq is a large, modern, heavily urbanized country. If we bomb it apart, are we going to be wise enough to put it back together? Have Mr. Wolfowitz and his fellow sunshine warriors calculated the effects of an American war on feelings among Arabs and other Muslims? What would follow Saddam? The nature of a post-Saddam government in Iraq is a crucial concern for Iran, Turkey, Syria, and others; but the Bush administration has shown no sign of having an answer to that question.

Jane Perlez of *The New York Times* spoke with women students at the United Arab Emirates University, an island of modern education in the Persian Gulf world. She found that although they saw Saddam Hussein as a dictator, they felt strongly that a war on him would be a war on them. Mr. Wolfowitz should read her story. He might also look at a September 17 *Financial Times* interview with Mahathir Mohamad, the prime minister of Malaysia for the last twenty-one years and no softy. War on Iraq "will lengthen the antiterrorist campaign," he said:

> It will undermine the world economy, it will create a sense of uncertainty and fear throughout the world. If America persists in removing Saddam Hussein by military means it will only anger the Muslim world. . . . There will be more willing recruits to the terrorist ranks.

American business leaders and economists have started to express their fears about the effect of rising oil prices resulting from a war on Iraq.

Mr. Wolfowitz may mean well. But he and his colleagues are members of that most dangerous breed of men, utopians. They think they can straighten out the untidy world in which we live, and they know they are right. To others, their certainty is arrogance. They have in George W. Bush an untutored believer in the verities of American goodness and American power. The odds are that, one way or another, he will press for war on Iraq. He will see it as the beginning of a great new opportunity for the United States to impose its views on the world: the Bush doctrine.

The power of a president to take this country into war is enormous. The fear of looking unpatriotic inhibits dissent, as congressional Democrats have demonstrated. But around the country there are a great many Americans who are fearful of this war. Opinion polls consistently show opposition to a unilateral American attack on Iraq, but polls cannot show the anguish being expressed at town meetings here and there.

Anatol Lieven of the Carnegie Endowment in Washington, writing in the *London Review of Books*, said the aim of the planned war on Iraq is not just to remove Saddam Hussein but to create there a ramshackle coalition of ethnic groups and warlords utterly subservient to the United States. The larger goal, he said, was "unilateral world domination through absolute military superiority." Then he wrote:

> The American people would never knowingly support such a programme— nor for that matter would the U.S. military. Even after September 11, this is not by historical standards a militarist country; and whatever the increasingly open imperialism of the nationalist think-tank class, neither the military nor the mass of the population wishes to see itself as imperialist.

We can only hope he is right.

The Unilateralist

James Fallows

The Atlantic Monthly | March 2002

When it comes to listing the most influential "neo-conservatives" in the Bush admin-
istration, Deputy Defense Secretary Paul Wolfowitz's name invariably appears at or
near the top. As the number two man at the Pentagon, he has been a leading hawk
on Iraq, and an active proponent of a muscular U.S. foreign policy aimed at encour-
aging the spread of democracy in the Middle East and elsewhere.

Wolfowitz's growing prominence is reflected in the amount of ink he's gotten in
the past year—including a lengthy piece in The New York Times Magazine *("The Sun-*
shine Warrior," by Bill Keller) and a recent Vanity Fair *profile, in which he ignited a*
media firestorm by admitting that the weapons of mass destruction issue was just
one of several reasons for waging war on Iraq. In this article, James Fallows catches
up with Wolfowitz early in 2002—a point in time when the Iraq invasion was still
just a gleam in the Bush Administration's eye. . . .

Soldiers wear ribbons on their uniforms to signal where they have been and
what they have done. People in Washington use photographs of themselves
with famous officials. The typical lawyer's or lobbyist's office is decorated with
trophy photos, on what has come to be known as the "I love me" wall. People
who have worked in White House jobs often display pictures of themselves
with the President in parts of their homes that guests will see.

The waiting room of Paul Wolfowitz's office at the Pentagon has half a
dozen pictures on the wall—Wolfowitz with the elder George Bush in 1991,
during the Gulf War; Wolfowitz with Ronald Reagan in the 1980s. The newest
and most interesting photo shows a grinning Wolfowitz with Donald Rumsfeld on one side and Dick Cheney on the other. Across the bottom is scrawled
"Paul—Who is the best Secretary of Defense you ever worked for? Dick." The
joke is that both the men flanking him are Defense Secretaries he has worked
for. Wolfowitz is now the deputy secretary of defense, No. 2 in the Pentagon
under Rumsfeld. During the Gulf War, when Cheney held Rumsfeld's current
job, Wolfowitz was an undersecretary there.

The Washington message the photo conveys is that Wolfowitz is well connected and that his relationship with Cheney is close enough for a bantering

inscription rather than "Thanks for your service to our nation!" But the photo seems worth noting for a less obvious reason: these three people really are a team, whose shared instincts and beliefs are of critical importance in the management of the war on terrorism.

Early in his time as President, Bill Clinton used to refer to "the conversation"—the ongoing discussions he'd had since the late 1960s with his wife and dozens of policy-minded friends about education, welfare, the Democratic Party's future, and so on. Any governor becoming President is ill prepared in certain ways, but on the topics they had long discussed the Clinton team did, as Clinton liked to point out, have a head start.

It is hard to imagine Wolfowitz, Rumsfeld, or Cheney using a term as self-conscious as "the conversation," but for thirty years they and several associates have been developing and applying the world view that mainly guides this war. Those associates include Richard Perle and Kenneth Adelman, who served in the Reagan Administration, and James Woolsey, a Democrat who was Bill Clinton's first CIA director. All three, from outside the Administration, have strongly made a case for carrying the anti-terrorist war to Iraq. The men inside the Administration are so familiar with one another's views, instincts, limitations, and strengths that they have been able to swing into wartime action with remarkably few blunders or amateurish moments.

Within the Administration there are still genuine disagreements about the next step, and the ultimate steps, in the war against terrorism. To those on the Rumsfeld team, the advantages of moving against Saddam Hussein in Iraq seem obvious—whether or not he can be directly linked to the September 11 attacks. The risk of letting his regime continue to develop chemical, biological, or nuclear weapons of mass destruction is too great. Political approval for a pre-emptive strike against terrorism can only diminish as time goes on—unless, of course, the United States suffers another devastating attack. Iraq's vaunted Republican Guard proved to be much less fearsome than advertised during the Gulf War; in the decade since then it has only grown weaker and American forces more powerful. Wouldn't it be shameful, one of Rumsfeld's supporters put it to me, if we suffered an attack and *knew* that we could have done something about it?

The counterargument, advanced mainly by Colin Powell and others in the State Department, is for a more methodical and cautious approach. Members of this camp are alarmed about the practical realities of a war in Iraq, where there is no counterpart to the Northern Alliance to do the actual fighting; they see more value in building an international alliance against

Saddam Hussein. But the operating skill of the Rumsfeld team has become a policy argument in itself, and if the United States attacks Saddam Hussein, it will be largely because the Pentagon team has bolstered U.S. credibility through its competence.

At fifty-eight, Wolfowitz is much older than Cheney or Rumsfeld was when running the Pentagon. (Cheney, who was Gerald Ford's chief of staff in his early thirties, became Secretary of Defense in the first Bush Administration at age forty-eight; Rumsfeld will turn seventy this year, but at forty-three he was the youngest-ever Defense Secretary, in the Ford Administration.) Yet Wolfowitz still has the air of a promising brainy student being groomed for great things. A character in Saul Bellow's novel *Ravelstein* (2000) is based on him; the novel is a roman à clef portrait of Allan Bloom, a mentor to Wolfowitz during his graduate studies at the University of Chicago. "It's only a matter of time before Phil Gorman has cabinet rank, and a damn good thing for the country," the Bloom character says, referring to the Wolfowitz character. "He has a powerful mind and a real grasp of great politics, this kid."

Wolfowitz, like Prince Charles, remains "this kid" partly because his elders are still filling the jobs ahead of him, but principally because of his bearing. He is serious-minded but not pompous or puffed up. Like Donald Rumsfeld, he looks comparatively young for his age; the film-actor version would be James Mason.

Cheney and Rumsfeld are two of the notable all-rounders in modern appointive politics, and Wolfowitz, too, has been well prepared for high office. He has held three jobs in the Pentagon and three in the State Department, and he worked in the Arms Control and Disarmament Agency (now part of the State Department) during the U.S.-Soviet arms-limitation talks. During the Carter Administration, when most of the government viewed the Shah of Iran as an island of stability in the turbulent Middle East, Wolfowitz led a Pentagon team that issued a prescient warning of upheaval in Iran. When Reagan arrived, Wolfowitz directed the East Asia office in the State Department, where he played a large role in swinging American support away from Ferdinand Marcos's regime in the Philippines. Then he was ambassador to Indonesia—a Jewish ambassador who was highly popular in the country with the world's largest (and perhaps least fanatic) Muslim population. I visited him in Jakarta near the end of his term. He was a genuine celebrity there, in part because his wife, Clare, who had been a high school exchange student in Indonesia, is an academic expert on Javanese language and culture. (The two are now divorced.) After that he was a crucial part of the original Gulf War team in the Pentagon.

In January, I talked with Wolfowitz under the watchful eye of Torie Clarke, the director of the Pentagon's press office, who kept glancing at her watch and finally said, "This is very interesting, but . . ." Given Wolfowitz's Clintonlike relish for the twists of an issue, this meant he was about an answer and a half into our conversation by the time our appointment was over. But, like Clinton, he had been chastised by friends for letting meetings turn into bull sessions and thus destroy his schedule, so he had learned to obey his timekeepers.

I wanted to ask about the evolution of the view that now guided the war. That view, as I understood it, was defined by pessimism, optimism, and impatience with procedure.

The pessimism lies in an insistence that the world is full of enemies who will hurt us if they can. This view is widespread in America since September 11. It was not before then—and the proof is the appetite for "Why do they hate us?" stories. Wolfowitz, I had been told by members of his camp, was less surprised by the attack than the public, because his formative experience was confronting the Soviet Union. Kenneth Adelman, who directed the Arms Control and Disarmament Agency in the Reagan years, told me, "I used to remind myself during the arms talks that if it was up to Karpov [his Soviet counterpart], I'd be in a gulag. When all is said and done, there really are people on the opposite side from us." Wolfowitz extended this view in several essays, including one in *The National Interest* in 1997 in which he compared the prosperity, optimism, and predictions of "global civilization" of the late 1990s to the very similar worldwide climate a century before, and warned that the risk of tragedy was just as great now.

The optimism lies in the conviction that if the United States confronts "evil" enemies, it can win. The proof is, of course, the Soviet Union's fall. Ronald Reagan came to office calling not for détente but for outright victory over the "evil empire." Ten years later the empire was gone. Nearly all the members of today's defense leadership were part of Reagan's team. The memory of that success lies behind George W. Bush's promises that terrorists will be not just contained, like drug traffickers, but beaten, like Nazis and Soviets.

As for impatience with procedure, around the world the Bush foreign-policy team is criticized as "unilateralist"—a group that scoffs at alliances and international organizations and doesn't take treaties seriously. To people who share Wolfowitz and Rumsfeld's views, these criticisms reflect a confusion of ends and means. If arms-control talks simply continue the arms race, these people think, then it's time to step away from the table. As long as the United Nations or NATO goes in the general direction the United States thinks wise, we should act through those alliances. But humoring allies counts for little in itself, and negotiating for its own sake has no appeal. The NATO countries complained when Ronald Reagan put intermediate-range missiles in Europe, and they complained when Bill Clinton took them out. The members of the current defense team "have made their careers by not being taken in by atmospherics or diplomatic niceties, not being deceived by lulls in the action," says Jay Winik, the author of *April 1865* (2001), whose previous book, *On the Brink* (1996), was about the conservative national-security establishment. "The whole nature of this terrorist war is that something terrible happens, and then it stops, and then something terrible happens again. In a very strong sense they are temperamentally right for this challenge."

I asked Wolfowitz about the experiences that had been most important in shaping his own strategic view. He sat and looked away for a long time. Then he talked about his early work at the Arms Control and Disarmament Agency.

"It's funny, if there's one thing that really separates my generation from the next generation, it's the Cuban missile crisis," he said. "People who lived through that can see the world in a certain way that people who didn't live through it can't, I guess. But one of the things that impressed me in the three years I worked on [arms control] was that nuclear wars are most likely to arise out of conventional wars. Preventing conventional war is the key, I came to think—even more important than simply looking at nuclear weapons in a vacuum. That actually led me to grab on very eagerly when I had the chance a few years later to come here [the Pentagon] for the first time."

Some politicians, such as George W. Bush and Ted Kennedy, are hard to quote directly because they don't finish their sentences. Wolfowitz is hard to quote directly because so many of his sentences have numerous internal clauses, like mathematical formulas with brackets. He went on to explain how his immersion in conventional power politics led him to realize that to conduct foreign policy, one must first know who one's allies are.

"You *do* have to treat your friends different from your enemies," he said. "I think that's a basic principle of international relations—and a lot of the rest of life, except in life you don't usually have enemies quite as nasty as you do in foreign policy."

During his time as an Asia hand Wolfowitz was known for applying pressure to "friends"—Ferdinand Marcos, the Korean generals—to encourage democratic reforms. What about applying that kind of pressure to the "friendly" dictators and tribesmen who are supporting us now? He said, "Well, first of all let's talk about the nondemocratic *enemies*. The fact is that all the regimes that sponsor terrorism terrorize their own people. For reasons that aren't obvious, we've tended—not just the United States but the world in general—to give a pass to, for example, the Syrian dictatorship that we never gave the South Korean dictatorship. I'm not saying that the South Koreans should have had it—but you sort of wonder at the ready acceptance of this kind of pass."

He said he really couldn't explain the double standard. But one reality was that through the 1980s "success built on success" in Asia as countries overthrew dictatorships, whereas in the Middle East "you might say failure has built on failure," with no examples of democratic reform like the ones in the Philippines, Korea, and Taiwan. "Also, if you stop and think about the penalties for being known to favor any kind of positive political change in, say, Iraq, it's not surprising that there are a million Iraqis who favor positive political change—and they're all outside of Iraq. Inside, you don't survive."

He thought that this pass system was about to change. "There has been . . . not tolerance but lack of intolerance toward support for terrorism until now," he said. "We had these terrorism lists, and countries were put on them for supporting terrorism. It was a bad thing to do, but it wasn't considered *intolerable*. I think that after September 11 it's intolerable. It seems to me that the political condition of the Muslim world and the Arab world was considered tolerable before. Not very nice, but you live with it. And I think that's not healthy—not healthy for us and certainly not healthy for them. Terrorists [and dictators] don't operate in a vacuum. They look at what happens to other terrorists. And hopefully now they are looking at what's happened to the people in Afghanistan. We're clearly getting very different responses from the Yemenis, for example, than we did a couple of months ago."

Part of changing the attitude toward terrorism, he said, is making sure that military action gets results. "It is important that you don't just think of military force as a way of 'signaling' things," he said. "I get very, very uncomfortable the minute we say we're going to 'send a message' with this or that use of military power. I find this funny coming sometimes from people whose formative experience was opposing the Vietnam War, which I would have thought would give them greater caution about it. You send a military message by having a military *effect*. We could have bombed Afghanistan for months and months and not sent any 'message' if we hadn't found a way, largely through getting Special Forces on the ground to coordinate air strikes, to make the air power devastating in its military effect."

The obvious question was how Wolfowitz viewed the Vietnam War at the time. But Torie Clarke and her associate Susan Wallace got me out before I could ask him, and he had no time for a follow-up e-mail exchange. The prevailing view of Vietnam among his colleagues is that it couldn't be fought effectively, because it was an attempt to fine-tune military efforts rather than go out and win. Therefore it was not worth fighting.

As I was leaving, I did manage to ask whether Wolfowitz, who a year before taking office had written in *Commentary* that a new round of "great-power conflict" would be the main threat to future peace, thought this was still true. He said he did.

A century ago, he said, the international problem was the appearance of new great powers—mainly Germany and Japan—whose appetites and grievances the existing world order could not accommodate. Now another crop of new powers was appearing.

"China is the most obvious one," he said. "In East Asia in general you have this stunning growth in economic power, which means ultimately, potentially, military power. A unified Korea is itself the size of a major European power. Only in Asia does Vietnam look like a small country—its army is tough and big. And then you've got the Indians. . . . It's a question of how to achieve balance of power in East Asia, among these growing powers, without going through the experience Europe went through to get there, because that's a little too costly."

Russia, the familiar "great power," would not be part of the new problem— "not at all, no," he said. "During the Cold War we were trying, with the opening to China, to help a weak China deal with a threat from a very powerful Soviet Union. I think in the future we may be trying to figure out how to help a weak Russia deal with an increasingly powerful China. I think we really are in a new era in U.S.-Russian relations. It will go through bumps and starts, and it's not a new era in the sense that suddenly they love us and we love them. But our interests coincide in so many ways that they didn't before." With that he was back to the current war.

White Lie

Lawrence Kaplan

The New Republic | April 10, 2003

One of the favorite Washington parlor games following the fall of Baghdad was, "Who's Next?" In particular, post-war rumblings from the Bush administration over Syria's supportive stance toward Iraq led some pundits to opine that Damascus was now number one on the Pentagon's hit list. Lawrence Kaplan, senior editor of The New Republic, *dispels this rumor, explaining that it's actually the paradoxical result of Syrian leader Bashar Al Assad's own wishful thinking. . . .*

Who's next? As Saddam Hussein's regime crumbled this week, that was the question being asked by commentators across the globe. And, when Secretary of Defense Donald Rumsfeld took to his podium to declare that the United States would hold Syria "accountable" for its weapons shipments to Iraq—a charge backed up by Secretary of State Colin Powell—it seemed the Bush team had finally provided the answer. The ubiquitous General Wesley Clark reported that "many 'policy types' in Washington are now speaking openly of Syria as the next target," while *New York Times* columnist Paul Krugman revealed that, having bested Iraqi forces, "a strong faction within the administration wants to go on to Syria."

Actually, there is no such faction. When President Bush insisted in the aftermath of September 11, 2001, that "either you are with us, or you are with the terrorists," he was said to have cast the international scene in "black-and-white" terms. This was meant as a criticism, a plea for nuance that took issue with the president's decision to place countries like Iran in the black column when they really belonged in the gray one. The more intriguing question, though, has always concerned countries that didn't merit inclusion in the axis of evil, such as Saudi Arabia and Syria, nations that simultaneously clamp down on and sponsor terrorism and to which neither toppling by force nor coddling without condition seem adequate responses. Nevertheless, the Bush team placed the Saudis and the Syrians in the white column and lavished them with praise for a year and a half.

If there was ever a regime that doesn't belong in the white column, it is Syria under Bashar Al Assad. But that does not necessarily mean it belongs in the black column either. As far as U.S. policy goes, there are two Syrias: a good one and a bad one. First, the good Syria. In the immediate aftermath of September 11, Assad provided the United States with what one administration official describes as a "treasure trove" of intelligence on Al Qaeda activities among Syrian nationals—principal among these Mohammed Haydar Zammar, an Al Qaeda commander living in Germany, and Mamoun Darkazanli, one of the organization's alleged financiers. Assad even sent President Bush a letter proposing that the two countries "establish sound bases of worldwide cooperation . . . to uproot terrorism in all its forms." Before long, Syrian intelligence operatives were meeting with the CIA and passing along warnings replete with details about likely terrorist targets. Even the administration's Syria hawks concede that one such warning, which alerted American policymakers to a plot against American forces in the Gulf, "saved American lives." Against all expectations, Damascus even voted for U.N. Security Council Resolution 1441, the U.S.-backed measure that sent weapons inspectors back into Iraq.

A grateful Bush team has responded with a steady diet of diplomatic carrots and blandishments. It excluded Syria from the axis of evil and barely uttered a peep when Syria was elected to the U.N. Security Council. On the contrary, Powell telephoned Assad to praise his cooperation in the war on terrorism; congressional delegations (and, last April, Powell himself) appeared at the Syrian dictator's palace gate; Vice President Dick Cheney called to chat; the administration kept mum about Syria's ongoing military occupation of Lebanon; and it even authorized the opening of a back channel to Damascus, conducted by members of the Bush père team under the auspices of Houston's aptly named James A. Baker III Institute for Public Policy. Not surprisingly, then, when Congress threatened to impose sanctions on Syria last year, the Bush team weighed in against the bill, reasoning, as Powell put it in a letter to the Senate Foreign Relations Committee, that "[n]ew sanctions on Syria would place at risk our ability to . . . change Syrian behavior." Employing similar logic, Bush's closest ally, Britain's Tony Blair, feted Assad at Downing Street and even ushered him in to meet the Queen.

It thus came as something of a surprise to many when, in the midst of the war with Iraq, Syria began supplying Saddam with anti-tank weapons, nightvision goggles, and suicide bombers. It shouldn't have. Because, even as the good Syria has been playing nice, the bad Syria has, if anything, gotten worse since the September 11 attacks. Balancing its need to stay out of America's bombsights with its domestic and regional aims, Damascus continues to play host to an alphabet soup of terrorist groups, including leaders from Hamas and Hezbollah, which Deputy Secretary of State Richard Armitage has branded the "A Team of terrorists." After Hezbollah intensified its cross-border attacks against Israel last spring, Bush demanded that Syria "choose the right side in the war on terror by closing terrorist camps and expelling terrorist organizations." Assad's reply came a week later, with his declaration that "Syria supports the Lebanese national resistance, including Hezbollah." As if to prove the point, the Syrian dictator has brushed aside even the restraints imposed by his father, Hafez Al Assad, who merely provided a conduit for Iranian arms destined for Lebanese terror camps, and has begun directly supplying Hezbollah with heavy weapons and integrating its units into the Syrian army.

If Syria's support for America's foes was confined to Hezbollah, the administration might still be touting Assad as a partner in the war on terrorism. Alas, the Syrian leader has a soft spot for Saddam, too. Unlike his father, whose enmity toward his Iraqi counterpart dated back decades and culminated in his decision to join the U.S.-led coalition against Iraq in 1991, the younger Assad has developed a full-blown alliance with the Iraqi leader in the three years since he took power. Strapped for cash, keen to prove his credentials to a rabidly anti-American public, and eager to emerge from his father's shadow, Assad reopened the Iraqi-Syrian pipeline in late 2000 and before long was funneling $1 billion worth of oil out of Iraq each year (in violation of U.N. sanctions); lifting visa, trade, and other border restrictions with Iraq; and even shopping for Saddam on the international arms market. Nor did Powell's 2001 plea to shut down Syria's illicit oil trade with Iraq or successive U.S. démarches make the slightest impression on Assad. Instead, the Syrian dictator pledged two weeks ago to "stand beside Baghdad" in its current war with the United States and, for good measure, had his foreign minister, Farouk Al Sharaa, assure the Syrian parliament that "Syria's interest is to see the invaders defeated in Iraq."

Even during the war, Assad's regime has been shipping military equipment across the Iraqi border, which prompted Rumsfeld's rebuke on March 28 [2003]. Nor did that rebuke come merely from Rumsfeld and his civilian advisers: It was cleared with the White House and reflected, if anything, frustration within the ranks of the U.S. military. That frustration, according to administration officials, stemmed from Syrian shipments of Russian-made Kornet anti-tank weapons and platoons of suicide bombers carrying Syrian passports. The traffic has continued despite repeated American protests and even a visit to Damascus by Assistant Secretary of State William Burns. The traffic has flowed in the other direction, too: As their regime collapsed around them this week, many of Saddam's lieutenants piled into caravans and scrambled to safety in Damascus.

So will Syria finally, as Rumsfeld insists, be held "accountable"? The Syrian regime seems to hope so. Over the past few weeks, a parade of its officials has fanned out on the Arab world's airwaves to predict, as Assad did two weeks ago, that Damascus will be Washington's "next target." He's not likely to get his way. "Pretending he's next, particularly after Saddam is gone, makes [Assad] look like a leader," says one Pentagon official. "But he's not even on the list."

Nor has the dictator's wartime conduct budged the administration's Syriaphiles from their attachment to Assad. At the State Department, where Burns and his deputy, David Satterfield, have been touting Assad as an Arab Gorbachev ever since September 11, opposition to sanctioning his regime still runs deep. As in Iraq, State Department officials have refused to meet with prominent Lebanese and Syrian opposition leaders and, in recent weeks, even prevented their counterparts at the Pentagon from doing so. The CIA's George Tenet along with Bush I veterans, such as former Secretary of State James Baker and former Ambassador to Syria Edward Djerejian, have also continued pushing the Bush team in the direction of diplomatic accommodation. As summarized by a State Department official who hears it daily, their argument is that, however imperfect he may be, Assad has provided invaluable assistance in the war against Al Qaeda, and the White House will need to call on him if it intends to revive the peace process between the Israelis and Palestinians. President Bush has also rung up a debt to Prime Minister Blair for his wartime support, and the British have been pushing the Bush team to make amends with Syria. Hence, when asked last week whether Rumsfeld's comments portend a less forgiving policy toward Damascus, British Foreign Secretary Jack Straw snapped, "We would have nothing whatever to do with an approach like that."

But the debate over who comes after Saddam again ignores the gray. America's diplomatic toolbox, after all, contains numerous options short of war, and it is exactly these options that are under consideration by officials less enamored of Assad. They run the diplomatic gamut, from pressing Damascus more forcefully—through diplomatic pressure and public denunciations—to oust the terror groups that call Syria home to elevating Syria's occupation of Lebanon in the hierarchy of U.S. policy concerns. That last option holds particular appeal for officials in the White House and at the Pentagon, who recall with disgust the quid pro quo that the elder Bush hammered out with the elder Assad in 1990. Under the terms of that agreement, the United States—in return for Syria's support for the Gulf war—agreed to turn a blind eye to its occupation of Lebanon. Washington does so to this day, and the mere suggestion of doing otherwise makes officials at Foggy Bottom apoplectic. Indeed, if policymakers at the Defense Department continue to flirt with speaking out about the occupation of Lebanon, the issue could easily become yet another flashpoint between the two agencies.

Unless, of course, the White House settles the matter first. Informed of Rumsfeld's denunciation of Syria, President Bush reportedly gave a monosyllabic response: "Good." But it would be even better if Bush made the denunciation himself. And better still if he did so for reasons that went beyond pique over Syria's wartime conduct. Here, after all, is a regime that, like Saddam's, tortures its own citizens, invades its neighbors, and supports terrorism abroad. True, it doesn't possess as many deadly weapons as its neighbor to the east. But, then, no one is advocating war with Syria. What Pentagon and White House officials are advocating is merely skepticism regarding the fantasy that the war on terrorism has transformed a longtime foe into a newfound friend. Candor on that point hardly requires toppling the regime in Damascus. It just means a few less love letters to Bashar Al Assad.

A Post-Saddam Scenario

Robert Kaplan

The Atlantic Monthly | November 2002

In this article, written several months before the invasion of Iraq, Robert Kaplan tries to envision how an American victory over Saddam Hussein will shape our future dealings in the region. One of his predictions—that the U.S. will take advantage of the opportunity to remove the American troops now stationed in Saudi Arabia—has already come to pass. Kaplan also suggests that a triumph in Iraq will give the U.S. more leverage in the Middle East peace process, and that Iraq will become the site of permanent American military bases. The accuracy of these calls is less clear. The Bush team is, in fact, moving to restart the Israeli-Palestinian peace talks, but the new initiative has quickly become mired in the same old cycle of violence. As to the second point, plans for the establishment of four major U.S. bases in Iraq have been leaked to the press, but this was promptly disavowed by the Pentagon. Kaplan's final prediction—that the commitment involved in rebuilding Iraq will be comparable to the post-World War II occupations of Germany and Japan—appears to be right on track, however. . . .

The constellation of overseas bases with which the United States sustained its strategic posture throughout the Cold War was a matter not of design but of where Allied troops just happened to be when World War II and its after-shocks—the Greek Civil War and the Korean War—finally ended. The United States found itself with basing rights in western Germany, Japan, Korea, the eastern Mediterranean, and elsewhere. In particular, our former archenemy, Germany, precisely because America had played a large role in dismantling its Nazi regime, became the chief basing platform for U.S. troops in Eurasia—to such a degree that two generations of American soldiers became intimately familiar with Germany, learning its language and in many cases marrying its nationals. If the U.S. Army has any localitis, it is for Germany.

A vaguely similar scenario could follow an invasion of Iraq, which is the most logical place to relocate Middle Eastern U.S. bases in the twenty-first century. This conclusion stems not from any imperialist triumphalism but from its opposite: the realization that not only do our current bases in Saudi Arabia have a bleak future, but the Middle East in general is on the brink of an epochal passage that will weaken U.S. influence there in many places. Indeed, the relocation of our bases to Iraq would constitute an acceptance of dynamic change rather than a perpetuation of the status quo.

Two features of the current reality are particularly untenable: the presence of "unclean" infidel troops in the very Saudi kingdom charged with protecting the Muslim holy places, and the domination by Israeli overlords of three million Palestinians in the West Bank and Gaza. Neither will stand indefinitely. President Bush's refusal to force the Israelis out of the West Bank has heartened neoconservatives, but it is a temporary phenomenon—merely a matter of sequencing.

Only after we have achieved something more decisive in our war against al Qaeda, or have removed the Iraqi leadership, or both, can we pressure the Israelis into a staged withdrawal from the occupied territories. We would then be doing so from a position of newfound strength and would not appear to be giving in to the blackmail of those September 11-category criminals, the Palestinian suicide bombers. But after the Israelis have reduced the frequency of suicide bombings (through whatever tactics are necessary), and after, say, the right-wing Israeli leader Ariel Sharon has passed from the scene, Bush, if he achieves a second term and thus faces no future elections, will act.

But first the immediate issue: Iraq. The level of repression in Iraq equals that in Romania under the Communist dictator Nicolae Ceaușüescu or in the Soviet Union under Stalin; thus public opinion there is unknowable. Nevertheless, two historical cultural tendencies stand out in Iraq: urban secularism and a grim subservience. Whenever I visited Baghdad in the past, the office workers at their computer keyboards had the expressions that one imagines on slaves carrying buckets of mud up the steps of ancient ziggurats. These office workers labored incessantly; a cliché among Middle East specialists is that the Iraqis are the Germans of the Arab world (and the Egyptians are the Italians). Iraq was the most fiercely modernizing of Arab societies in the mid-twentieth century, and all coups there since the toppling of the Hashemite dynasty, in 1958, have been avowedly secular.

Given the long climate of repression, the next regime change in Iraq might even resurrect the reputation not of any religious figure but of the brilliant, pro-Western, secular Prime Minister Nuri Said, who did more than any other Iraqi to build his country in the 1940s and 1950s. As in Romania, where the downfall of Ceaușüescu resurrected the memory of Ion Antonescu, the pro-Hitler nationalist executed in 1946 by the new Communist government, the downfall of Iraq's similarly suffocating autocracy could return the memory of the last great local politician murdered in the coup that set the country on the path to Saddam Hussein's tyranny.

Iraq has a one-man thugocracy, so the removal of Saddam would threaten to disintegrate the entire ethnically riven country if we weren't to act fast and pragmatically install people who could actually govern. Therefore we should forswear any evangelical lust to implement democracy overnight in a country with no tradition of it.

Our goal in Iraq should be a transitional secular dictatorship that unites the merchant classes across sectarian lines and may in time, after the rebuilding of institutions and the economy, lead to a democratic alternative. In particular, a deliberately ambiguous relationship between the new Iraqi regime and the Kurds must be negotiated in advance of our invasion, so that the Kurds can claim real autonomy while the central government in Baghdad can also claim that the Kurdish areas are under its control. A transitional regime, not incidentally, would grant us the right to use local bases other than those in the northern, Kurdish-dominated free zone.

Keep in mind that the Middle East is a laboratory of pure power politics. For example, nothing impressed the Iranians so much as our accidental shooting down of an Iranian civilian airliner in 1988, which they believed was not an accident. Iran's subsequent cease-fire with Iraq was partly the result of that belief. Our dismantling the Iraqi regime would concentrate the minds of Iran's leaders as little else could.

Iran, with its 66 million people, is the Middle East's universal joint. Its internal politics are so complex that at times the country appears to have three competing governments: the Supreme Leader Ayatollah Sayyed Ali Khamenei and the goons in the security service; President Mohammad Khatami and his Western-tending elected government; and the former President Ali Akbar Hashemi Rafsanjani, whose *bazaari* power base has made him a mediator between the other two. Sometimes Iranian policy is the result of subtle arrangements among these three forces; other times it is the result of competition. The regimes of Iraq and Iran are fundamentally different, and so, therefore, are our challenges in the two countries.

Vastly more developed politically than Iraq, Iran has a system rather than a mere regime, however labyrinthine and inconvenient to our purposes that system may be. Nineteenth-century court diplomacy of the kind that Henry Kissinger successfully employed in China with Mao Zedong and Zhou Enlai will not work in Iran, simply because it has too many important political players. Indeed, because so many major issues are matters of internal bargaining, the Iranian system is the very opposite of dynamic. Iran's foreign policy will change only when its collective leadership believes there is no other choice.

Iranian leaders were disappointed not to see an American diplomatic initiative in 1991, after the United States bombed Baghdad—which, like the shooting down of the civilian jet, had greatly impressed them. Also likely to have been impressive to them was President George W. Bush's "axis of evil" speech (Iran's orchestrated denunciations notwithstanding). Overtures to the moderates in Iran's elected government, as the White House has already admitted, have not helped us—we will have to deal directly with the radicals, and that can be done only through a decisive military shock that affects their balance-of-power calculations.

The Iranian population is the most pro-American in the region, owing to the disastrous economic consequences of the Islamic revolution. A sea change in its leadership is a matter of when, not if. But a soft landing in Iran—rather than a violent counter-revolution, with the besieged clergy resorting to terrorism abroad—might be possible only if general amnesty is promised for those officials guilty of even the gravest human-rights violations.

Achieving an altered Iranian foreign policy would be vindication enough for dismantling the regime in Iraq. This would undermine the Iranian-supported Hizbollah, in Lebanon, on Israel's northern border; would remove a strategic missile threat to Israel; and would prod Syria toward moderation. And it would allow for the creation of an informal, non-Arab alliance of the Near Eastern periphery, to include Iran, Israel, Turkey, and Eritrea. The Turks already have a military alliance with Israel. The Eritreans, whose long war with the formerly Marxist Ethiopia has inculcated in them a spirit of monastic isolation from their immediate neighbors, have also been developing strong ties to Israel. Eritrea has a secularized population and offers a strategic location with good port facilities near the Bab el Mandeb Strait. All of this would help to provide a supportive context for a gradual Israeli withdrawal from the West Bank and Gaza. A problem with the peace plan envisioned by President Bill Clinton and Israeli Prime Minister Ehud Barak, in the summer of 2000, was that coming so soon after Israel's withdrawal from Lebanon, it was perceived by many Arabs as an act of weakness rather than of strength. That is why Israel must be seen to improve its strategic position before it can again offer such a pullback.

Of course, many Palestinians will be unsatisfied until all of Israel is conquered. But in time, when no Israeli soldiers are to be seen in their towns, the seething frustration, particularly among youths, will turn inward toward the Palestinians' own Westernized and Christianized elites, in Ramallah and similar places, and also eastward toward Amman.

In regards to Jordan and our other allies, U.S. administrations, whether Republican or Democratic, are simply going to have to adapt to sustained turbulence in the years to come. They will get no sympathy from the media, or from an academic community that subscribes to the fallacy of good outcomes, according to which there should always be a better alternative to dictators such as Hosni Mubarak, in Egypt; the Saudi royal family; and Pervez Musharraf, in Pakistan. Often there isn't. Indeed, the weakening of the brutal regime of Islam Karimov, in Uzbekistan, will not necessarily lead to a more enlightened alternative. It could just as likely ignite a civil war between Uzbeks and the ethnic Tajiks who dominate the cities of Samarkand and Bukhara. Because Uzbekistan is demographically and politically the fulcrum of post-Soviet Central Asia, those advocating "nation-building" in Afghanistan should realize that in the coming years there could be quite a few more nations to rebuild in the region. For this reason some in the Pentagon are intrigued by a basing strategy that gives us options throughout Central Asia, even if some countries collapse and we have to deal with ethnic khanates.

Our success in the war on terrorism will be defined by our ability to keep Afghanistan and other places free of anti-American terrorists. And in many parts of the world that task will be carried out more efficiently by warlords of long standing, who have made their bones in previous conflicts, than by feeble central governments aping Western models. Of course we need to eliminate anti-American radicals (Gulbuddin Hekmatyar is a case in point) who are trying to topple Hamid Karzai's pro-Western regime. But that doesn't mean we should see Karzai's government as the only sovereign force in the country. Given that the apex of Afghan national cohesion, in the mid-twentieth century, saw the Kabul-based regime of King Zahir Shah controlling little more than the major cities and towns and the ring road connecting them, the prospects for full-fledged nation-building in Afghanistan are not only dim but also peripheral to the war on terrorism. We forget that the December 1979 Soviet invasion of Afghanistan did not spark the *mujahideen* uprising. The spark came in April of 1978, in the form of the Kabul regime's attempt to extend the power of the central government to the villages. However brutal and incompetent the methods were, one must keep in mind that Afghans have less of a tradition of a modern state than do Arabs or Persians.

In any case, the changes that may be about to unfold in the Middle East will clear Afghanistan from the front pages. In the late nineteenth century the Ottoman Empire, despite its weakness, tottered on. Its collapse had to wait for the cataclysm of World War I. Likewise, the Middle East is characterized by many weak regimes that will totter on until the next cataclysm—which the U.S. invasion of Iraq might well constitute. The real question is not whether the American military can topple Saddam's regime but whether the American public has the stomach for imperial involvement of a kind we have not known since the United States occupied Germany and Japan.

National Conversation: Winning the Peace

Our New Baby

Thomas Friedman

The New York Times | May 4, 2003

On May 1, 2003, just six weeks after the first U.S. missiles were launched on Baghdad, President Bush declared an official end to major combat operations in Iraq. The weeks that followed saw an uneasy peace, however, as widespread crime continued to plague Iraq's towns and cities, and sporadic guerrilla attacks claimed the lives of several dozen more U.S. soldiers. In this piece, published shortly after Bush's announcement of victory, Pulitzer Prize-winning columnist Thomas Friedman warns that where the rebuilding of Iraq is concerned, America's conservatives and liberals had better quickly put their differences aside and start pulling together. . . .

President Bush may have declared the war in Iraq effectively over. But, judging from my own e-mail box—where conservative readers are bombing me for not applauding enough the liberation of Iraq, and liberals for selling out to George Bush—the war over the war still burns on here.

Conservatives now want to use the victory in Iraq to defeat all liberal ideas at home, and to make this war a model for America's relations with the world, while liberals—fearing all that—are still quietly rooting for Mr. Bush to fail.

Friends, whether you like or hate how and why we got into this war, the fact is America—you and I—has assumed responsibility for rebuilding Iraq. We are talking about one of the biggest nation-building projects the U.S. has ever undertaken, the mother of all long hauls. We now have a 51st state of 23 million people. We just adopted a baby called Baghdad—and this is no time for the parents to get a divorce. Because raising that baby, in the neighborhood it lives in, is going to be a mammoth task. If both Republicans and Democrats don't start looking clearly and honestly at what is evolving in Iraq, we're all going to be in trouble.

How so? The pulling down of Saddam's statue was not the fall of the Berlin Wall. Sorry. That statue was pulled down by U.S. troops and a few Iraqi youths. What Iraqis were doing in much larger numbers that day was looting—not because they are criminal in nature, but because the war had left a power vacuum and people were so poor, desperate, hungry, and full of rage toward the old regime that they just wanted to grab anything.

We have not fully liberated Iraq yet—we have created the conditions for its liberation. That is still hugely significant. But the feelings of Iraqis right now are a jumble of liberation, hope, and gratitude, mixed with anxiety, humiliation, fear of lawlessness, fear of one another, grief for sons killed in the war and suspicion of America. Conservatives, though, are so intent on proving George Bush right and liberals wrong—so the Bush team can drive its radical right agenda at home—they have rushed to impose a single liberation story line on this much more complex reality. Eastern Europe was liberated when the wall came down, because the civil society and democratic roots were already there to fill the void. In Iraq, that order and self-governing civil society will have to be created from scratch. I believe that with enough effort, it can be done, and if it is done, Iraq will be liberated. If it isn't done, Iraq will be a mess.

One senses, though, that liberals so detest Mr. Bush that they refuse to acknowledge the simple good that has come from ending Saddam's tyranny—good for Iraqis and good for America, because it will inhibit other terrorist-supporting regimes. Have no doubt about that. If Democrats' whole analysis of this war is determined by whether or not it helps Mr. Bush, then they are never going to play the role they must play—constructive critics of how we rebuild Iraq.

This is such an important moment in U.S. foreign policy. How people view American power is at stake in the outcome in Iraq, and Democrats can't be missing in action. They have to help shape this moment, and not leave it to the Bush Pentagon. But it won't happen if Democrats are sulking in a corner, just trying to point to everything that is going wrong in Iraq, and not offering their ideas for making it better.

Why should Democrats trust the Bush people to win the peace in Iraq the way they won the war? It is clear the Bush team had no coherent postwar plan in place. This administration, with its deep mistrust for diplomacy and diplomats, may be way too ideological and Pentagon-centric for nation-building. We need alternative voices. What is the Democratic view on the proper role of the U.N. or NATO in rebuilding Iraq? How much emphasis do Democrats believe the U.S. should put into the Arab-Israeli peace process to support peace in Iraq? Is a principled and muscular internationalism now the private property of the Republican Party?

If conservatives exaggerate what has already been accomplished in Iraq, they're going to misread how much more needs to be done and blow the opportunity to meaningfully liberate Iraq. If Democrats underestimate the importance of what has already been accomplished by Saddam's removal, and its huge potential, they are going to miss the opportunity to shape—and help make happen—one of the most important turning points in U.S. foreign policy and the Middle East.

Giving Peace a Real Chance
Fareed Zakaria

Newsweek | June 2, 2003

In this opinion piece, Newsweek International *editor Fareed Zakaria offers some advice to the Bush administration on how to succeed in post-war Iraq. Among his prescriptions: Ease the strain on U.S. forces by inviting our NATO allies to share in the work, don't scrimp on funding, and be prepared to stay a good long while. . . .*

Why is an administration that was so bold, ambitious, and clearheaded about waging war so hapless, diffident, and error-prone when it comes to waging peace? With Jay Garner and other top officials fired before they had unpacked their bags, we can stop pretending that things are going smoothly in postwar Iraq. Of course, some chaos was inevitable and we will have to make many adjustments as we go along. Paul Bremer is already—shrewdly—asserting power, creating order, and restoring basic services. But superficial changes will not be enough. The Bush administration went into Iraq clinging to some ideological preconceptions. It needs to junk them to succeed.

The administration thought it could learn nothing from a decade of American and international efforts at nation-building—except to see them as utterly flawed. Kosovo was repeatedly cited as an example of the United Nation's bloated approach. In fact, the record has been mixed, in the precise sense of that word, with some success and some failure. In general, things got better over time. James Dobbins, a former assistant secretary of State, who was centrally involved in all such efforts for the past decade, says, "Nation-building was disastrous in Somalia, bad in Haiti, better in Bosnia, and better still in Kosovo."

Yes, Bosnia and Kosovo are not functioning liberal democracies with market economies. But they are a whole lot better off than they were, and than most poor and ethnically riven countries. If the base line is Germany and Japan—ethnically homogenous countries that had advanced economies before World War II—they have fallen short. If the base line is Somalia, they have done pretty well.

The key lesson of nation-building over the past decade is, don't leave. In Haiti and Somalia, we left. In Bosnia and Kosovo, we're still there. The corollary: keep sufficient force to maintain order. In Somalia and Haiti, the forces were too thin and too soon withdrawn; in Bosnia and Kosovo, large troop deployments remain for the long term.

And now? Dobbins, who was the Bush administration's policy coordinator for postwar Afghanistan, says, "After making progress for a decade in our capacities in nation-building, we have regressed in Afghanistan and—so far—Iraq." In Afghanistan, we have just 5 percent as many troops, per capita, as we do in Kosovo—and it shows. In Iraq, if we were to put as many troops as there are in Bosnia, per capita, the stabilization force required would be more than 250,000, about the number cited by the Army Chief of Staff Gen. Erik K. Shinseki. In Germany and Japan, five years after World War II, we had hundreds of thousands of troops stationed in each of those countries.

Iraq has oil, as we keep hearing. But it will take time and effort to get it on line. Meanwhile the country needs food, water, electricity, schools, police, and courts. In Bosnia and Kosovo—as in Germany and Japan after 1945—money poured in. Aid to Kosovo per capita is still 25 times higher than aid to Afghanistan. Without European and Japanese help, aid to Iraq is destined to be too little, too late.

The United States simply cannot sustain an effort of this magnitude without broad international support. The current efforts remain ad hoc and weak. Even if we want to keep half as many troops (per capita) as in Bosnia, that's 125,000, a crippling burden for the United States. Britain could contribute 10,000 or 15,000 soldiers. Countries like Pakistan and India could send some forces (for payment), but there still needs to be an integrated command and control with troops that have experience at peacemaking and -keeping. That means NATO; including France and Germany.

Similarly, in the administrative realm, the best way to help Iraq create a modern, democratic state is to thoroughly de-Baathize it and build new legal and administrative structures. Unless the United States plans to build a colonial bureaucracy of its own, with thousands of civil servants who can help run Iraq, it should use international agencies with expertise and experience. In some areas, the training of police for example, the United Nations has proved to be excellent. In others, such as finding weapons and trying Baathists, it would bring international legitimacy.

"On nation-building, people can be divided into three groups," says Dobbins. "Those who know something about the country involved. They tend to be mired in the local culture so that they believe nation-building is impossible. Next are those who know something about nation-building. They believe it's doable but tough and expensive. And then there are those who know nothing about either the country or about nation-building. They think it will be cheap and easy." On this one, it's worth spending big.

Missing in Action: Truth
Nicholas Kristof

The New York Times | May 6, 2003

The Iraq war may be more or less over, but it's already clear that the matter of Saddam Hussein's alleged nuclear, chemical, and biological weapons programs isn't going to go away any time soon. As of this writing, an intensive search has turned up little more than a couple of trailers, which may have served as mobile laboratories. The Bush administration—whose argument for invasion was based entirely on Iraq's reputed pursuit of WMDs—is now trying to downplay the issue. In this column, Nicholas Kristof raises the disturbing possibility that the American public (and the world) was intentionally misled by our government. . . .

When I raised the Mystery of the Missing W.M.D. recently, hawks fired barrages of reproachful e-mail at me. The gist was: "You *&#*! Who cares if we never find weapons of mass destruction, because we've liberated the Iraqi people from a murderous tyrant."

But it does matter, enormously, for American credibility. After all, as Ari Fleischer said on April 10 about W.M.D.: "That is what this war was about."

I rejoice in the newfound freedoms in Iraq. But there are indications that the U.S. government souped up intelligence, leaned on spooks to change their conclusions, and concealed contrary information to deceive people at home and around the world.

Let's fervently hope that tomorrow we find an Iraqi superdome filled with 500 tons of mustard gas and nerve gas, 25,000 liters of anthrax, 38,000 liters of botulinum toxin, 29,984 prohibited munitions capable of delivering chemical agents, several dozen Scud missiles, gas centrifuges to enrich uranium, 18 mobile biological warfare factories, long-range unmanned aerial vehicles to dispense anthrax, and proof of close ties with Al Qaeda. Those are the things that President Bush or his aides suggested Iraq might have, and I don't want to believe that top administration officials tried to win support for the war with a campaign of wholesale deceit.

Consider the now-disproved claims by President Bush and Colin Powell that Iraq tried to buy uranium from Niger so it could build nuclear weapons. As Seymour Hersh noted in *The New Yorker*, the claims were based on documents that had been forged so amateurishly that they should never have been taken seriously.

I'm told by a person involved in the Niger caper that more than a year ago the vice president's office asked for an investigation of the uranium deal, so a former U.S. ambassador to Africa was dispatched to Niger. In February 2002, according to someone present at the meetings, that envoy reported to the C.I.A. and State Department that the information was unequivocally wrong and that the documents had been forged.

The envoy reported, for example, that a Niger minister whose signature was on one of the documents had in fact been out of office for more than a decade. In addition, the Niger mining program was structured so that the uranium diversion had been impossible. The envoy's debunking of the forgery was passed around the administration and seemed to be accepted—except that President Bush and the State Department kept citing it anyway.

"It's disingenuous for the State Department people to say they were bamboozled because they knew about this for a year," one insider said.

Another example is the abuse of intelligence from Hussein Kamel, a son-in-law of Saddam Hussein and head of Iraq's biological weapons program until his defection in 1995. Top British and American officials kept citing information from Mr. Kamel as evidence of a huge secret Iraqi program, even though Mr. Kamel had actually emphasized that Iraq had mostly given up its W.M.D. program in the early 1990s. Glen Rangwala, a British Iraq expert, says the transcript of Mr. Kamel's debriefing was leaked because insiders resented the way politicians were misleading the public.

Patrick Lang, a former head of Middle Eastern affairs in the Defense Intelligence Agency, says that he hears from those still in the intelligence world that when experts wrote reports that were skeptical about Iraq's W.M.D., "they were encouraged to think it over again."

"In this administration, the pressure to get product 'right' is coming out of O.S.D. [the Office of the Secretary of Defense]," Mr. Lang said. He added that intelligence experts had cautioned that Iraqis would not necessarily line up to cheer U.S. troops and that the Shiite clergy could be a problem. "The guys who tried to tell them that came to understand that this advice was not welcome," he said.

"The intelligence that our officials was given regarding W.M.D. was either defective or manipulated," Senator Jeff Bingaman of New Mexico noted. Another senator is even more blunt and, sadly, exactly right: "Intelligence was manipulated."

The C.I.A. was terribly damaged when William Casey, its director in the Reagan era, manipulated intelligence to exaggerate the Soviet threat in Central America to whip up support for Ronald Reagan's policies. Now something is again rotten in the state of Spookdom.

Privatization in Disguise
Naomi Klein

The Nation | April 28, 2003

Is the post-war rebuilding of Iraq providing cover for a U.S. corporate gold rush? Nation *contributor Naomi Klein reports on the selling of a country. . . .*

On April 6, Deputy Defense Secretary Paul Wolfowitz spelled it out: There will be no role for the United Nations in setting up an interim government in Iraq. The U.S.-run regime will last at least six months, "probably . . . longer than that."

And by the time the Iraqi people have a say in choosing a government, the key economic decisions about their country's future will have been made by their occupiers. "There has got to be an effective administration from day one," Wolfowitz said. "People need water and food and medicine, and the sewers have to work, the electricity has to work. And that's a coalition responsibility."

The process of getting all this infrastructure to work is usually called "reconstruction." But American plans for Iraq's future economy go well beyond that. Rather, the country is being treated as a blank slate on which the most ideological Washington neoliberals can design their dream economy: fully privatized, foreign-owned, and open for business.

Some highlights: The $4.8-million management contract for the port in Umm Qasr has already gone to a U.S. company, Stevedoring Services of America, and the airports are on the auction block. The U.S. Agency for International Development has invited U.S. multinationals to bid on everything from rebuilding roads and bridges to printing textbooks. Most of these contracts are for about a year, but some have options that extend up to four. How long before they meld into long-term contracts for privatized water services, transit systems, roads, schools, and phones? When does reconstruction turn into privatization in disguise?

California Republican Congressman Darrel Issa has introduced a bill that would require the Defense Department to build a CDMA cell-phone system in postwar Iraq in order to benefit "U.S. patent holders." As Farhad Manjoo noted in *Salon*, CDMA is the system used in the United States, not Europe, and was developed by Qualcomm, one of Issa's most generous donors.

And then there's oil. The Bush Administration knows it can't talk openly about selling off Iraq's oil resources to ExxonMobil and Shell. It leaves that to Fadhil Chalabi, a former Iraq petroleum ministry official. "We need to have a huge amount of money coming into the country," Chalabi says. "The only way is to partially privatize the industry."

He is part of a group of Iraqi exiles who have been advising the State Department on how to implement that privatization in such a way that it isn't seen to be coming from the United States. Helpfully, the group held a conference on April 4-5 in London, where it called on Iraq to open itself up to oil multinationals after the war. The Administration has shown its gratitude by promising there will be plenty of posts for Iraqi exiles in the interim government.

Some argue that it's too simplistic to say this war is about oil. They're right. It's about oil, water, roads, trains, phones, ports, and drugs. And if this process isn't halted, "free Iraq" will be the most sold country on earth.

It's no surprise that so many multinationals are lunging for Iraq's untapped market. It's not just that the reconstruction will be worth as much as $100 billion; it's also that "free trade" by less violent means hasn't been going that well lately. More and more developing countries are rejecting privatization, while the Free Trade Area of the Americas, Bush's top trade priority, is wildly unpopular across Latin America. World Trade Organization talks on intellectual property, agriculture, and services have all bogged down amid accusations that America and Europe have yet to make good on past promises.

So what is a recessionary, growth-addicted superpower to do? How about upgrading Free Trade Lite, which wrestles market access through backroom bullying, to Free Trade Supercharged, which seizes new markets on the battlefields of pre-emptive wars? After all, negotiations with sovereign nations can be hard. Far easier to just tear up the country, occupy it, then rebuild it the way you want. Bush hasn't abandoned free trade, as some have claimed, he just has a new doctrine: "Bomb before you buy."

It goes further than one unlucky country. Investors are openly predicting that once privatization of Iraq takes root, Iran, Saudi Arabia, and Kuwait will be forced to compete by privatizing their oil. "In Iran, it would just catch like wildfire," S. Rob Sobhani, an energy consultant, told the *Wall Street Journal*. Soon, America may have bombed its way into a whole new free-trade zone.

So far, the press debate over the reconstruction of Iraq has focused on fair play: It is "exceptionally maladroit," in the words of the European Union's Commissioner for External Relations, Chris Patten, for the United States to keep all the juicy contracts for itself. It has to learn to share: ExxonMobil should invite France's TotalFinaElf to the most lucrative oilfields; Bechtel should give Britain's Thames Water a shot at the sewer contracts.

But while Patten may find U.S. unilateralism galling and Tony Blair may be calling for U.N. oversight, on this matter it's beside the point. Who cares which multinationals get the best deals in Iraq's post-Saddam, pre-democracy liquidation sale? What does it matter if the privatizing is done unilaterally by Washington or multilaterally by the United States, Europe, Russia, and China?

Entirely absent from this debate are the Iraqi people, who might—who knows?—want to hold on to a few of their assets. Iraq will be owed massive reparations after the bombing stops, but without any real democratic process, what is being planned is not reparations, reconstruction, or rehabilitation. It is robbery: mass theft disguised as charity; privatization without representation.

A people, starved and sickened by sanctions, then pulverized by war, is going to emerge from this trauma to find that their country has been sold out from under them. They will also discover that their newfound "freedom"—for which so many of their loved ones perished—comes pre-shackled with irreversible economic decisions that were made in boardrooms while the bombs were still falling.

They will then be told to vote for their new leaders, and welcomed to the wonderful world of democracy.

What Was Newt Thinking?
Patrick Buchanan

WorldNetDaily.com | April 30, 2003

Newt Gingrich may no longer be Speaker of the House, but the ex-Congressman is still a formidable Washington player. So when he gave a speech last April at the height of the Iraq war, attacking the performance of Colin Powell and the State Department, many people assumed he was acting as a proxy for Pentagon chief Donald Rumsfeld, and that his speech was evidence of an ongoing feud between State and Defense over the direction of U.S. foreign policy. In this column, Pat Buchanan—himself a canny veteran of the Washington scene—suggests that Newt's blast was actually aimed at a much larger target: President George W. Bush. . . .

Last week's pre-emptive strike by ex-Speaker Newt Gingrich on the State Department and Colin Powell may appear purest madness. But there is method in Newt's madness.

For in his attack on State, Newt—front man for the neoconservatives— fired a shot across the bow of the West Wing, i.e., you have blundered in backing off the threats against Syria, but do not believe you can pressure Israel, with impunity, into making concessions to the Palestinians.

Consider the site Newt chose to launch his attack.

The American Enterprise Institute, the creation of Lebanese-American William Baroody Sr., was begun as a think tank with ties to Taft-Goldwater Republicans. In the 1990s, it was captured by neocons and converted into their principal nesting ground inside the Beltway. It is now Centcom for the War Party.

Even before Bush took his oath, AEI issued an astonishing paper urging us to ally with Israel and "strike fatally" at Damascus, Baghdad, Tripoli,

Teheran, and Gaza, to "establish the recognition that fighting either the United States or Israel is suicidal."

"Crises can be opportunities," wrote AEI's David Wurmser. He urged us to be on the lookout for an opportunity to execute the joint U.S.-Israeli strikes. Opportunity knocked on 9/11.

Consider the issues on which Newt attacked Powell and State. The first was Powell's coming trip to Syria. Bellowed Newt: "The concept of the American secretary of state going to Damascus to meet with a terrorist-supporting, secret police-wielding dictator is ludicrous."

Ludicrous? But Powell's trip was personally approved by Bush.

State's second sin is in creating the "Quartet"—America, Russia, the United Nations, and the European Union—and approving its "road map" for a Middle East peace. To Newt, this is "a deliberate and systematic effort to undermine the president's policies . . . by ensuring they will be consistently watered down and distorted" by Russia, France, and the U.N.

But it was Bush himself who committed us to the "road map."

Thus, the White House rightly saw Newt's attack on Powell as an attack on, and warning to, the president himself.

Newt also blasted State for making us friendless in the world and failing to convince Turkey to let us use its territory in the Iraq war. But the man who failed to persuade Turkey was not Colin Powell but Paul Wolfowitz of Defense. And our alienated allies do not point to Powell as America's problem, but to the neocons clustered around AEI and to Newt's icon, Donald Rumsfeld.

In short, Newt savaged State for the failures of his own crowd and attacked Powell for pursuing the president's policies.

Whoever put Newt up to it, the speech backfired. Not only was he berated by old friends like Jack Kemp, he was dismissed by an assistant secretary of state as an "idiot" and by Deputy Secretary Richard Armitage as a nutball: "It is clear that Mr. Gingrich is off his meds and out of therapy."

And almost no one is defending Newt. Kemp says that Newt's speech did "enormous collateral damage." But the real damage appears to have been done to Newt himself, the neocons, and perhaps to Rumsfeld. For the attack on the Bush-Powell policy, many believe, had to be cleared by the Pentagon. And it is being taken as the opening thrust in a power struggle between State and Defense for the control of foreign policy.

But why would the neoconservatives, in their hour of power after victory in Iraq, attack the most popular man in Washington?

Answer: The Bush-Powell agenda and the neoconservatives' agenda, one and the same in Iraq, have diverged sharply—over Syria, over the road map, and over whether pressure should be applied to Prime Minister Ariel Sharon.

While the neocons may be powerless to force Bush to confront Damascus, they are not powerless to prevent him from pressuring Israel. And in standing by Sharon, they have powerful allies—in the Israeli Lobby, in the Amen Corner commentariat, among the Tom Delay-AIPAC Republicans, and with Evangelical Christians.

Moreover, Sharon is ready to resist. According to the *New York Times*, Sharonites consider the Bush-Powell road map to be only a "show" put on for the benefit of Britain and Tony Blair. And Israeli Finance Minister "Bibi" Netanyahu is confident Israel can handle the White House. "Pressure is expected, but we can and must resist it," says Bibi. "It is in our power to affect American policy."

In short, Bibi is warning the White House that if Bush tries to push Israel, Israel and its friends will push back, and show him who runs U.S. Middle East policy. Newt and the neocons were knocked down in Round One, big time, but they are by no means knocked out.

The battle for control of U.S. foreign policy has only just begun.

He's Out With the In Crowd
Maureen Dowd

The New York Times | April 27, 2003

In this column, Maureen Dowd gives her own reading of Newt Gingrich's assault on the State Department (see "What Was Newt Thinking?" p. 307)—and provides a useful Washington scorecard to help tell the Rummys from the Powellites. . . .

WASHINGTON—The swank cocktail party celebrating the fall of Baghdad was the hot ticket on Embassy Row.

The host was the Bush administration's vicar of foreign policy. The guests on Saturday, April 12, included Tony Brenton, acting head of the British Embassy, and dozens of ambassadors from the smaller countries that fashioned the fig leaf known as the coalition of the willing.

The ambassador of Eritrea was welcomed to the house on Kalorama Road, even as the French ambassador, who lives directly across the street in a grand chateau, was snubbed. The German ambassador is kaput, but the ambassador of the Netherlands mingled with Dick Cheney, Paul Wolfowitz, Doug Feith, and Gen. Richard Myers and Gen. Peter Pace of the Joint Chiefs. The winners were gaily lording it over the losers, sneering at the French.

Conspicuously absent was the nation's top diplomat. Asked if Colin Powell was invited, a State Department official replied, "No. People here didn't know about the party."

The host was Rummy, top gun of a muscle-bound foreign policy summed up by the comic Jon Stewart as, "You want a piece of this?"

Washington has a history of nasty rivalries, with competing camps. There were Aaron Burr people and Alexander Hamilton people; Lincoln people and McClellan people; Bobby people and Lyndon people.

Now, since Newt Gingrich aimed the MOAB of screeds at an already circumscribed Mr. Powell, the capital has been convulsed by the face-off between Defense and State.

There are Rummy people: Mr. Cheney, Mr. Wolfowitz, Mr. Feith, Bill Kristol, William Safire, Ariel Sharon, Fox News, *National Review*, *The Weekly Standard*, the *Wall Street Journal* editorial board, the fedayeen of the Defense Policy Board—Richard Perle, James Woolsey, Mr. Gingrich, Ken Adelman— and the fifth column at State, John Bolton and Liz Cheney.

And there are Powell people: Brent Scowcroft, James Baker, Bush 41, Ken Duberstein, Richard Armitage, Richard Haass, the Foreign Service, Joe Biden, Bob Woodward, the wet media elite, the planet.

The dueling secretaries made a show of having lunch Wednesday at the Pentagon. Meanwhile, Mr. Armitage said Newt was "off his meds and out of therapy"; Mr. Baker called Mr. Gingrich "someone with no foreign policy or national security experience . . . who was in effect forced to resign" as House speaker; a Powell aide said it was "inconceivable that Newt could have made this extraordinary attack on his own" without running it past Rummy; and a Powell friend said the hard-liners had tormented the frustrated diplomat and made his life "hellish."

Newt, amateur historian, is part of Rummy's brain trust. The defense chief regularly forwards blathering Gingrich e-mail about military strategy to irritated Pentagon officials.

This clash is epochal because it's beyond ego. It's about whether America will lead by fear, aggression, and force of arms or by diplomacy, moderation, and example.

Rummy may merely be a front man for Dick Cheney, who tangled with Mr. Powell for being too cautious in the first Persian Gulf war, and scorned Mr. Powell's strategy of going to the U.N. before the second.

Karl Rove scolded Mr. Gingrich for overreaching; W. still dislikes Newt for leading the revolt against Poppy for breaking his tax pledge.

But the president has not spoken up for Mr. Powell, allowing his credibility to be undermined as he heads off to the Middle East to build the peace. And Mr. Bush has never reined in Rummy's rabid fedayeen.

W.'s gut leans toward the macho Cheney-Rummy idea that America is not bound by history, that the U.S. can help Israel and reshape the Arab world and the rest of the world and not care who is run over, or worry about what will happen if we don't get cooperation on terrorism, proliferation, AIDS, trading, or if people everywhere get up in the morning thinking about how to get back at us.

Nerviness, absolutism, and smiting enemies are seductive. Nuance and ambivalence aren't.

The day before Rummy's party, senators were shown an organizational chart for remaking Iraq. Just below Jay Garner, who reports to Tommy Franks, was a line to Larry DiRita, who is a special assistant to the defense chief. Even the time on the chart was "1700," for 5 P.M.

Diplomacy in Washington now runs on military time.

Return of Bin Laden
Richard Cohen

The Washington Post | November 14, 2002

American troops may be decamped in Baghdad—but where do things stand with our war on Al Qaeda? In this column, Richard Cohen reminds us that Osama bin Laden is still at large, and still capable of striking with devastating force. Cohen's point was subsequently underscored by the recent bombings in Riyadh, Saudi Arabia, which have been attributed to bin Laden's terrorist network. . . .

Ever since the Pentagon blew the battle at Tora Bora last year and apparently allowed Osama bin Laden to slip the noose, the administration has been busy playing down his importance. "We've tried hard not to personalize it," Pentagon spokeswoman Victoria Clarke said of bin Laden and his Taliban sidekick, Mohammad Omar. "This is a lot more than bin Laden and Omar," she said.

Yes, it's about failure.

The decision to de-emphasize the hunt for the two, especially bin Laden, seems "linked"—that all-purpose Washington word—to the fact that the United States has been unable to find him, either "dead or alive," in George Bush's unforgettable phrase. Specifically, it seems that bin Laden escaped from Tora Bora, where, U.S. intelligence now believes, he was present. It was a spectacular fiasco.

Defense Secretary Donald Rumsfeld set the administration's tone when he implied it didn't matter all that much if bin Laden was dead or alive since, in either case, his days as a master terrorist were surely over. "Wherever he is, if he is, you can be certain he is having one dickens of a time operating his apparatus," Rumsfeld said.

The commander of U.S. ground forces in Afghanistan, Army Lt. Gen. Dan McNeil, struck a similar note. He said the really important target was al Qaeda itself—not its leader. "We don't have to find him, because we're going to shut down his terrorist apparatus," he said.

Now an audiotape purportedly from bin Laden has surfaced in the usual outlet for such things, the Arab satellite channel, al-Jazeera. Since the voice mentions such recent events as the bombing in Bali and the murder of a U.S.

diplomat in Jordan, the tape has to have been made fairly recently. And since the Bush administration cannot show that bin Laden is dead, he will continue to live—whether in fact, tape, or myth—in the imagination and yearnings of his followers, larger than life because he cannot be proven dead.

The obvious attempt to play down bin Laden's importance has a whistling-past-the-graveyard quality to it. In the first place, the existence of the new tape is a form of nose-thumbing. It shows the world—particularly the Islamic world—that the United States is not as all powerful as some people might suppose. It may be able to pound Afghanistan into rubble and possibly do the same to Iraq, but it is far weaker when facing terrorism—the ol' asymmetrical warfare business. This is a lesson Israel learns on almost a daily basis.

Second, there was no al Qaeda before bin Laden, and while it might continue to exist without him, it would certainly be far less formidable. He bankrolled the organization with his personal fortune, but more important, he is a rare charismatic leader. There is no point in calling him names—evil, for instance—when no matter what we may think of him (and evil he surely is) he is a hero in parts of the world. For many reasons, he has become the personification of extreme Islam's war against the West, modernity, and—a rational person would suggest—the welfare of its own people.

Last, I have to go back to Clarke, the Pentagon spokeswoman. She and her bosses may now choose not to "personalize" the search for bin Laden, but I—and countless others—feel differently. The man is a mass murderer who took more than 3,000 lives on Sept. 11 alone. He is responsible for other terrorist attacks as well, including the bombing of the USS Cole off Yemen.

Those of us who were in New York when the twin towers of the World Trade Center were hit, who were downtown when the buildings collapsed, can never forget that day. The sound of buildings snapping and then collapsing, people plummeting to their deaths or tumbling into an inferno of jet fuel, firefighters and cops rushing up stairs that would soon be pulverized, widows, orphans, a gash in the city that endures—all this makes Sept. 11 very personal indeed. To this day, every firetruck rushing by—the names of the dead embossed on the sides—is a reminder of what happened, a blur of a memorial.

Osama bin Laden laughed at all this, his cackle caught on an earlier videotape. Now, in effect, he laughs some more. The murder of innocents in Bali, in Jordan, in Tunisia, in that Moscow theater—the terrorism he applauds, if not supports, and which was mentioned on that tape, makes it imperative that he be captured or killed, and that we know for sure. That would be good policy—and satisfying as hell.

Part Five:
The Democratic Contenders for 2004

. . . and Sets the Tone

E. J. Dionne Jr.

The Washington Post | April 29, 2003

One of the keys to electability, as any candidate will tell you, is to have a "hook"— a signature idea that is innovative, appealing, and easily understood. Congressman Dick Gephardt, the former House majority leader from Missouri, was one of the later entries into the race for the 2004 Democratic presidential nomination, but he quickly grabbed headlines with his bold plan for extending health insurance coverage to all Americans. The proof of his idea's merit, as E. J. Dionne notes, was how little time the other Democratic hopefuls wasted in attacking it. . . .

Some of the Democrats running for president have found an issue that's gotten them really worked up.

Howard Dean, the former Vermont governor, called the idea in question "totally impractical" and "much too expensive." Florida Sen. Bob Graham offered a worldly wise retort. "We tried that before," he said, and "it just fell apart."

These guys were not responding with fierce partisanship to a George W. Bush initiative. They were going after one of their own, dismissing Richard Gephardt's sweeping proposal to guarantee health insurance coverage to almost all Americans.

Not wishing to swell the wave of publicity Gephardt won for introducing the first Big New Idea into the 2004 campaign, his other opponents left the work of criticism largely to nameless lieutenants. But Gephardt, the former House Democratic leader, has already succeeded. He has drawn a clean, clear line across American politics by challenging Bush on precisely the issue that should be at the heart of the domestic debate in 2004.

Bush has dedicated himself to the proposition that anything that's wrong with the American economy can be cured by large tax cuts, preferably directed toward the "investor class," i.e., the wealthy. Gephardt has shouted a loud "No!" He would repeal almost all of Bush's tax cuts and direct the proceeds to helping employees, businesses, and governments cope with rising health care costs.

Before Gephardt gave his health care speech on Wednesday, Democrats were offering many rationales for resisting Bush's tax cuts—the general need for fiscal responsibility; the particular importance of making the government solvent by the time the baby boomers retire; the imperative of avoiding cutbacks in this or that program; the sheer unfairness of lavishing so many benefits on the most well-off Americans.

Good reasons all, but all rather abstract. Gephardt would offer voters a plain choice: They can have Bush's tax cuts or they can have secure health coverage. They can't have both. Yes, universal health insurance would cost a lot of money. But so would Bush's tax plan. If we're going to dedicate hundreds of billions of dollars to a cause, which cause should it be?

Sure, there are objections to Gephardt's approach. For one thing, there is a constituency for fiscal responsibility, and many Americans have figured out that Bush's tax policies guarantee a fiscal train wreck by the time the baby boomers start retiring. Harnessing the entire Bush tax cut to health care would reduce the Democrats' opportunity to campaign as the party of balanced budgets.

And, yes, big health care plans don't have a great record of political success. That was Graham's point in his inevitable reference to the health care adventures of a certain couple named Clinton. But unlike the Clintons, Gephardt has avoided remaking the entire health care system. His core idea is to build on the employer-based insurance system by essentially doubling the current federal tax subsidy to companies that provide health coverage. For companies that don't now provide coverage, his plan would require them to accept the tax credit and offer their employees insurance.

He would subsidize health insurance for uncovered Americans with particularly low incomes. He would allow those aged 55 to 64—an expensive group to cover—to buy into Medicare. And he would have Washington underwrite 60 percent of the health insurance costs not just of the private sector, but also of the employees of state and local governments. By Gephardt's estimate, this would provide fiscally strapped states and localities with $172 billion in relief during the plan's first three years.

Yes, the plan would be expensive. Gephardt's own numbers peg its costs in 2007 at $247 billion. Yes, it further subsidizes Americans who are already insured. Dean, a physician who has been saying sensible things about health care for months, wants new money spent primarily on expanding help to the uninsured. And Gephardt's plan won't satisfy those who think the country needs to move away from employer-based health insurance.

But Gephardt is right about two things. First, that relieving employers of a larger share of their health costs will inevitably translate into new investment, higher wages or both. And a plan designed to cover everyone will minimize the problem of perverse incentives. Subsidies targeted to particular groups might simply draw those groups away from employer-based plans and increase the government's long-term costs.

If nothing else, Gephardt has broken the spell of the Clinton Syndrome, the affliction that sees all efforts to achieve universal health insurance coverage as doomed to the same fate as ClintonCare. Gephardt will stand or fall on his health plan, but at least he'll stand for something.

Candide
Jeffrey Toobin

The New Yorker | December 16, 2002

Senator Joe Lieberman of Connecticut has always been known as one of the more centrist Democrats in Congress. He drafted the legislation establishing the Department of Homeland Security, has been calling Saddam Hussein's overthrow for years, and was a big proponent of stock options. He's also a deeply religious man, who places values above all else. This profile, which appeared shortly before Lieberman officially declared his candidacy (a decision that hinged on Al Gore's withdrawal from the race) explores the question of whether it's possible for a nice-guy-moderate Democrat to get elected president....

Senator Joseph Lieberman, Democrat of Connecticut and Al Gore's Vice-Presidential running mate, is seldom happier than when he is talking about his own Presidential ambitions, even his much discussed pledge regarding Gore. Last year, Lieberman promised that he would not seek the Presidency if Gore tried again. One night in October, the issue came up at a small fundraiser in Miami Beach where fifty Lieberman supporters in south Florida had paid a thousand dollars each to hear the Senator in an intimate setting over dinner at a private house. The weather was hot and sticky, but Lieberman, mingling with the guests on the patio, never took off his jacket and tie, and his demeanor remained serious. After a brief talk, he took questions, mostly about Iraq and the Middle East. When one guest asked about his plans for 2004, Lieberman said, "Good question!" and beamed.

"I made a pledge last year that I wouldn't run if Al did in '04," he said. "It felt right then, and it feels right now. If there is a possibility for a Presidential candidacy by me, and I think there is, a lot of it comes back to him picking me. So I'm waiting to hear what Al decides. But here are some of the numbers that I'll share with you. There have been four big polls recently. With Gore in the race, Al always comes in first. With Gore out of the race, I have come in first in every one of the four." The audience applauded politely, urging him on. "So these numbers tell me that when I think about running for President I'm not 'inhaling.' " Much laughter.

With the joke, Lieberman was gently mocking his own reputation for sobriety, if not sanctimony. He may be a thoroughgoing moderate in his politics, but he is a true conservative in temperament and style. His world is an orderly place, where people wait in line, take their turns, and generally behave themselves. Lieberman wants badly to be the President, but decorum compels him to defer to Gore. Like Nick Carraway, Lieberman wants "the world to be in uniform and at a sort of moral attention forever." When he was just a little-known senator, picking and choosing the issues he wanted to speak out on, this sense of rectitude served him well, but now the stakes are higher and the fights are grittier, and he seems perpetually disappointed, even surprised, when other politicians don't play by his rules.

Shortly after the September 11th attacks, Lieberman introduced a bill to create a Department of Homeland Security. At first, the Bush Administration opposed the proposal, but then, in June of this year, the Republicans suddenly made creation of the new department the centerpiece of their antiterrorism initiatives, and the bill appeared headed for easy passage. As the floor manager for the Senate, Lieberman had the most high-profile assignment of his thirteen years in office.

When the Senate began debating specific legislative language, a problem arose. President Bush asked for a provision allowing him to waive certain civil-service protections for employees of the new department if he thought it was in the interest of national security. Bush sought, for example, the authority to hire and fire at will in the new department. (He would still be bound by anti-discrimination laws, including those barring favoritism based on political affiliation.) The President's proposal also allowed him, in the name of national security, to exempt certain workers from collective-bargaining agreements. He already had that kind of authority over other parts of the government, and he had used it earlier in the year to prevent a union-organizing drive at the United States attorney's office in Miami. "The unions got very agitated about this," Lieberman told me one day in September, while the issue was being debated.

Lieberman seemed bewildered that this relatively obscure issue had come to dominate the debate over homeland security. "If you asked me whether civil-service protection would be the stumbling block, I would have never guessed it," he said. In the Senate, he tried to finesse the issue, helping to draft compromise language that appeared to have the support of more than half the Senate. But by threatening a filibuster Senate Republicans kept the compromise amendment from coming to the floor. They insisted on an up-and-down vote on the whole bill. Fred Thompson, who managed the bill for the Republicans, said recently, "I'm kind of prejudiced toward Joe from a personal standpoint, because we've had such a good relationship, but I really don't understand what he did on homeland security. We kept asking ourselves, 'What is it they are seeing here that we don't see here? Why are they fighting us on this?' This is Presidential national-security authority—that ain't got two sides to it." As John McCain, the Arizona senator and Lieberman's close friend, said, "Very frankly, they should have gone ahead and caved on it. It gave the appearance of being unpatriotic and beholden to the unions. The Republicans got a twofer out of it."

The decision to fight Bush on the union provisions of the homeland bill reflected a broader ideological evolution that Lieberman has undergone since Gore selected him, two years ago. At that time, Lieberman ranked as one of the more conservative Democrats in the Senate. He had questioned affirmative action, supported public funding of tuition vouchers for private schools, and generally irritated some of the Party's most stalwart constituency groups. During the campaign, Lieberman hewed closer to the party line on those issues, and as he weighs entering the Democratic Presidential primaries—with their left-skewing voters—he has reestablished his bona fides with the heart of the Party. He voted against the Bush tax cut, denounced the Republicans' environmental policies, and, in homeland security, made a stand for unions.

While Lieberman and his fellow-Democrats were doing the bidding of the public-employee unions, President Bush, Vice-President Cheney, and other leading Republicans took the opportunity to accuse them of a lack of patriotism and a weakness on terrorism. On September 25th, Tom Daschle, of South Dakota, the Democrats' leader in the Senate, responded to this barrage with indignation. Lieberman, characteristically, did not. "Tom was quite right to blow the whistle on this politicization," he told me the next day in his office. "Would it have been right for me to say that the President sacrificed national security by not introducing a bill for eight months on this issue? The problem is, the Administration can't take yes for an answer. I'm the one who should be angry at Bush. It's my bill he's talking about when he's talking about Democrats who don't care about national security."

Lieberman couldn't bring himself to question the President's motives, because he doesn't like visceral politics. "Part of the conspiracy theory is that they want the homeland-security bill *not* to pass, so they can keep the issue alive before the election and blame it on us," he said. In the weeks that followed, of course, that is exactly what Bush and the Republicans did—with great success. In the Georgia Senate race, television commercials about the homeland-security debate were widely regarded as the key to the upset victory of the Republican Saxby Chambliss over the Democrat Max Cleland. Lieberman and his Democratic colleagues had been completely outmaneuvered.

Compounding the awkwardness for Lieberman was the other big issue of the fall—Iraq. Over the past decade, there has been no greater hawk on Iraq than Lieberman. If anything, he has been to the right of President Bush on the issue. Lieberman has long called for an American military effort to oust Saddam Hussein, with or without the support of the United Nations. In 1998, along with Senators McCain, Trent Lott, and Bob Kerrey, he sponsored the Iraq Liberation Act, which stated that it "should be the policy of the United States to support efforts to remove the regime headed by Saddam Hussein from power in Iraq." As Lieberman told me in his office, "I've said since the end of the Gulf War that I think we made a mistake not to take him out when his forces were in disarray." On Iraq, Lieberman was the President's biggest Democratic supporter.

When the White House decided to seek congressional authorization for an attack on Iraq, McCain and his fellow-Republican John Warner, of Virginia, asked Lieberman if he would join as the lead Democratic sponsor. Lieberman said yes, and persuaded other Democrats to sign on as well. At a ceremony on October 2nd in the Rose Garden, Bush read a statement announcing an agreement on the bipartisan resolution on Iraq. Lieberman lavished praise on the President, calling his statement "eloquent, powerful, and convincing."

Intentionally or not, Lieberman spent the fall doing the Republicans' bidding. His stature gave the President's policy on Iraq the shimmer of bipartisanship; his leadership on homeland security led to a political debacle and policy failure for the Democrats. (After the election, the final version of the bill, which Lieberman voted for, basically adopted the President's position.) I asked him whether he was uncomfortable serving simultaneously as a punching bag and a cheerleader for the Bush White House. "It's odd," he said without emotion. "It happens in politics."

Lieberman, who was born in 1942, bears the scars of a happy childhood; his parents, who were Orthodox Jews, held him to the highest standards, which, in their view, he clearly exceeded. His father owned a liquor store in Stamford, and his mother ran the household and raised Joe and his two sisters. "I once took a college roommate home to Stamford," Lieberman told me, "and he said, 'After meeting your parents, I have the feeling that they greeted you every morning with a standing ovation.' " Lieberman went on, "I learned a lot of lessons about how you are supposed to behave from my parents and from my rabbi. It was all about making things better—*tikkun olam*, improving the world. We had an obligation to reach out. The rabbi that I had was very involved in the community. It was a different time, in a way, for the Orthodox movement in the fifties—much more centrist, if I can put it that way. That was all in me. I was reading history and intrigued by biographies of people who had made a difference. And then John Kennedy came along and swept me and all my generation with him."

At Yale, Lieberman's nickname was Senator. "We called him that because he had the same calm, statesmanlike affect that he does now, but in an eighteen- or nineteen-year-old it was a unique thing," Pete Putzel, a college and law-school friend who is now a criminal-defense lawyer in New York, said. "Joe was, even then, something of an establishment person." Lieberman's college years revealed a man with a precocious understanding of his own goals and the skills to make them real. He was a student leader—chairman of the *Yale Daily News* and, at law school, an officer of the Yale Democratic Club—but he also kept an eye on the world outside New Haven. In his senior year, he entered a program that would allow him to spend all his time writing his thesis about the head of Connecticut's Democratic Party, John Bailey, who was then in his sixties, and had run the state party for twenty years. Widely described as a political "boss," Bailey actually had little in common with leaders like Mayor Richard J. Daley, in Chicago. Bailey came from a moneyed family, rarely faced questions about his personal ethics, and generally shunned media attention. He was best known as an early champion of John F. Kennedy's Presidential ambitions. Bailey cared little for issues, leaving them to such protégés as Abraham Ribicoff and Chester Bowles. Instead, he focussed on building coalitions, avoiding primary fights, and choosing ethnically balanced tickets. This paradigmatic figure of the establishment was more than just a thesis topic for Lieberman. He turned his college work into a meticulously researched and frankly admiring book, "The Power Broker," which was published in 1966. There was, Lieberman wrote, "one quality which characterizes John Bailey's address to politics. He enjoys it as a game. He likes to win. He thrives on personal relations in pressurized political situations."

After graduation, Lieberman remained in New Haven to attend Yale Law School. (While in law school, he married Betty Haas, with whom he had two children. They divorced in 1981, and two years later he married Hadassah Freilich Tucker, with whom he has a teenage daughter.) It was a tumultuous period on campus. The university chaplain, the Reverend William Sloane Coffin, nursed an early activism among students in those years, and Lieberman, in a modest way, joined up with the cause, even taking a brief trip to Mississippi in 1963, to assist in a "mock election" for black voters. But it was John Bailey, not the protest movement, who was the formative influence on the aspiring politician. "Joe was no student radical, that's for sure," Terry Segal, a Boston lawyer who was also a classmate, said. "He was what was known then as a 'regular.' He was cautious. There were people who wanted the Yale Democrats to take positions on things like Vietnam, but Joe supported the Administration." For Bailey, and later for Lieberman, politics was a pursuit in which reasonable people crafted acceptable compromises with one another. "I was intrigued by how one makes a complicated, pluralistic system like our democracy work, and Bailey seemed to know how it worked," Lieberman told me.

In 1970, after a short stint at a private law firm, Lieberman decided to put Bailey's lessons to work, and ran for a seat in the state senate, knocking on thousands of doors with a corps of campaign volunteers that included Bill Clinton, then a Yale law student. At the age of twenty-eight, Lieberman scored a notable upset, and within five years he was the majority leader of the state senate. In 1982, when Lieberman was forty, he ran for state attorney general. In a complex four-way battle at the Democratic convention in Hartford— the kind of struggle in which his hero John Bailey had excelled—Lieberman outfoxed his rivals and won the nomination and the general election. Even in the semi-obscurity of his new office, he managed to gain a reputation as a strong environmentalist, and by 1988 he was looking to move up.

Michael Adler, who has long been a leader in Jewish and Democratic organizations in south Florida, hosted the fund-raiser for Lieberman in Miami Beach, and he told me how he came to support Lieberman's race for the United States Senate against Lowell Weicker, in 1988. "Weicker had always been a big friend of Israel, and I would say about ninety-five per cent of the politically active Jewish community down here was for him. But Weicker was also known as Castro's biggest friend in the Senate, and there was a lot of anger about that down here. So I knew that Lieberman was running, but Jorge Mas"—Jorge Mas Canosa, the unofficial leader of the hard-line Cuban-exile community—"told me that he was being supportive of his cause, and we should get behind him, too. So that's how I started working for Joe." Lieberman has remained loyal to the anti-Castro cause. "Joe Lieberman is my hero," Joe Garcia, the executive director of the Cuban American National Foundation, said recently. "He understands the struggle of the Cuban people for freedom."

In 1988, Weicker, an independent-minded Republican seeking his fourth term, seemed to be perfectly in tune with the Connecticut electorate. But Lieberman argued that Weicker had become lazy and complacent in the Senate, sometimes missing votes in order to take well-paid speaking engagements. Lieberman remained behind in the polls until his political consultant, Carter Eskew, designed a series of television advertisements that portrayed Weicker as a cartoon bear, drowsing when he should be working. "We ran at him from the left *and* the right," Eskew said. "The message was that Weicker has his head in the clouds and Joe has his feet on the ground. The ads delivered something that was true about Weicker—that he was a big gruff guy who was kind of distant from ordinary people." A late surge pushed Lieberman past Weicker by less than one per cent of the vote.

In the Senate, Lieberman began to display a distinctive ideological pedigree. More important than any partisan affiliation, he had a reverence for American institutions—among them family, faith, private enterprise, and government itself. It was thus not surprising that Lieberman fell in with a group of moderate Democrats who were trying to remake the Party through the Democratic Leadership Council, which served as a sort of idea factory to revitalize the Party. "At that time, we were looking at why our party kept losing the Presidency," Al From, the longtime head of the D.L.C., told me. "It was because we were losing the heart of the electorate, the people who go to work every day and play by the rules. It was around that time that we came up with our slogan: 'Opportunity, Responsibility, Community.' "

"The New Democrat movement was originally started in the mid-eighties by people who were particularly concerned with two themes," Lieberman told me. "And these themes worked their way through the Clinton years—to regain the confidence of the American people as a party that not only understood and cared about national security but was prepared to protect national security, and to rebuild confidence in the Democratic Party as a party that not only cared about economic growth but knew how to help create economic growth and understood that to do that you couldn't be anti-business."

To demonstrate that he wasn't anti-business, Lieberman became a champion of stock options, a cause dear to many high-tech executives, who felt that the broader use of options would help motivate corporate leaders and thus spur innovation. The cause suited his New Democrat sensibility, and Lieberman liked and trusted most businessmen. In the mid-nineties, the Financial Accounting Standards Board announced that it was going to recommend that all companies report the costs of stock options as a business expense. Its argument was straightforward: stock options were an expense, which companies already reported for tax purposes, and omitting their cost from income statements deceived investors about companies' true financial condition. The corporate community rebelled, especially high-tech companies, which relied heavily on stock options to compensate their executives. Lieberman sided with them, while Arthur Levitt, Clinton's chairman of the Securities and Exchange Commission, backed the accounting board. Lieberman initiated a "sense of the Senate" resolution that passed almost unanimously, denouncing the accounting board for considering the proposed change in the rules. "After that, I went to the accountants and told them to back off," Levitt said to me. "There was too much heat, and I was worried that the Congress would kill all standard setting if we continued to pick a fight on this issue." As Levitt writes in his new book, *Take On the Street*, no one in Congress "was a more formidable foe than Senator Joe Lieberman of Connecticut."

In October, Sandy Robertson, a prominent California venture capitalist, threw a fund-raiser for Lieberman's political-action committee, ROCPAC ("Responsibility, Opportunity, Community"), at his house overlooking San Francisco Bay, and he introduced Lieberman to the group with thanks for "all your work on stock options." The Senator responded with a rueful smile.

"It's nice to be in a place where I'm not abused for supporting stock options," he said. In the financial scandals of the past year, the misuse of stock options has become a familiar theme. Even before a sympathetic crowd, Lieberman could muster only a sheepish defense of his position. "I continue to believe that stock options are a good idea, but they were abused by greedy and unethical executives. That wasn't clear to me then," he said. "Stock options democratize capitalism. As I heard from Silicon Valley and around the country, the industry was using options to attract people to small companies from big companies. Looking back, seven to ten million people got them." But, Lieberman acknowledged, "Clearly a disproportionate percent of the options went to a small percentage of executives. That was disappointing."

On stock options, Lieberman had trusted the corporate executives, and they had let him down. Powerful people had said they were doing the public's business, but they were just helping themselves, and Lieberman was shocked, just as he was when President Bush turned against him on homeland security.

Lieberman's awkward position on the business collapses of the past year illustrates a broader problem that he and other Democrats face. They lambaste Bush and the Republicans for the souring economy, but they have yet to produce much in the way of alternatives. In a speech at the Nasdaq market site, in New York, on October 18th, Lieberman challenged the centerpiece of Bush's economic program—sort of. He said that the Bush tax cut, which he had voted against, was "far more expensive than we could afford and far less effective than our economy required." But, instead of calling for its repeal, Lieberman proposed to "redirect" the tax cut to businesses that invest in new technology and to companies that hire new workers. He also called for a tax rebate for low-income taxpayers. It is a more progressive approach than Bush's, but it's not all that different. Like the Republicans, Lieberman thinks that the best way to revitalize the economy is through tax cuts.

His conservative approach on the economy has brought Lieberman into a testy, long-distance debate with Al Gore. During the 2000 campaign, Gore often invoked the phrase "the people, not the powerful." Lieberman told me, "I didn't like the phrase, and to the best of my knowledge I never used it in the campaign, because it didn't really reflect what Al's record was. It didn't reflect the Clinton-Gore years. Why didn't it? Because it suggested class conflict, and we were not about that. It's very much not the New Democratic message. We were about growing the economic pie."

This summer, Gore responded to the critique in an Op-Ed article in the *Times*, saying that he thought the business scandals of the past year showed that his message was exactly right. To some extent, there may be less to the controversy than meets the eye. At the moment, there seem to be few substantive differences between Gore and Lieberman on domestic issues, or among any of the other prospective Democratic Presidential candidates. Looking back on the 2000 campaign, Lieberman recalled a speech to union members. "One of the most satisfying experiences to me was to be in a union hall and to give the basic D.L.C. message about fiscal responsibility, balanced budgets, keeping interest rates low, creating economic opportunity, and to get a rip-roaring standing ovation," he told me. "I think people get it." But the acceptance of the D.L.C. message also presents a problem for Lieberman. If every Democrat subscribes to it, how then does Lieberman distinguish himself?

The answer, it appears, is values. "My record is that I have been more willing to talk the language of values and faith in politics than any other Democrat," he told me. "I believe it. It's central to my notion of how to be a good leader at this point, to find an appropriate, inclusive way to bring values and faith into the public dialogue. Some of this may be expressed through legislation, but a lot of it is the question of the leader as a spokesperson, as somebody who wants to lead by example." The invocation of values remains Lieberman's signature. In his second term, he and William Bennett, the conservative former Secretary of Education, began a crusade against violence and vulgarity in the entertainment business. And then, on September 3, 1998, shortly before the release of the Starr report, Lieberman gave his famous speech on the Senate floor about President Clinton's behavior with Monica Lewinsky. Noting his "deep disappointment and personal anger," Lieberman said that Clinton's behavior was "not just inappropriate, it is immoral and it is harmful, for it sends a message of what is acceptable behavior to the larger American family, particularly to our children."

This speech, more than anything, led to his selection as Gore's running mate, and it remains his defining moment in public life, just as his sense of values remains the touchstone of his political judgments. But the invocation of "values" seems a slender reed on which to base a Presidential campaign. As Lieberman defines them, they have almost no political content. Indeed, he is so worried that people will think he is trying to legislate morality that he insists his notion of values doesn't necessitate specific new laws. By condemning Clinton, Lieberman set himself up as the anti-Clinton, despite their similarities on many policy issues. This may have been enough to earn a Vice-Presidential nomination from Gore, who was trying to distance himself from Clinton's ethical travails, but Lieberman's judgmental nature may be less advantageous in a Democratic Presidential primary. "Clinton is revered among primary voters, and there are a lot of people who think Joe is sanctimonious on the whole subject," one Democratic strategist who is generally sympathetic to Lieberman says. There is also the question of whether talk of values—in the context of adultery and the like—will resonate in 2004 as it once did. Lieberman's belief in the importance of virtue in a politician's private life may not be justified in a post-September 11th world, where, for example, Rudolph Giuliani's colorful marital history was instantly forgotten.

For Lieberman, talk of values often leads to talk of religion, especially his own. "Part of my message has to do with just respect for faith, which continues to mean an awful lot to most people in this country," he said. "And that can be expressed through support of what's called faith-based initiatives, but that is, in my opinion, a small part of it. The larger part is just to be respectful of the constructive role that faith plays in the life of our country and in the life of a lot of people in our country."

Faith certainly plays a central role in Lieberman's own life. On a Sunday afternoon in October, at the Kings Point Performing Arts Center, just outside Fort Lauderdale, about twelve hundred residents of the retirement community there, nearly all of them Jewish, waited more than an hour to hear from Joe Lieberman. They smiled as they heard the sixty-year-old Senator introduced as "like a favorite younger brother." Lieberman had come to vouch for the Democratic nominee for governor, Bill McBride, a stolid corporate lawyer with a thick Southern accent. "Somebody asked me if Bill McBride was a mensch," Lieberman told the group. "I said, 'He's a *richtiger* mensch.' " The crowd gave a knowing laugh. (The Yiddishism means, roughly, "really great guy.")

Lieberman has an infectious enthusiasm for his Jewishness. He may at times be a humorless scold about virtue in general, but he embraces his religious identity with joy and wit. One day in his office, I teased him about whether he had accepted gifts of clothing from his supporters, as his colleague Senator Robert Torricelli has allegedly done. Lieberman rolled his eyes and said that he had bought the suit he was wearing at a Brooks Brothers in Connecticut. "The salesman told me to look at the tag. It said, 'Made in Israel.'

Unbelievable. Who ever heard of a suit made in Israel? Then he said, 'Be careful with the pants. Those Israelis are a little short with the fabric.' "

Among some Jews, Lieberman's nomination for Vice-President induced a kind of vertigo. On the one hand, the Anti-Defamation League chided him for excessive discussion of God and religion, including his invocation of George Washington's warning "never to indulge the supposition that morality can be maintained without religion." On the other hand, some in the ultra-Orthodox community complained when Lieberman was seen drinking water on Tishah-b'Av, a sombre day of fasting and reflection. Lieberman laughed about this minor flap. "It's the inner, inner world," he said.

These controversies now seem long forgotten, and Lieberman enjoys broad and deep support among Jews. If he runs, Jews, who make up an estimated four per cent of the national electorate, will likely provide the core of his financial support and a significant voting bloc in Democratic primaries. The broader question of whether any Jew can be elected President is more difficult. Most political observers seem to regard Lieberman's faith as more of an asset than a hindrance in a Presidential race. "You can't poll for this stuff — 'Would you vote for a Jew?' " one leading Democrat says. "But the consensus seems to be that being Jewish, at least for him, is not a disqualification at all." Oddly, perhaps, it was Jewish political professionals who seemed most skeptical of any Jew's chances. "A President who doesn't celebrate Christmas?" one told me. "Forget it."

The issue may be less Lieberman's heritage than his heart. Lieberman campaigned energetically in 2000, even making trips to Texas to criticize Bush's environmental record, but he did not assume the customary role of the Vice-Presidential nominee as hatchet man, which would have been out of character for him. At one key moment, in fact, Lieberman's gentlemanly bearing may have hurt Gore's chances. Lieberman's debate with Dick Cheney on October 5, 2000, in Danville, Kentucky, was a decorous standoff; the polite exchanges allowed Cheney to prove that he was not the right-wing ideologue that his voting record in Congress suggested he was. Lieberman remains defensive about his performance in the debate. In a brief memoir of the campaign, *An Amazing Adventure*, which will be published in January, he writes, "I was ready to get aggressive again in the debate with Cheney, because the differences between his record and mine and Al's were so stark. But surprisingly, the pollsters and consultants counseled otherwise." Today, some of these professionals remember their advice quite differently. "From the ticket's perspective, it would have been a more effective performance if he had constantly put Cheney on the defensive," one Gore adviser said. "It was a missed opportunity."

During the thirty-six-day post-election battle in Florida, Lieberman shied away from another fight. In the early days of the recount, he was a forceful behind-the-scenes advocate for insisting on the recount in the courts. "I was a hawk on the whole question of legal challenges, because I thought where we had a plausible right we should assert it and let the judge make a decision," he recalled afterward. But on Sunday, November 19, 2000, nearly two weeks into the recount, when political momentum began to swing against Gore, Lieberman switched tacks. On that day, the Bush campaign began assailing the Democrats for trying to exclude the votes of military personnel who were stationed overseas if their ballots did not comply with Florida law. Norman Schwarzkopf, the retired general and Bush surrogate, declared, "It is a very sad day in our country when the men and women [who] are serving abroad and facing danger . . . are denied the right to vote [because] of some technicality out of their control." The next morning, Lieberman appeared on *Meet the Press* to answer the charge.

Lieberman capitulated completely. "I would give the benefit of the doubt to ballots coming in from military personnel generally," he said. In the crucial days that followed, Republicans around Florida cited Lieberman's statement to persuade local canvassing boards to allow hundreds of invalid ballots to be counted. (A later investigation by the *Times* found that six hundred and eighty illegal absentee ballots had been included in the final total in Florida. The votes were divided in a way that would most likely have reduced, but not eliminated, Bush's margin of five hundred and thirty-seven.) Fighting the absentee-ballot issue, Lieberman told me, "seemed to me inconsistent with the over-all thrust of our campaign in Florida post-Election Day, which was to count every vote." The Republicans in Florida drew no such fine distinctions and clawed for every advantage. Lieberman's fastidiousness on the issue enraged many Democrats who were trying hard to elect him Vice-President.

In *An Amazing Adventure,* Lieberman and his wife, Hadassah, who contributed a few passages, have written an almost substance-free book, a collection of innocuous anecdotes about how nice people were to them around the country. Unlike most politicians, Lieberman has written good books in the past, so this one seems especially hollow. Characteristically, Lieberman has a kind word for almost everyone. Of the debate with Cheney, he writes proudly,

"Cheney and I disagreed on most issues, but we managed to disagree without being disagreeable." The book does accurately reflect Lieberman's philosophy about values, which amounts to little more than the exhibition of his virtuous personal life.

As for his Presidential candidacy, Lieberman seems to be modelling it roughly on his 1988 campaign against Weicker—taking on Bush from the right and the left. Lieberman remains more hawkish than Bush on Iraq, and more determined to bring the battle directly to the terrorists. And Lieberman will certainly use traditional Democratic issues like the environment and, to a lesser extent, tax fairness as well. As Lieberman put it to the ROCPAC group in Miami Beach, "internationalist, strong on defense, fiscally responsible, socially progressive—those are the key words."

It's a platform that shares a lot with the colleague Lieberman mentions most often: John McCain. "I love McCain," Lieberman told me. "I consider him one of my best friends in the Senate." McCain told me that he thought Lieberman would be a strong candidate. "He's a very decent, likable person who will wear well in a campaign," he said. "That is the kind of personality that does well in the retail politics of New Hampshire." I asked Lieberman whether he thought about asking McCain to be his running mate. "People have asked us that individually and together, and we always say we can't figure out which one of us would be Vice-President," he said, laughing. Then he turned serious. "You know, it's so far ahead. There's nobody I think better of, just in terms of integrity, purpose, honor, trustworthiness." McCain rejected the idea. "We will not run together," he said. "I won't leave the Republican Party, and he won't leave the Democratic Party."

I suggested to Lieberman that at least he and McCain feel the same way about George W. Bush.

"Exactly," he said. Then he corrected himself. "I probably don't feel as strongly negative."

Lieberman doesn't feel strongly negative about almost anyone in politics, and few seem to feel strongly negative about him. But in national politics that may be less of an advantage than it appears. Is civility really a political attribute that will mobilize an electorate? One of Lieberman's friends told me, "Joe's biggest problem is that he doesn't have any enemies."

Is John Edwards the Next Bubba?

Robert Draper

GQ | December 2002

On paper, John Edwards makes a near-perfect candidate for president: Young, wealthy, and articulate, with telegenic good looks and a built-in base of financial support among his fellow trial lawyers, he also hails from North Carolina at a time when Southern politicians seem to be the only ones capable of being elected to our nation's highest office. He also has the least political experience of any major presidential contender, having served less than one full term in the Senate. Then again, George W. Bush got elected President with a very similar resume. In this article, Robert Draper explores what lies behind this fresh new Democratic face. . . .

He used to jog in the cemetery. Scarcely a mile from where he had spent most of his legal career in Raleigh, it had looping swaths through one hundred acres of grass and granite irresistible to a young man long on energy but short on leisure time. He intended no irreverence. The cemetery welcomed tourists and admirers of mortuary art; it is a place of history, the Valhalla of North Carolina's ablest statesmen and defenders.

That said, he did not come here to meditate on man's greatness, folly, or brevity. He was only passing through. Born a poor boy, John Edwards was now a rich man, the state's most celebrated attorney. He loved his work and his family, and he had every reason to believe his good fortune would hold. And so it was with a certain impervious brio that he would circumnavigate the bleached monuments, glide past the 2,800 mounds irrigated by the tears of Confederate widows, disperse his sweat amongst the dead and then return to his neatly ordered existence.

One April afternoon in 1996, he buried his 16-year-old son, Wade, in the cemetery. An ill wind had literally blown the boy and his vehicle off Interstate 40. For months thereafter, John Edwards did not work. He did not jog. Instead, he and his wife, Elizabeth—the only woman in his life since law school—sequestered themselves in their Raleigh house. They still had their 14-year-old daughter, Cate, but a cosmic fulcrum had ruptured. From boyhood on, John Edwards had taken but a single errant step: He went to Clemson in the vain hope of becoming a football star so as to give his old man, a Tigers fan, a thrill. Otherwise, his path to success, from mill worker's son to titan of the North Carolina legal community, was swift and entirely sensible. When he was a kid, his parents gave him books about sports legends and one about Hitler. Heroes and evildoers occupied his world, along with regular decent folk and, yes, protectors from evil. John Edwards was one of the latter. He liked to say he stood up for the little guy against powerful interests. His favorite little guy, of course, was Wade. He was a sweet, shy boy yet full of surprises, and looking into his frail face John Edwards could not help but think hope for all humanity was incubating therein.

That winter John Edwards arose every morning before dawn and drove to the cemetery. Sitting on the marble bench engraved with the words AND I SEE YOU IN EACH SHINING STAR, he stared up at the gleaming statue of an angel cradling the likeness of Wade's face, and he spoke to his son and prayed. Then he went to the courthouse and defended another frail child. Her name was Valerie Lakey, and she had been effectively disemboweled while sitting upon an uncovered swimming-pool drain. During the opening day of testimony, when a witness described Valerie's screams, John Edwards began to cry. But he rallied. As the trial progressed, his evisceration of the drain manufacturer became a thing of archangelic beauty. At the end of his closing argument, John Edwards's voice plunged to barely audible depths as he quoted from an editorial about the recent death of a Raleigh boy: "Their loss is our loss. Their child is our child." He did not mention that the boy was his son Wade. But the jury heard enough and returned with an award of $25 million—a record in North Carolina to this day, though likely John Edwards himself would have eclipsed it had he not abruptly retired from defending frail children in the courtroom, just as he had quit jogging in the cemetery.

One day a close friend coaxed John Edwards out of his house and drove him northeast of town to William B. Umstead State Park. There, amid 5,500 acres of ragged forest, the friend showed John a trail where he and Wade had never been. John Edwards started to run again. Over time he found daylight, the death of his son less a pounding blow than an existential call to arms—leading him, in a sure if inarticulable way, to a conclusion he and his family, including Wade, had casually discussed for some time: that he should relinquish private life and run for the U.S. Senate.

The well-known Democratic pollster Harrison Hickman flew down from Washington at the end of 1996 to prod the neophyte. "Give me your biography," he said, meaning "tell me why I should be spending one minute with a nobody like you." John Edwards supplied it without blinking: *I grew up around ordinary folks, and as a lawyer I've stood up for them when the deck was stacked against them. I want to do the same thing on a larger scale—give a voice to those who have no voice.* Hickman walked away muttering, "This is the guy we want to work with."

Still, the pollster soon returned to Raleigh for the express purpose of warning John Edwards, "I have an obligation to tell you that the other side of this game is that you're going to lose your privacy, and people are going to say horrible things about you. You have a beautiful reputation and a lovely family, and it's not the worst thing in the world to say 'I don't want the millions of people in my state to think I'm a bad guy.'"

John Edwards paused to consider the risk—or perhaps he was only being polite, so that his reply would not jolt Hickman, though it did anyway: "Five years ago, that probably would've made a difference to me. But if you've ever had to get up on a table in a medical examiner's office and hug your son good-bye, you know there's nothing they can do to you."

The first time the Edwards family visited New Hampshire, on a college-scouting trip for Wade in 1996, Elizabeth requested iced tea at a restaurant only to be informed by the waitress that iced tea was "out of season." To a southerner, this is akin to conferring seasonality upon fried chicken or prayer. Today the Edwardses can still laugh at the memory, if bittersweetly. New wonderments supplement the old: Cate is a junior at Princeton, while 4-year-old Emma Claire and 2-year old Jack—blond-haired fruits of the hormone shots Elizabeth began receiving in her late forties—pillage the household. The Edwardses often travel to New Hampshire as a couple, attending an endless succession of "house parties," the gauntlets through which all presidential hopefuls must pass.

They blend in almost too well. The candidate's wife is unfussily attractive, with merciful pale eyes. Although she was once a brilliant lawyer and spends her idle time listening to college lectures on tape, she is both gabby and a generous listener, and she wears on her wedding finger the same $11 band John Edwards proffered as a penniless law student a quarter century ago. The partisan warhorses in attendance here are often surprised to learn she is the senator's wife. By the same token, it is a slight shock when one's eyes apprehend her willowy, cotton-clad husband, with his Dennis the Menace hairdo, clutching a Diet Coke and grinning like a jackass eating bees. The response elicited is not, as *People* magazine would have us believe, "How sexy!"

(Elizabeth: "They're not the kind of looks that just do it to me") but, rather, "So *young!*" In repose Edwards fits no one's image of a world leader, nor even of a high-priced lawyer. When he takes the floor, he is transformed only little by little. With the briefest of preambles, his undulating Carolina baritone launches into the log-cabin particulars: how he grew up in small towns, how his dad worked thirty-six years in cotton mills, how his mom's last job was delivering mail, how he was the first in his family to attend college. All true, but Edwards's regular-guy rhetoric doesn't captivate, in part because New Hampshirites have been led this way before but also because it's an awkward thing, standing in front of strangers and bragging about your humbleness.

Still, in this cozy New England cottage, the presumptive candidate is naked. Al Gore has been in such places, and his tendency to speechify is well remembered. George W. Bush was genial but uninformed and palpably homesick. Gradually, it becomes apparent that Edwards has nothing to hard-sell and nothing to hide. His footwork, though light, does not resemble a Liddy Dole promenade. His courtroom-inspired gesticulations are effusive but not Shakespearean. When he takes questions, he stuffs his hands into his front pockets, leans forward, cocks his head and frowns a bit in earnest consideration of the questioners' words. His responses are well formed but immediate; he's dying to say what he thinks. He opposed the Bush tax cut and now goes on record as saying the richest 1 percent should forgo their future breaks "as an act of patriotism." He opposes school vouchers, adding with a show of teeth, "I've got my reasons, but you've probably heard them, anyway." To an advocate of the single-payer health-insurance concept, Edwards breaks the news with a sympathetic smile: "It's just not gonna happen." On abortion Edwards is almost breathtakingly succinct: "I don't think it is for me—as a man or as the government—to tell women what they should do. It's just about that simple."

The obvious epiphany—he's working the jury!—is apt up to a point. One lawyer who tried a case with Edwards told me that in jury selection, Edwards could determine not only who would be on his side but also which potential juror would lead the others his way. Another colleague recalled that Edwards would imbue jurors with "something beyond themselves, so that when they decided the case they felt the decision was bigger than the case." This is the effect Edwards has on the Mont Vernon, New Hampshire, house party. The Vision has taken hold. If they vote for this man in 2004, they will be voting for levelheadedness and a basic social leveling. After the festivities wind down and the senator and his wife are whisked off into the horizon of pig roasts and coffee klatches, those left in Edwards's wake assume the formation of an admiring echo chamber as they reflect upon the stranger who came to town.

But a jury is not simply a limp wind sock that leaps at every tuneful gust any more than voters surrender in force to the canniest of orators. If either were so, lawyers would rule the world in fact, not merely in the shadowy imaginings of Republican Party tort-reform firebrands. Shortly after the house party had wound down, a few of us—the senator; his wife; his press secretary, Mike Briggs; and I—were driving through a hissing summer shower in a rented General Motors van, discussing populism and the prosperity gap, when I felt the need to pop an uncomfortable question: "Do you think it's illegitimate for people to view lawyers as a special-interest group?"

The career lawyer's untarnished face did not register surprise. Nor, however, did it flush with warmth. "No," he said quietly.

"Do you understand why so many people don't like lawyers?"

I had figured this to be an obvious question. But Edwards's answer had a tentative beginning. "I think I understand it," he said. "Mostly, what I've found to be a fairly common thing is that people have a distaste for lawyers in general—but they like their own lawyer. They don't really see what service lawyers provide, and they have this perception that lawyers make a lot of money and they don't do anything, they don't add anything. But when you talk to the people I represent—they see me working eighteen hours a day for them, sweating blood, and they have a totally different view. The way I always say it to my lawyer friends is, and it's a lot like politics: It's not about you. It's about the people you represent. If you ever think it's about you, you're going downhill."

Hitting his stride, the slender figure in the khakis, Izod shirt and loafers slouching just to my left encroached slightly into my airspace and, in a buoyant voice, continued, "When you think about the event we just went to, what are they thinking when someone's standing up and talking to them? They're thinking: Do I like this person? Are they honest? Are they being straight with me? Is this a bunch of crap? It's all about credibility and vision. *Trials* are totally about credibility. My trials, which last weeks or months at a time, they get to see everything that's right and wrong about you. They're sitting six feet away from you, eight hours a day. Now, just think about that. You can't fool those people. I mean, you can't! It's impossible! They'll figure out over time whether you're being straight with them, whether they can trust you. I think, by the way, that this concept pretty well applies to what I'm doing now."

It applies, at least, in New Hampshire. Which isn't nothing, as former senator Bob Kerrey reminded me: "You can't pull it off unless you finish first or second in New Hampshire. That's the most important thing to remember in presidential politics. If he's in third place, it's not a question of *if* he leaves the dance floor, only *when*." Kerrey has shared this opinion with his good friend from North Carolina. The Edwards strategy might thus proceed as follows: A cluster of lacklusterites—Senator Joe Lieberman, Senate Majority Leader Tom Daschle, Vermont governor Howard Dean, and House Minority Leader Dick Gephardt—will, in short order, give way to Edwards, Senator John Kerry and, if he seeks an encore performance, Gore. After New Hampshire, the primary action shifts to Edwards's kissing-cousin state of South Carolina. (He was, in fact, born in Seneca, South Carolina, in 1953.) Kerry, the Massachusetts liberal, so goes the playbook, will not fade the Dixie heat. That leaves Gore. Already, a host of former Gore staffers and financiers have aligned themselves with Edwards. Is it foolhardy to imagine that Democratic voters might do the same?

No—but wait. We are talking about a man who, by November 2004, will have held elective office for a grand total of six years—yes, yes, like Bush in 2000 but without W.'s political pedigree and Texas's thirty-two electoral votes. (North Carolina has fourteen.) Edwards's name recognition was so low in one poll—1 percent, half that of Al Sharpton's—the senator joked that taking the poll's margin of error into account, possibly a negative number of Americans know who he is. Unlike Bush in Texas, Edwards is not a beloved figure in his home state, though Bush is quite popular in North Carolina. Unlike the son of a president, he lacks the Rolodex by which hundreds of "pioneers" can be dispatched to gather $100,000 apiece. Edwards has further hamstrung his fund-raising efforts by pledging not to accept money from Washington lobbyists or political-action committees. He will, as Republicans delight in pointing out, take big checks from wealthy attorneys. The disciples of Karl Rove, the president's political consigliere, who feel about "predatory lawyers" the way the rest of us regard suicide bombers, may be mistaken in their conviction that John Edwards's previous career will repel voters by the millions. Then again, anyone who thinks Edwards will actually reap a windfall at the polls due to his having made millions bemoaning the plight of the injured is in serious need of medication.

Ironically, it is the specter of President Bush that not only illuminates John Edwards but also enlarges him. A Raleigh lawyer and Democratic Party activist who once employed Edwards, Wade Smith, told me, "There is a tide in the affairs of people that, when taken at its crest, makes all the difference. It's the time for John, whether he's ready or not. It's his time. The presidency has been thrust upon John more than John has thrust himself upon the presidency." I promptly disregarded Smith's musings as gaudy lawyer-speak. But the more time I spent rummaging through Edwards's personal history, the less absurd Smith's words seemed to sound. Could a one-term senator manage to beat *both* winners of the 2000 presidential election? Could this extraordinary time in our nation's history possibly be the time of a mill worker's son? Could America at its crest of patriotism abide anything so . . . American?

Should Edwards achieve the nomination, Rove and company will no doubt attempt to make him into an other slick-talking southerner with a law degree—Bubba redux. What should preoccupy them is not what Clinton and Edwards have in common but what Bush and Edwards have in common—and the point at which those similarities come to a jarringly definitive end.

W's proud anti-intellectual streak will not find an obliging foil in John Edwards. The landscape of Edwards's language is not freighted with "lockboxes" and other bureaucratic abstractions—nor, really, with abstractions of any kind. At one point during one of our conversations, he parried a personal question with a grinning "I'm not good at psychoanalysis," eerily refraining then governor Bush's comment to me four years ago that "I'm not a very good psychoanalyst guy." Like Bush, Edwards harbors a quietly persistent religious faith and a devotion to his family. Culturally, his taste runs to football. ("He's not read Dostoyevsky; he has no interest in reading Dostoyevsky; it's not gonna happen," says Elizabeth, who, like Laura Bush, is her family's serious reader.) As a lawyer, Edwards has a genius that lies not in the details but in his ability, as one legal observer remarks, to "put complex things in a simplified manner the jury could understand." Another attorney remembers watching Edwards instruct a jury that "there are four things you must remember." Edwards went through the first three points, paused, then shrugged and said, "Never mind. I guess there're just three." Recalls the observer with an admiring grin, "It just made him human."

At 49, Edwards is seven years younger than Bush. Both ambled through the counterculture of the late '60s and early '70s without accumulating battle scars. Edwards missed out on the draft and was fortunate to draw a high lottery number. While Bush spun the discs of George Jones, Edwards was partial to the Beach Boys—though by the end of college he had graduated to the

Allman Brothers. Edwards's college roommate, Bill Garner, recalls that Edwards registered as an Independent in 1972, had no affection for McGovern and did not truck with draft-card burners. (Edwards nonetheless insists, "No way did I vote for Nixon.") As a result, Rove's "oppo dudes" will find even less of prurient interest in Edwards's dorm closet than the Democrats found in George W.'s. Still, as Edwards told me, "I changed during the time I was in college"—he had taken in the somber lessons of Watergate and Vietnam and evolved his politics accordingly—unlike young George, who, by all accounts, left Yale precisely as flip and preppy as he entered it.

But an additional factor separates Edwards from the man he may challenge in 2004. While they mull over the obvious significance of his son Wade's death, observers have overlooked the strong possibility that, like George W. Bush, John Edwards is considering a run for the presidency largely because of his father. Through the fathers, in fact, one finds all the difference between these two men—the source of both Edwards's personal and political strengths.

Edwards was not trying to make this point the day we discussed Wallace Edwards, in the senator's ample space in the Dirksen Senate Office Building. He was simply expressing his admiration for his father, whom I had already met: a trim and easygoing fellow in his seventies, happily retired in the shuttered mill town of Robbins, North Carolina, after spending half his life working in seven Milliken textile plants throughout the South. The elder Edwards spoke without bitterness of how his lack of a higher education meant his workday often consisted of training college kids to be his eventual superiors. But ruefulness was evident in the son's voice as he told me, "I remember my father, when he'd work these long hours at the mill, he'd get up early in the morning—I wanna say five or six—and watch these shows on television to be better educated. I remember him sitting there, watching them. . . . It wasn't like an anger about it. But he always knew that not having a college education—or, more positively, having an education—was the key to doing things out there in the world.

"I still remember, we went into a restaurant in Georgia. It was a Sunday at lunch—this is the kind of thing you remember when you're young. We sat down; we're all dressed up; we'd come from church. And they handed us the menus, and my dad looked at it and said, 'We can't pay for this.' And I remember how embarrassing it was for all of us, how we had to get up and leave."

Eventually, the Edwardses were not poor. But to afford their firstborn a better life—to send him to college—the mother also had to work. And Bobbie Edwards did, always: stripping furniture, folding sheets, sewing bathing suits, typing voter registration cards, delivering mail. And so the ever-grinning boy with the silver-capped front tooth masking the equally steely competitive streak quietly resolved that his parents' labors would pay off. Like George Walker Bush, the boy christened Johnny Reed Edwards vowed not to disappoint his father. But there's a bit of a difference, wouldn't you say?

To be an Edwards rather than a Bush was to lack a safety net. Yearning to be a lawyer, Edwards nonetheless majored in textiles at NC State, just in case law school turned out to be as futile a fantasy as playing wide receiver for the Clemson Tigers did. He blitzed through undergraduate in three years, studied his ass off because he didn't know anyone of influence; absent his 3.8 GPA, he didn't have a prayer of getting into law school. Because his family couldn't afford tuition at Duke, he settled for second best, the University of North Carolina School of Law, where his mother's wages paid for the fall semesters and his father's Christmas bonuses covered the spring tuitions. After graduating with honors and spending three years as a corporate lawyer in Nashville, Edwards returned to Raleigh and signed on with the smaller but dynamic Tharrington Smith, where, recalls senior partner Wade Smith, "John quickly established himself as an excellent lawyer and the world beat a path to his door."

Bush inherited wealth and family connections; Edwards inherited a work ethic. How could he coast? "These people would come and sit on your couch, and they can't pay their bills. They don't know where their food's coming from. Something really bad has happened to them or their families. And they're describing what happened in their cases against, you know, some huge insurance company, or some corporate concern. And you realize then that it's a very disparate condition of life. Particularly in cases for the kids—they were probably the worst: I'd wake up constantly at three in the morning, before and during trial, saying I didn't do enough; I should've done this or that; if we don't do every single thing that can be done. . . . I mean, when you're representing some child who has a whole lifetime in front of him, I just couldn't stand that thought. It was just that simple. Trials, no matter how professional someone wants to portray them as—these trials are very, very, very personal. Especially when you're taking on their cause."

That cause, of course, he associated with the mill worker's cause. Over time his clients began to look startlingly familiar to him. It was not a Bush they resembled. "When I started doing these cases, spending time with people in mobile homes, out in the country—these were the same people I'd known *all my life.*"

Then Edwards added with a sly half grin, "By the way. Interesting enough, I realized over time that these were the same people who sat on juries."

No John Edwards speech is complete without the line "I'm proud of what I did for twenty years; for twenty years I walked into courtrooms and I fought for the little guy." In the 1998 U.S. Senate race, he pledged to do the same on a statewide scale when he came out of nowhere to coldcock Jesse Helms's ventriloquist dummy, the jowly pig farmer Lauch Faircloth. He arrived on Capitol Hill at a time when a lawyer's skills were particularly useful. Four weeks into his tenure, Edwards was supervising the depositions of Monica Lewinsky and Hillary Clinton aide Sidney Blumenthal. Two weeks later, he gave what was thought to be the most forceful evidentiary presentation in favor of Clinton's acquittal. As an attorney, Edwards told me, "most of your life isn't spent in the courtroom. It's spent figuring out how to bring two sides together in resolution." The freshman thus interposed himself between Senators Phil Gramm and Paul Sarbanes and with them worked round the clock to negotiate their seemingly intractable differences, leading to passage of a banking-reform bill that had been comatose literally for decades. That spring Edwards took to the Senate floor and vivisected a small-business-unfriendly Y2K bill—in the process outraging its cosponsor, John McCain, although later the Arizona senator spread compliments about the first-termer and would eventually join forces with him on campaign-finance reform and the Patients Bill of Rights.

In a matter of months, John Edwards had become one of the most effective legislators on the Hill. The following year, candidate Gore's flirtation with Edwards alerted the media to the latter's telegenicity. By early 2001, the Democrats had reclaimed the Senate and Edwards sat on five committees, including the prime-time judiciary and intelligence panels. Four years into his political life, Edwards is today a national media figure. As to whether the little guy back home rejoices in this, the jury is out. North Carolina is famously schizophrenic, as evidenced by Edwards's Senate seat, which an incumbent has not held on to in the past six elections. As seemingly every press release reminds us, the senator "has visited all one hundred counties during his first term." His dedication to local issues—hurricane relief, river preservation, textile-worker retraining—is assiduous and often passionate. Still, anecdotal evidence abounds that the national media's worship of John Edwards, though hardly of his doing, rubs North Carolinians the wrong way.

The tightrope upon which he balances duty and ambition will become increasingly threadbare as his presidential ambitions gain visibility. As he has increased his out-of-state forays, Edwards has stepped up his attacks on the Bush administration. He has seized upon the sagging economy as a failure of the Bush administration's imagination. "The president's plan is: Do nothing to promote economic growth in the short run, and pretend that deficit-exploding tax cuts for the wealthiest will promote economic growth in the long run. That is wrong for our economy and our security," Edwards said this past October. On these little-guy issues, the senator shoots comfortably from the hip. He is less acute in his foreign-policy critiques—including, most recently, the question of what to do about Saddam Hussein. In August, Edwards's remarks on the subject were limited to demanding that Bush seek international backing for a regime change in Iraq. But by October, Edwards was telling CNN's Wolf Blitzer that "sitting month after month listening to briefings" on the Senate Intelligence Committee had convinced him that "every single day that goes by, [Saddam is] increasing his chances of nuclear capability. He could be six to nine months from getting nuclear weapons." Edwards offered no evidence that Saddam was cozying up to Al Qaeda and is thus an urgent target in America's war on terrorism. Instead the senator was citing nuke lust as sufficient cause for intervention. Why, then, didn't Edwards join fellow presidential aspirant Joe Lieberman last year in calling for Saddam's ouster? Why did he step in line only when the midterm Republican drumbeats had distracted the little guy with talk of war? The downside to having a fresh face is that credibility is not easily won on the fly. In New Hampshire, a sarcastic Edwards asked, "Would the FBI know serious foreign intelligence if they saw it—and if they did, would they know what to do with it?" But he offered nothing in the way of thoughtful reform, just as his call to arms on education—"Every single one of your families should get as good an education as the richest family on earth!"—has no follow-up in policy proposals. This past summer, Edwards voiced concern about America's crime rate. His chosen area of attack, the nation's various parole and probation systems, is intriguing. But when I asked for details, he confessed, "It's complicated, a federal, state, and local deal. Right now I'm laying down the concept. We're working on it as we speak. And we don't know the cost of it yet."

But his greatest challenge involves tapping a vast but largely dormant populace that knows little if anything about him. It's safe to say that African-American voters will wish to know where a southern senator stands on matters dear to their hearts. Only very recently has Edwards begun to speak directly to that constituency, apart from writing letters of support to North Carolina black colleges seeking grants, and being among several cosponsors to award

Rosa Parks a Congressional Gold Medal and establish a national museum of African-American history. Asked if the state's African-Americans approved of Edwards's efforts, James Ferguson II, a civil rights lawyer in Charlotte and friend of the senator's, answered carefully, "I think he has strong support from those African-Americans who have gotten to know him."

Edwards faces a lot of house parties, in other words. But his reticence on race—the subtext of virtually every Senate campaign in North Carolina for the past half century *except* for his—is a curiosity that dogged me throughout the months I spent rummaging through his history. Edwards attended junior high just as desegregation began in Robbins. There had been Klan marches a few miles east and a torched school just to the north. How much of this had Edwards absorbed?

One day in New Hampshire, we drove toward Portsmouth in the middle of the afternoon. Two events were behind him and another two awaited, and although Edwards had been noticeably jazzed by his receptions, his Carolina drawl reflected a yearning for downtime. Asked to recall his early memories of racial inequity, the senator paused for a moment before replying, "I remember there was a teacher when I was in Georgia, sixth grade, who announced to the class that he was thinking of not teaching because they were going to let—and he used the N-word—come into our school. And I was disgusted by that."

"Had your parents talked to you about race?"

Again he paused. Then: "I just remember more an attitude of my parents. Which was that anyone and everyone deserved respect."

Fumbling through my notes, I said, "Do you remember at your high school when there was a protest among blacks that they ought to have their own homecoming queen?"

A slight smile. "Vaguely. I don't remember the details. I remember it happening."

"Do you remember," I prodded, "when your football team played a game near Chapel Hill and the other team taunted yours for having black players?"

"I thought I had a good memory," Edwards said, laughing. "I remember the incident. We were playing in Rockingham, and I don't think they had any black players. And I think they were throwing things at our bus, if I remember correctly."

He did. But that was all he said, and in two minutes' time, we had covered the trifling subject of race in the South in the time of John Edwards and were now on to the weightier matters of lawyers, FBI reform, and New Hampshire house parties. When we arrived in Portsmouth, I stepped out of the senator's van and into my rental car and drove out of town muttering to myself. Was he really that insensitive, or inattentive, or averse to introspection? James Ferguson had assured me that this was not the case, and my own experiences with the man simply did not square with his almost jarring unexpansiveness. Perhaps, I decided, Edwards preferred not to presume to understand a pain of which he was ignorant. Robbins had no black residents during his youth. A mere dozen graduated with him. Johnny Edwards's worldview spun out of the mill: Respect everyone. I gave up on the matter, not altogether satisfied with my conclusion.

It occurred to me only days later that I had been deaf to a continuing refrain espoused by virtually everyone who knew Edwards well, including him. The press had taken to fashioning the senator as a populist, even an us-against-them populist. Edwards understood how a listener could develop this impression of him. But, he told me, "in my mind, there's a difference between being for the little guy and against people who've done well." To Edwards, class warfare is demagoguery, and demagogues are, among other things, phonies. So it wouldn't be his nature to burn with outrage and stoke it in others. His cases, and now his policies, sought remediation—a leveling, not blind vengeance. And, I now remembered, Edwards did not always broadcast his remedies, any more than he politicized his grief over his son's death. Sometimes he just did what he had to do, as when he rented a U-Haul after a devastating hurricane, filled it with a thousand dollars' worth of food and provisions, drove it to Myrtle Beach, dropped off the contents at the Red Cross and drove back to Raleigh. I returned to my notes, wondering if I had missed anything.

A black classmate of the senator's had told me about the African-American protest for representation on the homecoming court, but he had offered no details. Then I remembered that another high school chum, Edwards's eventual college roommate, Bill Garner, had brought up the subject as well. The few blacks at North Moore High had staged a sit-in on the campus lawn, Garner told me. And, he said, Johnny Edwards had walked up to the group and spoken with them. Then he sat down with them.

Edwards had not volunteered that detail. Perhaps he didn't remember it. Perhaps he deemed it puny in scope. This was not, after all, a lunch counter or the front of a bus. Only a stupid homecoming-court sit-in. A little thing. That's all there was to do. So he did it—spur of the moment, sitting down for the little guy.

The Unlikely Rise of Howard Dean

Meryl Gordon

New York magazine | Feb. 24, 2003

Howard Dean is a pro-gun liberal Democrat, and one of the few presidential can-
didates to flatly oppose the war in Iraq. A physician who once worked on Wall Street,
he gave up medicine to become a five-term governor of Vermont, then quit the state-
house to run for president. In other words, he's not your typical candidate—which,
as Meryl Gordon discovers, may be just what the people want. . . .

Howard Dean is running for president as Jimmy Stewart. The buttoned-down
Democrat begins campaign speeches by conceding to his audience, "You don't
know me," before describing his transformation from medical doctor to Vermont's five-term governor. Instead of jetting around the country on chartered
planes, Dean flies coach on Southwest Airlines and JetBlue. Known for
padding around his governor's office with holes in his socks and plain, well-
worn suits, this frugal contender for the highest office in the free world avoids
$450 hotel suites on his travels, preferring to bunk at the homes of supporters,
even though it often means being shoehorned into kids' quarters. When he
comes to New York, as he does often these days, he stays at his mom's place.

It was there, in fact, that Dean, suddenly the hottest comer in the densely
bunched Democratic pack, entertained 30 moneyed and influential party stal-
warts last week, including superlawyer David Boies and JFK speechwriter
Ted Sorenson. Still, the crowd wasn't exactly slumming: The Dean family
homestead is a Park Avenue apartment serenely decorated with small African
sculptures and modernist paintings and prints.

Let his Democratic rivals hype their only-in-America humble origins—Joe
Lieberman is the son of a liquor-store owner; John Edwards's father worked
in the textile mills—Howard Brush Dean III is the proud patrician product
of Park Avenue and 85th Street, the son, grandson, and great-grandson of
investment bankers. After graduating from Yale, Dean, too, worked on Wall
Street before quitting to attend Albert Einstein medical school, where he met
his wife, Long Island-born physician Judith Steinberg. Dean didn't just summer
in the Hamptons; his parents belonged to the Maidstone Club, and his family's
Sag Harbor roots trace back to an eighteenth-century whaling captain.

He enjoys watching New Yorkers' attitudes change when they discover he's not a hick from the state of Ben & Jerry's. "New Yorkers are tough; they want to know what you've got," says Dean. "But I've never had people open their hearts to me more than when they discover that my wife is Jewish and I'm from New York. They look at you completely differently. It's flabbergasting."

What's even more surprising is Dean's brashness in setting his sights on 1600 Pennsylvania Avenue as an unknown without a national base of deep-pocketed supporters. The man's sole political experience has been governing an aging-hippie and dairy farmers' theme park of a state with a population—600,000—one third that of Queens. Even Dean's loyal mother assumed her oldest son couldn't be serious when he told her a year ago that he was planning to run for president. "I thought it was preposterous, the silliest thing I'd ever heard," says Andree Maitland Dean, a widow (her husband died in August 2001) who works as an art appraiser. "It seemed like such a quixotic quest."

But once Al Gore dropped out of the race in December, the contest became the most wide-open Democratic presidential competition in more than two decades, and Dean's campaign has gained momentum from his outspoken skepticism about war with Iraq. Dean is the most anti-war of the current Democratic contenders, with the exception of Al Sharpton: "I'm the only one of the four elected officials running at this point who did not support the president's Iraq resolution—and I still don't."

That said, the compact 54-year-old with graying black hair and piercing blue-gray eyes is more than a single-issue anti-war candidate. He's a strict fiscal conservative (he consistently balanced Vermont's budget); he's a staunch health-care advocate (he made sure the state provided health insurance for all children); he's a dedicated environmentalist (he protected thousands of acres of open lands); and he's a social liberal (he signed the controversial legislation permitting same-sex civil unions). In political style, he's notably candid, and he's got executive experience—he just stepped down as Vermont's governor after eleven years in office—no small thing given that four of our last five presidents have been governors.

All of this has suddenly vaulted Dean to the political forefront. "I'm hearing great things," says Terry McAuliffe, chairman of the Democratic National Committee, while stressing that he has no favorite in the race. "Howard's got a good message, and people are enthusiastic about him." Dean has also begun to draw opponents' attention. The Republican National Committee in January put out a seven-page document snarling that Dean is "an ultra-liberal" and "out of the mainstream." Dean's response: "I've arrived."

Now comes the work. He's making regular money-hunting forays into Manhattan, and visiting the critical early-primary states. Since it's less than a two-hour drive from his home in Burlington, Vermont, to New Hampshire, he's in the first primary state weekly: A recent poll of New Hampshire Democrats by the independent American Research Group showed Dean as the solid second-place finisher, nipping at Kerry's heels and garnering twice the support of Joe Lieberman, Dick Gephardt, and John Edwards.

An upbeat man with a ready smile, Dean exudes coiled energy and ambition when I meet with him for the first time, at the Regency Hotel, in January. Having reluctantly upgraded to a new Paul Stuart suit, he is wooing major Democratic fund-raisers—breakfast with hotelier Jonathan Tisch this morning, later a meeting with financier Roy Furman, and a dinner in his honor at the home of billionaire George Soros. I ask Dean for a preview of his political sales pitch, and it's like hitting the fast-forward button.

"I'm very direct and very blunt," he begins. "The pitch is that I'm different from every other candidate in the race, I'm a governor, I'm the only one who's ever balanced a budget, I'm the only one who doesn't support the president on Iraq. They can talk about health care; I've done it. They can talk about land conservation; I've done it. They can talk about early-childhood intervention; I've done it."

Dean isn't a physically prepossessing guy, he's not warm and cuddly, yet he has a mesmerizing impact once he speaks. Following up later on Dean's Manhattan foray, I learn that he'd scored. "Howard Dean impressed me as a serious candidate with a broad vision and a fresh voice," Soros says via e-mail. "Like Kerry, he is certainly a very attractive alternative to Bush." Furman, the vice-chairman of Jefferies & Company, was so enthused he agreed to dial for dollars for Dean. "Howard has magnetism. It doesn't bother me that my friends don't have the slightest idea who he is," says Furman, an early supporter of that other small-state governor turned presidential long shot, Bill Clinton. "Dean will be discovered."

The Left Coast Democratic cabal, too, is flirting with his insurgent candidacy. *The West Wing's* Martin Sheen—the fictional New England governor turned president who also has a practicing-doctor wife—has endorsed him. On a recent L.A. swing, Dean had an audience with Warren Beatty and Annette Bening at the Polo Lounge. (Dean's favorite movie is *Bullworth*, and he does a hilarious version of Beatty's money-rap speech.) The Vermonter-New Yorker also pitched his ideas to Rob Reiner, Larry David, Stephen Bing, Norman Lear, and Nora Ephron at a Spago lunch. "I liked him," Ephron says. "He has a modesty and a lack of razzle-dazzle that's charming."

It is bone-chillingly cold, a mere ten degrees out, when I arrive at Dean's recently leased campaign headquarters in Burlington a week after our Regency Hotel meeting. Furnished with beat-up desks and chairs purchased from the University of Vermont, the offices are located on the fourth floor of a redbrick building that houses a popular restaurant, the Vermont Pub and Brewery.

While some Dean staff members have offices with pretty views of Lake Champlain and the snow-covered Adirondacks, the candidate himself, who today is wearing a blue sweatshirt, corduroys, and boots, has chosen to work out of a cubby-hole overlooking the street. Dean moved to Burlington to do his residency in 1978. "My life isn't restaurants and theaters," he says. "It's skiing and hiking and camping." While building a medical practice, he lobbied successfully for the development of a bike path instead of condominiums hard on the shores of Lake Champlain. That whetted his appetite for politics, and in 1982, he was elected as a Democratic state representative to the part-time legislature. Four years later, he ran for and won the mostly ceremonial job of lieutenant governor. Dean abruptly became governor in 1991 when Republican incumbent Richard Snelling died of a heart attack. Dean got that news while examining a patient. "It was the ultimate medical emergency," he recalls. "I actually hyperventilated, and then I caught myself and thought, *You'd better stop this, or you're not going to be much good to anyone.*"

Dean looks at his watch; he has to interrupt our interview to meet his 17-year-old son, Paul, at home to help shovel snow off the backyard ice-hockey practice rink. Inviting me along, he jokes that his car—a rusted-out 1989 Chevy Blazer— is "not very presidential," and that his home is not grand, either. "Judy and I don't care much about material things," he says. The Deans have a net worth of $4 million, according to tax returns: He says he received $25,000 from his father at age 21 and made the rest through work, prudent investments, and frugal living. Driving along the icy streets, he expresses pride that his wife has maintained her own life as an internist, even doing house calls, opting out of the role of pol's wife. Unlike the wives of his rivals, "She's not going to campaign for me," he says. As we pull up in front of his tan two-story modern home, he casually mentions that since the once-a-week house-keeper comes on Thursday and this is a Monday, the place is a bit of a mess: "None of us is big on housekeeping."

Sure enough, the place looks like it's been ransacked. The garage is a jumble of bicycles, camping equipment, old campaign signs, and tools. Following Dean into the ground-floor rec room, I have to step carefully over an army of L.L. Bean boots, boxes of books and papers from the governor's office, and Dean's half-filled suitcase, dropped haphazardly the night before on his return from a weekend in Iowa. "I never bother to unpack anymore," he says.

He leads me up the stairs, covered with ripped ancient green shag carpet, to the sunny living area, with a soaring A-frame ceiling. He makes me a cup of herbal tea and introduces his gray three-legged cat, Katie (she had cancer). Excusing himself to join his son outside, Dean is half out of the room when he turns to say, "Feel free to look around."

This is such an astonishing offer from a man running for president that I toss it back at him: "You mean, look in the medicine cabinets and open the drawers?" Dean looks startled for a second, then grins and says, "I have no secrets." And then he leaves.

Ah, the tyranny of being trusted. I wonder for a second what Matt Drudge would do, but limit myself to inspecting things that are easily visible. It's a much-lived-in house, with an Oriental rug, a white couch and wing chair that need reupholstering, a chess set, and framed pictures on every flat surface showing the athletic Dean foursome (daughter Anne is a freshman at Yale) in outdoorsy activities that would look at home in a Ralph Lauren catalogue. A menorah is perched on a living-room shelf: Dean was baptized Catholic (as was his mother), was raised Episcopalian (his father's denomination), and became a Congregationalist ("I don't go to church a lot, but I pray at night"). But because Judaism is important to his wife, the family celebrates Jewish holidays and the kids consider themselves Jewish.

The cat rubs my leg, a silent chaperone, as I head downstairs to the ground floor. Dean's office is filled with mementos, including two beat-up guitars (he serenaded legislators with "On the Road Again" at a party last year, an in-your-face response to complaints he was away too much). A certificate from Yale's Pierson College hangs on the wall. He was a freshman in 1967, when George W. Bush was a senior, but the two didn't know each other. Still, there is a family connection: Bush's grandmother was a bridesmaid at the wedding of Dean's grandmother.

At Yale, Dean was a political-science major, but his college friend Ralph Dawson, now a Manhattan lawyer, says Dean wasn't politically ambitious then: "If he wanted to be president, he certainly didn't tell me." Dean opposed the war in Vietnam, but he wasn't an outspoken protester. He was classified 1-Y by his draft board because of an unfused vertebra in his back. Dean's sixties-era entry in his Yale yearbook lists his future occupation as "living" and quotes a favorite Neil Young song: "Don't let it bring you down . . ."

But the most revealing keepsake in this room is a collage of beer coasters, which Dean collected as an exchange student in England at age 17. It's a memory of another life. Asked about Dean's student hobbies, Dawson offers an amused reply: "Well, he drank."

Not anymore. "I quit drinking when I got married in 1981," Dean says later. "I didn't think I handled liquor well. Actually, I drank beer. I tended to misbehave." He won't elaborate but says he was never arrested for drunk driving, and there is no alcoholism in his family. "What's funny when you're 18 isn't funny when you're 30," he says. "So I just quit."

Arriving back at his campaign office, Dean—to the dismay of his staff— brings me into a meeting to plot out his schedule. It's a crash course in the insane logistics of a presidential campaign moving into warp speed: The biggest problem is allocating Dean's time, so he can get to the big-money Democrats before they pledge allegiance to another candidate. "Goddamn it, we have to meet everyone at once," he says in a rare moment of frustration. "If those guys go for Kerry before I even get to see them, I'm going to hit the ceiling."

Judith Steinberg's medical practice is located in a converted barnlike creamery along a well-traveled road in Shelburne, a short drive from Burlington. With her shoulder-length dark hair, glasses, and shy smile, this petite woman in a berry sweater set and conservative black skirt has the look of the smartest girl in med school; Dean says she was the far better student.

If her husband weren't running for president, Steinberg (she uses her maiden name professionally) would be perceived as a baby-boomer I-don't-know-how-she-does-it working mom who's too busy with a demanding job and a teenage son to pay much attention to her spouse's career. But in an era when Americans expect to see political wives standing by their men, it will be interesting to watch how voters react to Steinberg's decision to stay out of the fray. "I'm involved in Howard's life, but I'm not very involved in his politics," she says. "He is able to separate it and really respects what I do. I support what he does and we meet in the middle, and it seems to work so far."

Unlike every other political household in America, the Deans do not have cable TV at home ("We believe the less TV, the better"), so she hasn't watched his campaign speeches, as televised on C-SPAN, and is seemingly unaware of his surging wave of support. "I think he's happy," she says. "I guess I haven't really felt the groundswell."

Steinberg, 49, is the daughter of two doctors; she grew up in Roslyn and attended Princeton. Until her husband became governor, they worked side-by-side in these medical offices. When I ask about their styles as doctors, she smiles and says, "I'm a very methodical person; I do all the tests. Howard tends to jump to conclusions. He's usually right, but he just leaps."

In live-and-let-live Vermont, Steinberg has been able to maintain her privacy, with only occasional grousing in the press about the state's invisible First Lady. She's never campaigned in her husband's races, she's avoided reporters (Dean's veteran press secretary, Susan Allen, who accompanied me, had never been to Steinberg's office before), and she doesn't do political entertaining. "I hate to cook," she admits.

What kind of a First Lady would she be? Her radical notion: She wants to practice medicine in Washington. I can't resist joking about the challenge of the Secret Service screening her patients or the lobbyists eager to claim her as their internist. "I don't know that people would come to me because of who I was married to," says Steinberg.

It's Tuesday, February 11. The clock is ticking inexorably every day toward war, the troops are being airlifted overseas, the networks have staffed up in Qatar and Turkey, and Howard Dean is still loudly proclaiming, at candidate forums in New York and Iowa and New Hampshire, that attacking Iraq is a mistake. "I'm not a dove," he hastens to add; he just doesn't believe this particular battle is one that America should take on alone. "I don't think the president has made his case. He's got to show Saddam possesses nuclear weapons, and I don't think there's a shred of evidence for that." Dean says he sees biological and chemical weapons as insufficient grounds for a unilateral attack, and he favors the French proposal to triple the inspectors and further pressure Iraq rather than launching missiles in March, adding that he would back an invasion if authorized by the United Nations. "Nobody can run for president without being willing to use the full and maximum power of the United States," Dean says. "But I'm one president who would be very careful if I had the opportunity."

If he's more passionate about restraint than the other Democratic candidates, it's partly because he has a personal reason for wanting to spare families the agony of body bags and MIA phone calls. Back in 1974, his younger brother Charlie, 24, was traveling through Laos, paddling with a friend down the Mekong River taking pictures, when the two were seized by the Communists and charged with being American spies. Months later, word came back that they had secretly been executed; the bodies have never been recovered.

Dean never mentions this family tragedy in speeches and usually moves through the topic briskly with reporters. Unsure what to say, I tell him that my own brother died—of an asthma attack—and that I am still haunted by his death. Dean gives me a look of recognition—which leads to a running conversation over several days about the agony of losing a sibling, how it changes you, the pain of watching your folks suffer. "It was awful for everyone, but it was worse for my parents," says Dean, who shared a childhood bedroom—complete with bunk beds—with the irrepressible Charlie. "It just wastes you. Everyone falls apart; they just fall apart in different ways."

His mother recalls the family's desperate efforts to save Charlie; the Deans have long believed that their globetrotting son worked for the CIA but have never gotten confirmation. Her husband flew to Laos and knocked on all the diplomatic doors, trying to ascertain at what jungle location Charlie was being held; Andree Dean followed a month later. "I kept going from person to person," she recalls. "It was so awful." Thinking back now, she also regrets the family's stiff-upper-lip reaction afterward, wondering about the impact on her other three sons—Howard; James, now a Fairfield, Connecticut, market researcher; and William, a Boston bond trader. "We could never discuss it at home, because Howard's father would get so upset," she says. "That wasn't the era when you talked about things."

Dean's wife tells me he rarely spoke about Charlie for years. Dean's father died in August 2001, and that event combined with the cataclysm a few weeks later of September 11—Dean came to Manhattan three days after the attacks to see the damage—spurred him to examine his own past. So he went to Laos last February, visiting what's believed to be his brother's burial area joining vol-

unteers excavating other sites for American remains. Dean spoke with a witness who claimed he had seen his brother's body dumped in a foxhole. "It gave
me closure," he says, but his voice grows husky: "It never goes away. It gets
better, but it never goes away." Then he snaps back to the present, linking these
feelings to his opposition to invading Iraq: "Most people have no idea, except
people who lost their kids in combat. That's why I think my fellow politicians
running for the Democratic nomination are wrong on Iraq."

The next morning, Dean is driving to the Burlington airport, sweet-talking
a prospective donor on the cell phone: "Now that Al Gore and Tom Daschle
aren't running, I was hoping . . . You will? It's $2,000 a couple. And I want
to hear more about that idea . . ." He's so caught up in the conversation that
he misses the entrance to the parking garage; for the past eleven years, he
had state troopers driving him everywhere. At the newsstand, I suggest buying
two copies of the New York *Times* for the flight, and he stares at me disap-
provingly. "I'm a fanatic recycler," he says; we will share and leave the paper
later in an airport-lounge seat for other travelers.

This trip to Washington, to appear at a NARAL [National Abortion and
Reproductive Rights Action League] dinner in honor of the thirtieth anniversary of legal abortion, was a last-minute invite that has already screwed up
his schedule. So when US Airways announces that our Washington plane has
been canceled, Dean is not a happy man; we're hustled onto a flight to
Philadelphia.

Changing planes in Philly, Dean decides to race-walk several concourses
rather than wait for a shuttle bus. Because of confusing signs, we end up going
through security again. Unlike in Burlington, where Dean is famous, no one
recognizes him here despite his appearances on *Meet the Press* and *Face the
Nation*. The guard unzips his suitcase and rummages through his stuff. Dean
hums under his breath to control his tension; he makes the flight.

At the Omni Shoreham a few hours later, it's controlled pandemonium,
with anti-abortion protesters waving placards outside, a heavy police presence, and 1,300 guests milling around. Tonight is the first time that all six
candidates have appeared together on a stage. Dean is scheduled fifth on the
program, not an auspicious slot, and he looks comically short (he claims 5
feet 8¾ inches) standing next to the craggy Kerry (6 feet 4). John Edwards
leads off, warning that a "chill wind blows tonight," followed by Joe
Lieberman, who comes across as well-meaning but sonorous. Reverend Al

wins huge cheers as he describes telling an anti-abortion protester: "Young lady, it's time for the Christian right to meet the right Christian." Next comes Richard Gephardt, who gets a chilly reception as he apologizes for his early opposition to abortion.

Dean starts off awkwardly, venturing a Taliban joke, proposing that the Bush administration is so regressive that soon girls won't be allowed to go to school. No one laughs. Uh-oh. But then he starts to build. He talks about why he's against laws demanding parental consent for minors who want an abortion, how as a doctor he once had a pregnant patient who was 12 and he suspected the father was her father. The crowd applauds—he's winding up, ad-libbing. People are waving light wands from the tables and jumping to their feet. It's Dean's moment. Poor Kerry, with laryngitis, follows and can't score.

"Dean was electrifying," a political consultant working for a rival candidate concedes moments later. A TV anchorman shares the same view: "The headline tonight: DEAN." The instant verdicts are repeated in newspapers and magazines in the next few days: *The New Republic's* Ryan Lizza, for example, writes that Dean's "style is to grab the political live wire that everyone else is terrified of touching."

It's one thing to dazzle the liberals in Manhattan, Los Angeles, or Washington, but winning the hearts and minds of voters in Live-Free-Or-Die New Hampshire is a tougher proposition. Flying to the Granite State the next morning, Dean starts off at the Havenwood-Heritage Heights Retirement Community, in Concord, with a decent turnout of 50 people. Citing his accomplishment in balancing Vermont's budget, he attacks Bush's tax cut and soaring deficits, rips the administration for despoiling the environment, and promises to pass universal health insurance, thundering his tag line again and again: "We can do better."

But what these senior citizens want is to hear Dean's explanation of the most controversial Vermont legislation passed on his watch: same-sex civil unions. One elderly man asks, "How do you convince people that civil unions aren't gay marriages?"

"The only people who call civil unions 'gay marriage' are poorly informed reporters and the right wing of the Republican Party," Dean replies. "Civil unions mean gay people get to have the same rights I do. Such as if I get sick, my wife can visit me in the hospital; if I die, my wife gets the estate without probate."

He's trying to sell this emotionally loaded topic as a civil-rights issue, neutralizing the stereotype of guys and gals in heavy leather setting up housekeeping: "Marriage is between a man and a woman. I agree with you—most Americans aren't going to support gay marriage, but most Americans will support equal rights." And then he closes with the phrase that makes him beloved in the gay community: "If you're brave enough to go to Afghanistan, and brave enough to rescue people at the World Trade Center, you're brave enough to have your own rights."

When the Vermont Supreme Court ruled in 1999 that gay couples were entitled to the same legal rights as heterosexuals, Dean was thrust reluctantly into an ugly battle. This was not his crusade, but he did the right thing and took the heat, receiving hate mail and death threats as he traveled not-so-quaint Vermont talking up the civil unions legislation. (Many lawmakers who courageously voted in favor were defeated in the next election.) "I marched with Howard in a Fourth of July parade," says State Attorney General William Sorrell, "and people were throwing things and screaming, 'You fucking cocksucker.'" Dean quips that being called "a child molester" and "queer" was great training for a presidential campaign: "Given some of the things the Republicans do, what the right wing does on a national level, I figured now that I had a taste of it, I was ready to run."

As the lone Democratic contender who has an A rating from the National Rifle Association, Dean is also questioned frequently about his position on gun control. He supports existing legislation (the Brady bill, closing the gun-show loophole, banning the sale of assault weapons) but doesn't favor national gun-control laws, insisting it's a state issue. Citing Vermont's low crime rate, he likes to note that his rural hunting state has only two gun laws: "You can't bring a loaded gun to school, and you can't have a loaded gun in the car. We don't want people to shoot deer out of the window of a moving car; we don't think that's fair for the deer." He usually gets a laugh from that line but doesn't necessarily win converts. "If gun control is your only issue, I'm not going to be your candidate," he tells a woman who presses him on the topic at a Manhattan gathering. "If you can get over that, I can give you health care, a balanced budget . . ." She looks skeptical but says, "I'll try."

It's impossible to know whether Dean's newfound visibility is a blip or represents the first stage of an out-of-nowhere Democratic insurgency. Dean goes into the race as the most underfunded of serious candidates: While his Washington rivals have multimillion-dollar war chests and are aiming to raise $15 million to $20 million this year, Dean, who pulled in a mere $315,000 in January, is already behind on his goal of $10 million. "I think he's a very attractive guy, and he has bold convictions," says Harold Ickes, the veteran Clinton strategist, "but I just wonder if he can raise the money."

Along with momentum, however, he does have the gift of time. Dean's only job right now is running for the presidency, compared with the three senators and the congressman who must spend several days a week in D.C. A rival-campaign staff member has ruefully calculated that Dean will have four extra months on the road to raise money and woo voters—no minor advantage, since personal contact matters in the vital early states. "Dean has made eighteen trips here and counting," says Iowa state Democratic chairman Gordon Fischer, noting that the other candidates have logged half that time. "He's getting good crowds and reactions."

More outspoken than front-runner Kerry, more liberal than the charming Edwards or the well-known Lieberman, a fresher face than Gephardt, and without the baggage of Sharpton, Howard Dean, at least for the moment, has the attention of the chattering classes. "You can't move people unless you stand for something," he said that night in his mother's living room. "When I get done with this campaign, I don't know if I'm going to win or lose, but everybody in America will know what I stood for."

The Long War of John Kerry

Joe Klein

The New Yorker | December 2, 2002

Senator John Kerry was still a couple of years shy of thirty when Morley Safer of 60 Minutes asked him point-blank, "Do you want to be president?" It's taken another thirty years to get Kerry's final answer. In this in-depth profile, ace political scribe Joe Klein offers a revealing look at the war-hero Democrat from Massachusetts and his long-distance quest for the White House. . . .

On a rainy October morning, the day after Senator John Forbes Kerry, of Massachusetts, announced that he would reluctantly vote to give President George W. Bush the authority to use lethal force against Iraq, the Senator sat in his Capitol Hill office reminiscing about another war and another speech. The war was Vietnam. The speech was one he had delivered upon graduating from Yale, in 1966. Kerry was twenty-two at the time; he had already enlisted in the Navy. As one of Yale's champion debaters and president of the Political Union, he had been selected to deliver the Class Oration, traditionally an Ivy-draped nostalgia piece. But the speech he gave, hastily rewritten at the last moment, was anything but traditional: it was a broad, passionate criticism of American foreign policy, including the war that he would soon be fighting.

I'd been trying to get a copy of this speech for several weeks, but Kerry's staff had been unable to find one. There seemed a parallel—at least, a convenient journalistic analogy—to his statement the day before about Iraq: two questionable wars, both of which Kerry had decided to support, conditionally, even as he raised serious doubts about their propriety.

Kerry bristled at the analogy. He assumed that a familiar accusation was inherent in the comparison: that he was guilty of speaking boldly but acting politically. And it is true that from his earliest days in public life—a career that seems to have begun in prep school—even John Kerry's closest friends have teased him about his overactive sense of destiny, his theatrical sense of gravitas, and his initials, which are the same as John Fitzgerald Kennedy's. "I signed up for the Navy in 1965, the year before the Class Oration," Kerry said now, with quiet vehemence. He repeated it, for emphasis: "I signed up for the *Navy*.

There was very little thought of Vietnam. It seemed very far away. There was no connection between my decision to serve and the speech I made."

But there was a connection, of sorts. Kerry had made the decision along with three close friends, classmates and fellow-members of Yale's not so secret society, Skull and Bones: David Thorne, Richard Pershing, and Frederick Smith. All came from families with strong traditions of military and public service. Pershing was the grandson of General John Pershing, the commander of the American Expeditionary Force in the First World War. (Richard Pershing was killed during the Tet offensive.) "Our decisions were all about our sense of duty," Fred Smith, who went on to found Federal Express, recalls. "We were the Kennedy generation—you know, 'Pay any price, bear any burden.' That was the ethos."

The week before John Kerry delivered the Class Oration, the fifteen Skull and Bones seniors went off on a final jaunt together to a fishing camp on an island in the St. Lawrence River. Fred Smith remembers spending the days idly, playing cards and drinking beer. David Thorne, however, says that there was a serious running discussion about Vietnam. "There were four of us going to war in a matter of months. That tends to concentrate the mind. This may have been the first time we really seriously began to question Vietnam. It was: 'Hey, what the hell is going on over there? What the hell are we in for?' "

Kerry's reaction to these discussions was intense and precipitate. He decided to rewrite the speech. His original address, which can still be found in the 1966 Yale yearbook, was "rather sophomoric," he recalled. "I decided that I couldn't give that speech. I couldn't get up there and go through that claptrap. I remember there was no electricity in the cabin. I remember staying up with a candle writing my speech in the wee hours of the night, rewriting and rewriting. It reflected what I felt and what we were all thinking about. It got an incredible reception, a standing ovation."

The Senator and I were sitting in wing chairs in his office, which is rather more elegant than those of his peers—the walls painted Chinese red with a dark lacquer glaze and covered with nineteenth-century nautical prints. There is a marble fireplace, a couch, a coffee table, the wing chairs: in sum, a room with a distinct sensibility, a reserved and private place. Kerry seemed weary. Our conversation was interrupted, from time to time, by phone calls from his supporters—most of whom seemed unhappy about his Iraq vote. At one point, he had to rush over to the Senate chamber to vote on another issue. When he returned, we began to talk about his time in Vietnam. He served as the captain of a small "swift boat," ferrying troops up the rivers of the

Mekong Delta. He was wounded three times in four months, and then sent home—the policy in Vietnam was three wounds and you're out. He received a Bronze Star, for saving the life of a Special Forces lieutenant who had fallen overboard during a firefight, and a Silver Star. The latter, a medal awarded only for significant acts of courage, was the result of a three-boat counter-attack Kerry had led against a Vietcong position on a riverbank. He had chased down, shot, and killed a man that day. The man had been carrying a B-40 rocket-propelled grenade launcher. "You want to see what one of those can do to a boat?" he asked. "A couple of weeks after I left Vietnam, a swift boat captained by my close friend Don Droz—we called him Dinky—got hit with a B-40. He was killed. I still have the photo here somewhere."

Kerry began to rummage around his desk and eventually pulled out a manila folder. "Here it is," he said. The boat was mangled beyond recogni-tion. "Oh my, look at this!" He held up a sheaf of yellowed, double-spaced, typewritten pages. It looked like an old college term paper, taken from a three-ring binder. "It's the original copy of my Class Oration. What on earth is it doing here?"

He sat down again and studied the speech, transfixed. Then he began to read it aloud, curious, nostalgic, embarrassed by, and yet impressed with, his undergraduate eloquence. He read several pages. Worried looks passed between the two staff members who were in the room: Was he going to read the whole damn thing? " 'It is misleading to mention right and wrong in this issue, for to every thinking man, the semantics of this contest often find the United States right in its wrongness and wrong in its rightness,' " he read, swiftly, without oratorical flourish. " 'Neither am I arguing against the war itself. . . . I am criticizing the propensity—the ease—which the United States has for getting into this kind of situation—' "

He stopped and looked up, shaking his head, "Boy, was I a sophisticated nabob!" The two staff members exhaled. "You have to laugh at this now. . . . Do I even want this out?"

But he continued reading, unable to stop himself. He skipped several pages in the middle, then recited the entire peroration.

The Class Oration says a lot about John Kerry, who will soon announce his intention to run for President of the United States. It is a nuanced assess-ment of American foreign policy at a crossroads—delivered at a moment when the political leaders of the country should have been questioning basic

assumptions but weren't. Kerry did, however—a year before the antiwar movement began to gather strength and coherence. The speech was notable for its central thesis: "The United States must . . . bring itself to understand that the policy of intervention"—against Communism—"that was right for Western Europe does not and cannot find the same application to the rest of the world."
Kerry went on:

> In most emerging nations, the spectre of imperialist capitalism stirs as much fear and hatred as that of communism. To compound the problem, we continue to push forward our will only as we see it and in a fashion that only leads to more mistakes and deeper commitment. Where we should have instructed, it seems we did not; where we should have been patient, it seems we were not; where we should have stayed clear, it seems we would not. . . . Never in the last twenty years has the government of the United States been as isolated as it is today.

There is, nonetheless, something slightly off-putting about the speech. The portentous quality, the hijacking of Kennedyesque tics and switchbacks ("Where we should have instructed . . ."), the absence of irony, the absence of any sort of joy—all these rankle, and in a familiar way. This has been the knock against John Kerry for the past thirty years, ever since he captured the nation's attention as the spokesman for Vietnam Veterans Against the War, a group whose members staged a dramatic protest in Washington in April of 1971, camping out on the Mall and tossing their medals and combat ribbons onto the Capitol steps.

He seemed the world's oldest twenty-seven-year-old that week, even though he was dressed in scruffy combat fatigues, his extravagant thatch of black hair gleaming, flopping over his ears and eyebrows—he looked a bit like the prehallucinogenic George Harrison. Kerry spoke to the Senate Foreign Relations Committee in much the same style as he'd spoken at Yale. His testimony was brilliant and succinct: "How do you ask a man to be the last man to die in Vietnam? How do you ask a man to be the last man to die for a mistake?"

He was an immediate celebrity. He was also an immediate target of the Nixon Administration. Years later, Chuck Colson—who was Nixon's political enforcer—told me, "He was a thorn in our flesh. He was very articulate, a credible leader of the opposition. He forced us to create a counterfoil. We found a vet named John O'Neill and formed a group called Vietnam Veterans for a Just Peace. We had O'Neill meet the President, and we did everything we could do to boost his group."

Kerry launched a national speaking tour; he spoke to the National Baptist Convention, was named an honorary member of the United Auto Workers, and spoke on campuses across the country. He was the subject of a *60 Minutes* profile. Morley Safer asked him if he wanted to be President of the United States. "No," he said with a chuckle, after an instant's surprise and calculation.

Serious as all this was—he was, for a moment, as Colson suggests, the most compelling leader of the antiwar movement—there was something uneasy, and perhaps even faintly risible, about it, too, particularly the ill-disguised Kennedy playacting. Even as Kerry delivered his Senate testimony, he distorted his natural speech to sound more like that earlier J.F.K.; for example, he occasionally "ahsked" questions. (Kerry had befriended Robert F. Kennedy's speech-writer Adam Walinsky and consulted him about the speech, bouncing phrases and ideas off the old master.) This sort of thing had been a source of merriment for his classmates ever since prep school, where the joke was that his initials really stood for "Just For Kerry." He had volunteered to work on Edward Kennedy's 1962 Senate campaign, had dated Janet Auchincloss, who was Jacqueline Kennedy's half sister, had hung out at Hammersmith Farm, the Auchincloss family's estate in Newport, and had gone sailing with the President. A practical joke—one of many, apparently—was played on him in the 1966 Yale yearbook: he was listed as a member of the Young Republicans. After his 1971 antiwar debut in Washington, his fellow-Yalie Garry Trudeau lampooned him in the "Doonesbury" comic strip.

The jokes have never really abated. William Bulger, a state senator from South Boston and the dean of that city's clever politicians, nicknamed Kerry Live Shot, for his homing instinct when it came to television cameras. Indeed, Kerry's every move—the fact that he tossed his combat ribbons, not his medals, onto the Capitol steps; the fact that he had corrective jaw surgery (to fix a clicking sound, which had been compounded by a hockey injury); the fact, most recently, that he married the wealthy widow Teresa Heinz, whose late husband, Senator H. John Heinz III, was an heir to the ketchup fortune—all these were assumed to be political and were subjected to ridicule. "We were pretty rough on him over the years," Martin Nolan, a recently retired member of the Boston *Globe*'s mostly Irish and extremely raucous stable of political writers, says. "He was an empty suit, he was Live Shot, he never passed a mirror without saying hello."

Indeed, John Kerry has always looked as if he had been requisitioned from central casting: preposterously dignified, profoundly vertical. He is six feet four inches tall, and his narrow frame, long face, and sloping shoulders make him seem even taller. His face is a collection of strong features that inaccurately suggest an Irish heritage, as does his name: his father's family was mostly from Austria. He has a practically endless jaw, a prominent nose, and eyebrows that hang like a set of quotation marks beside grayish-blue eyes. And then there is the hair, which is so melodramatically profuse and puffy that it seems an encumbrance almost too weighty for his long, thin neck.

"He's cursed to look like that," says Bob Kerrey, the president of New School University, who served with Kerry in the Senate and is a fellow combat veteran of Vietnam. "His looks say something about him that is different from what he actually is. He's very easy to hang out with. There isn't an excessive use of the pronoun 'I.' There's a genuine person there, a very approachable person, a very honorable person." Other friends reflexively assume a defensive posture when describing him: He's not the loner that he once was, he's not as aloof, he's more comfortable than he used to be, he's grown as a person—although people have been saying these sorts of things about him, especially at election time, for the past twenty years.

Kerry's aristocratic reserve, his utter inability to pose as a populist, is not a quality recently associated with successful candidates for President of the United States. His voice and manner are cultured, Brahmin; he seems the sort of person who might ask for a "splash" of coffee, as George H. W. Bush did, to his political embarrassment, at a truck stop during the 1988 campaign. That Kerry is a Massachusetts liberal does not recommend him highly, either: the last three such candidates were Ted Kennedy, Paul Tsongas, and Michael Dukakis, and the latter's campaign has become shorthand for the disastrously effete, National Public Radio tendencies of the Democratic Party. Kerry has consistently voted for gun control, for abortion rights, and for environmental protection, and has opposed the death penalty; he has voted with Kennedy about ninety-six per cent of the time.

"But it's important to look at that other four per cent," David McKean, his chief of staff, says. Kerry does tend to be more fiscally conservative than Kennedy. He was one of the first Democrats to sign on to the Gramm-Rudman-Hollings balanced-budget proposals of the eighties; he favors free trade; he voted for welfare reform; he has even, on occasion, delivered

speeches that raised questions about such bedrock liberal dogma as affirmative action and guaranteed tenure for public-school teachers.

His great strength is his mastery of foreign affairs and military policy. His
willingness to criticize the Bush Administration on these subjects has distinguished him from the other eminent Democrats who wandered the country
during the recent election season, hoping to make a Presidential impression
on the Party faithful. In fact, he often derided "a new conventional wisdom
of consultants, pollsters, and strategists who argue . . . that Democrats should
be the party of domestic issues only."

Kerry's criticism of the Bush foreign policy is meticulous and comprehensive. It begins with the Administration's gratuitously ideological diplomatic actions in the year before the September 11th terrorist attacks. On
Bush's decision to simply walk away from the Kyoto global-warming treaty,
for example, he told me, "One hundred and sixty nations spent ten years
working to get to a certain place and the United States just stands up and
dismisses it out of hand. The Administration doesn't say we're going to try
to fix it, doesn't say we respect your work, doesn't say we're going to try to
find the common ground where we do have some differences. It just declares
it dead. Now, what do we think those presidents of those countries, those
prime ministers and those finance ministers, those environmental ministers
are? Are they all dumb? Are we telling them they are absolutely incapable
of making judgments about science, that the ten years of work that they've
invested in conference after conference, many of which I attended, was
absolutely for naught? That makes us friends in the world?"

Kerry extends this argument beyond the usual liberal critique: the unilateralist approach, he says, damages America's ability to do the intelligence
gathering and wage the unconventional warfare that are at the heart of an
effective campaign against terrorists and rogue states. He is critical of both
the Clinton and Bush Administrations for their uncertain, and too frequently
unsubtle, use of American power. Although he voted against the Gulf War
in 1991, he has supported military action against Iraq in the years since—
indeed, he was a cosponsor of the resolution that threatened force against
Iraq in 1998, when Saddam Hussein sent the United Nations weapons inspectors home. But he is a critic of the Pentagon's old-fashioned Cold War doctrine of overwhelming air power, its overcautious use of ground troops, and
its skepticism about the efficacy of unconventional war-fighting assets, like
the Special Forces. Early on, he criticized the Bush Administration for its
tactics in Afghanistan, its slapdash and unsuccessful effort to trap the Al Qaeda

leadership at Tora Bora—and particularly its decision not to use American troops to surround the mountain redoubt. "When given the opportunity to destroy Al Qaeda, the President turned not to the best military in the history of man," he said in July, "but rather turned to Afghan warlords who only a week earlier were on the other side."

Kerry's foreign policy seems a muscular multilateralism: active, detailed engagement with the countries in the Middle East and elsewhere; less pompous rhetoric and more of the patient scut work—the diplomatic consultation, the building of direct relationships with local intelligence and police agencies—that will make an occasional use of force by America more palatable. There is an implication that much of the Bush Administration's bombast has been for domestic political consumption, an attempt to sound tougher than Bill Clinton did. "The Administration mistakes tough rhetoric for tough policy," Kerry told me. "They may gain short-term domestic advantage as a result, but they are damaging the long-term security of the country. This is a far more complicated world than the ideologues of the Administration care about or understand."

Finally, Kerry broadens his practical critique of Bush's foreign policy to add some vision. Specifically, he says that the President missed an opportunity, in the weeks after September 11th, to call the nation to a larger cause: energy independence. In October of 2001, Kerry proposed a concerted energy-conservation campaign, including higher fuel-efficiency standards in automobiles and a "Manhattan Project" to develop renewable sources of energy. "No American son or daughter should ever again be sent abroad to die for oil," he often says on the stump, invariably to ovations from the Democratic faithful.

This is a complicated message, and—except for the one sound bite—a difficult one to deliver at a political rally. But Kerry's knowledge and conviction, and the fact that his words sound different from the market-tested slogans that other Democrats were rehearsing this autumn, gave him a credibility that his competitors in the larval Presidential race were missing. For the first time in his career, he didn't seem precocious. "I think he's had a hell of a year," James Carville, the political strategist, said. "Why? Because he's actually saying something. People do notice that, you know. The other thing is, 9/11 made the Commander-in-Chief part of the Presidency important again, and that's helped him, too, because of his military background. And, finally, he's not conflicted about this. He's not testing the waters. He's immersed in the waters. He's growing gills."

In late September, Kerry went to Charleston, South Carolina—the site of the first Southern primary in 2004 and a newly crucial state in the Presidential process—to campaign for Phil Leventis, the Democratic candidate for lieutenant governor. Leventis served as a pilot during the Gulf War, and various veterans' groups had gathered to announce their support for him. It was a perfect, cloudless Saturday. Kerry and Leventis stood in Marion Square, posed before a carefully arranged group of Vietnam combat veterans, most of whom wore blue knit shirts and boonie hats. Kerry gave a short but passionate speech about the service and sacrifice of the vets, about the Bush Administration's attempt to stint on some promised benefits. But he was speaking into a void. There was no audience. There was a single television camera, standing like a scarecrow in an empty field.

The real business of the day was transacted afterward. Kerry mingled easily with the vets, who were mostly African-American; he cussed and joked and talked about places like Da Nang and Da Lat. A pink-faced overweight man approached. "I'm Jim Gunn," he said to Kerry. "Do you remember me?"

Kerry nodded warily. Gunn was the leader of the Coalition of Retired Military Veterans and had attacked Senator John McCain during the 2000 Republican Presidential primary in South Carolina. Kerry had written a letter protesting the charges that another veterans' group had made against McCain—essentially, that McCain was "anti-veteran"—and he had got the other Vietnam combat veterans in the Senate to sign it. Now Jim Gunn said to him, "I just want you to know, Senator, that you were right about McCain and I was wrong. Bush lied to my face, and I'll never support him again." Gunn proceeded to file a bill of particulars against the President on veterans' issues. Then he sighed and said, "I wish there was a machine that could really say when someone is telling the truth, but you sound sincere when you talk about our issues. I represent seventeen thousand vets in South Carolina—I'm like their union boss—and if you run for President next time we're with you."

The scene was a striking reversal from the first time I'd seen Kerry campaign—in 1972, when he ran for Congress from a district that centered on the old mill towns, like Lawrence and Lowell, north of Boston. Crowds were easy in those days, especially crowds of young people; the Kerry campaign was a portable protest march. But the candidate didn't spend much time trying to find common ground with older veterans, like Jim Gunn, who still favored the war, and their enmity was a factor in his eventual defeat. In fact, Kerry was a fairly awful candidate, if I remember correctly—stiff, pompous, delivering the functional equivalent of his Senate testimony to elderly Portuguese shoe workers worried about their jobs and looking for some human contact. "That sounds right," Kerry told me recently. "If there's a balance like this in politics"—he held his two hands evenly in front of him—"issues over here and personal politics over here, I came into this business heavily on the issues side. I wanted to end the war." He raised his right hand and lowered his left. "I never had a mentor. I never worked beside a Tip O'Neill, I didn't have a Honey Fitz," he said, referring to the late Speaker of the House and to John Kennedy's grandfather. "I just came from a different place. I had to learn by making mistakes."

Kerry had won a tough Democratic primary that year and coasted, ten points ahead, into what seemed an easy election campaign against an unknown Republican named Paul Cronin. But he neglected to do his homework with the ancient, feudal Democratic Party organizations in the mill towns—that was considered the "old" politics—and the Lowell *Sun* launched a withering assault against him. "It was an overwhelming feeling of powerlessness," he says now. "There was nothing we could do to reverse it."

By all accounts, the loss was devastating. It was the first deviation from the career trajectory he had imagined for himself in prep school. "He came to my home in New Hampshire that weekend," his friend George Butler, a documentary filmmaker who was then a freelance photographer, recalls. "He wouldn't say a word to anyone. He sat there Friday night and built an entire model ship from scratch. On Saturday, he and I climbed a mountain together. He still wasn't talking. At the top of the mountain, I took a picture of him—I must have taken five thousand pictures of him over the years, but that was one of the best. He was the most despondent-looking human being I had ever seen."

Kerry has never been the most sociable fellow. He grew up lonely: his father was a foreign-service officer who was rarely home; his mother was a member of the aristocratic Forbes family—they made their fortune in the China trade—but she was one of eleven siblings and the fortune had been subdivided into insignificance by the time John Kerry's generation came along. He was brought up among the wealthy, but his was a threadbare, erstwhile aristocracy. There were many houses, most of them other people's houses: in Brittany (a Forbes family estate, where his mother had spent much of her youth); on Naushon Island, just off Cape Cod (another Forbes retreat); in Washington; in Groton, Massachusetts. He had been sent to boarding school in Switzerland, and hated it (he speaks fluent French and some Italian). He was then sent to boarding school in the United States, to St. Paul's, in Concord, New Hampshire. He was one of a handful of Catholic students; they were sent to Mass on Sunday in a taxi.

In one of our conversations, I asked Kerry how he became interested in politics. His interest was a result, he replied, of seeing the impact of the war in Europe as a child. "My very first memory—I was three years old—is holding my mother's hand and she was crying, and I didn't know why, as we walked through the broken glass and rubble of her childhood house in France, which the Germans had used as a headquarters and then bombed and burned as they left. I remember a staircase going up into the sky, and I remember a chimney into the sky. Those were the two images—that was all that was left. I remember going to the beach at Normandy on a subsequent trip, in 1951, and seeing burned-out landing vehicles, and the bunkers, and playing in those bunkers. And then we lived in Berlin for a brief period of time, with the Communists right on the other side of the sector. The Cold War was very real to me, more so than for most people my age."

There were constant policy discussions, and guests from the diplomatic community, at the dinner table; for Kerry, talking politics was the best way to communicate with his father. "John grew up in Europe, as I did," David Thorne, his friend from Yale, says. "He grew up around a lot of fancy people, as I did. But I think he grew up very much alone, and it showed. He rubbed a lot of people in school the wrong way—but then it was rare to see someone so intent on a career in public service at such a young age." Indeed, many of Kerry's friends joke that he was acting as if he were President in high school.

These days, the Senator is quite conscious of that ever-earnest image. "Look, I was a very serious guy except for when I was a non-serious guy," he said. "I knew how to have a lot of fun, sometimes too much. There were plenty of times when I was disengaged, frivolous, four sheets to the wind on a weekend." (Kerry has admitted to smoking marijuana a few times, but, sadly, he claims to have been bothered by the smoke.)

"We did do some wild things together—flying planes, running with the bulls in Pamplona," Thorne recalls. "He was very gutsy, always pushing—let's do this, let's do that." Kerry's physical daring—as a skier, a windsurfer, a motorcycle rider, a stunt pilot—remains a source of wonder among his friends. He was, apparently, something of a cowboy in Vietnam as well. His old crewmates remember that he played rock music over the boat's loudspeaker system—the Doors, the Stones, Jimi Hendrix—before they went on patrol. "He starred in that Marlon Brando movie, *Apocalypse Now,* long before they ever made it," Gene Thorson, a former crewmate, says.

To release the tension after a trip up the river, Kerry would often instigate chicken races between the swift boats, cutting over each other's wakes. He also organized water-balloon battles. Once, his three-boat squadron attacked an American supply ship at night with flares. "The brass was not too happy about that," Kerry recalled. "But what were they going to do to us, send us to Vietnam?"

Admiral Elmo Zumwalt later joked that he wasn't sure if he should give Kerry the Silver Star or court-martial him for his actions on February 28, 1969. Kerry had ignored standard operating procedure as his squadron ferried troops up the river that day. "He had talked to me about trying something different," Mike Medeiros, a crew member from San Leandro, California, said. "He said he was tired of just going up the river and getting shot at. He asked me what I thought about turning to attack the enemy positions if we took fire and no one was hurt. I said it might not be a bad idea."

If he turned his boats toward the shore, Kerry believed, he would transform a long, horizontal target into a narrower, vertical one. "It would concentrate both of our machine guns directly on the point of fire and surprise the hell out of them," and it would keep the twenty soldiers each boat was carrying astern out of the line of fire, Kerry recalled. "When the firing began, I gave the order to turn and—*phoom!*—we just went in and beached and took them by complete surprise, and we routed them and we didn't take a wound."

As Kerry's boat crashed ashore, a lone Vietcong stood up holding a B-40 rocket-propelled grenade launcher. "When he first stood up, he froze, because he didn't expect to see us staring him in the face, literally ten yards away." The man was wounded by one of Kerry's crewmates and began to run; Kerry leaped off the boat and chased him. "I didn't want to let him get away. I didn't want him to run away and turn around with an active B-40 and take us out. There but for the grace of God . . . The guy could have pulled the trigger and I wouldn't be here today."

It has been widely, and inaccurately, reported that Kerry filmed this and other actions with an 8-mm. movie camera. The films were in fact mostly travelogues and clowning-around shots on the boat. More than a few other vets recorded their adventures in Vietnam. "We did it for our families," Kerry told me. "We wanted to have a record of where we'd been. We wanted them to know what it had been like if we got killed."

As always, however, there was a sense that Kerry saw these home movies as part of a larger, more heroic film. "He was very much aware of the stage," David Thorne says. "He knew that his actions in Vietnam might have some bearing on his future life. But none of us could anticipate the impact—the psychological trauma—the war would have on us. John's been able to to live with the demons of combat, but they are there and they've given his life shape and meaning in a way that he never anticipated." Thorne went on, "In a way, it was harder coming back than being there. You know, we got home, and it was, 'What the fuck was that all about?' Vietnam Veterans Against the War was one big T-group. People like Jane Fonda wanted to make it into a political movement, but all we wanted to do was hug each other."

The second reel of John Kerry's Heroic Life Story, the twenty years from 1972 to 1992, turned out to be somewhat less heroic than the protagonist might have hoped. His celebrity evaporated with the congressional defeat in 1972. But the residue of the war remained—he had nightmares, at times so intense that he'd wake up screaming, leap out of bed, and slam into walls—and there was now a life to be constructed. Kerry didn't abandon his political dream, but he revised it prosaically: he would pay his dues. He went to Boston College law school; he became an assistant district attorney in the Middlesex County District Attorney's office. He built a reputation as a successful prosecutor, raised money for other Democrats, and waited for his moment.

In 1970, Kerry had married David Thorne's twin sister, Julia; they had two daughters, born in 1973 and 1976. According to friends, Julia was not a typical political wife. "There were times at dinner parties when John would be very pompous, unable to control his impulse to make a speech," one acquaintance said. "It was all slightly laughable, and Julia was one of those who laughed. She'd say things like, 'What the fuck did you just say?' "

Kerry is understandably loath to talk about the details of the marriage; his reticence is compounded by the fact that Julia was suffering from severe depression. She eventually wrote a book about the illness, called *You Are Not Alone*. It began:

> February 1980, five months after my thirty-sixth birthday, my mind ravaged by corroding voices, my body defeated by bone-rattling panics, I sat on the edge of my bed minutes from taking my life. . . . I could no longer pretend I was of use to my husband or my children. . . . I knew that, once I was gone, my family and friends would be relieved of the burden of my incompetency.

They separated in 1982, after Kerry decided to run for lieutenant governor of Massachusetts. Julia's mental condition was precarious, but Kerry chose to push ahead with the race. "When I get focussed and set out to do something, I'm pretty good at staying focussed," Kerry told me. "You don't want to let yourself down, you know what I'm saying? One loss is enough. You don't have to screw up everything else." He went on to say that there were days during the campaign when he and Julia would have wrenching morning discussions about their children and their future living arrangements, "and then, in the afternoon, I'd have to put on a smiling face and say, 'Hi, I'm John Kerry, I'd like you to vote for me,' and I'd feel empty inside doing it. It was not an easy process."

David Thorne calls the separation "an extended psychodrama." There were, apparently, several attempts to reconcile, but the divorce became final in 1988. Julia is now living in Montana.

John Kerry's first two statewide election campaigns, for lieutenant governor, in 1982, and, two years later, for United States senator, were successful, but not exactly triumphant. He was a more personable campaigner than he'd been in 1972; he worked hard, debated well, raised money relentlessly (and he had to spend more time raising it than most, because he refused to take contributions from political-action committees), but he was accepted only grudgingly by the state's Democratic Party establishment. "He was yesterday's hero, and he was frustrated by the fact that, every time he ran, the liberals would find some other darling," a close associate says. "In 1982, it was a woman, Evelyn Murphy, whom Michael Dukakis wanted as his running mate. In 1984, it was Jim Shannon."

Shannon was the sort of candidate the Boston *Globe* loved: blue-collar background, a member of Congress, charming, a Tip O'Neill protégé. The primary contest was brutal. "He was not a very likable guy," Shannon recalls of Kerry. "But he knew how to run a statewide campaign and I didn't. There were no real differences between us on the issues."

Kerry was so distressed by the newspaper coverage that he invited the *Globe*'s editor, Michael Janeway, to breakfast after the election. "He wanted to know why we were so rough on him," Janeway recalled. "I reminded him about Sam Rayburn's classic political categories. I said, 'John, there are workhorses and show horses, and I guess our staff considers you a show horse.'"

Ted Kennedy, who has now served as a United States senator from Massachusetts for forty years, is both a workhorse and a show horse. He dominates the Senate's domestic-policy agenda, but he has also come to be considered, in his old age, something of a card. He is a devilish tease—and, according to Senate colleagues, John Kerry has been a perfect pigeon. "Their relationship is good, far better than it was with Kerry's predecessor, Paul Tsongas," a former Kennedy aide said. "In fact, Kerry has been very skillful when it comes to playing Teddy. But Teddy sure knows how to torture John."

A few weeks ago, I asked Kennedy about his junior colleague. He launched a series of respectful encomiums, but couldn't resist a tiny jab. I mentioned that he and Kerry had very different styles, even though both were New England aristocrats. Kennedy's style was more emotional, I suggested—at which point the Senator interrupted me, saying, "John comes from a great Massachusetts tradition as well: Leverett Saltonstall, Henry Cabot Lodge . . ."

"Senator, you're naming only Republicans," I noted (and rather stuffy Brahmin Republicans at that).

Kennedy smiled slightly and replied, "Yes, but they made their mark. They were winners."

When John Kerry arrived in the Senate, in 1985, his first challenge was to figure out how to coexist with Kennedy. There were two possible strategies. One was to settle back and take a seat on the Appropriations Committee, a sure ticket to perpetuity in the Senate. The job of appropriators is to decide how to spend federal money; as politicians, they tend to be as blowsy and lugubrious as the bills that stumble out of their committee. Obviously, this was not the sort of career John Kerry had intended for himself, and so he chose the Foreign Relations Committee, which, by the mid-eighties, was not nearly as glamorous as it had been during the Vietnam era. The public was no longer very interested in foreign policy, and for a politician it held little practical allure—no taxing, no spending, no hardware to buy, no regulations to set. "But it was about war and peace," Kerry said. "We were entering an illegal war in Latin America. One of the lessons of Vietnam was about lying, about people who hide the truth from the American people, and there was a real parallel in Latin America."

Kerry started a series of investigations into the Reagan Administration's involvement with the Nicaraguan Contras, a guerrilla group opposed to the left-wing Sandinista government. His subcommittee on narcotics and terrorism revealed that Oliver North, a junior Marine officer assigned to the White House, was in charge of funnelling arms to the Contras; and suggested that some of the C.I.A. operatives who supplied the Contras were flying narcotics back to the United States (a fact that the C.I.A. finally acknowledged almost a decade later); and then that Panama's dictator Manuel Noriega had been involved with the arms-running, the drug-running, and the C.I.A. From there, Kerry began to investigate Noriega's money-laundering operation, which was run through the Bank of Credit and Commerce International, in the Cayman Islands. The B.C.C.I. trail led to its partner, First American Bank, in Washington, D.C., which was represented by Clark Clifford, who had served every Democratic President from Harry Truman to Jimmy Carter. "John wasn't a very popular guy when he called Clark Clifford to testify," David McKean, the committee's chief investigator at the time, said. "Most of the other members of the committee were uncomfortable with it. I remember that one senator cornered Kerry in the elevator and said, 'What are you doing to my old friend Clark Clifford?' But those hearings were the first real look at how terrorists, drug dealers, and international criminals conducted their business."

Indeed, Kerry was soon about as popular in Washington's political community as he'd been in Massachusetts. "He was a very driven, very relentless guy, and that could be off-putting to his colleagues," Timothy E. Wirth, who was a senator from Colorado at the time and later became Kerry's friend, recalls. "He was an outsider. In fact, you never saw him around much, with good reason—he was up in Boston with his girls. My sense is that Julia wasn't always reliable during those years, and John took a lot of responsibility for raising the kids. He would rush up there for every school play and soccer match. You had the sense that he was a very lonely guy. He was being hacked to death by the *Globe*, and others, and he never had anyone to share it with."

Kerry was easily reelected to the Senate in 1990, but his political career was in remission. His Presidential ambitions seemed vestigial; he wasn't even mentioned as a possible candidate in 1992. At times, Kerry's name appeared more often in the gossip columns than on the editorial pages; rumors about his romantic life were frequent, and occasionally disdainful.

But the third reel of John Kerry's Heroic Life Story was about to begin; and it started where the first had ended, in Vietnam.

"When he ran for lieutenant governor in 1982, John didn't want to have anything to do with Vietnam," Cameron Kerry, the Senator's younger brother, who managed the campaign, says. "He didn't even want us to show a picture of him in uniform in the campaign ads."

Vietnam was inescapable, of course. In 1984, Jim Shannon had deployed a group of anti-Kerry veterans; their attacks were effective and discomfiting. The Kerry campaign found no effective response until after the final debate, and then the antidote arrived by accident. Shannon brought up Vietnam and, in effect, called Kerry a hypocrite because he'd fought in a war he didn't believe in.

The next day, Kerry headquarters was deluged with calls from infuriated veterans: Shannon hadn't fought in Vietnam; they hadn't been so lucky—and they hadn't "chosen" to go to war, either. In their final debate, Kerry asked for an apology, and Shannon said, "That dog won't hunt."

An emotional rally of Vietnam veterans had already been held at the State House, and now a flying squad, which called itself the Doghunters, was organized to confront Shannon. It has been a fixture in every Kerry campaign since. "After the 1984 election, the Doghunters had a black-tie dinner at my house, and the only thing we didn't drink was the Aqua Velva," John Marttila, a political consultant who has worked on every Kerry campaign, says. "They've had regular dinners ever since. When you see John with those guys, you realize what bullshit the stuffy, aloof caricature of him is. I think he may be at his best, his most comfortable, with other Vietnam veterans."

Over time, that proved to be true in the Senate as well. In 1991, the Majority Leader, George Mitchell, of Maine, asked Kerry to chair a committee to investigate the possibility that American prisoners of war were still being held in Vietnam. The Rambo films were in vogue then; various paramilitary charlatans were raising money from the families of those missing in action to go on "rescue" missions in Vietnam; *Newsweek* had published, on its cover, a photograph of three Americans allegedly held in a Vietnamese prison camp (the picture was soon found to have been doctored).

"Nobody wanted to be on that damn committee," Bob Kerrey said. "It was an absolute loser. Everyone knew that the P.O.W. stories were fabrications, but no one wanted to offend the vet community." George Mitchell and John Kerry began twisting arms. Kerrey, John McCain, Chuck Robb, and Hank Brown—all the other Vietnam combat vets then in the Senate—agreed to serve on the committee, as did Daniel Inouye and Bob Dole, who were Second World War veterans. (Al Gore was the only Vietnam-era vet who refused.)

"I wasn't very close to John before that," John McCain recalls. "I thought he was standoffish and pedantic. Actually, no—I was the standoffish one, because I didn't agree with what he'd done, the protest where they threw away their medals." In fact, McCain had campaigned against Kerry during the general election of 1984. "But I gained a great deal of respect, and affection, for John during those P.O.W.-M.I.A. hearings. He was a lot more mature, a lot more patient than I was." Kerry was especially helpful when some of the more extreme P.O.W.-movement types testified before the committee. "I'd see the way some of these guys were exploiting the families of those missing in action, and I'd begin to get angry," McCain went on, "and John would sense it and put his hand on my arm to calm me down before I'd lose"—McCain paused and smiled—"my effectiveness."

Kerry and McCain went to Vietnam together; they visited the cell where McCain had been held as a prisoner of war. "Just to stand there alone in this tiny cell with McCain, just to look at this guy who was now a United States senator, and my friend, in the very place where he'd been tortured, and kept for so many years, not knowing if he might live," Kerry began a sentence one day, sitting in his Capitol office—and then he seemed unable to finish the thought, unwilling to break through his public reserve. "We found this common ground in this far-off place."

After more than a year of research and eight trips to Vietnam, Kerry managed to cajole a unanimous vote from his committee—including two Republicans, Bob Smith, of New Hampshire, and Chuck Grassley, of Iowa, who had been banging the P.O.W. drum the loudest—in favor of a report saying it was very unlikely that any Americans had been left behind in Vietnam. It was the sort of labor-intensive, quietly useful work that other senators notice and respect. The committee's unanimity made it possible for Bill Clinton to normalize relations with Vietnam, in 1995. In a practical way, Kerry had at last brought an end to the war that had dominated so much of his adult life.

There was a personal consequence as well. The time Kerry spent with McCain—and, to a lesser extent, with Bob Kerrey and Chuck Robb—completed the transformation that the Doghunters had begun. He was no longer a political loner; he was, finally, part of a distinct, bipartisan, and emotionally intense group: the Vietnam combat veterans in the United States Senate. (Max Cleland, of Georgia, and Chuck Hagel, of Nebraska joined the group in 1996; Kerrey and Robb departed in 2000.) They took common positions on veterans' issues, and sometimes on questions of war and peace, but they were most passionately united when one or another of them was attacked.

Remarkably, most have had aspects of their service called into question over the past decade—evidence that Vietnam remains the primary political battlefield of the baby-boom generation. Kerry's service was questioned during his 1996 Senate race against Governor William Weld; a column in the Boston *Globe* asserted that his actions had been imprudent and excessive in the battle for which he received the Silver Star. Earlier, in 1984, the *Wall Street Journal* reported that Kerry had tossed away his combat ribbons, not his medals, at the 1971 protest in Washington. Kerry had never implied otherwise (indeed, the protesters that day had tossed all sorts of things—dog tags, photographs, discharge papers, insignia), but he had complicated the story with an excess of honesty, recalling that he'd also tossed several medals that had been given him by veterans who were unable to make the trip. The journalistic short-hand became: Kerry tossed someone else's medals.

The Doghunters came to Kerry's defense in both cases, and the stories had little impact. Others in the Senate caucus didn't get off so easily. There were the attacks on McCain by pro-Bush veterans in 2000, which helped scuttle his Presidential campaign in South Carolina. And then, in the spring of 2001, Bob Kerrey was accused of participating in a massacre of Vietnamese women and children. "John called and asked me to go to New York to help Bob get through it," Tom Vallely, a veteran and longtime Kerry friend who advised the P.O.W.-M.I.A. committee, said. "I stayed there for several weeks, helping Bob with the press strategy, doing whatever I could."

Kerry, Cleland, and Hagel defended Kerrey in a Washington *Post* op-ed column; they were joined by McCain to defend Kerrey on ABC's Sunday-morning political program *This Week*. "I just thought people were piling on after the fact, making judgments they had no knowledge about, that they had no right to make," Kerry told me later. "And I felt very much concerned about Bob personally, because he's a friend and I love him dearly."

"Love" is not a word often tossed around by United States senators, par-ticularly with regard to other United States senators. But Bob Kerrey uses it as well: "The feeling we all have is the closest guys get to love."

Finding his place among comrades was John Kerry's first step in from the political cold. There were two others, frequently cited by friends: his victory over William Weld in the 1996 Massachusetts Senate race and his improb-able second marriage, to Teresa Heinz.

The notion that John Kerry married Teresa Heinz for political reasons—specif-ically, to use her money to run for President—is put to rest within nanosec-onds of meeting her: this is a flagrantly impolitic human being. The marriage is bursting with strong emotions and ill-concealed conflicts, and much too complicated for the facile armchair psychologizing that goes on during a Pres-idential campaign. It is not the sort of relationship that an ambitious politi-cian, in his right mind, would want; it is likely to be a distraction for the press corps, an easy way to obscure the campaign's "message." One can only con-clude, it must be love.

Heinz will not be censored. "John went on too long," she said the day I met her, after watching her husband deliver his Iraq speech in the Senate Chamber on C-SPAN. "But that's what happens when he starts thinking about history."

We were sitting in the study of Mrs. Heinz's Georgetown home—the walls were painted in the same darkened, glossy Chinese red as Kerry's Senate office, but they were covered with priceless art, in particular Dutch still-lifes from the seventeenth and eighteenth centuries. We were not alone. Chris Black, formerly of the Boston *Globe* and CNN, sat with us—she was hired to help Mrs. Heinz with the press after a Washington *Post* story, widely regarded in the political community as disastrous, described the quirky quality of the marriage. The story emphasized Mrs. Heinz's enduring devotion to her first husband, John Heinz, who died in a plane crash in 1991. There are pictures of Heinz throughout the house, and Kerry's staff refer to her as "Mrs. Heinz." And so I began by asking a slightly wicked question: "How did you meet your husband?"

"You mean John—John Kerry," she said. We spent the next several hours talking, much of the time taken up by Heinz's long monologues about her past—she grew up in Mozambique, the daughter of a Portuguese doctor—and her work as an environmentalist and as a social-policy expert, which is quite impressive (among other things, Massachusetts recently adopted a means-tested prescription-drug plan for senior citizens that was developed by the Heinz family foundation).

But Heinz's descriptions of the courtship with Kerry, which began when they were both delegates to the 1992 Earth Summit, in Rio de Janeiro, were cautious and dispassionate. She seemed to be trying out a new, more politic story line; she had clearly been rehearsed, but she was unrehearsable. She went to Mass with Kerry in Rio, she recalled, and heard him singing in Portuguese. "I found that interesting," she said. (He explained that he knew some Italian and had been faking it.) They were joined for dinner by Senators Frank Lautenberg and Larry Pressler, neither of whom is known as a barrel of laughs, but the meal somehow turned out to be riotous fun. They spent the evening, she said, mocking the inanities of public life.

Months later, in Washington, there was another dinner, and Kerry offered to drive her home. They stopped at the Vietnam Veterans Memorial; he showed her the names of his friends on the granite wall. When he dropped her off in Georgetown, he didn't accompany her to the door, which irked her. (Kerry claims that he was double-parked, with a bus coming up behind him.) "I thought he was interesting, but . . . a specimen who'd been out in the woods a long time," she said, in her softly accented English. "He was like having a pet wolf who comes in and you say; 'Yeh, cute.'" She made a face and pulled away. "I need to teach him a couple of things. I think many people who get married late in life and who haven't been married have adjustment problems." (Several times, Heinz noted that Kerry "had never been married," an odd elision, which one friend attributed to her Catholicism: "She is not comfortable with the fact that he was married and divorced.")

Heinz's eccentricities and her awkward candor are indeed an easy target, but they are also misleading, according to friends, who are vehement in their support of the marriage. "She is incredibly loving and involved in his life," says former Senator Tim Wirth, who, with his wife, Wren, has been among Heinz's closest friends. "She won't let him get away with the things he used to keep to himself. She forces him to talk, to express emotions. This has been terrific for him."

Heinz is five years older than Kerry, and there is a motherly quality to her descriptions of him: "John has an elegant mind. His thinking is not brutish. He really likes to take his time, talk things through, to deliberate." In fact, his interests in the world are "insatiable," she said. "We see a beautiful sunset and he says, 'I really want to know how to paint that.' He's learning the classical guitar, he's learning windsurfing, he's learning sky-whatever-it-is, and I say, 'You got married, remember. What else do you want to learn?'"

I asked her once more about their courtship. "I think what happens when you're older and you've had a relationship like the one I'd had"—she was referring to her twenty-five years with John Heinz—"your measurements aren't quite the same. You find the things that are comfortable, like old shoes. Talking about a lot of issues, that was comfortable. It was nice to do that again. There were other things that were familiar, like languages, like having lived in Europe. . . . And then you get to the point where you like somebody so much that when you're not with him you miss him. We were careful. I certainly was careful. It's not like you're eighteen and it's *ahhh*." Mrs. Heinz paused, and changed the subject slightly. "And then, of course, we got married, and we had that wonderful Senate race. That was our wedding present."

The 1996 Senate campaign between John Kerry and William Weld was the rarest of events in latter-day American politics: a civil, closely contested, intelligent, and wildly entertaining brawl. "Both candidates were incredibly popular," the Kerry consultant John Marttila said. "Both had sixty-percent favorable ratings, and negatives in the twenties. And they maintained their popularity throughout the race."

Both were Brahmins, but Weld, with a shock of strawberry hair and irony to burn, seemed an honorary Hibernian—once again, Kerry was faced with an opponent bound to be favored by the reportorial romantics at the Boston *Globe*. "We were both comers," recalls Weld, who had just been reelected governor, with seventy-one percent of the vote. "We were both at the height of our powers. If I'd won that race, I was going to turn straight around and run for President in 2000. I think he was, too—although I guess he eventually decided that Gore had too big a head start."

The campaign began with a remarkable agreement to limit campaign spending, negotiated face to face by the two candidates in Kerry's Beacon Hill mansion. They also agreed to a series of eight debates, some of which would be Lincoln-Douglas style, with the two candidates questioning each other directly, without a mediator. Weld figured that his issues—crime, welfare reform, and tax cutting—and his charm would see him through, but mostly his charm. "John isn't really a cold person, but he does seem aloof," Weld said recently. "The truth is that he's courtly to the point of gentility. We were pummelling him through August, but his campaign turned on a dime when Bob Shrum was hired as his consultant. It went from flaccid to sharp in a week."

Kerry's aides insist that it was more than Shrum. They say that Kerry was distracted in Washington, that he didn't really focus on the campaign until the Senate recessed. "It wasn't a lack of focus," Kerry says. "It was a strategy. I figured people wouldn't really be paying attention until the fall debates."

The last four debates were fabulous political theatre—two very smart men having at each other. "John's at his best under pressure, when he's being seriously challenged," Paul Nace, an old Navy friend, says. "He gets really cool, very calm. He really is a warrior—he just loves it. I took one look at him as he was walking into Faneuil Hall for one of the last debates and I thought, Bill Weld has no idea what's about to hit him."

Weld—who calls the debates a "bloody draw"—says that Kerry successfully attached him to the national Republican Party. (Weld had said some embarrassingly positive things about Newt Gingrich two years earlier.) "The turning point came when he asked me if I'd vote to keep Jesse Helms as the chairman of the Senate Foreign Relations Committee. That was a killer."

I asked Weld how he responded. "I ducked it, of course," he said, with a smile. "I mean, I hated Jesse Helms. But what could I do?"

Kerry won the election by eight percentage points. "John has always been underestimated politically," Marttila says. "But that race had the quality and intensity of a Presidential campaign, and he won. I don't see how they can underestimate him anymore, but they probably will."

John Kerry will not be the only Democrat running for President in 2004, of course, and the race will turn, more than any campaign in recent memory, on events outside the control of the politicians—war in the Middle East, a terrorist event at home, a sluggish economy (or the opposite: a Bush boom). Any attempt to handicap an outcome would be foolish in the extreme.

But it is possible to sense a mood. There is a frustration with the mechanical, poll-driven, consultant-managed politics of recent years. The mood is particularly easy to discern in New Hampshire, a state that John McCain took by storm in 2000. "People have had it," Rick Katzenberg, a Democratic activist from the town of Amherst, said a few weeks before Election Day. "They've just been overwhelmed this year. They're sick of all the telemarketing—the phone calls to get out to vote, the opinion surveys, the push polls. I don't even trust polling results anymore, because people are so quick to hang up. The television ads have no impact, except to get people angrier. It's a very tough atmosphere."

John Kerry understands the mood, and he particularly understands what his friend McCain accomplished in 2000. He is also aware that McCain supporters—the Republicans and Independents who can cross over and participate in the Democratic primary—will be a significant voting bloc in 2004, when the Democrats are likely to be the only party in town. He also knows that he could not ever, not even remotely, pass for John McCain. He doesn't have McCain's outlaw sensibility, for one thing, or his Borscht Belt comic timing. But the McCain campaign is the model Kerry thinks about most seriously: "People are jaded, people are cynical—there's been a breach of faith. You have to reestablish a way to connect with people. John McCain did that." We were riding back to Boston after a long day on the stump in mid-October. "He succeeded in building some trust in New Hampshire," Kerry went on. "I think it was built partly on his manner, his approach, and partly on who he was, the story of his life." Kerry stopped and sighed. "Whether I can do that, I don't know. I'm not cocky enough to say that, absolutely, I can do what he did. But I know it's worth trying."

Kerry is a much smoother candidate than he was thirty years ago, when

I first watched him work. There are times when he can even rouse an audience, get them to stand and cheer; more often, however, the reaction is attentive silence. His audiences, almost entirely Democratic activists at this point, follow his foreign-policy formulations closely, but sometimes they grow impatient with him. One Sunday in Nashua, New Hampshire, a woman named Marilyn Peterman actually interrupted Kerry in mid-disquisition on Iraq. "You're letting Bush hijack the debate!" she yelled. "What about the economy? What about the war on terrorism?"

Peterman was angry, she later told me, about Kerry's Iraq vote—and about the Democrats' general lameness. She was disappointed by Kerry's explanations; he didn't come close to reflecting her anger. "I'm trying to keep an open mind," she said. "I was going to support him, especially when he was speaking out against Bush last summer, but now I'm not so sure."

Kerry, when given the chance, pleads consistency on Iraq. He has been making the same argument since 1998: that there needs to be an aggressive multilateral effort to remove Saddam Hussein's arsenal. He believes that pressure from the Democrats—and, of course, from Secretary of State Colin Powell—convinced President Bush to work through the United Nations; and that Bush has been, essentially, on the right path since his speech to the United Nations on September 12th. If so, it has been a substantive victory and a political loss: if Bush proceeds to act prudently for the next two difficult years, he will deserve to be reelected.

It takes passion to defeat a sitting President. Ronald Reagan had it in 1980; Bill Clinton in 1992. The Democrats have been notable for their lack of passion in recent elections. They have become the party of tactics, of risk-averse appeals to targeted, reliable constituencies, like the elderly. Their crimped, boring pessimism is a long, sad distance from John Kennedy's vigor and idealism—and I asked Kerry, as we rode back from New Hampshire that night, if there was anything from the Kennedy experience that could be resurrected profitably now. He reacted defensively, fearing a trap. He had spent years working to bury the invidious J.F.K. comparisons; in recent elections, he had even excised the "F." from his bumper stickers. "That was a once-in-a-lifetime moment," he said, curtly, of Kennedy, "and I think anyone who tried to mimic it, reinvent it, reach it, or touch it would be making a mistake."

Several weeks later, after the Democrats' election losses, Kerry revised and amended his remarks on the phone. "I guess I was responding to the Camelot thing, the romanticism," he said. "But there are other aspects of the Kennedy era that are applicable. I think that asking people to be part of something larger than themselves, asking the country to do something better and more important—those are aspects of the Kennedy legacy that are applicable now."

Inspirational politics seems an oxymoron after thirty years of public scandal and cynicism. But any Democrat who hopes to have a chance in 2004 must find a way to rebuild the Party intellectually, and to reach new constituencies, particularly the young people who have been boycotting elections in droves. This will require a new political style and vocabulary. It will certainly require a break from the past as dramatic as John F. Kennedy's 1960 campaign was. It is quite possible that Kerry's thoughtful manner and complicated answers will be wrong for the moment. But it is also possible that his calm maturity will seem Presidential, particularly if he somehow manages to combine it with a touch of McCain, the exhilaration of candid, inconvenient positions on the issues of the day—and, no small irony, he will need a touch of Kennedy as well. Indeed, John Kerry may have to become the politician he once dreamed of being. He may have to do all those old Kennedy things: sound the trumpet, pick up the fallen standard, and see if an army is lurking about, waiting to respond.

"I've reached the point where I'm just going to do what I'm going to do, and to hell with whatever the conventional wisdom is," Kerry told me last summer, as we cruised in his speedboat off Naushon Island. It seemed the sort of thing politicians always say at the beginning of a campaign, but then he added, "I mean, if I screw up, what are they going to do to me—send me to Vietnam?"

How the Dems Created Al Sharpton

Michelle Cottle

The New Republic | February 17, 2003

While everyone agrees that Democratic presidential hopeful Al Sharpton has no chance of winning his party's nomination, a lot of people are fretting that the eloquent civil rights leader may peel off a large number of black voters in the primaries, causing the already disenchanted African-American community to stay home rather than vote for the eventual Democratic nominee in the general election. In this profile of Sharpton on the campaign trail, Michelle Cottle suggests that these fears are actually a reflection of the poor job the Democrats have done in reaching out to their African-American base—and also of the gaping political hole left in this regard by the departure of Bill Clinton. . . .

GREENVILLE, SOUTH CAROLINA

It's 8:45 A.M., and the growing entourage in the lobby of the Hilton is drawing curious stares from passing guests. A half-dozen black men, dressed to the nines, have been hovering at the elevator bank for the past half an hour, laughing, chatting, and scanning the Sunday papers. Every so often a newcomer joins the huddle to be greeted with clasped hands and cries of welcome. Out in the parking lot, several dark luxury cars stand at the ready, clustered around a long, white Cadillac limousine. A driver pops his head in from the cold to see when the group will be ready to roll. No one knows. The caravan was supposed to be on its way to the Reedy River Missionary Baptist Church by 8:30 to catch the tail end of early worship service. But Democratic presidential aspirant Al Sharpton is running late this morning—a not infrequent occurrence—and no amount of gentle prodding can rush the good reverend. As the men anxiously check their watches and pull cell phones from their coat pockets, a middle-aged white guy ambles over. "You're all waiting for someone, aren't you?" he posits with a goofy grin. "Mind if I guess who?" The group looks decidedly not amused. "Al Sharpton!" the man crows. "I knew it! I heard on the news that he was in town!"

Indeed, as Sharpton began his unofficial campaign swing through South Carolina over the Martin Luther King Jr. weekend, most upstate residents caught their first glimpse of the infamous New York agitator on the Saturday and Sunday local news, where Sharpton expressed dismay at Greenville County's refusal to observe the holiday honoring the slain civil rights leader. (Unlike city workers, county employees don't get the day off.) Others first spotted the jowly reverend in the Sunday papers, which carried reports of Sharpton's Saturday-night rally at a nearby church, where he criticized political leaders for turning their backs on civil rights issues and made a particular point of accusing Democrats of taking the black vote for granted. Though not overtly negative, the coverage was pretty much what you'd expect from a visit by Sharpton: heavy on themes of racial injustice and inequality. It was, in short, precisely the sort of Sharpton campaign story that's giving national Democrats nightmares.

Well aware of the havoc wreaked by the bomb-throwing reverend in many a New York election, party strategists are exceedingly nervous about Sharpton taking his racialist political theater to the national stage. Many fear that, if not shown the proper obeisance by the party and its eventual nominee, he will use his oratorical gifts and trademark grievance politics to convince minority voters that they might as well stay home on Election Day. At the same time, Dems worry about what will happen if their party gets too snuggly with the reverend. In the early '90s, Bill Clinton helped erase his party's association with identity politics; a return to the old sectarian ways could drive itchy swing voters straight into the compassionately conservative embrace of George W. Bush. With Sharpton in the race, warns one Democratic player, "the question is whether he will destroy the national party the way he did the Democrats in New York."

But, as much as Democrats might point the finger at Sharpton, he is more a symptom than a cause of the party's racial woes. Since Clinton left center stage, larger forces have propelled the Democrats back toward the kind of racially divisive infighting that plagued them in the 1980s. A combination of factors—the absence of racially unifying figures, black or white; the Democrats' electoral disappointments of 2000 and 2002; the GOP's recent racial controversies; and the early South Carolina primary—pretty much guaranteed that race would loom large in the Democratic primaries. Opportunist par excellence that he is, Sharpton has simply stepped into the breach.

Despite his technicolor reputation, in person Sharpton isn't an especially electric figure. He does not radiate energy or charisma or even personableness. When the reverend finally rolled out of the hotel elevator just before 9 A.M., he had no handshakes, smiles, or warm words for the men who'd been standing around waiting for him for the past hour. Cell phone clutched to his ear, Sharpton barely glanced their way as he ambled across the lobby. It was left to his lawyer and erstwhile campaign counselor, Sanford "Sandy" Rubenstein, to herd the puzzled group into the waiting cars. Sharpton even seems a little uncomfortable with one-on-one retail campaigning. While he will stand still for an endless stream of cheek kisses and photos, his manner often appears a bit strained, his smile a bit forced as well-wishers file past. He recognizes that people need to express their appreciation of his work, but he doesn't seem to enjoy the interaction. Much of the time, Sharpton looks bored, sleepy, and just the teensiest bit surly.

When the reverend steps into the pulpit, however, the result is pure magic. At his two Sunday sermons in Greenville—one at Reedy River and one at Jesse Jackson's old church, Tabernacle Baptist—Sharpton displayed the awesome oratorical gifts that had him dubbed "the boy wonder preacher" by the tender age of ten. He works without notes and insists he doesn't know what he'll say until he steps to the microphone. Eyes heavy, face solemn, he starts slowly, his voice harsh and gravelly as he introduces the morning's theme: Black America risks forgetting how far it has come and at how high a price. He then weaves in personal anecdotes, news items, statistics, bible verses, and gospel lyrics to illustrate his point. His voice warms; his eyes grow wide and bright; he waves his arms and glides around the pulpit, whipping the crowd into a frenzy. Calls to "Tell it, preacher!" and "Say so!" fill the sanctuary. At Reedy River, a woman in a glorious purple hat stands and flings her lace hanky at Sharpton in exultation. Slipping into the home stretch, the reverend draws the crowd into a call and response—a staple among many black ministers but rarely executed as well as by Sharpton. His voice soaring more in song than in speech, Sharpton establishes a hypnotic rhythm: "I don't know what you read in the newspapers!" Pause a beat. "But this is my story!" Beat. "This is my song!" Beat. "Praising my savior!" Beat. "All the day long!" (With these well-known hymn lyrics, Sharpton can wrap even the controversies of his past in the gospel.) "I been up!" Beat. "I been down!" Beat. "I been stabbed!" Beat. "I been criticized!" Beat. "But through it all!" Beat. "I-I-I-I learned to trust in Jesus!"

As recent weeks have shown, Sharpton can modulate his oratorical gifts to woo audiences well beyond his base. Even skeptical party strategists and media types expressed admiration at Sharpton's crowd-wowing performance a few weeks ago at the NARAL Pro-Choice America gathering in Washington. "It was bizarre," notes a colleague, "to see all those upper-class white women cheering for him." Sharpton, of course, delights in having delivered a wake-up call to the competition: "The other night they got their first warning that they had better start paying attention to me."

There's little danger of Sharpton being ignored in this race. Many Dems shudder at the thought that the reverend could draw enough support—especially down South, where Democrats rely heavily on the black vote—to carry a slate of delegates to the national convention. Party activists point anxiously to the racial divide that emerged during Jesse Jackson's 1988 presidential run. Careful, eleventh-hour negotiations were required at the Atlanta convention that summer to get Jackson supporters on board with nominee Michael Dukakis. A similar scenario starring Sharpton could prove considerably worse, say Dems. After all, by 1988, Jackson had moderated his image and enjoyed multiracial support. Just as importantly, he was willing to negotiate for the good of the party. (Or, as some Dems less charitably put it, he could be bought off for a few million dollars and the use of a campaign jet.) Sharpton, by contrast, has shown repeatedly in New York a great willingness to sink his party over a perceived lack of ideological purity or even personal pique. Says one alarmed presidential campaign veteran, "Going hat in hand to Jesse Jackson is one thing, but owing Al Sharpton is quite another."

But, if Democrats are forced to go begging to Sharpton, they largely have themselves to blame, having failed to anticipate and respond to the many factors conspiring to return racial politics to the forefront of the party. First among these is Clinton's departure from the White House. Donna Brazile, the Democrats' go-to gal where the black vote is concerned, points out that, fair or not, part of the problem the party now faces "is that the bar was set so high under Clinton." Nowhere were Clinton's consummate political skills more evident than in the overwhelming, unwavering support he enjoyed from black voters. The appeal was partly political, partly personal, and near impossible to define completely. Some Dems point to Clinton's record in Arkansas and his credentials within the civil rights community. Clinton went to all the civil rights meetings, says Brazile, "and, when he was governor, he would invite all the leaders to come and brief him and talk to him." He thus arrived on the national scene with an existing "Arkansas posse" of black compatriots—Ernie Green, Rodney Slater, and Carol Willis, just to name a few. But, ultimately, Clinton's appeal was grounded less in his civil rights background and ties to black leaders than in his deep personal comfort with black America. He didn't just tap blacks for his Cabinet and staff, says former Gore speechwriter Kenneth Baer. "When he was palling around on the golf course, Vernon Jordan is who he chose to hang out with." Many attribute this comfort to Clinton's Southern roots. "Southerners are generally just more comfortable around black people because they were around black people so much growing up," says Democratic campaign veteran and South Carolina native Donnie Fowler. Adds Brazile, "He knew the walk. He knew the talk. He even knew the food." At a 2000 fundraiser featuring celebs like Lionel Ritchie and Quincy Jones, Brazile recalls with a chuckle, "When it came time for people to pick out their meal from the buffet, Clinton went straight for the black-eyed peas." This intimacy with the community allowed Clinton to pursue policies others would never have dared. "There was an element of respect," says Brazile, "so that, even when people disagreed with him on something like welfare reform or the three-strikes laws, there was always the knowledge that Bill Clinton was on our side." Republicans' impeachment efforts against Clinton only solidified his black support. "People said, 'There must be something good about this guy if Republicans are so hell-bent to get him,'" says Fowler. As a result, when Clinton was the face of the Democrats, no black leader could credibly argue that the party took black voters for granted—as Sharpton now charges daily.

The second factor contributing to the Dems' racial predicament is the departure of Clinton's chosen heir, Al Gore. Though lacking Clinton's personal magic, Gore enjoyed tremendous advantages from his association with the president. And Gore had his own long-standing ties to the black community, in part thanks to his father's record on civil rights. "Ben Hooks, former executive director of the NAACP and a native Tennesseean, grew up very close to the Gore family," recalls Brazile. And, of course, Gore's biggest defeat— the Florida recount battle—sealed his reputation among black voters. Virtually overnight, he became, as one Democratic strategist put it, "the most aggrieved man in America." Black Americans felt his pain especially acutely, because of the allegations that Republicans had conspired to keep black voters from the polls. Gore's defeat became black America's as well.

While Gore enjoyed the history and credibility with black voters to challenge Sharpton's racial strategy (it's notable Sharpton didn't run against him in 2000), the current crop of Democratic candidates lacks this advantage. Each campaign, of course, has its prepared spin about why its guy will appeal to black voters. Lieberman's people point to his association with the Florida fiasco, his involvement with civil rights marches in the 1960s, and his religiosity; Edwards has the Southern thing going for him, as well as his championing of the little guy during his years as a trial lawyer; Gephardt has his ties to the Congressional Black Caucus, for whom he has done many favors over the years; and so on. And all of the 2004 contenders are scrambling to hook up with the black staffers, opinion leaders, and local politicians who can help them plead their case with black voters. But none of them has the range of deeper, long-term associations that Clinton or Gore could call on. "They just lack that natural [connection]," says Brazile.

Yet another reason for the political vacuum Sharpton has stepped into is, of course, the fall from grace of his onetime mentor Jesse Jackson. For years now, Sharpton has been positioning himself to inherit Jackson's mantle as the voice of black America—an inheritance that Jackson himself sped along with a series of scandals both personal and financial. If Jackson were running this time, or (more likely) still had the credibility to help rally black voters behind one of the other candidates, there's little chance Sharpton would have jumped into the fray. But, with Jackson's decline from prominence, Sharpton has been free to pitch his own run as the sequel to Jackson's historic 1988 showing.

Once upon a time, it looked like Jackson's 1988 bid might lay the ground-work for something better. Though largely forgotten, the first sequel to Jackson's candidacy was the 1992 presidential bid of former Virginia Governor Doug Wilder. Wilder's campaign lasted about 15 seconds but nonetheless seemed to offer a compelling model in which black elected politicians, accustomed to working from within the system, could take a larger role in national politics, marginalizing racial firebrands like Sharpton. This, obviously, hasn't happened—and the reason is straightforward. The majority of viable presidential contenders come from the ranks of senators and governors, and today—more than a decade after Wilder's candidacy—there is not a single black senator or governor in the country. To some extent, say some Dems, this is because many of the party's most talented black pols hail from the South, where increasingly any Democratic candidate—especially a minority one—faces an uphill battle for statewide office. Others point more specifically to the racial gerrymandering of congressional districts, arguing that perversely it can hurt a minority representative's chances for higher office. "The center of gravity is so different in a majority-minority district," says one party strategist. "To win statewide office, you'd then have to turn around and reinvent yourself." What's more, says Brazile, even talented black candidates often get overlooked when money and resources are being distributed by the party. (She cites Oregon State Treasurer Jim Hill's gubernatorial primary run last year as a prime example.)

Internal party politics have proved to be another sore point of late. Many blacks—including Sharpton—were upset by the way the Democratic National Committee archly dismissed former Atlanta Mayor Maynard Jackson when he challenged Terry McAuliffe for committee chairman in 2001. Likewise, there was grumbling after new House Minority Leader Nancy Pelosi ignored Louisiana Representative William Jefferson's interest in being named head of the Democratic Congressional Campaign Committee, instead tapping her California chum Representative Robert Matsui. Both decisions may have been correct on the merits, but more than a few black leaders felt they should have been more involved in the consultation process. (Of course, such recriminations are always strongest when the party loses—and doesn't have the White House patronage machine to dole out goodies to keep constituent groups happy.) Brazile even points to a January Associated Press story about the candidates' top campaign advisers in which "not one campaign had the good sense to list the number of prominent African-Americans supporting their candidacies." It was a strategic error, says Brazile, "and why the Al Sharptons of the world will always have a foothold for sticking their finger in the eye of the Democratic Party."

In the coming election, Democrats have only heightened the racial anxiety by scheduling the South Carolina primary right on the heels of Iowa and New Hampshire. At least 40 percent of the state's Democratic primary voters are black, and Sharpton—who will be hard-pressed to make more than a token showing in lily-white Iowa or New Hampshire—intends to take full advantage. His white competitors, meanwhile, are scrambling to establish their racial bona fides. Already, we're seeing the absurd spectacle of John Edwards vowing to uphold the NAACP's economic boycott of South Carolina to protest the presence of the Confederate battle flag on the grounds of the state capitol—a boycott that many of the state's black leaders, including powerful Representative Jim Clyburn, have rejected. (As the other campaigns snickered of Edwards's pandering, "How are you supposed to run a primary campaign without spending money in the state?")

The Democrats are also suffering, ironically, from the GOP's racial controversies. The past few months have seen the Bush administration's decision to reintroduce affirmative action into the public debate by coming out in opposition to the University of Michigan's affirmative action program, now before the Supreme Court; Trent Lott's unfortunate—and costly—remarks at Strom Thurmond's one-hundredth birthday party; and the White House's nomination and subsequent renomination to the federal bench of Mississippi Judge Charles Pickering, whose position in a cross-burning case has made him anathema to the civil rights community. Cumulatively, these incidents signal that the era of good feelings and harmony proclaimed in the wake of the September 11 attacks is officially over. The country has returned to its usual divisions—race central among them.

All of which, one can only presume, is just fine by Al Sharpton, who, after all, made his name by fueling racial discord. When asked, Sharpton denies he's running to be the spokesman for black America and insists that his message will resonate well beyond his traditional base. But, at times, even he can't help cracking wise about just how alien he is to white voters. After a mad dash between campaign stops in Greenville, the reverend tucked into a late lunch at an all-you-can-eat food bar. As he chowed down on veggies and fried chicken, a stream of well-wishers—all black—wandered over for autographs and pictures. As Sharpton rose to leave, the white manager of the restaurant stopped him for a quick photo. The reverend obliged, and then, cruising past his waiting entourage on his way to the restroom, mumbled dryly, "He thought I was John Kerry." For the rest of the Democratic field, race is nothing to joke about this season. And, unless Democrats begin to deal with the structural forces threatening to re-create the racial fratricide of the '80s, it may not be a laughing matter in the party for a long time to come.

Contributors

Jack Beatty is a senior editor at *The Atlantic Monthly*. He is the author of several books, including *Colossus: How the Corporation Changed America*.

Richard Brookhiser is a senior editor at *National Review* and a columnist for *The New York Observer*. He has written numerous books, including *America's First Dynasty: The Adamses, 1735-1918*, and *Founding Father: Rediscovering George Washington*.

Patrick Buchanan is a columnist for *WorldNetDaily.com*. He served as White House Communications Director under Ronald Reagan, and was a candidate for the 1992 Republican presidential nomination. He is the author of numerous books including, most recently, *The Death of the West*.

Elisabeth Bumiller is the White House correspondent for *The New York Times*, and has written two books: *May You Be the Mother of a Hundred Sons: A Journey Among the Women of India*, and *The Secrets of Mariko: A Year in the Life of a Japanese Woman and Her Family*.

George W. Bush is the 43rd President of the United States.

Robert Byrd has been a U.S. Senator from the state of West Virginia since 1958.

James Carney writes about politics for *Time* magazine. He has also worked as a special correspondent for CNN.

John Cassidy is a staff writer for *The New Yorker*. He is the author of *Dot.con: The Greatest Story Ever Told*.

Jonathan Chait is a senior editor at *The New Republic*. He has also written for *The New York Times*, *The Wall Street Journal*, *The American Prospect*, *Slate*, *Time* and other publications.

Eleanor Clift is a contributing editor and columnist at *Newsweek*. She is also a regular panelist on the *The McLaughlin Group*, and a political analyst for the Fox News Network. She has co-authored two books with her husband, Tom Brazaitis, including *Madam President: Shattering the Last Glass Ceiling*.

Richard Cohen is an op-ed columnist for *The Washington Post*. He is the co-author, with Jules Witcover, of *A Heartbeat Away: The Investigation and Resignation of Spiro T. Agnew*.

Michelle Cottle is a senior editor at *The New Republic*.

John Dickerson is a White House correspondent for *Time* magazine.

E. J. Dionne Jr. is an op-ed columnist for *The Washington Post*. He is the author of *Why Americans Hate Politics* and *They Only Look Dead: Why Progressives Will Dominate The Next Political Era.*

Maureen Dowd is an op-ed columnist for *The New York Times*, where she was awarded the 1999 Pulitzer Prize for distinguished commentary.

Robert Draper is a writer-at-large for *GQ* magazine.

James Fallows is a national correspondent for *The Atlantic Monthly* and a contributing editor to *The Washington Monthly*. He is the author of several books, including *Breaking The News*.

Benjamin Forest is an assistant professor of geography at Dartmouth, where he teaches courses on political, legal, and cultural geography, as well as a public policy class on voting rights and political representation.

David Francis is the senior economics correspondent at *The Christian Science Monitor*.

Thomas Friedman is the foreign affairs op-ed columnist for *The New York Times*. He won the Pulitzer Prize for international reporting in 1983 and in 1988, and was awarded the 2002 Pulitzer Prize for commentary. He is the author of several books, including *From Beirut to Jerusalem*, the 1989 National Book Award winner for non-fiction.

Meryl Gordon is a contributing editor to *New York* magazine.

Mark Green is a former New York City Public Advocate and Consumer Affairs Commissioner, and in 2001 was the Democratic candidate for Mayor of New York City. He is the author of several books, including *Selling Out* and *Who Runs Congress?*

Bob Herbert writes a twice-weekly op-ed column on politics, urban affairs, and social trends for *The New York Times*.

Christopher Hitchens is a columnist for *Vanity Fair* magazine and a contributing writer to *Slate.com*. He has written numerous books, including *Why Orwell Matters* and *The Trial of Henry Kissinger*.

Michael Ignatieff is the Carr Professor of Human Rights Practice and the director of the Carr Center of Human Rights Policy at Harvard's John F. Kennedy School of Government.

Lawrence Kaplan is a senior editor at *The New Republic*. He is the co-author, with William Kristol, of *The War Over Iraq: Saddam's Tyranny and America's Mission*.

Robert Kaplan is a correspondent for *The Atlantic Monthly*. He has written numerous books, including *Warrior Politics: Why Leadership Requires a Pagan Ethos* and *Balkan Ghosts: A Journey Through History*.

Michael Kinsley is the founding editor of the webzine *Slate.com*, and a contributing writer to *Time* magazine. He also served for six years as the co-host of the CNN program *Crossfire*. He has written several books, including *Big Babies: Vintage Whines*, a collection of essays.

Joe Klein is a columnist for *Time* magazine, and a contributing writer to *The New Yorker*. He is the author of several books, including *Primary Colors* and *The Natural: Bill Clinton's Misunderstood Presidency*.

Naomi Klein is a Toronto-based journalist and television commentator. She is the author of *No Logo: Taking Aim at the Brand Bullies* and *Fences and Windows: Dispatches from the Front Lines of the Globalization Debate*.

Nicholas Kristof is an op-ed columnist for *The New York Times*. Previously he served as Associate Managing Editor of the *Times*, responsible for the Sunday editions. In 1990, he and his wife, Sheryl WuDunn, were awarded a joint Pulitzer Prize for their coverage of the Tiananmen Square democracy movement in China.

Willam Kristol is editor of *The Weekly Standard*. He also appears regularly on Fox News Sunday and the Fox News Channel. He is the co-author, with Lawrence Kaplan, of *The War Over Iraq: Saddam's Tyranny and America's Mission*.

Paul Krugman is a professor of economics and international affairs at Princeton University, and writes a twice-weekly op-ed column for *The New York Times*. He is the author of numerous books, including *Fuzzy Math: The Essential Guide to the Bush Tax Plan*.

Lawrence Kudlow is a contributing editor at *National Review* and the economics editor of *National Review Online*. He is also chief economist for CNBC (where he co-hosts *Kudlow & Cramer*), a regular panelist on *The McLaughlin Group*, and is the author of *American Abundance: The New Economic and Moral Prosperity*.

Robert Kuttner is a founder and co-editor of *The American Prospect*. He also writes a syndicated column on political economy, and is a contributing columnist to *Business Week*. He is the author of several books, including *Everything For Sale* and *The End of Laissez-Faire*.

Lewis Lapham is the editor of *Harper's Magazine*. He has written numerous books, including *Theatre of War*, *Fortune's Child*, and *Money and Class in America*.

Simon Lazarus is a Washington-based lawyer and writer. He previously served on President Jimmy Carter's White House Domestic Policy Staff, covering regulatory and legal-policy issues.

John Leo is a contributing editor and columnist at *U.S. News & World Report*. He is the author of *Two Steps Ahead of the Thought Police* and *How the Russians Invented Baseball and Other Essays of Enlightenment*.

Anthony Lewis was an op-ed columnist for *The New York Times* from 1969 to 2001. He won the Pultizer Prize for national reporting in 1955, and again in 1963. He is the author of several books, including *Gideon's Trumpet*.

Ryan Lizza is the White House correspondent for *The New Republic*. His writing has also appeared in *The New York Times Magazine* and *The Washington Monthly*.

John McWhorter is an associate professor of linguistics at the University of California, Berkeley. He is the author of several books, including *Losing the Race: Self-Sabotage in Black America* and *Authentically Black: Essays for the Black Silent Majority*.

Stephanie Mencimer is a contributing editor at *The Washington Monthly*. She has also worked as an investigative reporter for *The Washington Post*, and was a recipient of the 2000 Harry Chapin Media Award for reporting on hunger and poverty.

Michael Moore is a documentary filmmaker and writer. His latest film, *Bowling for Columbine*, won the 2002 Academy Award for Best Documentary. He is the author of *Stupid White Men* and *Downsize This!: Random Threats From an Unarmed American*.

Ralph Nader was the Green Party candidate for President in 2000. He has authored or co-authored numerous books, including *Crashing The Party: How to Tell the Truth and Still Run for President*.

Kenneth Pollack is a senior fellow and director of research at the Saban Center for Middle East Policy. He was director for Persian Gulf Affairs at the National Security Council from 1999 to 2001, and has also served as a military analyst for the CIA. He is the author of *The Threatening Storm: The Case for Invading Iraq*.

Anna Quindlen is a contributing editor and columnist at *Newsweek*. In 1992, as a columnist for *The New York Times*, she was awarded the Pulitzer Prize for Commentary. She has written numerous books, including the novels *Black and Blue* and *One True Thing*.

William Raspberry writes a twice-weekly op-ed column for *The Washington Post*, for which he was awarded the Pulitzer Prize for Distinguished Commentary in 1994. He is the author of the book *Looking Backward at Us*.

Gregory Rodriguez is a senior fellow at the New America Foundation and a contributing editor to the *Los Angeles Times* Opinion section.

Ron Suskind is national correspondent for *Esquire* magazine. He also writes for several other publications, including *The New York Times Magazine*, and is the author of the book *A Hope in the Unseen*. In 1995, while working for the *Wall Street Journal*, he was awarded the Pulitzer Prize for feature writing.

Matt Taibbi is a contributing writer to the *New York Press*.

Jeffrey Toobin is a staff writer for *The New Yorker*, and a legal analyst for ABC News. He is the author of several books, including *A Vast Conspiracy* and *Too Close to Call: The Thirty-Six-Day Battle to Decide the 2000 Election*.

Karen Tumulty is the national political correspondent for *Time*. She has previously served as *Time*'s White House correspondent, and also covered Al Gore's 2002 campaign for the magazine.

James Wolcott is a contributing editor to *Vanity Fair* magazine, and the author of the novel, *The Catsitters*.

Michael Wolff writes the column "This Media Life" for *New York* magazine, where he is a contributing editor. He has written numerous books, including *Burn Rate: How I Survived the Gold Rush Years on the Internet*.

Bob Woodward is an assistant managing editor at *The Washington Post*. He is the author of numerous books, including *Bush at War* and *The Agenda: Inside the Clinton White House*.

Fareed Zakaria is the editor of *Newsweek International*, and a columnist for *Newsweek*. He is also a regular member of the roundtable for *This Week with George Stephanapoulos* on ABC, and has written several books including, most recently, *The Future of Freedom: Illiberal Democracy at Home and Abroad*.

Permissions

"W. and the 'Boy Genius'" by James Carney and John Dickerson. Copyright © 2002 by TIME Inc. Reprinted with permission. Originally appeared in the November 18, 2002 issue of *Time*.

"Why Are These Men Laughing?" by Ron Suskind. Copyright © 2003 by Ron Suskind. Reprinted with kind permission of the author. Originally appeared in the January 2003 issue of *Esquire*.

"The Mind of George W. Bush" by Richard Brookhiser. Copyright © 2003 by Richard Brookhiser. Reprinted with kind permission of the author. Originally appeared in the April 2003 issue of *The Atlantic Monthly*.

"Special K" by Jonathan Chait. Copyright © 2002 by The New Republic, LLC. Reprinted by permission of *The New Republic*. Originally appeared in *The New Republic*, December 30, 2002.

"The Ideological Imposter" by Robert Kuttner. Copyright © 2002 by Robert Kuttner. Reprinted by permission of *The American Prospect*. Originally appeared in *The American Prospect*, June 3, 2002.

"With Signals and Maneuvers, Bush Orchestrates an Ouster" by Elisabeth Bumiller. Copyright © 2002 by The New York Times Co. Reprinted with permission. Originally published in *The New York Times*, December 21, 2002.

"What Is He Thinking?" by Eleanor Clift. Copyright © 2003 by Newsweek Inc. All rights reserved. Reprinted with permission. Originally appeared in *Newsweek*, February 7, 2003.

"Partisan Lines Harden in Debate Over Tax Cuts" by David Francis. Copyright © 2003 by David Francis. Reprinted by permission. Originally appeared in *The Christian Science Monitor*, March 31, 2003.

"Wealthy Choice" by Ryan Lizza. Copyright © 2003 by The New Republic, LLC. Reprinted by permission of *The New Republic*. Originally appeared in *The New Republic*, January 20, 2003.

"From Baghdad to Iwo Jima" by Lawrence Kudlow. Copyright © 2003 by Lawrence Kudlow. Reprinted by permission. Originally appeared in the *National Review Online*, April 15, 2003.

"Bushonomics" by John Cassidy. Copyright © 2003 by John Cassidy. Reprinted by kind permission of the author. Originally appeared in *The New Yorker*, May 12, 2003.

"The Faces of Budget Cuts" by Bob Herbert. Copyright © 2003 by The New

simplehome

simplehome

calm spaces for comfortable living

mark & sally bailey

photography by Debi Treloar

LONDON · NEW YORK

Senior designer   Paul Tilby
Editor   Delphine Lawrance
Location research   Sally Bailey, Jess Walton
Production controller   Toby Marshall
Art director   Leslie Harrington
Publishing director   Alison Starling

Styling   Mark Bailey

First published in 2009
This edition published in 2017 by
Ryland Peters & Small
20–21 Jockey's Fields
London WC1R 4BW
and
341 E 116th Street
New York, NY 10029
www.rylandpeters.com

ISBN: 978-1-84975-803-1

10 9 8 7 6 5 4 3 2 1

Library of Congress Cataloging-in-Publication Data
for the original edition of this book is as follows:

Bailey, Mark.
  Simple home : calm spaces for comfortable living
/ Mark & Sally Bailey ; photography by Debi Treloar.
     p. cm.
  Includes index.
  ISBN 978-1-84597-915-7
  1. Interior decoration--Psychological aspects. I.
Bailey, Sally. II. Treloar, Debi. III. Title. IV. Title: Calm
spaces for comfortable living.
  NK2113.B34 2009
  747--dc22

2009010301

Printed and bound in China.

contents

introduction

The simple home is about keeping things plain and useful – it is a chance to get back to basics, to consider ideals of good design and the forgotten traditions of craftsmanship and then think how they can be adapted to a more modern approach. This way of living feels refreshing in a time when things seem to have a tendency to get over-complicated.

That is not to say the simple home has to be hard-edged or overly austere, with no cats, crumbs or kids allowed. Instead, it is the key to comfortable, relaxed living – it allows for flexibility and endless options, giving you the chance to curate your home like a personal museum. Reconsider your belongings and only surround yourself with things that you really love. Objects that have been well crafted can make everyday life a pleasure; from sweeping the stairs with a beautifully constructed wooden

right A marble sheet propped up on two ornate but very weathered former French café table stands makes a great resting place for some daffodils and woven wicker trays.

opposite A room infused with natural daylight and clean white paint is the perfect spot for two simply upholstered white chairs to sit quietly side by side.

brush to relaxing on a soft, linen-covered sofa at the end of a hard day. The traditions that lie behind the manufacture of these things are all about using the best materials for the job, perhaps making them by hand – even if it takes longer this way, and ensuring that the end product will last for years. Well-made, well-designed things grow old gracefully. But as well as these industrious objects, be sure to include others that are cherished because they remind you of a person, place or time; these are the treasures that will make your home unique.

Another aspect of the simple home way of thinking is the ability to find beauty in the imperfections that come with age and wear and tear. Old furniture that has been loved and looked after enough to stand the test of time has a reassuring, timeless elegance, no matter how battered, scraped and scratched it may appear now. So choose pieces that have a history; not necessarily antiques but items that have been rescued and given a new purpose in life, or new furniture that has been crafted out of found objects and old pieces of wood. Such things have a natural honesty and integrity that makes them desirable rather than fashionable.

this page The essence of simplicity in a quiet corner – two bentwood ash stools and a handmade porcelain lamp slung casually over a nail. The wire basket is filled with old lavender twigs for a sweet-scented fire.

opposite left An unusual twist on tradition, here old wooden curtain rings are used for keeping vintage linen napkins in place.

opposite right Utensils stored tidily in a glazed jar. Casually posed postcards soften the Sicilian marble.

opposite Scaffolding poles form the simple skeleton of this bed, while the nonchalantly slung, graphic handwoven textiles and white patchwork blanket make a great contrast. Ticking rugs on the floor mirror the graphic theme neatly.

below Copper piping makes a functional and honest-looking towel warmer. Strings of pebble and stone collected on beachside holidays add to its rugged charm.

Light plays an important part in a home with a pared-down, simple style – it makes your space feel clear, uncluttered, light and airy. In an understated way, a room filled with natural light will be the first thing you notice and will certainly leave a lasting impression, long after the furniture and the fixtures and fittings have faded away. Light can make an even better impression if the backdrop is calm and quiet. Choose colours that are inspired by nature rather than fashionable colour charts, or colours that just turn up from underneath layers of paint. With this in mind, the shades found in the simple home are soft and chalkily pale, but they retain a feeling of freshness that comes about when things are stored away and the space is neat, tidy and as free from clutter as possible. So once you have taken all those articles that you don't really need to the grateful ladies at the charity shop, you will need to invest in decent storage – though not just mass-produced, ugly plastic boxes. Think in a more creative way and your home will look all the better for it.

In the end, you can't really go wrong if you follow the assertion of American architect, interior designer, writer and all-round man of wisdom, Frank Lloyd Wright:

'Study nature, love nature, stay close to nature and it will never fail you.'

philosophy

colour

above A worn, weather-beaten wall, showing off its different layers of texture and subtle tones, and an old outdoor verdigris copper tap demonstrate how colours change and mature over time.

above right Piles of ticking cushions and blankets provide contrastingly sharp stripes of colour in simpler surrounds.

opposite An assortment of collected maps, photos, lumpy-textured wall and nature are all subtle ways to bring a glimpse of colour into your home.

On first glance, the simple home may appear to be devoid of colour, but that is to dismiss the subtleties of an understated, more natural approach to the subject. The colour scheme is not dictated to by the whims of what's in fashion, colour charts or the rules and regulations of the colour wheel. In this way, it is much more personal, with colour coming from the addition of one or two of your favourite things. The simple home is predominantly filled with soft colours that quietly complement each other and envelop your surroundings with a sense of calm. Think of the colours and texture of handmade paper and you'll be well on the way to the perfect palette for your home.

A subtle colour range of classic neutral colours like soft, milky whites, tree-bark beige, creamy ivory and silvery greys forms the perfect painterly backdrop to your space, bathing your home in gentle tones that generously allow other splashes of colour to take centre stage. This might be your favourite painting, a vividly printed cushion or simply a farmhouse jug of flowers.

The deliberately limited colour scheme of your walls reflects the natural, honest materials of your home – beautiful grainy wooden floors and furniture, as well as the undulations and dimples of old, worn stone and tiles. Neutral colours welcome the infusion of warmth from the tones and textures found in such enduring signs of construction.

Choosing white to paint your walls is not a step backwards into the glaringly harsh white of monochrome, minimalist colour schemes. The look is easily softened by what you choose to surround yourself with; go for slubby linens or chunkily hand-knitted blankets coloured with natural dyes rather than the hard edges of minimalist furniture (or lack of it). Sunlight plays a large part too, bringing out the best in the world of white. With light falling through your windows, the varieties of tone become almost infinite; think of white cotton sheets drying in the sunlight and flapping in the breeze. White and sunlight are the best of flexible friends, with white changing tone depending on the time of day, like the colours of nature changing depending on the season.

Other colours that work well with soft neutrals are generally those that are mixed with generous quantities of white. Think back to days at school spent mixing paints in a palette – you hardly need to add any coloured pigment to give white a delicious hint of something else. These colours have a faded feeling of worn-out softness; just like a child's soft toy that has been washed hundreds of times but remains the favourite among the hoards of shinier plastic toys, or comforting milky drinks that warm your hands in the depths of winter.

opposite left The beautifully textured wall is almost like an Impressionist painting of a cloudy sky. The soft folds of the loosely covered armchair enhance the subtle blue shades.

opposite centre Artworks are another way to introduce small flashes of colour into the home.

opposite right The stripey grain of this white-washed table shows off the surprisingly myriad tones of white, while a platter of old varieties of English apples adds another gently colourful element.

this page A gently faded denim-covered armchair looks like the perfect spot to rest by the creamy Aga. Its washed-out blues are the perfect partner to the terracotta floor tiles.

You are unlikely to find huge expanses of shout-out-loud bright colours in the simple home. There might be the odd burst of it here and there, sometimes planned or sometimes more unexpectedly found by chance – maybe discovered hidden under layers of flaky paint – or more deliberately in the detail of a cushion or cosy woollen throw. Nature is also a good place to start when considering flashes of brighter bits of colour. Think about how colour changes as things age – like the way copper oxidizes when left to the elements, going from bright shiny orange to soft verdigris (like the Statue of Liberty). Or bring in the innate brightness of nature such as the crazily dazzling orange of

CHOOSE COLOURS THAT ARE INSPIRED BY NATURE RATHER THAN FASHIONABLE COLOUR CHARTS.

autumn leaves, acidic lemony yellows of old-fashioned varieties of apples or bright bunches of flowers casually displayed in old French confit jars. These small splashes of colour add contrast to the larger areas of chalky whites, soft greys and comforting light browns, but at the same time they make you even more aware of the gentleness of your overall colour scheme. The neutral colours harmonize with the brighter flashes of colour and give you and your home a feeling of relaxation and well-being.

above A set of monochrome plates sits on an unusual patchwork tablecloth. The ensemble is softened by the dried grasses.

left A worn music case and shiny boots create a simple still life.

opposite The vivid shades of autumn bring bold colours into the home – the fig leaves are in fact made of rusting steel.

above left Concertina paper lanterns, left undecorated, are hung on long, supple bamboo canes to create an unusual point of interest on a gently sloping ceiling.

above centre The dappled patchwork of colours of these steel bistro chairs shows the licks of paint lavished on them over time and are beautiful signs of age, which should not be shied away from.

above right The sturdy bench against a weathered wall reveals the amazing textures of stone.

opposite With its turned brass handle, this door shows the honesty of wood as it wears through use.

We don't often consider the materials our houses are made from; we notice them every now and then as we slide our hands along a smooth wooden handrail or feel a cool tiled floor under bare feet as we run to collect the pile of post pushed through the letterbox. In the simple home, however, the materials of construction are proudly displayed rather than hidden away under layers of paint and plaster. Stone floors and fireplaces, bare, uncovered brickwork, old tiles, wooden floors, doors and beams are star materials – especially when set off by softly neutral colours. In previous years they would have been hidden or disguised; now is the time to restore them to their former glory and proudly reveal the inner workings of your house.

materials

WOOD AND STONE ARE HARD-WEARING, ROUGH, TOUGH MATERIALS. THEY ARE WELL AND TRULY CAPABLE OF STANDING THE TEST OF TIME.

Floors and walls form the bare bones of your home – celebrate their construction, leaving them unpainted or scraping off layers of paint and plaster to reveal their inner beauty. It is an honest way to 'decorate', despite being almost the exact opposite of decoration. Leaving them freshly unadorned shows what your home has been through before you came along and how these ancient materials are well and truly capable of standing the test of time and ever-demanding families.

Scratches, flaky paint, speckles, freckles, raw edges and nail and pin heads left on display are the hallmarks of authenticity and craftsmanship – these are signs of age and belong to materials that have been well cared for, repaired and not left to quietly rot. While wood and stone are hard-wearing, rough, tough materials, they do have their points of weakness and require a little TLC. Their continued existence shows that they've been loved and this gives us a cosy warm glow inside.

above left A simple wooden shelf with metal rod supports is home to a pile of Vietnamese bamboo sieves. The little bird on a wire adds humorous detail.

above right Unusually curvaceous apothecary bottles with stemmed bases hold linear-looking twigs, bringing the more delicate materials of nature into the home.

opposite Contrasting materials holding kindling work well together. The wirework basket was rescued from an abandoned park rubbish bin.

Invite more modern materials into your home too; the unexpected combinations of textures they introduce make our homes a sensory pleasure. Recycled rubber has an honest durability and is up to the hardest of tasks in your home. Stainless steel and aluminium are other materials that are ignored at your peril. They are shiny but not too shiny or brash, and provide the perfect contrast to more roughly hewn materials. Another up-and-coming star is concrete, somewhat surprisingly if you have memories of brutalist 1960s architecture. Rugged-looking poured concrete makes for a floor with an amazing surface.

When looking for furniture, choose skeletal wooden chairs and go for tables either with skinny, tapered legs or sturdy, extra-chunky ones – extremes like these make much more of a statement than in-between compromises. Another surprising material to consider is paper, such as paper lanterns or lampshades. Its delicate nature plays with the sturdiness of other, more solid materials in the home.

MATERIALS OF CONSTRUCTION ARE PROUDLY DISPLAYED RATHER THAN BEING HIDDEN AWAY UNDER LAYERS OF PAINT AND PLASTER.

above Wood shows its signs of age and wear and tear with pride – whatever you do, don't cover them up with new paint.

right A sliding door made from sturdy sheet metal panels has been brushed with tourmaline to make it less shiny and to speed up the aging process.

far right A closer view of the door shows how the panels have been riveted together. Delicate paper decorations soften the industrial backdrop.

opposite Scratchy-looking rusty metal and concrete contrast beautifully with the polished floor, glass balustrade and smooth cupboard doors.

this page The mixture of natural shapes and textures creates a restful corner in this room. The unruly swirl of twigs in the fireplace provides another piece of nature in the home.

opposite right Wonky, hand-thrown porcelain vases by Bridget Tennant crowd together on a simple angular fireplace. Light diffusing through Perspex shades adds to the sense of calm pervading the room.

opposite left A sculptural paper shade hung from a length of bamboo.

We seem to be so busy all the time, rushing around with long lists of things to do. The constant surrounding bombardment of random snippets of noise only serves to raise our stress levels further still. With this going on around us every day, our homes really need to be a haven of tranquillity and relaxation. The good news is that if you choose to create an interior that embraces the idea of simplicity, you will infuse your home with a sense of calm without really having to think too much about it.

The ice cream-soft colour scheme of the simple home, with its tones of whites, honey browns and silvery greys, goes a long way to creating this tranquil idyll. These

colours are easy on the eye and gently whisper in contrast to the bright colours that shout at us during our working day. Choosing tones that are close together in the colour spectrum creates a feeling of harmony, as nothing jars or leaps out at us. Instead, they relax the senses, and as the colours react to the differing qualities of seasonal daylight, they can feel either cosy and warming like a creamy lambswool sweater or, on a hot day, deliciously cool.

calm

far left A late-Victorian daybed re-upholstered in plain linen provides a place of rest by the window. The elaborately turned table adds to the air of refined elegance, but the bare washed floorboards ensure that the room remains fuss-free.

left The theme of relaxed elegance is continued in this room, with a squashy-looking sofa and simple metal-framed daybed piled with silky wheat-filled cushions and blankets. The tones of white add to the sense of calm.

YOUR VERY FAVOURITE THINGS, HOWEVER INSIGNIFICANT THEY MAY SEEM, SHOULD BE WELL MADE AND DO THEIR JOB WITHOUT BEING OSTENTATIOUS.

Taking time to find the beauty in small, seemingly ordinary things makes daily life a pleasure. Make sure that absolutely everything in your home has a place in your heart. Your very favourite things, however insignificant they may seem, should be well made and do their job without being ostentatious. Don't save your good taste for books and paintings; everyday items such as soft, fluffy piles of towels in the bathrooom or the mug you drink your morning coffee from can bring you joy. In this way, the simple act of opening a cupboard can make you smile, be it a cupboard stacked with sheets and blankets in your favourite colour combinations, a shelf of simple Japanese-looking drinking vessels or neat piles of monochrome plates and bowls.

this page The sheer curtain, subtly embroidered with a quote from writer and film-maker Marcel Pagnol, softens the light flooding through the large window and creates a tranquil setting for reading. The naturally curving stool has been hand-wrapped with thick, undyed twine.

opposite A paint-splattered ladder resting against a plain white wall contrasts well with the shelves holding 'Seven Cups on Floating Grounds' by ceramicist Julian Stair.

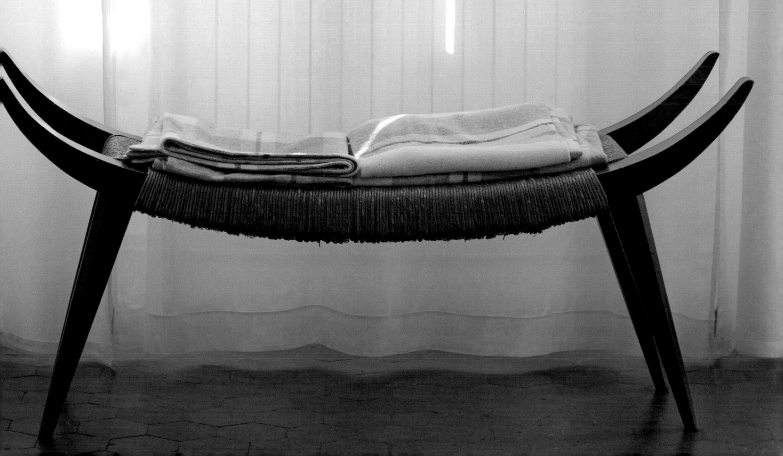

'les mots qui ont en son noble contiennent toujours de belles images.'

Marcel Pagnol

DECORATING YOUR HOME WITH HANDMADE OBJECTS MAKES YOU FEEL GOOD – THEY TAKE TIME TO CREATE AND PROMOTE A SENSE OF PEACE.

above left The clean lines of the room remain unbroken by leaning the prints on the table rather than a more conventional wall display.

above right Delicate flowers contrast well with a sturdy, recycled rubber bucket.

opposite The symmetry of this space creates a wonderful feeling of serenity, enhanced all the more by the subdued colours and soft textures.

The well-worn materials of your home have an easy, timeless grace, and as well as reminding us of a time when life wasn't so hectic, they provide us with a connection to nature. Sitting on a beautiful wooden floor transports us back to the last time we took a moment to sit under a tree in a sunny park. Collections of pebbles and seashells from summers spent beachcombing have a similarly calming effect. Decorating your home with one or two handmade objects makes you feel good; they take time to create, and this quality promotes a sense of peace. Having a disciplined cleaning routine and well-considered storage helps your home to be clutter free, clean and tidy. As a result you get a cleansing, calming space that is liberated from reminders of household chores yet to be done. The same goes for overly embellished interiors that are too fussy or frilly; all that frippery gets in the way.

Purposefully create your own small oasis of calm. All it takes is a pile of soft, unbleached cotton cushions in a cosy corner, or a favourite armchair placed in a daylight-infused room, with sheer curtains wafting in the breeze. They're perfect places to sit and quietly take in your home's beauty.

opposite These handwoven twiggy platters highlight the untamed nature of craft. Set on a smooth marble surface with an elaborate base, their wonky charm is all the more evident.

right Redundant pieces of print block have found the perfect resting place in a hand-carved Ethiopian wooden vessel, which was probably used for some kind of game in its former life.

far right Mahatma Ghandi watches over piles of hand-stitched books covered in offcuts of raw Indian cotton.

below An old tailor's dummy is put to good use as a stand for strings of jewellery.

When thinking about craft and handmade objects, it's important to get as far away from memories of garish crocheted tea cosies at Sunday craft fairs as possible. These days, craft can be viewed as a rebellion against the ubiquity of mass production. We've all had more than enough of seeing the same things over and over, in one home to the next, with the same short life span. Choosing something handmade by an artisan is a celebration of individuality, durability and simple beauty.

craft

above Exquisite examples of the highest form of quality craftsmanship. A collection of plain, unglazed ceramic vessels and sculptural looking teapots by Julian Stair. The centre teapot sports a wisteria handle. The pared-down palette and simple shapes lend these beautiful pots a refined air.

right Ever so slightly wonky, tall, skinny, fat, thin and tiny porcelain vases hand thrown by Bridget Tennant. Together they create a monumental, almost Stonehenge-like display.

CHOOSING SOMETHING HANDMADE BY AN ARTISAN IS A CELEBRATION OF INDIVIDUALITY, DURABILITY AND SIMPLE BEAUTY.'

The influence of craft and all things handmade in the simple home can be felt in every room. Handmade objects of all shapes and sizes have a myriad of uses, from tables made from reclaimed wooden floorboards, handwoven naturally dyed textiles and tactile hand-thrown ceramics to beautifully intricate jewellery made from a collection of seed pods. These things are made to be used or worn, not just looked at; form and function go hand in hand with aesthetic pleasure. Objects such as these are what make our homes personal and unique. We generally buy something that is handcrafted because we love it and this is a big part of the simple home – to carefully choose well-made, useful things because they please us, not just because they are cheap and easily obtainable. In this way, the everyday becomes infinitely more pleasurable.

The elements of the handmade are an essential part of the ideals of the simple home. They have an inherent individuality – quirks, flaws and a certain wonkiness reveal how they have been made and set them apart from things that have been mass produced and can be found everywhere. The materials used are recognizable, honest and relate to nature: wood, glass, clay and textiles. It is clear that much thought, care, time and attention to detail have gone into the production of handmade objects and this is a large part of their appeal, as it seems to infuse them with a sense of calm and makes them a delight to use.

this page A collection of plain, antique ceramic pots. From left to right – a white stoneware cup from China, a stoneware faceted bowl from Japan, a porcelain offering plate from Korea, a stoneware amawori bottle and stoneware bowl, both from Japan and a stoneware jar from China.

right An old tin truck is neatly parked on a table made from aged pieces of wood board. The unexpected flash of orange adds a sense of fun, along with the floating globe.

far right This scratchy zinc-plated number two probably once adorned a shop front.

below A pile of handmade books covered in patchwork scraps of Indian cotton.

opposite top left These sculptural ceremonial paper hats are amazingly crafted by hand entirely out of paper.

opposite top right A cast-iron star-shaped wall plate watches over some wooden print block.

opposite centre A misty painting atop a marble fireplace.

opposite left A pair of mosaic ceramic hands by Cleo Muzzi.

opposite right A delicate pair of handmade paper wings.

DON'T RELY ON OTHER PEOPLE FOR YOUR CRAFT ITEMS; REDISCOVER SUCH OLD HOBBIES AS MAKING CARDS, KNITTING OR EMBROIDERY.

Handcrafted objects are more often than not made using traditional skills that have been handed down through the generations; by inviting craft into your home, you are keeping these old skills alive. Also, look out for things that were handmade years before, as they tend to be so well constructed that they still have a job to do today. They may need a bit of looking after to bring them back to life, but the time this takes will be well worth it. They feel good to use, some areas smoothed away where they were held by previous owners, plus they're so much more tactile than their modern-day cousins.

Some objects relating to craft may have outlived their previous use, such as wooden print block, but they remind us of an era before the digital age when processes took a little longer and our lives were less hectic. Collections of print block look lovely, with their worn and slightly ink-stained edges, and as well as their aesthetic appeal they can be used on a much smaller scale to make handmade cards – just take time out to do it! Don't rely on other people for your craft items; rediscover such old hobbies as making cards or knitting, embroidery or, if you can find the necessary facilities, ceramics. These crafts have long since shed their old-fashioned image. There are all sorts of inspirational contemporary craftspeople (or makers as they prefer to be known) out there creating amazing items. It's a much better use of time than relying on huge televisions for entertainment.

this page A classic Ercol rocking chair shows off its skeletal clean lines and looks all the more refined as it sits beside a scuffed and scratched set of drawers rescued from a workshop. A French brioche tin has been adapted to create a recycled light shade.

far left A curved wooden cupboard, once hard at work in a shop, has been stripped of its paint to show off its grainy features. It provides a resting place for tin trucks and print block made into an artwork, with its original thin print drawer acting as a frame.

left A detail of the wonderfully worn wooden print block.

below A collage of old and new maps makes a recycled version of wallpaper.

recycling

We all know that we should recycle as much as we can, carefully separating jam jars from cereal packets and newspapers. In the same way, reconsider how you shop for furniture; it's time to rescue, re-think and reuse – visit flea markets, bazaars, antique fairs and reclamation yards. People throw too much stuff away, so encourage an end to this culture of disposability. Other people's junk could be your perfect table, chair, piece of storage and so forth.

Have an open mind and don't stop searching until you find something to fall instantly in love with. It's probably not going to be about the task you need them to perform in your home; it's more likely to be down to texture, a flash of bright colour peeking out from layers of flaky paint or the signs of quality craftsmanship. If you're prepared to think differently about what goes where, then any piece of furniture has a role to play in all the rooms of your house.

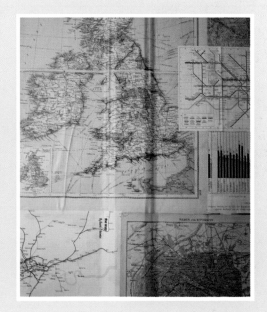

below A stripey patchwork blanket made from strips of suiting fabric is used to cover the blemishes of an old chair.

right A jacket made from military canvas kitbags.

It goes without saying that old furniture will have flaws, blemishes and imperfections, especially if you find something hidden under piles of junk at a flea market. These signs of wear and tear should be seen as qualities – proof of age and individuality; characteristics you're not going to find in mass-produced, flat-packed convenience furniture. Take the trouble to repair if necessary, but don't fuss with invisible mending. If you find a comfy looking chair with worn-out upholstery,

throw on some vintage fabric cushions, or a handcrafted patchwork blanket. In this way, you hide the small imperfections and create the perfect place to curl up with a mug of coffee and a good book. Don't be fooled by appearances – give outdoor furniture a treat and use it inside your home instead; it will thank you for it! A weathered garden bench makes ideal seating alongside a chunky wooden kitchen table, and if you need extra seating, a curly ironwork chair provides decorative contrast too. Don't be afraid to mix old and new; worn, faded furniture looks even better next to a sleek, shiny stainless steel

DELIBERATELY MISMATCHING GIVES YOUR HOME INDIVIDUALITY AND A MORE RELAXED ELEGANCE.

above left Hide the signs of overuse with a simple white linen throw, but don't cover up outstanding features of beauty such as clawed feet. The industrial-looking angular lighting has been given a more contemporary twist by removing the shade in favour of a bare curly-wurly filament light bulb.

above right Antique linen from Provence, recently dyed using natural vegetable dyes, shows the versatility of the recycled approach – adapt what you find to suit your needs.

oven or fridge, or when it's providing a resting place for an up-to-the-minute television or music player. Be creative; even a worn-out old door has its uses – try it as an unusual shelf. If you have a collection of postcards hidden away, old wooden rulers make amazing skinny shelving that is perfect for showing them off. Pieces of floorboard and architrave make beautiful patchwork frames for mirrors or paintings, or tabletops. Surprise yourself by turning an old

French brioche tin or jelly mould into an unusual lampshade – just get someone who knows what they're doing with electricity to help you! The list is endless once you have thrown out pre-conceived ideas and learned to see the potential in absolutely everything.

The simple home is not about feeling stressed out because you can't find the right set of dining chairs or cutlery. Deliberately mismatching gives your home individuality and a more relaxed form

top left Take a closer look – an old door has been put to good use here as an elevated shelf for well-read novels.

centre Two creative examples of recycling – an oversized galvanized catering colander and an old brioche tin have been turned into ingenious and interestingly shaped light shades.

below A decorator's trestle table has been brought into the home and makes a surprisingly elegant dining table, especially when accompanied by a station waiting-room bench.

opposite Reconsidering how you use things creates an element of surprise in your home, as shown here by a row of wooden-spoon hooks.

SIMPLICITY IS THE WATCHWORD HERE – DON'T FILL YOUR HOME WITH TOO MANY THINGS, AS IT CAN QUICKLY DESCEND INTO CLUTTER.

of elegance – pick things that you really, really love; not just because they go with the other five chairs parked around your table or forks nestling in your kitchen drawers.

An added bonus to furniture recycling is that it means you don't have to be too precious about your furniture finds. They've already aged pretty well, and with just a little bit of cleaning, care and attention from you, they'll keep on growing old gracefully, whatever you or your family throws at them.

Do be choosy when perusing flea and antique markets or even the internet – there are lots of good websites out there selling vintage furniture. Remember that simplicity is the watchword here. Don't fill your home with too many things, as it can quickly become overwhelming and descend into clutter. Recycled finds need space in order to fully show off their beautiful imperfections. One or two well-considered larger items provide an unusual talking point, while smaller finds, such as kitchenware, storage jars, old suitcases or stationery, do their jobs with quiet, understated elegance.

comfort

opposite One huge sofa covered in loose linen sits opposite a Chesterfield that is covered unusually in dark linen. The reassuringly sturdy stone fireplace, complete with a log-burning stove and Cornish granite floor, give the room a comfortingly timeless quality.

above left Generous amounts of daylight are allowed into this room by the parting of a pair of simple linen curtains.

above right An inviting pair of squashy, feather-filled cushions in contrasting fabrics.

Your home should be a serene and tranquil domestic landscape in which to sit back and relax, giving you the chance to forget the stresses of the day. The kind of comfort you seek ultimately depends on the season, but whatever the time of year, you can't go wrong with a huge, squashy sofa piled high with plump cushions – then it's up to you and the elements as to whether or not you light the fire.

The components that make up the look of the simple home – colours, materials, handicraft and recycling – all add up to a comfortable, happy habitat. Be sure to throw them all into the mix, otherwise your home could end up hard-edged, overly minimal and off-puttingly austere.

below An assortment of cushions of varying textures, shapes and sizes invites you to curl up on this sofa. The heavily textured knitted cushions lend a cosy feel, while the others add pattern and colour.

inset Patches of bright neon orange embroidery provide a vivid flash of contrasting colour on this cushion covered in an old linen tea towel.

opposite A few crumples add to the textural values of the easy, elegant home.

The natural materials that predominate in both the structure and furniture in your home – stone, wood and raw brickwork – bring the outside in. They remind us of ruddy-cheeked walks in the country, happily trudging through golden autumn leaves, knowing that a fireside Sunday lunch isn't far away. They're like super-sized versions of the small treasures you might collect on one of these idyllic rambles – skinny twigs, shiny conkers, feathers and pebbles. They are instilled with memories that make us feel warm and ready to hibernate on less clement days, when the rain beats against the windows.

right Soft folds of lightweight fabric wrapped around a bed piled with pillows create a cosy comfort zone in this compact Parisian apartment.

opposite top left Extra-large stitching gives a reassuringly handcrafted feel to this chunky sofa. The roughly woven tapestry behind brings another warm, textural dimension.

opposite centre A pile of Egyptian cotton-filled floor cushions, covered in mousy-coloured linens creates an impromptu resting spot.

opposite top right Shelves of simply decorated, handwoven Indian cotton.

opposite below Everything about the creative process of this beautiful handwoven Indian linen with tribal embroidery speaks of serene simplicity; from the planting of the cotton to spinning it by hand into an uneven yarn.

The milky-soft, natural colours in your home are reminiscent of large mugs of hot chocolate and add to the feeling of relaxation. Make sure that you use paint with a matt finish, as it has a velvety feel, and avoid glaringly shiny plastics, which are more in keeping with the sterile look of a doctor's waiting room. A rich mix of contrasting textures adds to the comforting mood.

Use expanses of easy-to-find utilitarian fabrics such as ticking or canvas to cover your sofa or as a hard-working tablecloth. Add richer, velvety fabrics and a few vintage textiles, softened over time and washing cycles. As with recycled furniture, a flea-market find of well-loved vintage fabrics that have been cared for over the years will give you a warm, cosy glow. As long as they're fresh, a few frayed edges here and there won't matter at all – in fact, they lend an air of relaxed grandeur. Then place your texture-rich sofas and chairs around the fireplace, making it the heart of your living room rather than the television, light a fire and snuggle up under a chunky hand-knitted blanket. All you need to complete the picture is a cup of tea and maybe a gently purring cat. Meeeow!

natural cleaning

above left A waffle-textured cloth and a well-crafted wooden nail brush are ready to hand, resting on an old wall tap.

above right A wooden-handled bristle broom rests against the wall after a hard time sweeping this beautiful hardwood floor. Its utilitarian nature is effectively contrasted with the delicately carved chaise.

opposite An array of wiry bottle brushes are stored in vintage milk bottles. There is one for every occasion and shape of bottle.

If your house is clean and tidy, it's a sign that you treat it with the respect it deserves. A spick and span house is also the perfect foil for the graceful imperfections of the natural materials that make up your home. There's no denying that cleaning is a constant chore, but it can be less painful and better for the environment if you make your own cleaning products. It feels good to be safe in the knowledge that there's nothing with too high a chemical content in your cleaning cupboard. Use beautiful tools too; it's much more pleasing to employ a well-constructed beechwood brush with soft horsehair bristles or an ostrich feather duster, and makes cleaning feel almost glamorous.

BEESWAX POLISH

Beeswax polish is the very best choice for keeping wood looking good, or for perking up any tired wooden furniture. All you need to make your own creamy polish are equal amounts of turpentine and beeswax – and a wide-mouthed jam jar with a lid. If you have a favourite essential oil, you could also add a few drops to the polish.

Get in touch with your local beekeepers' association for advice on buying beeswax. Turpentine should be available from good art shops or hardware stores – make sure you get the real thing, not turps substitute.

The absolutely simplest way to make it is to combine the two ingredients in the jam jar, screw on the lid and leave it in a warm place for a few days. Eventually the beeswax will dissolve in the turpentine.

If you're in more of a hurry to get polishing, you can speed up the process by melting the beeswax first. If you do, be extremely careful. Melt the wax the way you would melt chocolate – by setting the container of wax over a saucepan of hot water. Have a damp tea towel to hand in case disaster strikes.

Apply the finished polish with a cloth or soft brush, leave for about 20 minutes, then polish with a soft cloth – you don't need to use much so it should last a while.

left Beeswax is easily made at home and is the most superb polish possible for bringing out the best in wood.

below An ostrich feather duster hangs out with a variety of wire food covers and trays and an industrially huge colander. Its signs of wear and tear are proof of its fine cleaning pedigree.

To clean well, cheaply and safely throughout the home, all you need are the recipes included here and some basic ingredients – distilled white vinegar, bicarbonate of soda (baking soda) and lemons. Those and a little bit of elbow grease should go a long way. It's also worth reusing items such as old toothbrushes to clean hard-to-reach corners and squares of old cotton t-shirts or sheets as dusters. Just remember to wash or boil them regularly and you need never buy another duster again.

Distilled white vinegar has a myriad of cleaning uses, as well as being an effective disinfectant and deodorizer. It is safe to use on most surfaces (apart from marble) and is incredibly cheap. Use it in the bathroom to clean the bath, shower, toilet, sink and taps. To

From left to right – a vintage banister brush, a goat-hair dusting brush with extra soft bristles for delicate dusting, horsehair brush, a sturdy stainless steel dustpan, a vintage cornice brush, an old banister brush for reaching dizzy heights, a sculptural-style behind-the-cupboard brush and an ostrich feathered duster.

FURNITURE POLISH

This is perfect for everyday cleaning, and is handily made from simple storecupboard ingredients.

Mix together the juice of one lemon with a teaspoon of olive oil (ordinary olive oil is best here; save the fancy extra-virgin variety for salads) and a teaspoon of water. The lemon cuts through any greasy grime and smells deliciously fresh; the olive oil conditions and polishes the wood.

This polish needs to be made fresh every time.

get rid of limescale deposits around a shower head, fill a bowl with hot vinegar heated in a saucepan and immerse the shower head for no longer than an hour, then scrub off the loose limescale with an old toothbrush. Run the shower to remove any excess vinegar.

To remove limescale from taps, wrap paper towels around the base of the taps where it usually gathers, then pour hot vinegar onto the paper towel sheets until saturated. Again, leave for about an hour, then rinse thoroughly and buff to a shine. Vinegar also

LINEN WATER

Going to sleep in freshly laundered sheets is one of life's simple pleasures and can be made even more luxurious if you've used softly scented linen water. It's easy to make and you can add your favourite essential oil to sweeten your dreams.

You will need 90ml high-proof vodka (80+ is best and make sure that it's not flavoured), 750ml distilled water (totally pure water, available from most grocery or hardware stores) and a teaspoon of essential oil (lavender is often used and is said to aid a good night's sleep).

Pour the ingredients into a clean, dry glass or plastic bottle, ideally one with a spray top. Close the bottle and shake to mix the oil and alcohol (the vodka emulsifies the oil to give an evenly mixed solution). Shake well before each use.

works wonders in the kitchen – use it to clean all work surfaces and appliances. As well as having cleaning power, vinegar can also eliminate lingering cooking odours – simply simmer a solution of vinegar and water in a pan for five minutes. For gleaming windows, mix one part vinegar with three parts warm water. Dunk an old cotton tea towel in the solution and rub on the windows before using some scrunched newspaper to buff them.

above A tiny pair of antique embroidery scissors hangs above piles of freshly folded crisp white linen.

left Simple stripey linen tea towels hang from a row of 'S' hooks, ready for action.

opposite Linen water can be made at home from a surprising storecupboard ingredient – vodka (well it might be in your cupboard if it's your favourite tipple)! Once you have blended the basic constituents, add your favourite essential oil to lightly scent your ironing.

Use bicarbonate of soda (baking soda) in the bathroom and kitchen. Put it on a damp cloth to clean all surface types and use for cleaning the oven – make a paste with equal parts salt, bicarbonate of soda and water, paste onto oven walls and leave for a while (preferably overnight), then wipe off. It also works well as a deodorizer; place a box in the fridge to absorb odours.

Finally, lemon juice is a multi-tasking miracle worker too. Use it in the recipe for furniture polish or mix with bicarbonate of soda to make a cleaning paste for all manner of surfaces.

By keeping things natural, you'll cut back on costs and waste, and reduce the number of harsh chemicals at work in your home.

this page These sturdy wooden chairs double as casual tables holding treasure-filled lacquered deed boxes. The white wood-panelled wall feels contrastingly clean and fresh.

opposite above Chunky colonial-looking chairs sit at the end of the bed. Their solid frames have an air of Bauhaus angularity about them.

opposite below A couple of handcrafted bamboo chairs sit side by side in a roughly hewn hallway.

Furniture makes your home work; it can offer a place to sit, eat, sleep, work or rest, but also does all manner of other important jobs too – like hiding washing powder and looking after your books. A well-chosen collection of furniture adds colour and detail to your home, provides textural contrast or complements what you already have in place on your walls and floors.

Recycled furniture from salvage yards, antique shops and flea markets is usually the most sympathetic to the simple home style. Make sure everything is in working order, or at least nothing that a few minor repairs can't fix.

Remember to keep an open mind about what you can use where and be choosy; you don't want to overstuff your attempted shrine to simplicity. It's a good idea to choose furniture that allows plenty of light to flood around it – it fits in with the mildly minimal ethos of simple style and it goes for all your furniture, from leggy metal bar stools to glass-fronted medical cabinets mounted on long limbs.

furniture

CHAIRS ARE THE SOCIAL ANIMALS OF THE FURNITURE WORLD, SO PLACE THEM IN FRIENDLY GROUPS. THEY DON'T HAVE TO MATCH IN ORDER TO GET ON WELL.

Alternatively, team up chunkier items with skinnier friends, as their contrasting characteristics create the perfect match. The same goes if you come across a must-have item that is a little more elaborate – make it a talking point by leaving everything else plain. If your decorative find is a little bit battered around the edges, then leave it this way as it will ooze timeless elegance much more so than a shiny, repaired version of its former self.

Tables are where people gather for mealtimes, to read the papers or just to chat over a pot of fresh coffee, so seek out the largest one you can fit in your space. Choose sturdy tables that have seen some action and are up to the rigours of daily life, be they overenthusiastic finger painting or red wine spillages; you don't want to be constantly worrying about perfect polishing. If you can't find one big enough, then get two and join them together; it really doesn't matter if they don't match. Long wooden refectory tables are timeless classics and look great. If legs are a little wobbly, replace them with contrasting skinny metal ones. Circular café tables or tables rescued from the garden are well worth considering if you're short on space.

Chairs are the social animals of the furniture world, so place them in friendly groups. Again, they don't have to match; all manner of different chairs get on marvellously. Look out for chairs that are keen to show off just how comfortable they are. Slightly worn seats and arms are sure

above A myriad of different textures are at work here, with a glass-fronted cabinet of curiosities perched on a chest made from rescued wooden boards and a block of wood acting as a simple low table.

this page A trio of mismatched antique chairs are connected by their plain linen upholstery. The decorative nature of the turned double seat and traditional gateleg table are balanced by the huge inglenook fireplace.

opposite Don't neglect shelving! A wooden trolley on wheels from a shoe factory neatly stores recycled cardboard boxes of paperwork and files.

left A set of shelves brought in from the cold of the potting shed holds a collection of glass cake plates. Its rough edges and flaky paint highlight the fragility of the glass.

above right An Indian shelving unit formerly used to hold jars has come to rest in the nursery, holding recycled cardboard wastepaper bins, which in turn store a zoo full of brightly coloured toy animals.

right A metal-framed factory trolley makes excellent kitchen storage. Every aspect has been used, with the addition of hooks to hold an oven glove.

signs that someone once thought they were good to sit in – over and over again! Take a seat and try it for size before finally deciding it's the one for you – even if it needs a lick of paint or a slim cushion to hide less attractive comfy credentials. Canvas or stripey ticking are perfect fabrics for covering chairs that need a bit of attention, as they are more than up to the wear and tear of family life and are also ideal for making heavy-duty, hard-wearing cushion covers. Chairs with a variety of past lives come alive once more when invited into your home. Wooden church pews, chapel chairs and garden benches are great for parking a number of people around your kitchen table. Cinema seats, café chairs or

wooden lab stools all have a part to play too. Don't forget about the classics either – if you're lucky enough to find some 1950s gems such as a skeletal Antelope chair by Ernest Race or a wiry Bertoia chair, made by Harry Bertoia for Knoll then snap it up without a second thought.

Sofas are an extremely important investment purchase and worth spending a little bit extra on if you can. The unofficial rule of thumb with a sofa has to be to buy one that you can stretch out on and that will accommodate you and your friends for an afternoon of classic film watching. You'll also need cushions to hide behind and a coffee table close to hand – though it doesn't

this page Soft geometric shapes in the form of a silvered leather pouf and a metal-framed daybed offer informal seating options in this pale but interesting corner.

opposite Classic chairs work well in all situations. Here, a wiry Bertoia chair sits with a similarly leggy friend around a table piled with treasures, all reflected in an 18th-century French mirror and lit by a bare bulb suspended from a long, knotted cord.

this page An extra-long table with a beautifully scuffed painted surface stands elegantly in a sunny kitchen. A pair of simple wooden benches provides ample seating for hungry hoards.

above A chunky stainless steel surface with integral hob has been cleverly engineered to suspend from the steel ceiling prop. This makes the most of the available space and emphasizes the industrial style of the rescued factory chairs.

right A scrubbed wooden top on curvy steel legs gives a sculptural twist to this informal dining table, and reflects the graphic nature of the extra-large steel Crittal window.

necessarily have to be a table; an old tin trunk provides the perfect perch for a Brown Betty teapot and a plate stacked with chocolate cookies. It's probably wise to go for a brand new sofa; there are so many well-crafted slouchy sofas out there and really old ones might poke you in the behind with a sharp spring while you're perusing the Sunday papers! However, leather sofas do

age gracefully and lend an air of old-school sophistication and charm to your home. If you find one that fits the bill but is a little too well worn in places, then throw on a cosy blanket to hide the more significant blemishes.

Shelves are often an afterthought when hunting for furniture, which is a shame as they offer so much. Redundant factory

A WELL-CHOSEN COLLECTION OF FURNITURE ADDS COLOUR AND DETAIL TO YOUR HOME, AS WELL AS PROVIDING TEXTURAL CONTRAST.

rejects are a good place to start if you can track one down. Their slightly bashed wooden frames are ideal for all the rooms in your house. They'll hold everything, from neatly labelled boxes of stationery in your home office to wonky piles of plates and glasses in your kitchen or a host of stuffed toys in the nursery. Even better news is that they're usually set on wheels, making them even more flexible. For fixed shelves, get a friendly carpenter to make you some bespoke ones out of abandoned pieces of wood; weathered railway sleepers or old reclaimed floorboards are ideal for this job. If you want to close the door on your piles of paperwork or eco-friendly canvas shopper collection (you know you've got one), then freestanding cupboards are the answer. Don't feel restricted by their previous employment. Formerly glamorous wardrobes and armoires take on the challenge of kitchen storage. Sturdy wooden beasts previously used as storage for hammers and nails, covered in all manner of historical paint splodges and splashes, look at ease in more elegant surroundings.

above left This sturdy glazed dresser from the 1800s was discovered in an antique shop in Provence. It provides ample storage space in its many drawers, while the faded charm and original blue paintwork easily stands up to the grandeur of the carved marble fireplace.

above right An old decorative 1800s French armoire has a lovely feeling of faded elegance with its original, worn painted surface. The linen loose cover on the chair and lightly creased tablecloth add to the relaxed atmosphere of the room.

this page It seems someone started to cover up the beautiful worn wooden surface of this curved cupboard with paint before realizing the error of their ways. The shell-like shapes of the decorative ceramics are reflected in the well-chosen line drawing hanging above.

this page Your private gallery space can be anywhere in your home. Here, a stairwell has been used to house a collection of unusual found objects. The scuffed tiles and weathered wooden board are in stark contrast to the white steps and grey cushions, but the matching tonal values keep a balance.

opposite left Extra-long simple stems lined up in a mismatched collection of old lemonade bottles make a feature of an open-plan staircase.

opposite right Wooden print block, an oversized atlas and the bold silhouette of an old office fan share a strong graphic theme. A Michelin man figure watches the world go by.

curating your home

Curating collections of art, found objects or cherished travel mementos is the fun part of creating the simple home – to live simply doesn't mean that you can't build up a vast collection of your favourite things. What you have to do is think of yourself as a museum or art gallery curator and your home as your very own personal museum. In this way, your prized possessions remain a constant source of delight rather than degenerating into mere piles of clutter. In the real world of museums and galleries, the curator is responsible for the acquisition and care of objects. When adopting this role in the home, the same applies. Happily, what you have in your personal collection or how you acquire it is less restrictive than it is for actual museums. Just about anything can become a collection; it could be triggered by coming across a beautiful object in an antique shop and deciding to collect other similar things.

You could decide to turn your one or two postcards into a more substantial assortment. Wooden print block, old tins or other quirky examples of vintage packaging, play-worn toys or even typewriters could be the obsession for you. Found objects, bits of weathered wood, feathers, even fragments of animal skull collected on walks in the country or seashells amassed on family holidays make lovely displays and are imbued with memories of special moments; they match the natural warmth of the materials in the simple home, and what's more they're free! Look around – you may already have a collection without even realizing it. All it takes is to sort your items into some kind of theme.

this page Putting unexpected items together can create a surprisingly eloquent still life. Here, the fragility of the dried leaf emphasizes the timeless elegance of this collection of antique silverware.

opposite A lovely little booklet on moths and butterflies by artist John Dilnot accompanies the pressed ferns perfectly.

Coming up with a strategy for your display is another hugely important part of the curator's job description. In the home it elevates your potentially disparate array of goodies into something special. Decide on a theme and stick to it, but not forever or things could get a bit tired; people wouldn't keep returning to the Tate gallery if the display never changed. Take a good look at what you've got; consider texture, colour, materials, matching content or anything that works for you and your particular collection.

far left A collection of oddly shaped ceramic pots, vases and vessels sit comfortably with piles of well-read paperbacks. Whether by design or good luck the ensemble works very well, creating a perfectly colour-matched assembly.

left Unusual jugs of all shapes and sizes, including one with an unusual glaze that has the look of wet clay, are displayed on plain wooden shelves, with informally leaning black and white prints and photographs. The unexpected addition of a large spring adds an extra linear quality, which reflects both the subjects and style of the artworks.

above right A cupboard lined with a quirky collection of man-made versions of nature – lettuce leaves and oysters. Shells add warmth to these unexpected small treasures.

below right A black and white collection of wobbly piles of kitchenware, graphic pictures, postcards and a McDougalls flour man are thoughtfully arranged on a skinny steel shelf and a rescued factory trolley.

Once you have a theme, the next step is how to show off your assortment. This can be another way of bringing your collection together, as well as keeping the dust off. If you display objects in a row of glass domes, cloches or even glass cake covers, it brings a sense of unity, no matter how incongruent your items are.

this page An interesting array of objects congregate on this table – insect drawings, votive candles, a broken porcelain lamp, a plaster bust and an iPod, all surveyed by a man peering from a dark painting.

opposite above left A collection of old wooden shoe lasts paraded on metal shelves.

opposite above centre Frames of pressed seaweed and leaves hang on a rough wall with a similar texture to lichen.

opposite above right Various misty Victorian mirrors gently reflect light, while guarded by a pair of beautifully carved wings.

opposite below left A travel theme is created by the pile of old trunks and a London Routemaster bus blind. A reused brioche tin makes a lampshade, while a hanging chair awaits guests.

opposite below right Old food larders and safes store toys. Printed cushions sit on a slatted wooden seat from a 1950s bus.

this page The glass domes, framed seaweed and a brown apothecary bottle bring a scientific feel to this table of strange treasures. The overall whiteness of the display adds to the clinical effect but this is ultimately softened by a pile of old black and white postcards and ceramic bowls.

Glass-fronted medicine cabinets are perfect for the job – they keep everything together, thus denying the descent into clutter, and are usually lockable, giving the collection a certain mystery – turning mundane objects into a Renaissance-style cabinet of curiosities. Keep an eye out for glazed wooden boxes too; they are very museum-like and give you the opportunity to turn your everyday bits and pieces into magical, mini works of art in the manner of the American surrealist Joseph Cornell. The items you put next to each other under your domes or in your display cupboards or glass-covered boxes are all important. This is curating as alchemy – two objects arranged next to each other magically transform both and create a third thing – which has the power to trigger cascades of thought and reaction.

Collections of art or photos don't always have to be framed and hung on your walls. You can create a more relaxed feel by casually leaning small groups of them against your walls instead, either on a tabletop or on the floor. If you find a piece of art that you like but

BY KEEPING YOUR DISPLAYS WELL CONSIDERED, YOU WILL HAVE MORE BREATHING SPACE AND IT WILL MAKE YOUR ROLE AS CURATOR ALL THE MORE CHALLENGING.

in a frame that you don't, simply free it from the offending frame and mount it on a piece of cut-to-size plywood instead or suspend it from small, shiny bulldog clips and string. If you do decide to hang them suitably framed on your wall, then go for small, dynamic groups, with images playing off against each other.

Something to keep in mind, especially in view of the clutter-free ideals of the simple home, is that at any given time museums display only a small portion of their collection. You don't have to show everything off at once. By keeping your displays well considered, you will have more space and it will make your role as

Various silver-plated hotel dishes crowd together on a vintage Hungarian linen table runner. Their shininess contrasts well with the chunky black stone bowls from India. In the alcove sit three mercury glass vases. The delicate wall hanging is made from thin pieces of porcelain.

A scattering of silver-plated
hotel ware gives the sense that
this kitchen shelf holds untold
treasures – it does in fact
include a vintage soda siphon
and cocktail shaker.

WHAT YOU HAVE TO DO IS TO THINK OF YOURSELF AS A MUSEUM OR ART GALLERY CURATOR AND SEE YOUR HOME AS YOUR VERY OWN PERSONAL MUSEUM.

opposite far left Circuit boards mounted onto a panel become an artwork in their own right. When seen like this, the intricate detail that goes into them can be appreciated. Its elevation into the art world is emphasized by the framed drawings and paintings leaning next to a shapely wooden chair.

opposite top right A vintage tailor's dummy creates a still life while it works. Piled next to it is a collection of old cotton shirts.

opposite below far left A vintage globe sits on an unusual turned wooden base.

opposite below centre An old theatre spotlight is poised to flood a late night game of table soccer with light.

opposite below right A close-up view of the game in action.

curator all the more challenging. Safely store away some of your cherished collection in boxes, corrugated paper or tissue. If you are worried about aging, use acid-free tissue or clear archival holders, available from specialist art shops. Then you can rotate and change your displays as and when you feel like it, which will keep the rooms in your home fresh. Once you have adopted this innovative idea there's endless fun to be had, but whatever you decide, it's always a good plan to introduce the odd unexpected element to give a sense of fun and keep people looking.

Ultimately, lots of the more mundane everyday things can become a less precious kind of collection if they've been well designed and most things look good in quantity. Look out for nicely packaged groceries and store them on open shelving in a way that turns them into still lifes from every angle. Or, if the packaging isn't up to much, then decant into glass storage jars. Rather than alphabetizing your books, rearrange them into waves of colour. Whatever makes you happy – it's your museum!

above left A themed collection of star shapes.

above centre The tagua beads and polished seed heads give this mirror a soft, feathery feel.

above right Print block spells out the all-important theme!

spaces

We all want to make a good impression, and that goes for your home as well. Wading through piles of newspapers and mounds of unwanted junk mail waiting to be recycled is not going to put your home in a good light with visitors, neither is tripping over discarded shoes and boots.

For an inviting entrance and clear hallway, all it takes is some care, organization and considered storage. Hooks keep hats, coats, scarves and bags out of the way and off the floor. They don't have to be conventional – there are all sorts of quirky hooks out there. But get creative; all manner of things could work if you're feeling a little bit experimental. Try a row of wooden spoons or thick twigs. Alternatively, a curvy classic Café Daum coat stand,

above This busy entrance brings you straight into the heart of a hard-working kitchen. Baskets stand ready for more fruit and veg collecting.

below left Glass panels in the front door allow light to flood this narrow hallway. A white floor adds to the sunny feel.

below right The walls in this entrance have been painted in gradients of soft grey, which give a feeling of light flowing into the furthest reaches of the space. The geometric lines add to the graphic feel of the tiles.

opposite Panels of sheer fabric suspended from cables add softness to this narrow entrance with its solid stone floor. An industrial wall light adds to the contrast of textures.

entrances & hallways

designed by Michael Thonet, solved the 'where to put my coat' dilemma for Viennese café society, so why not let it do the same for you? If there's space, fit a narrow shelf for keys and all those other things you can never find when you're in a hurry. If you are lucky enough to have a little extra space, then a skinny chair is a treat for putting on shoes. A blackboard in your hallway or on the landing between rooms is the ideal way to get important reminders and messages across.

Entrances and hallways should ideally be light-filled spaces, and obviously glass-fronted doorways are a great idea as long as safety or laminated glass is used. But a small amount of glass goes a long way in a slim entrance hall, and if you are worried about nosy neighbours, choose a piece of etched or opaque glass; it can become a subtly decorative feature if you get it right. Sticking to a fairly monochrome palette can help to make entrances and hallways seem larger (in the same way as wearing the same colour shoes as your tights can create the impression of longer legs!). Painting the floors and walls in a pale, light-reflecting shade makes them almost seamless.

above Contrasting white wooden boards lead down to a natural-coloured hallway; the balustrading has Shaker-style hearts cut out of it. A skeletally framed chair is a handy spot for tying shoelaces.

below left Beautiful sawn wooden boards follow the curves of the staircase, leading you up the stairs as they wind around the corner.

below right Stairs worn down the middle through years of use. Their sturdiness contrasts with the delicate wall embroidery.

this page The family dog guards the landing (though he doesn't appear to be too ferocious). The addition of a blackboard provides the perfect spot for leaving messages, as well as cute drawings of birds. A collection of glass vases filled with pebbles and shells are reminders of holidays spent joyfully beachcombing.

this page A series of interconnecting rooms in this French apartment shows the different functions of floors, as you step from roughly hewn stone flooring through to glazed floor tiles.

If you're lucky enough to have inherited beautiful Victorian floor tiles in your entrance hall, don't even think about getting rid of them, even though they may feel too vivid for a simple interior. If you keep everything else as plain and tidy as possible, these tiles will help create the perfect first impression of your home, as well as being true to its history. Victorian floor tiles are usually made from pretty robust ceramic, but may be suffering from hundreds of years of wear and tear. If this is the case, unfortunately it will take a bit of elbow grease to clean them. Avoid harsh chemicals that will add to their worn feel and plump for a natural cleaner with bicarbonate of soda (baking soda) or distilled white vinegar as a base instead. Don't get the tiles too wet and scrub them with the kind of non-scratch scourers you would use on your best pans. For further tips and recipes, refer to the natural cleaning chapter.

STICKING TO A FAIRLY MONOCHROME PALETTE CAN MAKE ENTRANCES AND HALLWAYS SEEM MORE SPACIOUS.

above right Smooth white floors sweep you seamlessly from room to room. The lower half of the corridor walls are painted black to match the monochrome kitchen.

below left Beautiful French parquet flooring with its classic herringbone pattern is a fine feature in this Parisian flat, belonging to architects Anki Linde and Pierre Saalburg.

below right Bert the cat peeks out from behind the laundry room door. The sanded floor helps lighten a dark hallway.

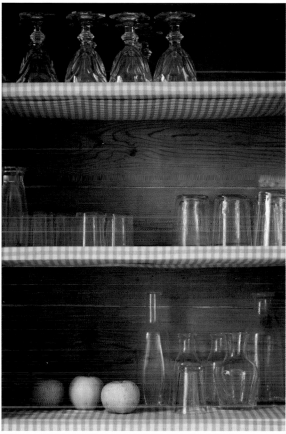

cooking & eating

opposite An ample, nearly floor-to-ceiling dresser provides generous storage for cream-ware jugs, plain white plates, wobbly carafes and café-style glasses. The table shows off its age with a surface worn smooth over the years. A row of hand-printed polar bear tags strung above the table adds humour.

above left Old rescued floor tiles act as a splashback and provide a battered contrast to the sleek mixer tap.

above right Shelves are given some colour with gingham linen.

As the whole house becomes less and less compartmentalized, the recent trend for combining kitchens and dining rooms makes perfect sense, as it results in much more versatile, casual spaces for cooking and eating. This way, the member of the family providing the evening meal doesn't feel cut off from the fun going on in the rest of the house and cooking becomes more of a sociable leisure activity. With the aid of a kitchen island, the chef can take centre stage while cooking and entertaining. As well as that, it's a much more practical design solution, as the food can quickly go from stove to tabletop and arrive piping hot without the need for an awful 1970s-style hostess trolley.

TAPS SHOULDN'T BE OVERLOOKED – GO FOR ONES THAT YOU MIGHT FIND IN A PROFESSIONAL KITCHEN, THAT YOU CAN EASILY TURN ON AND OFF.

Before the cooking, eating, working, playing or whatever else you think might happen in your space starts, plenty of consideration needs to go into the planning stage. This is certainly one area of the house that demands any extra cash to be lavished on one or two essential appliances. Indulge yourself in the biggest and best oven you can afford and fit into your kitchen; go for something rugged and industrial so that it becomes a long-term investment that will stand up to the demands you put on it. The same goes for the fridge – the roomier the better and a shiny stainless steel or pale pastel American-style one won't need to be slyly hidden away behind a false door. Taps shouldn't be overlooked either. Again, go for ones that you might find in a professional kitchen; those that you can easily turn on and off, even when your hands are covered in flour or sticky clumps of pastry. Ones with an extendable hose attachment make washing up after a big meal or pre-dishwasher rinsing easier to deal with too.

Expensively fitted kitchens that are more of a status symbol than an actual place to work are definitely not what is required in the simple home. Once your cooker and fridge are in place (and

this page Space is at a premium in this apartment, but the owners, architects Anki Linde and Pierre Saalburg, have come up with the ideal solution – a cantilevered brushed aluminium work surface, which extends into a useful dining and workspace. This ingenious space saver also provides shelter for a Smeg oven and a gang of six contrastingly classic French stools designed by Xavier Pauchard in 1934.

opposite Brushed aluminium adds a surprising softness to this efficiently designed kitchen.

this page This light and airy kitchen space boasts surprising contrasting details. The smooth, olive green cupboards, shiny oven and sleek marble surface are offset by a flakily painted wall cupboard and wide, unfinished floorboards. If you should look upwards, the intricate cornicing has been left undisturbed by paint.

KITCHEN ISLANDS ALLOW THE HARD-WORKING COOK TO KEEP CHOPPING WITHOUT TURNING THEIR BACK ON VISITORS.

above left Split bamboo provides the backdrop to this utilitarian space, which is filled with an array of shiny steel tea urns, teapots and an industrial coffee machine. Just the thing for shots of dark espresso, drunk leaning against the extra-thick, wooden tabletop.

above right The contrastingly rustic detail of the bamboo is shown in detail here.

be sure to work out exactly where the very best place is) freestanding cupboards, old wooden dressers and open shelves are the eye-pleasing, natural alternative. They allow you to mix and match as you wish and give a much more pared-down feel to your kitchen rather than the often sterile, over-designed feel of its uptight fitted cousin. Kitchen islands are increasingly popular too, as they mean that the hard-working cook doesn't have to turn their back on visitors while they chop away. Ignore convention and look out for extra-large cupboards or chests of

drawers to act as your island. Not only will you (or your sous chef) be able to face the hungry audience, but there will also be some sneaky extra storage into the bargain for all those rarely used kitchen gadgets.

It is almost impossible to have a minimalist approach to your cooking space – unless you want to become a very familiar face at your local restaurant or spend all hours cleaning. However, this doesn't mean that the ideals of the simple home can be ignored altogether. Far from it – there are plenty of opportunities to employ natural materials that will add to the overall warmth of the space. These come in the guise of tables, chairs and one-off pieces of furniture, as well as old wooden chopping boards and spoons. Again, it's best to decorate with low-key, milky colours. Anything brighter might put you off your food! The simple pale colour palette sits quietly in the background, feels wonderfully fresh and allows light to reflect off its surface, flooding your kitchen and dining space with all-important natural light. A lick of well-chosen eggshell paint can work wonders and harmonize the desired look. Or alternatively, take a complete about-turn and scrape off all the paint, then polish the plasterwork for the ultimate in simple style; just keep textures matt everywhere except for your sleek, shiny cooker.

After the oven and fridge, the table is probably the hardest-working element of your cooking and eating space. Think of all the activities that are likely to take place around the kitchen table – you'll quickly come to the conclusion that it is much more than a place for mealtimes. So the bigger the table you can find and have space for, the better. Wouldn't it be

above A skylight illuminates this space dominated by honey-toned wood. An artwork by Julian Stair's father, Bill Stair gives textural contrast while ceramics by Julian and Richard Batterham sit on the shelf.

left Slim shelves are a great way to make room for storage.

wonderful if your table was long enough to push half-finished crosswords, homework, pens and piles of books to one end, allowing you to dine at the other without feeling overwhelmed? Chunky wooden refectory tables are perfect for this particular role, as are long tables with drawers, which provide essential extra storage. Lovely weathered wooden tables such as these age well and don't need constant polishing – just the occasional rub with some homemade beeswax polish. They can stand up to the challenge of hot pans or poster paint-covered fingers and give you extra food preparation space too. Long benches mixed up with industrial steel stools and curly but slightly rusty garden chairs are the perfect seating partners for such charmingly rugged tables.

THE RECENT TREND FOR COMBINING KITCHENS AND DINING ROOMS RESULTS IN A MUCH MORE VERSATILE CASUAL SPACE FOR COOKING AND EATING.

below left A vast kitchen island allows the chef to take centre stage, while a pair of roughly edged slate roof tiles act as a splashback and a handy message board.

below right A collection of beautiful textured teapots nestle on a grainy wooden shelf.

If space doesn't allow for never-endingly long tables, then look to your favourite café for inspiration. High stools around an extended counter give your kitchen area a more industrial edge and can be the ideal solution to a lack of space. They may also get you even closer to the cooking action (though if this is the case, be prepared to lend a helping hand).

If you inherit your kitchen long after the planning stage, when it's too late or just not the right time for major structural changes

or refits, it's good to remember that little changes can make all the difference. Think of ways that you can add extra storage including, if possible, open-plan shelving for your more loved kitchen bits and pieces. Cooking and eating spaces are another place where you can indulge a passion for collecting, and in this case the collection has a purpose too. These kitchen collections could range from teapots or jugs to stacks of wobbly white crockery (the quirky French design duo Tsé & Tsé create beautiful,

this page An enormous cantilevered stainless-steel surface, housing a hob, sink and classic manual Italian espresso machine, dominates this open-plan loft space. It is supported by a hard-working single bracket on the scuffed steel pillar, which lets light from the wrap-around Crittal windows flow in and add to the airy feel.

opposite A well-appointed wooden shed has been turned into an understatedly glamorous dining space. The white painted wooden boards give a feeling of extra space and light. Their sleek surface is in contrast to the flaky French bistro table stand and the well-scrubbed wooden shelves, which sit solidly under the window. The table has been covered with a plain antique French linen table cloth, while sewing machinists' stools have been made more comfortable with pastel soft Welsh woollen blankets. A rusty brioche tin acts as a suitably themed light shade.

top left A collection of well-used wooden utensils sits in an old brown ceramic jug.

top right Earthy brown salt-glazed pottery contrasts with a shelf of frilly-edged porcelain.

centre left Antique cutlery is ingeniously displayed on a flattened dressing table mirror.

contre right Very plain wooden shelves allow the decorative fluted-edged plates and serving dishes to take the spotlight.

below right Traditional glazed jugs hailing from Apt in the south of France create a still life with some green tomatoes.

deliberately wobbly plates and bowls). What you need to do is decide what things you want to hide away behind cupboard doors and what is going to be out on display. In this case, it's not just down to a matter of taste but one of practicality too – certain items need to be close at hand – knives, for example, are stored perfectly on a professional kitchen-style strong magnetic strip. Track down beautiful old earthenware jugs, creamware pots or old chemists jars in which to store your essential utensils and tomato sauce-stained wooden spoons. They definitely need to be on show, as they're a badge of honour; a sign that you actually do cook in your kitchen! Easily installed slatted metal shelves lend an industrial edge to your kitchen and are great because not only can you stack pots, pans or plates on them but, with the addition of some butcher's-style 'S' hooks, you can suspend things too. Indeed, any hooks that you can fit in your kitchen are sure to be used at some stage. They make the most of the space and work well both in and out of cupboards.

this page A delicious cream
Aga is the perfect fit for this old
fireplace. A display of silver
cups, a candlestick and graphic
aluminium letters, along with a
string of silvery white shells,
lend a relaxed atmosphere to
this Cornish kitchen. This feeling
is added to by a loosely denim-
clad armchair warming itself
in the cosy corner.

opposite left Brass lever taps
make light work of floury hands.

Choosing a simpler style in your kitchen area means that you don't have to rely on conventional materials or ways of installing them. If you find some beautiful old tiles that you really love but they're a bit too chipped or not in plentiful supply, they will work just as well leaning casually behind your sink space. Or you could decide to ditch tiles altogether; pieces of slate or small, wooden-framed blackboards work well too and are easily cleaned into the bargain. All they need is a quick dunk in a sink full of soapy suds. Extra, flexible storage is always handy. Scratchy metal 'work-in-progress' trolleys on wheels are great for storing everything from plates and stacks of sturdy Duralex café glasses to the contents of your organic vegetable box. They have the obvious benefit of being mobile too. Worn wooden crates are also very useful,

above right Peek into this kitchen and be rewarded by the sight of a pale blue aga. The collection of kettles hints that a cup of tea may be on offer.

as they can be shoved under tables or dressers or stacked neatly in a corner. They could even be mounted on the walls to make an attractive storage area for your vast collection of cookery books, which is handy, as many of us have more of these than we've made hot dinners!

There's nothing better than eating in the garden. A long wooden trestle table is perfect; when the sun comes out you can easily grab the tabletop and its legs from your shed and crowd as many chairs around it as you need. On other, cooler occasions, you might wish to dine in a bit more style than perched on the edge of your kitchen table. Simple textiles such as a slightly crumpled vintage linen makes a great plain tablecloth, allowing your crockery collection and bone-handled cutlery to take pride of place. Wooden curtain rings make unusual napkin holders too, and while on the subject of napkins, old linen tea towels give a little extra coverage for stray crumbs and spills. Folded old Welsh woollen blankets soften the edges of industrial stools or wirework garden chairs. As a finishing touch, add a few candles in confit jars, or decorate the table with a couple of wiry stems in a milk bottle or generous bunches of flowers in a large French ceramic jug or two. It's the perfect setting for an informal, stylishly simple dinner party – all you need now is the food.

THERE'S NOTHING BETTER THAN EATING OUTSIDE. A LONG TRESTLE TABLE IS PERFECT – YOU CAN GRAB IT EASILY FROM THE SHED AND CROWD A STACK OF CHAIRS AROUND IT.

above Make the most of sunny days and take meals outside.

left A long row of curvaceous pastel-painted wooden chairs waits patiently for guests.

right A group of folding chairs gather around a large leafy tree, ready to be collected for lunch.

opposite Weathered Tolix chairs, once painted white but now with a time-worn dappled effect, provide informal seating around a trestle table.

this page A cantilevered lamp by Paolo Rizzatto illuminates this corner, making it an ideal space for reading. The 1930s sofa has been re-covered in beautiful soft brown silk velvet.

opposite above An old gilt-framed mirror, with a mottled silvered surface, sits on a carved marble fireplace. A woven rug and chunky log baskets give the room a more relaxed feel.

opposite below A grouping of objects on a brushed aluminium table creates an unusual still life, lit by a shiny desk lamp.

Living spaces should be a serene and tranquil domestic landscape where you can escape from the more stressful and busy events of the day, as you sink into the deep, feather-filled cushions piled high on your sofa. They are a place to indulge in your favourite pastimes and guilty pleasures, from listening to music (at full volume if the neighbours don't mind) to quietly reading novels, curled up on your much-loved velvety-soft armchair. They are also often the favoured room for household members to meet up for a cup of tea and a gossip or, if the music is still playing, to dance around energetically until exhaustion strikes and the sofa beckons once more.

Keeping things simple doesn't mean that your home has to be hard-edged or minimal, especially in the one room in the house where you want to kick back and

relax. It's a case of carefully choosing your furniture and colour scheme so that nothing jars or feels over the top, and having plenty of storage. The clean lines and light-filled atmosphere of clutter-free spaces are much more relaxing than overly stuffed, overly fussy ones; there's less to worry about as you're not constantly scanning the room for things that need dusting or frills that need flouncing.

living

Don't overload your senses with the latest gadgets or entertainment consoles. It's not that such things are unnecessary or should be banned from stylishly simple homes; sometimes there's nothing better than virtually skiing in your living room on a Sunday afternoon! It's just a

CREATE A COMFORT ZONE BY MAKING THE FIREPLACE THE HEART OF YOUR LIVING SPACE. POSITION YOUR SOFA AND CHAIRS AROUND ITS WARM GLOW.

matter of storing them out of the way when you're not feeling so sporty. Old wooden fruit crates, wicker fishermen's baskets, tin trunks or deed boxes provide contrastingly timeless storage options.

Create a comfort zone by making the fireplace the heart of your living space rather than the television. Position your sofa and chairs around its warm glow. Other than a generously filled log basket, keep the fireplace the very centre of attention. Resist the temptation to fill the mantelshelf with all manner of clutter. Instead, let the simple home ideas of display come into play. If you do feel the need to break up the hard-edged geometry of the fireplace, carefully choose one or two cherished objects that share a certain theme or colour range. They become all the more special this way and the fireplace remains the main attraction.

A generous floor-to-ceiling window means that this huge, light-filled space is the perfect quiet spot for a bit of easy reading. The decorative features such as the fireplace and the cornicing, as well as the antique chair and mirror, are offset by more rustic elements in the room – woven baskets and an enormous rug, a chunky unvarnished table and a casually leaning print – giving the room a relaxing atmosphere.

this page This is a room of pleasing contrasts. Two leather-clad antique chairs on wheels sit on a scrubbed flagstone floor in front of a vast hole-in-the-wall fireplace. The delicate Venetian glass chandelier and abstract painting emphasize the well-loved, time-worn feel of these things.

opposite A utilitarian-looking wood-burning stove sits in a simple marble fire surround. The mantelshelf provides a perch for a group of similarly coloured jugs and a seascape in muted tones. Wide wooden floor-boards add a touch of colour with their warm honey shades.

If your home doesn't come with architectural gems such as a sculptural stone fire surround, a carved wooden one or a decoratively tiled cast-iron Victorian beauty, don't attempt to make up for it by installing replicas. Be true to your home and don't force it into anything that looks unnatural. In any case, a plain, unframed fireplace is the perfect foil for other, more obviously decorative pieces, such as bright cushions or chunkily hand-knitted blankets.

Once you've found your central focus, the sofa, or two sofas if you've got the funds or the space, is the most important piece of furniture in your living area. This is the all-important place to unwind, and needs to be as comfortable as possible. Definitely sit down on any sofas that take your fancy while furniture shopping; you need them to be enduringly comfortable for those long winter evenings or Sunday afternoon movies. A sturdy wooden frame that can withstand the rigours of family life and deep seats with plenty of room for lounging are the hallmarks of a good sofa. A mix of goose and duck feathers makes the most luxurious cushion

this page An inviting slouchy chair encourages relaxation. The whitewashed floorboards and chunky woven seagrass rug add to this feel, along with the soft tones of the painting. Wire in-trays parked by the door are re-employed to hold more fun reading matter than they did in their office days.

opposite This living space is a perfect study in black and white. A deliberately frayed-edged armchair sits next to a more upright classic Robin Day chair. The shelves hold a well-considered collection of monochrome pieces.

opposite Roof lights infuse this small living space with much-needed light. The concrete beam contrasts with the unusual glass chandelier.

above A Barcelona chair and stool sit in this light-filled space. The Crittal windows give the room an industrial edge.

filling. They may require a little extra plumping, but it's not the worst job in the world and is definitely worth it. There is a huge array of options out there for covering your sofa – slubby linens and cotton are the most durable choices and in their undyed state sit quietly in a simply decorated living space. But why not take the opportunity to showcase a collection of

vintage textiles that you may have amassed over the years? If you have enough, turn them into a beautiful patchwork sofa cover (if you're not overly familiar with the ways of a sewing machine, find someone who is). Make the most of stitches and seams; these simple details are honest signs of creation, and shouldn't be hidden away. If your textile collection is rather more limited it is easy to create cushion covers that are unique to you and your sofa. Even vintage tea towels can become eye-catching additions to your comfort zone. Old leather sofas add a timeless decadence to your living space, and the older they are, the better they look, proudly showing off the signs and scars of life. Their warm, honey-coloured hues work well with the other natural materials and colours of the simple home.

Always make sure that there are enough cushions to go round and remember that every now and then the floor is the best place to spread out the various sections of the weekend papers. When space is limited or you prefer the look of more upright chairs, it is amazing how easily a cosy woollen blanket casually thrown over one edge of a more austere chair can soften such refined features. If you want to create a slightly more decadent extra seating area, a chaise longue takes up a little less space than another sofa but is a better option for stretching out than an armchair; it looks more relaxed too. An old chaise longue can make a decorative addition to the simplicity of other pieces of furniture in your living space.

As for other furniture, such as low tables that are an essential resting place for trays of coffee and biscuits, go for something with the character that is inherent in antique or rescued pieces, or furniture crafted from recycled elements. Spindly-legged tables with strong shapes that allow light to flood round them are an ideal addition to a living room.

A simple steel-framed daybed with a generously plump mattress covered with Egyptian cotton is a cosy resting spot in this refreshing white space. Extra informal seating is thoughtfully provided with a soft metallic leather pouf and a pile of wheat-filled cushions.

LIVING SPACES SHOULD BE A SERENE AND
TRANQUIL DOMESTIC LANDSCAPE WHERE
YOU CAN ESCAPE FROM THE MORE
STRESSFUL AND BUSY EVENTS OF THE DAY.

DECORATE YOUR LIVING SPACE GENTLY, USING A SOFT PALETTE OF LIGHT-REFLECTING CREAMY WHITES. IT WILL FEEL DELICIOUSLY RELAXING.

Decorate your living space gently, using a soft palette of light-reflecting creamy whites. Large mirrors add sparkle and extra light, while their shabby gilt frames lend them an air of laid-back grandeur. If you can't find a large mirror, hang smaller ones in groups; 1930s-style bevelled-edged ones are particularly good in this situation, as they come in a variety of shapes and sizes.

Getting the lighting right is essential for a relaxing atmosphere. Bright overhead lights seem too harsh when all you want to do is read on the sofa, so fit a dimmer switch; it gives you greater control and is better for the environment. Extra task lighting adds a softer glow just when and where you need it. Articulated anglepoise lamps lend an industrial edge and work surprisingly well with other, more glamorous lighting. A classic crystal chandelier adds elegance to a frugally furnished living space. Its sparkling good looks are all the more elevated when it is the most decorative feature. Chandeliers don't necessarily have to fit into conventional expectations though; well-made plastic or dark flock-finished numbers add an unexpected twist as well as humour.

opposite Black and white makes a dramatic statement, but it doesn't need to feel too austere. A couple of paintings leaning against the wall help to soften the look, along with the quirky addition of a fire bell, presumably there to call for emergency cups of tea.

this page A small writing desk tucked into a corner is an example of well-used space. The tranquil atmosphere of the room is sure to result in well-written letters.

this page Layers of good-quality white linen bedding make for a restful night's sleep. An articulated anglepoise lamp is ideal for bedtime reading, despite its office associations.

opposite above Enclose your bed in soft folds of fabric for an extra-cosy night's sleep.

opposite below Scaffolding poles make a reassuringly sturdy bed frame. Here, woven African textiles and an old grain sack create a fabric headboard and soften the industrial look. The bed is covered with creamy soft linen, and extra warmth is on standby in the form of a pile of striped ticking quilts.

Without a doubt, the bedroom is the one room in the house where comfort is of the uppermost importance. It is the most private space that we have – a comforting place to retreat to at the end of the day – and it is likely that we spend more time there than we do anywhere else. It goes without saying that the bed is the most important piece of furniture in the room. In keeping with the simple home, the best combination is the pairing of a recycled frame, or simply something plain made from wood, with a springy new mattress – a hard-wearing ticking-covered one means that it's ok if its stripey edges are on display. Invest time in researching and selecting the most comfortable mattress for your bed that your budget will allow so that it stands the test of time. If you want something a little more ornate to aid sweet dreams, decorative cast-iron bedsteads often crop up at antique fairs or reclamation yards, though don't expect perfection; these pieces look better and less girly with signs of age and worn-out paint. Also, don't worry if you can't find a matching pair. Not only does this give you the opportunity to think creatively about what could be used in its place but the mismatched arrangement looks all the more relaxed and individual. Just make sure that everything else in the room is kept as pared-down as possible.

bedrooms

Scaffolding poles can be turned into a minimally sculptural bed frame and their hard-edged austerity provides the perfect balance with indulgent piles of super-soft bedding. Their flexibility and extendability means that they could even be used to create a surprisingly fuss-free four-poster, with the addition of some sheer fabric casually draped around the frugal frame. A simple wooden frame, ideally one with a worn, scrubbed surface, has an air of warmth, and the inherent solidity that comes with wood is deeply comforting and reassuring.

Layer upon layer of differently textured textiles turn your bed into a soothing nest; be it a cosy

LAYER UPON LAYER OF NATURAL LINENS AND HANDWOVEN COTTON TURN YOUR BED INTO A SOOTHING NEST.

haven to snuggle deep into during cold winter months or with the option to kick off a layer or two in warmer seasons. Natural linens and handwoven cotton are perfect, as they're unfussy and in their natural state. Their muted tones are soothing and will make your bedroom look more spacious than a bed wrapped in darker shades. Unless you're a particularly heavy sleeper, anything too crazy could be insomnia inducing. The layering of waffle sheets or knobbly knitted blankets on your quilt adds a little something for your senses, while a soft Welsh blanket brings a little muted colour.

Undulating folds of fabric divide the living and sleeping areas of this Parisian apartment. Along with a soft furry throw, they help to create a restful, nest-like sleeping space. The cleverly designed bed incorporates a shelf for bedside lighting, bits and bobs, and the all-important book at bedtime.

this page A simple steel-framed four-poster with buttery linen curtains and layers of feather-filled quilts creates the ultimate classic comfort zone. Draw the curtains and enjoy a quiet, undisturbed night's sleep.

above left This comfortable-looking bed boasts layers of soft brown-coloured quilt covers and sheets, as well as a variety of pleasingly tactile textures, including an extra-chunky hand-knitted blanket in soft porridgey hues. Unusual Perspex shutters allow soft light to filter gently in.

above right The calming stripes of the ticking mattress and softly crumpled linen give an added feeling of relaxation. The stripes on the mattress cover are picked up in the piped cushion edge.

By keeping the walls plain and painting them in pale chalky colours that match your choice of bedding, you are sure to fall asleep quickly.

Windows do need the addition of curtains, but don't choose anything too heavy. It's all the more relaxing to have a little light gently filtering into the room and it keeps us in touch with the rhythms of the seasons. Sheer blinds or panels of muslin draped easily over a curtain pole are the ideal solution if your home is overlooked. To light your way at night, unobtrusive bedside lights set on low tables are just the ticket, especially if they can be angled to the perfect reading position. Make sure that your bedside

table has room for a book at bedtime and your morning cup of tea – if you happen to be lucky enough to have one delivered to your bed! In an ideal world, this would be all the furniture you would have in your cosy bedroom. In this perfect world, you would also have a separate room dedicated to your clothes. However, not many of us are that fortunate, so to house your garments in the style they undoubtedly deserve, look out for an antique French armoire or old shop fittings that have preferably seen slightly better days and are therefore imbued with relaxed grandeur. Your bedroom should now be a beautifully calm haven for a good night's sleep.

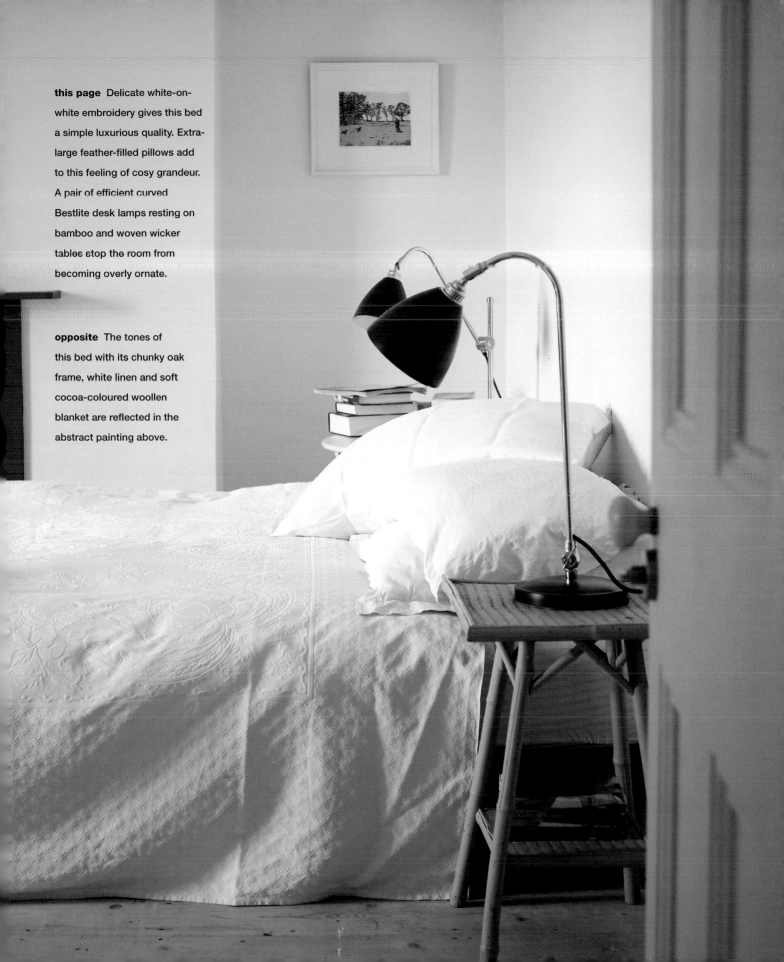

this page Delicate white-on-white embroidery gives this bed a simple luxurious quality. Extra-large feather-filled pillows add to this feeling of cosy grandeur. A pair of efficient curved Bestlite desk lamps resting on bamboo and woven wicker tables stop the room from becoming overly ornate.

opposite The tones of this bed with its chunky oak frame, white linen and soft cocoa-coloured woollen blanket are reflected in the abstract painting above.

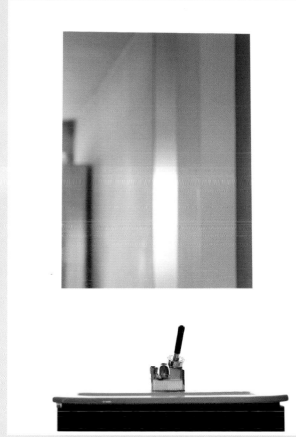

bathrooms

opposite The owners of this Parisian apartment were lucky enough to find this deep, roll-top bathtub at a flea market – it was resurfaced to ensure it lasts another few hundred years. The sink stand was commissioned to reflect the qualities of the tub in a contemporary style.

above left An architectural tap sits below a simple unframed mirror, made by sandwiching it between sheets of glass.

above right Wall-mounted taps add to the illusion of extra space in your bathroom.

The bathroom is the perfect place in which to further your campaign of simplicity. Apply the simple home philosophy for a bathroom with a clean, fresh feel and transform it into a place of sanctuary rather than one of hurried necessity. A well-considered, light, spacious and clutter-free environment is just what you need as you stumble out of bed and begin your bleary-eyed morning ablutions.

Make the most of your space. If you have the room and budget, invest in an ornate roll-top bathtub with clawed feet. It brings old-time glamour into your bathroom and gives you much more room to lie back and relax than narrow, modern acrylic baths.

this page An enormous claw-footed, roll-top bathtub takes pride of place in this bathroom. Its ornate features are contrasted with a sleek Philippe Starck tap, as well as a recycled bath rack made from a sawn piece of ladder cheekily topped with a wire in-tray. A long-handled scrubbing brush sits on a three-legged stool, crusty with layers of splattered paint.

If you want the decadent style of a freestanding bath but want to keep the look a little less ornate, then mount a tub onto sturdy wooden planks. Allow your fabulous bath to take pride of place by paring down other details, otherwise your bathroom might start to feel over the top. The desired look has more in common with rustic simplicity rather than anything too romantic or self-indulgent. Be honest about the functionality of the bathroom; don't box in pipes, as their coppery sheen is another contrasting element in the bathroom and they could be a good place for hanging towels too.

The bathroom is the ideal arena for highly contrasting textures. Wood is a perfect partner for sleek, shiny bathroom fixtures and fittings. Its pleasing weathered warmth brings a nautical feel in a watery context. Introduce pieces of wood creatively, perhaps in the form

top Driftwood makes an unusual splashback with the print block creating a pattern to match. The exposed plaster gives the walls a chalky feel.

centre A curvy cast-iron sink sits on turned legs, allowing light to flow round the room. The tiles against the wall are classic Delft pottery.

of a recycled version of a bath rack made from a sawn section of ladder with a wooden seed tray centre. Also, look out for well-loved wooden stools with flaky paint, splashes and scratches, crates to store your towels or bath-time treats in or an A-frame ladder that makes a simple towel rail leaning casually against the wall. Larger expanses of wood come with your choice of flooring – wooden boards are a good option,

this page Mounted shells and pebbles sit on a simple olive-green cupboard in this nautical, white wood-panelled bathroom. The drop-leaf mahogany table is unusual as these are usually highly polished – this one has a more relaxed feel and fits the room perfectly.

opposite A rescued bath with classic ball and claw feet shows off its essential pipe-work with pride. The theme is continued with the copper pipe towel rack, which sits well next to the rather scientific botanical print.

this page The light in this bathroom is diffused through a sheet of unbleached tissue paper hanging from the window. The old cast-iron and enamel mirror leans casually on the window ledge and provides the perfect counterbalance to the solidly geometric modern sink, as does the large curved shell.

opposite left Old enamel hooks are a useful addition to any bathroom.

either painted white or left in a more natural state. They cope surprisingly well with splashes and spillages; just mop them regularly. It will also help if your bathroom is well ventilated. Poured concrete is another good flooring choice, as its industrial good looks contrast with the more indulgent aspects of bathroom life and it is hard-wearing. Again, just make sure that you look after it properly. Treat with a water-resistant clear sealant; your contractor will help with the details. Also, make sure the finish isn't too smooth or over-polished, as it could be a bit slippery. Whatever you decide, don't be too hard on yourself. A knobbly woolly rug to step onto as you emerge from the bath is warm underfoot and gives your toes a chance to acclimatize.

Sleek modern basins make the most of the space in your bathroom, especially if they are wall-mounted. Their hard-edged modernity

contrasts well with more ornate elements. They can also be adapted to fit in with your particular take on simple style. Mount them on skinny legs to allow light to flood all around, or if you need extra storage, have one fitted onto a cupboard. Basin-style sinks that echo the old porcelain

above Piles of clean, fresh white linen await use. A tiny pair of scissors is an amusing touch, tucked away in the back of this spacious cupboard.

above left Add an air of opulence to your bathroom. Here, a wiry-stemmed bunch of flowers is arranged in a hammered Syrian silver cup resting on a chunky, bleached wooden block.

below left This freestanding bathtub is unusually mounted on pillar-like legs. The extra-wide wooden floorboards and simple towel rail give the room a more relaxed feel in contrast to the imposingly large tub.

A WELL-CONSIDERED, LIGHT, CLUTTER-FREE ENVIRONMENT IS JUST WHAT YOU NEED WHEN YOU STUMBLE OUT OF BED FOR YOUR MORNING ABLUTIONS.

bowl-and-jug washing custom of Victorian times are also an option; you could even go as far as placing two next to each other, his and hers style! Designer chrome taps work well in the simple bathroom too, as their style tends to be pared-down and minimal looking. If you can mount them onto the wall, then do; they look even better when hovering above your basin or tub.

Small details turn your bathroom into your own personal spa. Choose fluffy, undyed organic cotton towels, and find somewhere for a huge, comforting pile of them. Decant bath oils into recycled glass bottles so as to avoid garish plastic packaging spoiling the view from the depths of your tranquil tub. Bathrooms can be another place to display collections of shells and pebbles, or even wooden boats. Put your beachcombing treasures to work; pieces of driftwood lined up behind taps look much more interesting than overly clinical tiles. Don't store your soap in a ready-made soap dish; bowls rescued from the kitchen do the job just as well and often much more stylishly. Beautifully packaged aromatic soaps look like oversized sweets when piled together. Larger metallic bowls give your room an exotic air of the Turkish hamam. Just make sure that you keep the other details plain; one shiny specimen looks all the more special when contrasted in this way.

this page If you have the space, an armchair is a luxurious extra in a bathroom. This one holds a pile of soft towels. Its fuss-free, plain white loose cover adds to the clean lines of this spacious room.

workspaces

this page Patchwork wooden chairs on curved steel former factory frames sit by the window in front of piles of print block. The print block obsession continues on the window blinds, as a couple of pieces have been used as blind pulls.

above left Chunky silver pencils are gathered together in a French confit jar, which sits neatly on a small floating shelf.

above right An array of brushes are organized in small ceramic jars in this studio. Piles of sieves tower above them.

Whether you work at home on a daily basis or just need somewhere to sit and sort out bills, write emails or even actual letters, make sure that this area is in keeping with the rest of your home. The dull grey conventions and uniformity of corporate offices, ugly plastic furniture and flimsy partitions should be avoided at all costs. Choosing more inspirational furniture will aid creativity and won't jar with your personal style. Workspaces can be cleverly tucked into a small corner or even under the stairs or in the garden shed if space is really tight. If this isn't an issue, then devote a whole room to it so that you can close the door on the commotion of family life and get down to business.

The desk is the most important piece of furniture in your workroom, no matter where this happens to be. First of all, choose one that fits into the space. A pair of trestles is particularly flexible; wooden ones are relatively inexpensive and allow light to flow around your table so that it feels less clumpy. But a couple of skinny drawers do the job equally well and provide all-important storage space at the same time. You don't have to stick to conventional tops either. Get the right size piece of wood, patchworked floorboards or maybe a discarded door and you've got a surface on which to work. Old office furniture rescued from obscurity will settle happily into its former habitat; stainless steel 1950s desks are particularly hard-working, or old school-desks

MAKE SURE YOUR WORKSPACE IS IN KEEPING WITH THE REST OF YOUR HOME. CHOOSING MORE INSPIRATIONAL FURNITURE WILL AID CREATIVITY.

may be easier to get your hands on. If not, a simple kitchen table is just as well suited to the task. Old swivel chairs on wheels are much better looking and just as comfortable as modern-day ergonomic alternatives. But it is important to have the right seat at your desk, especially if you're going to be there all day (except for the occasional tea-making trip to the kitchen). Make sure that it's the right height and

your back is properly supported. The addition of linen cushions or maybe a folded blanket will offer extra comfort and soften your workspace.

It's important for both the look of your home and your brain to keep your workspace as clutter free as possible. Keep unruly paperwork at bay by tracking down old filing cabinets. Stripped of their paint they reveal a lovely scratchy, shiny patina, that sits comfortably in

above Sit your desk by a window if possible – natural daylight and an interesting view make working from home a pleasure. In this cleverly appointed writing corner, a large wirework waste basket awaits crumpled mistakes. The spindly legs of the chair and table ensure that the corner doesn't feel over-cluttered.

this page A large desk is constructed from ware boards, rescued from a closed-down pottery factory. A matching pair of steel display cabinets encase treasures, while a shelf close to the roof holds a collection of 1960s vases in various soft shades of blue. These colours are reflected in the sea of the globes sitting on the desk.

enter

This Card is Temporarily Out of Stock

this page This extravagantly articulated draughtsman's table was found in an antique shop in L'Isle sur la Sorgue, Provence.

the simple home. Tin trunks, battered leather suitcases or discarded wooden drawers can also file away your papers with timeless flair. Call on old wire in-trays to store items that you need to be instantly available. They are slim enough to slot under a trestle on the floor or they can rest stylishly on your desk. Pens, pencils and paintbrushes of all shapes and sizes look great gathered together in old jam jars or attractive food tins – much better than in ugly, grey plastic pen holders from the office.

this page The essential paperwork, pencils and pens of the office are tucked away in an old tin trunk, leaving the desk tidy and ready for work. A neat laptop takes less room than an unwieldy computer if space is tight.

BY LIVING WITHOUT EXCESS AND SURROUNDING YOURSELF WITH JUST ENOUGH OF THE RIGHT THINGS, YOU WILL FEEL AN AMAZING SENSE OF SATISFACTION.

above left A quirky desk made from recycled wooden boards on top of a tubular steel sewing machine base creates a neat little workspace. The clever use of space is continued by using the door as a handy blackboard.

above right Why put your pencils in an ugly plastic holder when they could be happily housed in a drilled piece of driftwood?

Decent lighting is vital for your workspace. If you can, place your desk next to a window to make the most of natural daylight; beams of afternoon sun streaming through the window can jolt you out of the worst case of the doldrums. Just don't get too distracted by the goings-on outside. For dark winter days, a desk light is a must. Again, the classic anglepoise is best or you could even go for a trio like on the previous page to make a display of your desk.

Simply styling your workspace and surrounding yourself with well-made, inspirational items will undoubtedly produce the best work. And this goes for the whole of your home. By living without excess and surrounding yourself with just enough of the right things – objects that are personal to you and are thoughtfully designed – you will feel an amazing sense of satisfaction, as well as making your home appear refreshing, relaxing and simple; an easy place to be.

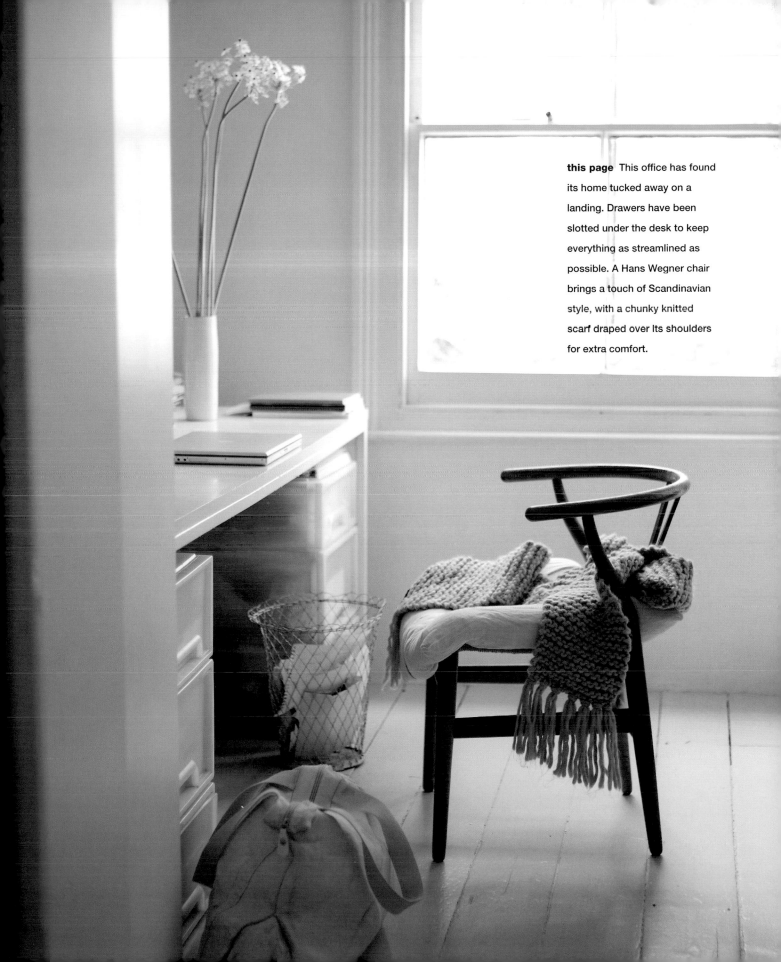

this page This office has found its home tucked away on a landing. Drawers have been slotted under the desk to keep everything as streamlined as possible. A Hans Wegner chair brings a touch of Scandinavian style, with a chunky knitted scarf draped over its shoulders for extra comfort.

sources in the UK

Shops and art spaces

The Art Shop
8 Cross Street
Abergavenny NP7 5EH
www.artshopandgallery.co.uk
+44 (0)1924 832631
Artists' materials and books.

Baileys
Whitecross Farm
Bridstow
Ross-on-Wye
Herefordshire HR9 6JU
+44 (0)1989 563015
www.baileyshome.com
Our store – an amazing mix of everything simple (we are biased).

Caravan Style
www.caravanstyle.com
Always fascinating. A place to look at flea-market style.

The Cloth House
47 & 98 Berwick Street
London W1F 8SJ
+44 (0)20 7437 5155
www.clothhouse.com
Fabrics from all over the world, made using and supporting local craftspeople.

The Conran Shop
www.conranshop.co.uk
Contemporary furniture, lighting, home accessories and gifts.

Contemporary Applied Arts
2 Percy Street
London W1 1DD
+44 (0)20 7436 2344
www.caa.org.uk
The best of British craft. They also provide a commissioning service.

Damson & Slate
www.damsonandslate.co.uk
Welsh art and craft, including cushions, blankets and fabrics.

Frank
65 Harbour Road
Whitstable
Kent CT5 1AG
+44 (0)1227 262500
www.frankworks.eu
Hand- and home-made craft, decorative pieces and artworks.

Hauser & Wirth Somerset
Durslade Farm
Dropping Lane
Bruton BA10 0NL
+44 (0)1749 814060
www.hauserwirthsomerset.com
Gallery and multi-purpose arts centre set in a restored 18th-century farm and with a landscaped garden by Piet Oudolf.

Kettle's Yard
Castle Street
Cambridge CB3 0AQ
+44 (0)1223 748100
www.kettlesyard.co.uk
This beautiful and unique gallery showcases a distinctive collective of 20th-century art and hosts contemporary exhibitions. Currently closed for renovations but due to reopen some time in 2017.

Le Chien et Moi
60 Derby Street
Nottingham NG1 5FD
+44 (0)115 979 9199
www.lechienetmoi.com
A constantly evolving stock of unusual and beautiful things.

Liberty
Regent Street
London W1B 5AH
+44 (0)20 7734 1234
www.liberty.co.uk
Stylish modern furniture, tableware and accessories from this historic London department store.

Material
www.materialmaterial.com
Limited-edition prints, books, homewares and stationery.

Mint
2 North Terrace
Alexander Square
London SW3 2BA
+44 (0)20 7225 2228
www.mintshop.co.uk
An eclectic and innovative selection of contemporary furniture, ceramics and accessories.

The New Craftsmen Gallery
34 North Row
London W1K 6DG
+44 (0)20 7148 3190
www.thenewcraftsmen.com
Showcases the materials, skills and craft products of the British Isles.

Ruthin Craft Centre
Park Road
Ruthin
Denbighshire LL15 1BB
+44 (0)1824 704774
www.ruthincraftcentre.org.uk
A state-of-the-art craft centre with studios, workshops and three galleries.

St Jude's
Wolterton Road
Itteringham
Norfolk NR11 7AF
+44 (0)1263 587666
www.stjudesgallery.co.uk
Specializing in British art, craft and design.

SCP
135-159 Curtain Road
London EC2A 3BX
+44 (0)20 7739 1869
www.scp.co.uk
Large range of modern furniture and contemporary design.

Selvedge
www.selvedge.org
A magazine about contemporary art and crafts.

Yew Tree Gallery
Keigwin
near Morvah
Pendeen
Cornwall TR19 7TS
+44 (0)1736 786425
www.yewtreegallery.com
Sculpture, jewellery and ceramics exhibits.

Yorkshire Sculpture Park
West Bretton
Wakefield WF4 4LG
+44 (0)1924 832631
www.ysp.co.uk
A showcase of contemporary craft and applied arts.

Antiques and flea markets

There are many regular antique fairs around the country. For information, visit www.antiques-atlas.com and www.gbaw.co.uk

London Markets:

Portobello Road Market
Portobello Road
London W11
www.portobelloroad.co.uk
Saturdays 8am–5pm.

Brick Lane Market
London E1
www.visitbricklane.org
Sundays 10am–5pm.

Bermondsey Antiques Market
Bermondsey Square
London SE1
www.bermondseysquare.net
Fridays 6am–2pm.

Camden Market
Camden High Street
London NW1
www.camdenmarket.com
Open daily.

Greenwich Market
Greenwich High Road
London SE10 9HZ
www.greenwichmarketlondon.com
Antiques and collectables on Mondays, Tuesdays, Thursdays and Fridays 10am-5.30pm.

Paint

Auro Organic Paints
+44 (0)1452 772020
www.auro.co.uk
Natural emulsions, eggshells and chalk paints in muted colours. Also floor finishes and wood stains.

Earth Born
+44 (0)1928 734171
www.earthbornpaints.co.uk
Environmentally friendly paints.

sources in the US

Furniture and accessories

ABC Carpet & Home
888 Broadway
New York, NY 10003
+01 212 473 3000
Visit the website for details of their
other stores.
www.abchome.com
*An eclectic collection of furnishings,
linens, rugs, and other home
accessories.*

Anthropologie
www.anthropologie.com
*One-of-a-kind home accessories,
including decorative hooks, boxes,
cupboard knobs, and racks.*

Counter Space
www.shopcounterspace.com
*Beautiful, simple and functional
products; both modern homewares
(including Japanese kitchenware)
and thoughtfully chosen vintage
furniture and accessories.*

Fishs Eddy
889 Broadway
New York, NY 10003
+01 212 420 9020
www.fishseddy.com
*Overstock supplies of simple plates
and other tableware.*

Home Stories
148 Montague Street
Brooklyn, NY 11201
+01 718 855 7575
www.homestories.com
*Elegant minimalist furnishings and
accessories with a European flavor
in a beautifully curated store.*

Knoll
www.knoll.com
*Iconic modern classics plus modern
and ergonomic lamps.*

Ochre
462 Broome Street
New York, NY 10013
+01 212 414 4332
www.ochre.net
*Contemporary furniture, antiques,
accessories, and lighting.*

Pottery Barn
www.potterybarn.com
*Contemporary furniture and
accessories for the home.*

R & Company
82 Franklin Street
New York, NY 10013
+01 212 343 7979
www.r-and-company.com
*Mid-century furniture as well as
lamps and lighting fixtures.*

Restoration Hardware
www.restorationhardware.com
*Reproduction hardware, lighting,
furniture, bathroom fixtures, and
accessories for the home.*

Antiques and flea markets

Brimfield Antique Show
Route 20
Brimfield, MA 01010
www.brimfieldshow.com
*This famous flea market, which
features dealers from all over the
U.S. and from Europe, runs for a
week in May, July, and September.*

Englishtown Auction Sales
90 Wilson Avenue
Englishtown, NJ 07726
+01 732 446 9644
www.englishtownauction.com
*This 100-acre market attracts
professional and amateur dealers.
Open Saturdays and Sundays
8am–4pm.*

Hell's Kitchen Flea Market
West 39th Street at 9th Avenue
New York, NY 10018
www.annexmarkets.com
Saturdays and Sundays 9–5pm.

Rose Bowl Flea Market
100 Rose Bowl Drive
Pasadena, CA 91103
+01 323 560 7469
www.rgcshows.com
*On the second Sunday of every
month, everything from retro kitsch
to fine furnishings.*

Architectural fittings, salvage, and antiques

Architectural Accents
2711 Piedmont Road NE
Atlanta, GA 30305
+01 404 266 8700
www.architecturalaccents.com
*A vast stock of antique light fixtures,
door hardware, garden antiques, and
other reclaimed items.*

Caravati's Inc.
104 East Second Street
Richmond, VA 23224
+01 804 232 4175
www.caravatis.com
*Restoration materials and
architectural details reclaimed from
old buildings.*

Harrington Brass Works
+01 201 818 1300
www.harringtonbrassworks.com
*Reproduction brass fixtures for
kitchen and home, especially faucets.
Also bathroom products.*

Old Good Things
Union Square
5 East 16th Street
New York, NY 10003
www.ogtstore.com
*A chain of stores specializing in
architectural antiques. Outlets in
NYC, Los Angeles, Pennsylvania,
and Texas.*

Ruby Beets Old & New
25 Washington Street
PO Box 1174
Sag Harbor, NY 11963
+01 631 899 3275
www.rubybeets.com
*Decorative antiques as well as
contemporary furniture, lighting,
accessories, art, and photography.*

Salvage One
1840 W. Hubbard
Chicago, IL 60622
+01 312 733 0098
www.salvageone.com
Architectural salvage.

Vermont Salvage
www.vermontsalvage.com
*Architectural salvage including
radiators and mantels.*

Signature Hardware
2700 Crescent Springs Pike
Erlanger, KY 41017
+01 866 855 2284
www.signaturehardware.com
*Authentic reproduction clawfoot
tubs, farmhouse sinks, pedestal and
console sinks, Topaz copper soaking
tubs, and more.*

Paint

Benjamin Moore Paints
www.benjaminmoore.com
*Manufacturers of the Colonial
Williamsburg collection of historic
American colors, based on original
pigments developed more than
250 years ago.*

The Old Fashioned Milk Paint Company
436 Main Street
Groton, MA 01450
+01 978 448 6336
www.milkpaint.com
*Natural pigment paints that replicate
the color and finish of Colonial and
Shaker homes.*

Old Village Paint
www.old-village.com
*Manufacturers of paint since 1816,
producing color reproductions from
the Colonial, Federal, and Victorian
periods and stains and varnishes.*

picture credits

Key: **a**=above, **b**=below, **r**=right, **l**=left, **c**=centre.

All photography by Debi Treloar.

Page 1 Khadi & Co., by Bess Nielsen; **2** Hélène & Konrad Adamczewski, Lewes; **3** Mark & Sally Bailey's home in Herefordshire; **4** The London home of stylist/designer Janie Jackson of Parma Lilac; **5** The London home of one of the owners of Ochre; **6** The London home of stylist/designer Janie Jackson of Parma Lilac; **7** Hélène & Konrad Adamczewski, Lewes; **8al** Mark & Sally Bailey's home in Herefordshire; **8br** Hélène & Konrad Adamczewski, Lewes; **9** The London home of stylist/designer Janie Jackson of Parma Lilac; **10** Mark & Sally Bailey's home in Herefordshire; **11** The family home of Julia Bird in Cornwall; **12–13** The home and studio of Julian Stair in London; **14** The family home of Julia Bird in Cornwall; **15l** The home of the designer Edith Mézard in Lumières; **15r** Mark & Sally Bailey's home in Herefordshire; **16l** The family home of Julia Bird in Cornwall; **16r** Hélène & Konrad Adamczewski, Lewes; **17** The family home of Julia Bird in Cornwall; **18** "Chambre de séjour avec vue…", Saignon in Luberon; **19al** The home and studio of Julian Stair in London; **19ar&br** The family home of Julia Bird in Cornwall; **19bl** The home of the designer Edith Mézard in Lumières; **20bl** The home of the designer Edith Mézard in Lumières; **20br** "Chambre de séjour avec vue…", Saignon-en-Luberon; **21l** Hélène & Konrad Adamczewski, Lewes; **21r** Khadi & Co., by Bess Nielsen; **22** "Chambre de séjour avec vue…", Saignon-en-Luberon; **23l** Mark & Sally Bailey's home in Herefordshire; **23c** "Chambre de séjour avec vue…", Saignon-en-Luberon; **23r** Sharon & Paul Mrozinski's home in Bonnieux, France; **24l** Le Café Chinois, 7 rue de Bearn, 75003 Paris, owned by Catherine and Pierre Langlois; **24r** "Chambre de séjour avec vue…", Saignon-en-Luberon; **25** The London home of stylist/designer Janie Jackson of Parma Lilac; **26al** Sharon & Paul Mrozinski's home in Bonnieux, France; **26ac** Hélène & Konrad Adamczewski, Lewes; **26ar** "Chambre de séjour avec vue…", Saignon-en-Luberon; **26bl** Le Café Chinois, 7 rue de Bearn, 75003 Paris, owned by Catherine and Pierre Langlois; **26br** The home and studio of Julian Stair in London; **27** Sharon & Paul Mrozinski's home in Bonnieux, France; **28–29** The London home of the owners of Ochre; **30 & 31r** The London home of stylist/designer Janie Jackson of Parma Lilac; **31l** Le Café Chinois, 7 rue de Bearn, 75003 Paris, owned by Catherine and Pierre Langlois; **32–33** Hélène & Konrad Adamczewski, Lewes; **33r** The London home of stylist/designer Janie Jackson of Parma Lilac ; **34** The home and studio of Julian Stair in London; **35** The home of the designer Edith Mézard in Lumières; **36** The London home of stylist/designer Janie Jackson of Parma Lilac; **37l** Hélène & Konrad Adamczewski, Lewes; **37r** Khadi & Co., by Bess Nielsen; **38** Hélène & Konrad Adamczewski, Lewes; **39al** Mark & Sally Bailey's home in Herefordshire; **39ar** Khadi & Co., by Bess Nielsen; **39b** The family home of Julia Bird in Cornwall; **40a & 41** The home and studio of Julian Stair in London; **40b** The London home of stylist/designer Janie Jackson of Parma Lilac; **42al** Khadi & Co., by Bess Nielsen; **42ar** Mark & Sally Bailey's home in Herefordshire; **42c** Hélène & Konrad Adamczewski, Lewes; **42bl** Mark & Sally Bailey's home in Herefordshire; **42br** The home of the designer Edith Mézard in Lumières; **43al** Mark & Sally Bailey's home in Herefordshire; **43ar** Hélène & Konrad Adamczewski, Lewes; **43b** Khadi & Co., by Bess Nielsen; **44–45a** Mark & Sally Bailey's home in Herefordshire; **45b** The London home of Richard Moore; **46r** Mark & Sally Bailey's home in Herefordshire; **47** Sharon & Paul Mrozinski's home in Bonnieux; **48a&cl** The London home of Richard Moore; **48cr** Mark & Sally Bailey's home in Herefordshire; **48b** "Chambre de séjour avec vue…", Saignon-en-Luberon; **49** Mark & Sally Bailey's home in Herefordshire; **50** The family home of Julia Bird in Cornwall; **51l** The home of the designer Edith Mézard in Lumières; **51r** Caravane by François Dorget; **52** Caravane by François Dorget; **53** Sharon & Paul Mrozinski's home in Bonnieux; **54al** Caravane by François Dorget; **54ac** The London home of stylist/designer Janie Jackson of Parma Lilac; **54ar&b** Khadi & Co., by Bess Nielsen; **55** The Paris home of architects Anki Linde & Pierre Saalburg of lsl architects; **56** Mark & Sally Bailey's home in Herefordshire; **57l** The home of the designer Edith Mézard in Lumières; **57r** Hélène & Konrad Adamczewski, Lewes; **58a & 59** Mark & Sally Bailey's home in Herefordshire; **58b** The family home of Julia Bird in Cornwall; **60** Mark & Sally Bailey's home in Herefordshire; **61l** Khadi & Co., by Bess Nielsen; **61r** The home of the designer Edith Mézard in Lumières; **62** The London home of stylist/designer Janie Jackson of Parma Lilac; **63l** Le Café Chinois, 7 rue de Bearn, 75003 Paris, owned by Catherine & Pierre Langlois; **63r** "Chambre de séjour avec vue…", Saignon-en-Luberon; **64** The family home of Julia Bird in Cornwall; **66–67** Mark & Sally Bailey's home in Herefordshire; **67br** The London home of Richard Moore; **68** The London home of stylist/designer Janie Jackson of Parma Lilac; **69** Mark & Sally Bailey's home in Herefordshire; **70** Sharon & Paul Mrozinski's home in Bonnieux, France; **71** The London home of one of the owners of Ochre; **72** Sharon & Paul Mrozinski's home in Bonnieux, France; **73** Hélène & Konrad Adamczewski, Lewes; **74 & 75l** The London home of stylist/designer Janie Jackson of Parma Lilac; **75r** The London home of Richard Moore; **76** The family home of Julia Bird in Cornwall; **77** The London home of stylist/designer Janie Jackson of Parma Lilac; **78l** The home and studio of Julian Stair in London; **78–79** The London home of Richard Moore; **79ar** The family home of Julia Bird in Cornwall; **79br & 80** The London home of Richard Moore; **81al** Mark & Sally Bailey's home in Herefordshire; **81ac** The family home of Julia Bird in Cornwall; **81ar** Sharon & Paul Mrozinski's home in Bonnieux, France; **81bl** The London home of Richard Moore; **81br** Mark & Sally Bailey's home in Herefordshire; **82–83** The family home of Julia Bird in Cornwall; **84–85** The London home of stylist/designer Janie Jackson of Parma Lilac; **86al** The Paris home of architects Anki Linde & Pierre Saalburg of lsl architects; **86ar** Khadi & Co., by Bess Nielsen; **86b** The London home of one of the owners of Ochre; **87l&r** Mark & Sally Bailey's home in Herefordshire; **87c** The London home of one of the owners of Ochre; **88–89** Hélène & Konrad Adamczewski, Lewes; **90** "Chambre de séjour avec vue…", Saignon-en-Luberon; **91bl** The London home of Richard Moore; **91br** Sharon & Paul Mrozinski's home in Bonnieux, France; **92a** The home and studio of Julian Stair in London; **92b** The home of the designer Edith Mézard in Lumières; **93** The family home of Julia Bird in Cornwall; **94** Sharon & Paul Mrozinski's home in Bonnieux, France; **95a** The London home of Richard Moore; **95bl** The Paris home of architects Anki Linde & Pierre Saalburg of lsl architects; **95br** Hélène & Konrad Adamczewski, Lewes; **96** Mark & Sally Bailey's home in Herefordshire; **97** The home of the designer Edith Mézard in Lumières; **98–99** The Paris home of architects Anki Linde & Pierre Saalburg of lsl architects; **100** Hélène & Konrad Adamczewski, Lewes; **101–102l** Le Café Chinois, 7 rue de Bearn, 75003 Paris, owned by Catherine and Pierre Langlois; **102r–103** The home and studio of Julian Stair in London; **104–105** The London home of one of the owners of Ochre, www.ochre.net; **106** Mark & Sally Bailey's home in Herefordshire; **107al, cr&b** Sharon & Paul Mrozinski's home in Bonnieux, France; **107cl** The London home of stylist/designer Janie Jackson of Parma Lilac; **108al** Mark & Sally Bailey's home in Herefordshire; **108ar&c** Le Café Chinois, 7 rue de Bearn, 75003 Paris, owned by Catherine and Pierre Langlois; **108bl** The London home of Richard Moore; **108br** The home and studio of Julian Stair in London; **109** Mark & Sally Bailey's home in Herefordshire; **110** The family home of Julia Bird in Cornwall; **112–113** "Chambre de séjour avec vue…", Saignon-en-Luberon; **114–115b** The Paris home of architects Anki Linde & Pierre Saalburg of lsl architects; **115r–117** Hélène & Konrad Adamczewski, Lewes; **119–120** Hélène & Konrad Adamczewski, Lewes; **121** The London home of Richard Moore; **122–123** The London home of one of the owners of Ochre; **124–125** The London home of stylist/designer Janie Jackson of Parma Lilac; **126–127** Hélène & Konrad Adamczewski, Lewes; **128** The family home of Julia Bird in Cornwall; **129al** Sharon & Paul Mrozinski's home in Bonnieux, France; **129br** Mark & Sally Bailey's home in Herefordshire; **130–131** The Paris home of architects Anki Linde & Pierre Saalburg of lsl architects; **132&133r** Sharon & Paul Mrozinski's home in Bonnieux, France; **133l** The London home of stylist/designer Janie Jackson of Parma Lilac; **134l** The London home of one of the owners of Ochre; **134–135** Hélène & Konrad Adamczewski, Lewes; **136–137** The Paris home of architects Anki Linde & Pierre Saalburg of lsl architects; **138–139 a&bl** Mark & Sally Bailey's home in Herefordshire; **140–141** The family home of Julia Bird in Cornwall; **142&143l** Hélène & Konrad Adamczewski, Lewes; **143r** The home of the designer Edith Mézard in Lumières; **144a&145** The London home of stylist/designer Janie Jackson of Parma Lilac; **146–147l** Mark & Sally Bailey's home in Herefordshire; **147r** The home and studio of Julian Stair in London; **148** Hélène & Konrad Adamczewski, Lewes; **149** Mark & Sally Bailey's home in Herefordshire; **150** Sharon & Paul Mrozinski's home in Bonnieux, France; **151–152** Mark & Sally Bailey's home in Herefordshire; **153** The London home of stylist/designer Janie Jackson of Parma Lilac. **Endpapers:** The family home of Julia Bird, Cornwall.

businesses whose work is featured in this book

Adamczewski

196 High Street
Lewes
East Sussex BN7 2NS

*Pages 2, 7, 8br, 16r, 21l,
26ac, 32–33, 37l, 38, 42c, 43ar,
57r, 73, 88–89, 95b, 100,
115r–117, 119–120, 126–127,
134–135, 142 & 143l, 148*

Baileys

Whitecross Farm
Bridstow
Ross-on-Wye
Heretordshire HR9 6JU
+44 (0)1989 563015

www.baileyshome.com

*Pages 3, 8al, 10, 15r, 23l, 39ar,
42ar, 42bl, 43al,
44–45a, 46r, 48cr, 49, 56, 58a,
59, 60, 66–67, 69, 81al, 81br,
87l&r, 96, 106, 108al, 109,
129br, 138–139a, 139bl, 146,
147l, 149, 151–152*

bird...inspired by nature

3 Custom House Hill
Fowey
Cornwall PL23 1AB
+44 (0) 1726 833737
&
49 Molesworth Street
Wadebridge
Cornwall PL27 7DR

info@birdkids.co.uk
www.birdkids.co.uk

*Pages 11, 14, 16l, 17, 19ar &
br, 39b, 50, 58b, 64, 76, 79ar,
81ac, 82–83, 93, 110, 128,
140–141*

Le Café Chinois

Café Salon de Thés
Boutique Objets d'Asie
7, rue de Béarn
75003 Paris
+33 (0) 1 42 71 47 43

www.lecafechinols.fr

*Pages 24l, 26bl, 31l, 63l, 101,
102l, 108ar, 108c*

Caravane

6 rue Pavée
75004 Paris
+33 (0) 1 44 61 04 20
Pages 51r, 52, 54al

**"Chambre de séjour avec
vue…" – Demeure d'art et
d'hôtes**

84400 Saignon-en-Lubéron
France
www.chambreavecvue.com
*Pages 18, 20br, 22, 23c, 24r,
26ar, 48b, 63r, 90, 112–113*

**Khadi & Co
By Bess Nielsen**

Emporium
37 rue Debelleyme
75003 Paris
France
Open Wed–Sat,
11am–7pm
+33 (0) 1 42 74 71 32
fax +33 (0) 1 44 59 84 65
khadiandco@hotmail.com
www.khadiandco.com

*Pages 1, 21r, 37r, 39ar, 42al,
43b, 54ar&b, 61l, 86ar*

Isl architects

33 rue d'Hauteville
75010 Paris
+33 (0) 1 48 00 09 65
fax +33 (0) 1 48 00 09 31
www.lslarchitects.com

*Pages 55, 86al, 95bl, 98–99,
114–115b, 130–131, 136–137*

Edith Mézard

Chateau de L'Ange
84220 Lumières
France
Shop open daily,
3pm-7.30pm
*Pages 15l, 19bl, 20bl, 35, 42br,
51l, 57l, 61r, 92b, 97, 143r.*

Richard Moore

Creative Consultant to the
Retail Industry
Scenographic
+44 (0)7958 740045
www.scenographic.blogspot.com

*Pages 45b, 48a, 48cl, 67br,
75r, 78–79, 79br, 80, 81bl,
91bl, 95a, 108bl, 121*

Sharon & Paul Mrozinski

The Marston House
Main Street at Middle Street
PO Box 517
Wiscasset
Maine 04578
+ 1 207 882 6010
fax + 1 207 882 6965
sharon@marstonhouse.com
www.marstonhouse.com

*Pages 23r, 26al, 27, 47, 53, 70,
72, 81ar, 91r, 94, 107al, 107cr,
107b, 129al, 132, 133r, 150*

Ochre London Ltd.

+44 (0)870 787 9242

www.ochre.net

*Pages 5, 28–29, 71, 86b, 87c,
104–105, 122–123, 134l*

Parma Lilac

98 Chepstow Road
London W10 6EP.
(Visits by appointment)
+44 (0)20 7912 0882
info@parmalilac.co.uk
www.parmalilac.co.uk

*Pages 4, 6, 9, 25, 30, 31r, 33r,
36, 40b, 54ac, 62, 68, 74–75l,
77, 84–85, 107cl, 124–125,
133l, 144a, 145, 153*

Julian Stair

Studio
52a Hindmans Road
London SE22 9NG
+44 (0)20 8693 4877
studio@julianstair.com
www.julianstair.com

*Pages 12–13, 19al, 26br, 34,
40a, 41, 78l, 92a, 102r, 103,
108br, 147r*

index

acknowledgments

This book was a hectic scramble around London, Paris, Cornwall, Herefordshire and the south of France. There was much refilling of London parking meters and losing our way in narrow cobbled streets in Paris, while staggering under the weight of all the bags and photographic equipment! But it was definitely worth it as we were allowed into some perfect simple spaces – so a big thank you to all those people who let us take over their homes for a day…especially:

Hélène & Konrad Adamczewski, a lesson in restraint. Thank you for lunch.

Richard Moore, creative consultant, an amazing lesson in how to use a small space.

Janie Jackson, Parma Lilac showroom open by appointment.

Solenne da la Fouchardière, designer & part of the Ochre co-operative, London & New York.

Julian Stair & Claire Wilcox, we'd like to be buried in one of Julian's stunning sarcophagi.

Gum & Julia Bird, good luck with the new shop. A huge thanks for supper and lunch.

Ken & Susan Briggs, so kind and generous, huge patrons of the arts.

Pierre Jaccaud, Chambre de séjour avec vue. Bed, art and breakfast – a lesson in curating.

Bess Nielsen of Khadi & Co., the veritable queen of hand-spun, hand-dyed textiles.

Anki Linde & Pierre Saalburg of lsl architectures, we are in awe of their attention to detail.

Edith Mézard, who let us into her home, showroom and studio with the added bonus of her son's neighbouring restaurant, Le Garage.

Caravane, inspirational furniture and textile showroom.

Sharon and Paul Mronzinski, just brilliant.

Mark and Sally would also like to thank Alison, Leslie, Delphine, Paul and Jess (thanks for putting up with us again) and everyone else at Ryland Peters & Small.

Debi Treloar – a brilliant photographer and calm in all situations, which makes her a joy to work with. Also her assistant Lorna, who made us laugh, while remaining amazingly focused.

Huge thanks to Charlotte Farmer who wrote the words over copious coffees in our café.

Last but not least, thanks to Ben, Lucy, Laura, Kirstin and everyone at Baileys.